Carnival

The Harriet Tubman Series on the African Diaspora

Paul E. Lovejoy and Toyin Falola, eds., *Pawnship, Slavery and Colonialism in Africa*, 2003.

Donald G. Simpson, *Under the North Star: Black Communities in Upper Canada before Confederation (1867)*, 2005.

Paul E. Lovejoy, *Slavery, Commerce and Production in West Africa: Slave Society in the Sokoto Caliphate*, 2005.

José C. Curto and Renée Soulodre-La France, eds., *Africa and the Americas: Interconnections during the Slave Trade*, 2005.

Paul E. Lovejoy, *Ecology and Ethnography of Muslim Trade in West Africa*, 2005.

Naana Opoku-Agyemang, Paul E. Lovejoy and David Trotman, eds., *Africa and Trans-Atlantic Memories: Literary and Aesthetic Manifestations of Diaspora and History*, 2008.

Boubacar Barry, Livio Sansone, and Elisée Soumonni, eds., *Africa, Brazil, and the Construction of Trans-Atlantic Black Identities*, 2008.

Behnaz Asl Mirzai, Ismael Musah Montana, and Paul E. Lovejoy, eds., *Slavery, Islam and Diaspora*, 2009.

Carolyn Brown and Paul E. Lovejoy, eds., *Repercussions of the Atlantic Slave Trade: The Interior of the Bight of Biafra and the African Diaspora*, 2010.

Ute Röschenthaler, *Purchasing Culture in the Cross River Region of Cameroon and Nigeria*, 2011.

Ana Lucia Araujo, Mariana P. Candido and Paul E. Lovejoy, eds., *Crossing Memories: Slavery and African Diaspora*, 2011.

Edmund Abaka, *House of Slaves and "Door of No Return": Gold Coast Castles and Forts of the Atlantic Slave Trade*, 2012.

Christopher Innes, Annabel Rutherford, and Brigitte Bogar, eds. *Carnival: Theory and Practice*, 2012.

C·A·R·N·I·V·A·L

THEORY AND PRACTICE

EDITED BY

Christopher Innes,

Annabel Rutherford

AND *Brigitte Bogar*

AFRICA WORLD PRESS
TRENTON | LONDON | CAPE TOWN | NAIROBI | ADDIS ABABA | ASMARA | IBADAN | NEW DELHI

AFRICA WORLD PRESS
541 West Ingham Avenue | Suite B
Trenton, New Jersey 08638

Book and cover design: Saverance Publishing Services

Library of Congress Cataloging-in-Publication Data

Carnival : theory and practice / edited by Christopher Innes, Annabel Rutherford, and Brigitte Bogar.
    p. cm.
  Papers originally presented at an international conference on "Carnival, a people's art and taking back the streets," held in Toronto, July 30-August 3, 2008, to coincide with the Caribana Festival.
  Includes bibliographical references and index.
  ISBN 978-1-59221-848-6 (hardcover) -- ISBN 978-1-59221-849-3(pbk.)
1. Carnival--Congresses. 2. Carnivals--Congresses. 3. Festivals--Congresses. I. Innes, C. D. II. Rutherford, Annabel. III. Bogar, Brigitte.
  GT4180.C29 2011
  394.25--dc23
                    2011018915

The Harriet Tubman Institute for Research
on the Global Migrations of African Peoples

Table of Contents

Acknowledgements   vii

INTRODUCTION Christopher Innes   ix

1. CONTEMPORARY CARNIVAL IN PERSPECTIVE

Peter Minshall: Nignorance and Enwhitenment   3

2. THE AFRICAN HERITAGE

Modesto Amegago: Interrogating the Roots, Elements, and Crossovers of the Caribbean Carnival: A Case of West African Celebrations   25

Henry Lovejoy: The Transculturation of Yoruba Annual Festivals: The *Día de Reyes* in Colonial Cuba in the Nineteenth Century   35

Sabrina Ensfelder: The African Heritage in Trinidad's Carnival: From Cultural Resistance to Identity Negotiation in Earl Lovelace's *The Dragon Can't Dance*   53

3. CARIBBEAN CARNIVAL

Jeff Henry: Carnival/Masquerade in Trinidad: Resistance through Performance   65

Teruyuki Tsuji: The "Other Half": The Articulation of Carnival in Nineteenth-Century Trinidad   79

Jeffrey Chock: The Mas I Know   93

Suzanne Deborah Burke: Policing the People's Festival – State Policy and the Trinidad Carnival Complex   107

4. THE CARNIVAL DIASPORA

Paul Lovejoy: Transformation of the *Ékpè* Masquerade in the African Diaspora   127

PHIL SCHER: The Power and Pitfalls of Carnival as Cultural
Heritage   153
UNITED STATES
BRUCE BOYD RAEBURN: Too Hip to Hop(e)? Post-Katrina
Brass Bands and New Orleans Carnival   165
BRITAIN
LESLEY FERRIS: Designing for the Diaspora: Images of Africa
in Contemporary British Carnival   177
CANADA
JERRY & LEIDA ENGLAR: Shadowland and Ecological Protest
in Carnival/Caribana   189
DONNA COOMBS-MONTROSE: Building the Carnival Arts in
Western Canada – The Cariwest Experiment   197

5. STEELPAN AND CARNIVAL
KAREN CYRUS: Why They Play Pan: Steel Band Communities
in the GTA   207
LIONEL MCCALMAN: Pan-Around-Neck Steel Band Tradition,
The London Notting Hill Carnival, and the Concept of Com-
munity Cohesion in the UK   217
HAROUN SHAH: Nostalgia Steel band and the Impact of "Pan-
round-Neck" at Street Carnivals in Europe   233

6. CALYPSO AND CARNIVAL
EVERARD PHILLIPS: The Political Calypso – A Sociolinguistic
Process in Conflict Transformation   251
RAY FUNK: Sir Lancelot : Taking Calypso from Carnival to
Nightclubs, Hollywood, and the World   271

7. DESIGNING AND PRODUCING CARNIVAL
LOYCE ARTHUR: Artists Who Dare: Contemporary Carnival
Designers   287
TONY HALL: Jouvay Popular Theatre Process [JPTP]:
Finding the Interior   299
PETER MINSHALL: Masman/Artist   315
Contributors' Biographies   339
Index   345

Acknowledgements

Without the organizational help of the two co-editors of this volume, Annabel Rutherford and particularly Brigitte Bogar, the conference from which this volume comes could not have been successfully held, nor would the essays here be so readable or accurate. They were responsible for budgeting at the conference, correspondence with speakers and the organization of everything from transport to coffee; and in preparing this volume have checked every reference, as well as unifying a range of formats.

In addition, the conference was made possible by generous funding from the Social Sciences and Humanities Research Council of Canada, and from the Faculties of Arts and Fine Arts, together with the Academic Vice-President at York University. The conference was also supported by Caribana, whose organizers made tickets to the various events available to conference delegates, and arranged for a ceremony honouring the keynote speaker, Peter Minshall, for his contributions to Mas. An exhibition of carnival art was provided by Ohio State University in conjunction with the Director of Swizzlesticks Theatre in Toronto; George Maharaj exhibited his Calypso collection, while the directors of various carnival-related films and CDs generously gave permission for them to be shown at the conference. In addition, support for the publication was generously provided from the Canada Research Chair in African Diaspora History and the Canada Research Chair in Performance and Culture. Without all these people and institutions the inspiring unity of the conference could not have been provided, and this collection of essays would never have come together.

Introduction

Carnival has developed into one of the most important global expressions of popular identity, yet relatively little scholarly attention has been paid to it. This volume is a step towards recognition of the significance of this popular art form.

Both as celebration and as resistance art, Carnival builds on the collision of cultures of Catholic European colonizers and enslaved West Africans, and has spread from Trinidad through the Caribbean, to England, the United States and Canada, as well as Germany, and with analogues elsewhere, becoming a truly global movement. Both as celebration and as resistance art, historically it builds on the collision of cultures of Catholic European colonizers and enslaved West Africans. The claiming of public space in the use of the street is a statement of presence that is as much political as artistic. Since Carnival is a global popular phenomenon, it can only be studied in an international context, while its nature requires a combination of disciplines. As a popular expression, taking place on the streets and, outside Trinidad or Brazil, frequently marginalized by social authorities, if not commercialized, the study of Carnival also requires the intersection of researchers with practitioners.

This collection of essays is the result of an International Conference on "CARNIVAL, 'A PEOPLE'S ART' AND TAKING BACK THE STREETS" held in Toronto, July 30-August 3, 2008 to coincide with the Caribana Festival. One of the major Caribbean diaspora annual events, this includes not only a Parade, but a Kings' & Queens' Competition, a steel-band competition, Pan Alive!, and a Junior Carnival Parade, as well as the traditional "limes" (parties) following the formal displays. People from across the world participated in the conference, with a line-up of Carnival experts from Trinidad, and academic speakers from South Africa, Singapore and Scandinavia, as well as the UK, Europe and North America, in addition to the Caribbean. It was held in collaboration and involved a wide range of disparate institutions: the Graduate Centre for Drama at the University of Toronto, Ohio State University, the International Steelpan Association & British Association of Steelbands (ISA/BAS), World Carnival Congress (WCC), and the Harriet Tubman Research Centre on the African Diaspora at York University. The full program can be seen at www.CarnivalConference.ca.

The essays in this volume are all drawn from papers and presentations at this Conference. However a selection has been made to give a clear focus. While the conference included presentations on carnival in Ancient Egypt and Rome, Denmark, Venice, Russia, South Africa and Asia, it was not possible to give a full global overview of carnival as a popular expression. So it was decided to focus solely on Caribbean Carnival, the links between this tradition and its African heritage, and on the Caribbean diaspora, with specific emphasis on carnival developments in London, New Orleans and Toronto.

At the same time, while there had been another conference on Carnival at Trinity College, Hartford, Conn. ten years before, this was the very first to attempt to unite discussion of Mas (Masquerade) design and dance, with the other aspects of Carnival, steelpan music and Calypso. Increasingly – whether in London or Toronto – recorded music from sound systems mounted on trucks has taken the place of live music as an accompaniment to the Mas bands' parade. And while Calypso songs share much of the same challenge to the social establishment and satiric aims as the traditional Carnival figures (the Blue Devils, Dames Lorraine or Pay-Wo Grenade, who are discussed in various of the essays in this volume) as well as having a similar musical background, Calypso is no longer presented in the same frame as the Mas Parades at all. There is also a lively Carnival sculptural tradition, mainly created out of bent wires and representing Mas figures, which is never part of the parades, although it is sometimes included in exhibitions of the carnival arts. So one of the aims of this conference was to challenge this separated artistic isolation; to discuss and by contiguity illustrate the interdependence and mutual benefit of the different Carnival expressions. Not only did the various panels at the conference focus on all the different carnival arts. In addition, the formal conference papers and panel discussions were accompanied by concerts of steelpan, a display of stilt walkers and Mas dancers, an exhibition of Calypso posters and record-covers, and an interactive exhibition on the Notting Hill Carnival – 'Midnight Robbers' – first presented at London City Hall in the UK, which was combined with visual material illustrating the history of Caribana. There were also videos and films shown: Alberto Guevara's

Dalits, *Dramas, Dreams*, Richard Fung's *The Art of Christopher Cozier*, Seth Feldman's *Caribana*, Dalton Narine's *Mas Man*.

The line-up from Trinidad equally illustrated this attempt at re-integration: the leading Mas designer of the post-World War II era, Peter Minshall; the playwright Tony Hall, who has both participated in Mas and written dramas about Carnival; the photographer Jeffrey Chock, who has spent a lifetime documenting carnival; Nestor Sullivan, founding member manager of Pamberi Steel Orchestra. Making this unification literal, Minshall and Hall, together with Roz Roach, the leader of the Toronto Mas band 'BazODee,' joined together in a group discussion on "Producing Carnival." And indeed, this initial attempt at re-integration of the carnival arts has inspired a further attempt in another conference in October 2011, specifically on "INTEGRATING THE THREE ELEMENTS OF CARNIVAL. STEELPAN, CALYPSO AND MAS" and mounted at the University of East London by Dr. Haroun Shah, a participant at the 2008 Carnival conference.

On the academic level, the aim was equally to bring into dialogue many widely separated disciplines. So the areas of expertise represented by the speakers – and reflected by the essays in this volume – range from Political Scientists, Cultural Historians, Sociologists and Anthropologists, to professors in Women's Studies, Diaspora, South American and Caribbean Studies, and Literature, as well as Art and Design, Music, Film, Theatre and Dance. The area highlighted in the program, which are also represented among the essays here, are:

* Carnival and theatricality
* The Trinidad Carnival Tradition
* Gender / Economics and Carnival
* Popular Art, Globalization & Copyright
* Caribana: history, performance
* Cross-Cultural Influences: Brazil, Bolivia, UK, America, Berlin, Toronto
* Images of Africa / Carnival in Africa
* Myth, Magic and Religion
* Social Activism & Carnival/Street Theatre
* Syncretism, Hybridity and Identity
* The Carnival Diaspora

Indeed the essays in this volume explore the anthropological, social, political and cultural aspects of Carnival and street theatre, as well as themes of exclusion/otherness, exoticism and cross-cultural acceptance, diasporic links, connections/comparisons between Carnival in Africa, the Caribbean, South and North America, Europe and the UK. While taking the African Masquerade traditions and its spread across the Caribbean to other continents as its base, this conference is also intended to focus on the widest socio-cultural aspects of this performative street art: hybridity and the negotiation of identity in the post-colonial context; anthropological assessment of historical developments, the politics of carnival and street theatre, economic and commercial pressures. So the conversation not only crossed artistic boundaries, but was also interdisciplinary. And in addition, in bringing together writers and academics with artists and those concerned with the production of carnival bands and parades, the Conference was concerned with bridging theory and practice – which is reflected in the title to this volume of essays.

The title of the 2008 conference, "CARNIVAL, 'A PEOPLE'S ART' AND TAKING BACK THE STREETS", also has a political edge. Already, citing "A People's Art" as a quotation (from Claudia Jones, the "mother" of Notting Hill Carnival) was an intentionally provocative statement; and while in fact it referred specifically to the origins of the London Carnival (which had been started at St. Pancras Town Hall in 1959 in response to a series of racially motivated murders in the Notting Hill district, and moved out into the streets of Notting Hill in 1966), "Taking Back the Streets" could also be seen as an image of the earliest Caribbean Carnival Masquerades before the abolition of slavery, when it was the only expression of freedom allowed to the black populations by the white authorities, and a seedbed for rebellion and emancipation. The history of the Diaspora, through which African traditions of magic and masquerade – the roots of Caribbean Carnival – were spread around the Americas, and then to Britain, is also the history of slavery; and a number of the essays here deal with this aspect. But other essays extend the political discussion to such important issues as globalization and commercialization, the formation of Diasporas, pan-cultural hybridity, Gender and Racism, the nature of Post-colonialism today, carrying the political discussion in the present.

This volume on CARNIVAL – THEORY AND PRACTICE is book-ended by pieces featuring Peter Minshall. A towering figure who revolutionized mas in the 1970s, leading to a series of extraordinary mas-bands that can be seen as political and ecological pageants through the 1980s and 1990s, and also and served as designer and artistic director for the ceremonies of the Olympics in Barcelona and Atlanta, as well as an anti-nuclear protest Mas in Washington D.C., Minshall sets the tone for the other essays – as indeed he did for the conference itself. He opened with a diatribe about the commercial corruption and political emasculation of contemporary carnival in Trinidad and elsewhere, which was greeted with repeated laughter, interrupted by applause, and given a standing ovation at the end. At the same time, Minshall draws on his long and brilliant experience to illuminate the problems the carnival arts have to overcome, and suggests possible solutions. As he says, Mas he designs may be primarily for the Caribbean, but it is also for all the people of the earth because "it is an extraordinary, universal form of expression that is not dependent on language. There is no art form like the Mas that is so profoundly a relationship between the artist, the participants and the audience." In this ideal, the Carnival Mas is a fertility ritual, but it is also a unique and original form of theatre (and Minshall began his career as a designer for the stage). For him it is not the designs but the Mas as a whole that is the work of art; and while movement, mime, and gesture were still the primary means of expression, in his iconic Mas bands beginning with *Paradise Lost* in 1976, Minshall integrated speech (*Santimanity*, 1989) collaborating with David Rudder and Charlie's Roots, or other calypsonians, reviving the "chantwell" tradition of songs to reflect the theme of the masband – making his work itself a prime example of the re-unification of carnival arts. His iconic Mas bands also encapsulated highly political messages, as with his two-Act 1983 *River*, where, Mancrab represented rapacious industrialism, seducing the people with the bright colours of bling and brands, and symbolizing the pollution of the water, and killing the Washer Woman as the spirit of the water.

So Peter Minshall is in many ways representative of the themes of both the conference and of this book that comes out of it. And as Minshall commented: how can anyone expect the art of Mas "to take a step forward when no one is brave enough to write in terms of world culture the truth about what is happening out there?" This volume is provides at least a beginning answer to his challenge.

Christopher Innes
Canada Research Chair in Performance & Culture
York University, Toronto

September 2010

1

Contemporary Carnival in Perspective

Nignorance and Enwhitenment

Peter Minshall

[*Minshall puts on a black velvet hat*]. I had made a big Robber hat to bring because today I am playing Minshall the mighty Robber Man. But it wasn't so much the Robber hat was too big to fit in the plane. It was too heavy for the plane to carry. It was so weighed down with skulls and bones, the coagulated blood of so many. The funny thing is I had the spirit and the dread to manage to carry it, but I was 'fraid for the plane, or the people from in front of the plane saying, "You are a terrorist!" [*Laughter*].

I ain't start yet, you know. I have a little prologue and I have a little epilogue, both from the op-ed of the *New York Times* in recent days. Here is the little prologue, just an excerpt from a piece on Barack Obama entitled "Bad in Berlin, Perfect in Paris." (Cohen: July 28, 2008)

"Obama looks like America reinvented; he summons from Europeans that imagined land of opportunity, foreign to their tired shores and confined spaces, that F. Scott Fitzgerald rendered at the end of *The Great Gatsby*: 'For a transitory, enchanted moment man must have held his breath in the presence of this continent, compelled into an aesthetic contemplation he neither understood nor desired, face to face for the last time in history with something commensurate to his capacity for wonder.'"

And I thought, yes, as with that continent so with my island. And the little prologue ends. (I will take off the miniature version of the Robber hat. Please remind me to put it back on at the end for a little epilogue, also from *the New York Times*.)

"There is a vitality, a life force, a quickening that is translated through you into action. And because there is only one of you in all time, this expression is unique. If you block it, it will never exist through any other medium and be lost. The world will not have it. It is not your business to determine how good it is, nor how valuable it is, nor how it compares with other expressions. It is your business to keep it yours, clearly and directly, to keep the channel open. You do not even have to believe in yourself or your work."— Martha Graham to Agnes De Mille. It makes such sense to me. Who am I to keep my channel open? "You have to keep open and aware directly to the urges that motivate you. Keep the channel open. No artist is pleased, there is no satisfaction whatever at any time. There is only a queer, divine dissatisfaction, a blessed unrest that keeps us marching and makes us more alive than the others."

To me and my fellow islanders a good artist is a priest. By the same token, a good priest is an artist. But there is a difference. The priest ministers established dogma to a congregation of believers. The priest plays by a rigid set of unbroken rules. The artist, by contrast, is always restless, always breaking and remaking rules, always eager for the next turn of the page, always trying to write a new chapter, seeking to deliver the unfettered future from the chains of the present and the ponderous baggage of the past.

Marcel Duchamp maintained that no work of art has a relevant life span longer than about forty years. After that, he said, it became art history. Artists are always on the move, pushing and shoving society off its accustomed path, away from the beaten track, breaking old hardened habits, often causing discomfort, nudging their congregation into sometimes blinding new ways of seeing and experiencing the world. The Caribbean "art world" is an island paradise for purveyors of exotic, decorative merchandise of the gilded Hallmark greeting card variety, some of it parading as pretty high-sounding intellectual tribal stuff. It sells. It is pretty. It is pretty shallow. It communicates little or nothing. It communicates little or nothing to art or art history. The artist-priest is driven by the needs of his community and by his own need to communicate. He gives his community its sense of being. On their behalf, he struggles to make a mark on the vast, incomprehensible canvas of the universe. A mark. A symbol. A sign of some sort, that declares and communicates their existence.

"Art is the highest form of human communication, and music is the highest form of art."—Maria Callas. This is a challenge to arms on all fronts on a small island adrift in the twenty-first century that doesn't know its art from its elbow or its mas. The terrain is hugely daunting. The tools for creative communication on the island range from the ancient power endowed to the spiritually uplifting stilts of a traditional Moko Jumbie stalking the streets in giant phantom steps, to the miraculous contemporary obeah of a hand-held effigy. [*feigns holding cell-phone to ear*] The Caribbean artist-priest accrues of necessity, as a matter of simply being who he is where he is, an extraordinary collection of ritual masks through which he undergoes transformation to become a truly rare hybrid. He is by chance and by choice a multi-layered richly textured creature. He is simultaneously Buddha, Jesus, Shiva, Shango and Dionysus. He is Africa, India and Europe. He is middle-America Bible-belted. He is Mecca. He is pre-Columbian, Oriental and Egyptian. His resources are readily and easily drawn from the raw theatre of highly charged out-of-door open-air collectives, the theatre of the streets, the potency and spontaneous vitality of primitive ritual performance symbolism. He is also drawing from the most highly refined, meticulously staged and ordained classicism. It is a most uncommon combination. If he is true to his cause, and his core, the artist embraces with equal fervour and energy that which is considered and disdained as coarse and primitive, and that which is regarded as refined and therefore more desirable. Seeming opposites: black and white. He endeavours to construct a single and complete whole, which marries the exciting immediacy of the defining moment with the worthy promise of long hours of meditative contemplation.

The next part of the Robber speech is going to be like a bit of jazz, heavy impro, and I have a sheet of notes here, some hotel scrap here and a little notebook here which, since Mr. Christopher[1] first talked to me, I started writing under the heading "Nignorance and Enwhitenment," which is really Scylla and Charybdis.

They say you should not judge a book by its cover. In the same breath they say I am white. But . . .

I am not a European.
I am not an African.
I am not an Indian.
I am not Chinese, Syrian, Amerindian, American—North or South.

---

1   Christopher Innes, organizer of the "Carnival" conference, and chair of
     the Minshall session.

I am none of these.
Yet I am all of these.

I am a Caribbean.

I am a rare hybrid.
I am a richly textured, multi-layered creature.
I am precious as a pearl.
The world is my oyster.
I see the world clearly from my island vantage.
  I do not harbour the vanities of a big city dweller or someone from a vast continent.
  I am at the tip of the spear that leads into the future.

They say the Caribbean is a sea.
Yes. I am an island in it.
Much blood has spilled in that sea.
All the waters of humanity wash my shores.

I am a Caribbean.

Most of my ancestors were sold into slavery for a handful of brightly coloured beads. [*extends handful of imaginary beads*] I look at the carnival of today and what do I see? [*broad gesture indicating same handful of imaginary beads—laughter*] Most of my ancestors would sing and dance in preparation for the hunt, would sing and dance in the planting of the crops, would sing and dance as they reaped the crops, as they feasted, as they cooked the food, as they married one to the other. As they initiated the young men, they would sing and dance. They would only go inside the house at night when they were damn tired. And it is amazing, with a bone marrow ancestral memory, even unto this very day, at the drop of a hat, all of my people would sing and dance. But my fellow artists—have you seen it? have you noticed?—they have abandoned their people because they have gone inside of the house to write novels or poetry, or to make plays or paintings inside of the house. And the people are outside, in Trinidad and all up the islands and wherever they go—in London, in New York and Miami and here in Toronto—they are singing and dancing outside. But the artists, the trained minds, the given spirits, are in the house, being refined. Not out of wickedness, eh.

Not out of spite. But out of Nignorance, ignorance of self, and out of a very confused and confusing world environment of Enwhitenment.

I just have to tell people, but oh God, all you don't see? White people's art is about keeping the dead alive. All those marble busts, every single painting is still life on the wall. And black people's art is in the living "now." Don't make the mistake of thinking I like one in preference to the other. I pray at the altar of the contemplative thought but I also pray at the altar of the living moment. On my island, early days I was taught immense spiritual value, not of placing art on the wall but of placing it on myself and bringing it alive to people as close as the road is to the pavement. Not in some house called a theatre, which is lovely, where everybody sits passively to see other people act out their business. [gesturing round, indicating the lecture theater in which they are gathered—laughter] I want to act out my own business.

Here! [gestures to the left of him] Here we have a man who awakes in the morning and washes his naked body and reaches into the earth, extracting the raw pigment, and meticulously makes marks on his skin, and dances in celebration of his gods and in communication with his fellows. And this is called art. And here [gestures to the right] we have another man, who awakes in the morning, washes his naked body, puts on his clothes, reaches into the earth, extracts the pigment, encases it in a box or a little tube, and for a small exchange of money, gives it to a colleague who goes home and makes marks meticulously on a piece of paper or a board or a canvas and hangs it on the wall in celebration of his gods and in communication with his fellows. And this too is called art. But our received knowledge in the Caribbean is that this art [on the right], and therefore this man, is refined. And that art [on the left], and therefore that other man, is coarse and primitive.

Well, I am here to tell you today that within the belly and the bosom and the phallus of the "Coarse and Primitive" reside potency and vitality, which "Refined" is very hard pressed to produce. And there is much talk from the political throne of the Caribbean about visions for the future, which really has to do with artifacts like skyscrapers and prime-ministerial palaces. But my vision for the future of my people is that it is our duty, not just to ourselves but to all of humanity, to embrace this brother [on the right] and to embrace that brother [on the left] and to be the liberty spear that leads into the future [embracing both] and shows the way. It's such a task to find that fine, exquisite balance between the divine moment of experience and the extended moment of the meditative.

A few actual examples: Reviews are written in our island newspapers for a multitude of sex comedies. I am yet to see a single review in my thirty years as masmaker of my work or that of any other masmaker. Never once have I seen a review of the Trinidad Carnival. How do you expect Toronto Caribana's Kings and Queen's Competition last night [which conference delegates had attended] to take a step forward when no one is brave enough to write in terms of world culture the truth about what is happening out there? When not a single designer and, I bet money on it, not a single artist who designed all the stuff we saw last night has been to an art school or a theatre school or a university. Well, maybe one, maybe two. But you understand what I am saying. "Oh, that is only mas." And where are the people who have gone to the university or gone to the art school? Oh, they are over here doing conceptual art and they are destined for the New York or the London art gallery or for Broadway or the West End. It took Richard Schechner to come to Trinidad the year we did *Tapestry* [1997] to say: Don't ever compare yourselves to Broadway. Where you are now as an island people is where the Greeks were when they were making plays. You are doing divine work. Broadway needs to come to Trinidad to learn.

Not only the mas. We're really caught in a downward spiraling deathtrap. When I was a little boy there was what we used to call a coconut cart on the Savannah[2]. And this is not nostalgia. The coconut cart by the Savannah was so named because that is what it was. It was a cart with a donkey with a man on top of the cart with a cutlass and a pile of coconuts. It had integrity. It had "islandness" which is not necessarily backwardness. But caught somewhere as we are between Desperados and Disney—they used to be called the Gay Desperados, by the way, until they went to New York, and ah-ah, better cut the "Gay" [*laughter*]—caught somewhere between Desperados and Disney, we now have institutional coconut carts by the Savannah for all the world to see that look like Cinderella's royal coach going to the ball with golden curlicues. [*booing from the audience*] Yes, disgusting. I'm not saying that we really need a law to keep things as they were. But if San Francisco can keep cable cars, wisely, and Bali keeps Bali, why can't Trinidad keep Trinidad? That is a severe case of enwhitenment. I would rather keep a plain old truck the fellow had, to replace his cart, than this golden curlicue thing. Some of you who haven't been to Trinidad please block your eyes when you're passing. [*laughter*] No, it's the difference between truth and lies.

---

2   The Queen's Park Savannah, the central park of Port of Spain.

We lose our integrity.

When I was a young fellow growing up, I used to lime with a group of people who gravitated to a house on Richmond Street [in Port of Spain] that was owned by Mr. and Mrs. Hinkson and their family. There was something about the house that was magical to us. It had no race, no gender, no age. Yes, respect for your elders. And the Hinkson brothers, and Kevin Arthur, with Minshall and Rampersad, and a few others, were glued together by the wonderful human substance that was in this old grey house with Demerara windows and an unkempt yard.

And Arnold Rampersad I remember especially. I was just fascinated by this young, what we in Trinidad call light-skinned fellow—not white but light-skinned—you know, we have all sorts of strata and layers of identification. Arnold Rampersad was just a brilliant linguist.[3] He read so many books and he just knew everything. Like me, early, because he spoke well, he went into radio. But the thing I remember most about Arnold Rampersad—the fellows would have a cricket bat and a cricket ball after a game in the Savannah, and Arnold Rampersad would be reciting and singing every word, tune perfect, from every song in Lerner and Loewe's *My Fair Lady,* in the 1950s, on the Caribbean island of Trinidad. "Let a woman in your life..." down around the Savannah. "The rain in Spain falls mainly..." from the beginning to the end. Well, Arnold Rampersad himself went from Eliza Doolittle to being the Professor Henry Higgins of black American biography. He wrote on Langston Hughes, Arthur Ashe; a whole bunch of people. Somebody last night tells me he's writing the life of Obama. I hope Obama knows that!

Just the other day, my island invites Professor Rampersad to come back to the Central Bank to do the commemorative Eric Williams speech. For those of you who don't know, Eric Williams is the father of our nation. He was an intellectual, a brilliant man who literally fathered us from Britain to being ourselves. Arnold, of course, makes sure that Minshall gets an invitation. I go with a young fellow artist, Che Lovelace, the son of the renowned writer.[4]

And we're sitting there. And I am catatonic. I cannot believe what I am seeing. The people of the Central Bank, believing themselves to be doing a marvelous thing, have prepared a set—and it must have cost thousands. (Well, we have money now.) There, from the floor of

---

3   Arnold Rampersad is Professor of English and Sara Hart Kimball Professor in the Humanities at Stanford University

4   Earl Lovelace, one of Trinidad's most prominent authors.

the stage to the ceiling, was one big-arse photographic blow-up, in full colour, of the Red House [the parliament of Trinidad]. And on the side of the stage, what I presume was supposed to be a representation of the bandstand in Woodford Square in which Eric gave his great speeches to the university,[5] for all the audience to see, something that looked like a miniature Japanese pagoda, for my friend, my great biographer of black America to come and deliver a speech entitled "The Road to Obama."

Now talk about inappropriate. This does not need scenery. It's not a piece of theatre. It's not pretend. Why are you doing this? They were so pleased with their scenery. A lady came up and said, "Haven't we done well?" And I am thinking, would that you had given it to Tony Hall or even Raymond Choo Kong.[6] It's they who are doing theatre! [*laughter*] And it's the same thing about the coconut cart. Another real telling case of enwhitenment. We're going to have scenery like we're going to have skyscrapers. When in fact, we have a great advantage now with the world, at the edge of environmental disaster, saying no, no, no, no, no more tall air-conditioned concrete and glass edifices for this tropical island. We will not build another building here taller than a coconut tree unless it is spectacularly unique and Caribbean in the world.

In the same way that we do scenery for lectures which don't need them, so we have a propensity for handing out titles. Now I really don't want this to reflect against the recipients of these titles. But I have always felt awkward when this little island, with so much else that needs encouragement and promotion, we don't yet have an Academy of the Mas, but we do have a Poet Laureate! And we do have—and I say this not about the recipient, it's about the society—we do have a Master Artist, and he ain't dead yet... I'm not saying that awards aren't correct, and last night I was deeply touched. [The previous evening Peter Minshall had been given an award at the Caribana Kings and Queens Competition.] It was only this morning that I fully read the text and the text brought water to me eye. Just a little piece of wood but it says the warmest things: "Thanks for your decades of work in the business." At

---

5   This public venue for Williams' series of pre-independence speeches became known as "the University of Woodford Square." Eric Williams was Trinidad's first Prime Minister (1956-1981).
6   Directors respectively of Trinidad's Lordstreet Theatre, known for its carnivalesque style (Hall was also in the conference audience), and of RCK Productions, whose repertoire is mainly foreign plays transposed to the local setting.

the same time I really do feel—not to seek pity—but when I look at last night—that I think my life's work is wasted. [*the audience protests*]

Please. Please. It was not.

The artist, that first man who made a mark on a wall in a cave, did it for one reason: to say to this blackness [*indicates the universe*]: "I am." That's the job of the artist on behalf of his community. And on a little island, it's so much more important and so much more difficult. We exist. I am. I am.

In my experience there is no history but knowledge. In the twentieth century it's remarkable. I experienced it. I looked at it. No one taught me it. The people who most made a mark on the twentieth century: the Blacks, the Jews, the Gays. Why? Obvious. What do they share? Persecution. No, you don't exist! No, you are lesser! No, you can't come to the same dining table or sit in the same part of the bus as us! You don't have the same rights!

I am a very conservative fellow and am very late arriving at the business of gay rights to marriage. I think, oh God, leave the people with their marriage nah. [*laughter*] Until just by chance in a conversation on TV, Ellen DeGeneres with John McCain—a slight disagreement there—she said, "But wait a minute. Are you saying that gay people in terms of marriage have to sit in the back of the bus?" Not her words, mine; but that was the sense of her meaning. And I thought, mm, she has a point.

Even so, I stray from mine.

My first band, *Paradise Lost* [1976]. It was epic. It was Cecil B. DeMille. It was my thesis for what was to become my life's work. If you look at *Paradise Lost*, you will see the beginning of everything I ever did. It was all there in *Paradise Lost*, right up to Tan Tan and Saga Boy.[7]

There was a big row because of an agreed prototype. Miss Elsie and Mr. Peter had agreed, ok, we'll put five beads on the sleeve. Three days later, the sewing girl brings the hundred costumes and lays them on the table and all the hundred costumes have two beads on each sleeve. How did that happen? "Miss Elsie say to put two." Mr. Minshall: "Elsie, what happen here?" Turns out Elsie took three beads off to put more pennies

---

7   The over-life-sized, fully-articulated mas puppets in Minshall's 1990 band, *Tantana*, which marked his breakthrough in his characteristic designs.

in her pocket. So there was a big row about the integrity of the work and so on, a big, big row. A Chinese gentleman comes up to Mr. Minshall. Hear what he says: "Oh Peter, why are you getting so excited? After all, it is only mas." And then I really did get excited. And the sum total of what I said to him—in words that cannot be repeated—is, "What you are saying is about yourself. It is ONLY you." And I—my life's work has been to eradicate the word "only" from the saying. And from the self.

"IT IS MAS!" And I really do feel that way.

Reel the tape forward from 1976 to 2008.

There is a young man with a brave and big heart who wants to record everything great about the Caribbean and I can call his name: Rubadiri.[8] He lionizes the Caribbean artist or Caribbean creativity in whatever way it expresses itself. He did a big magazine which I saw recently and it was on the table. I asked him, please sign it. I didn't look at the magazine until a few days afterwards and I was confounded. The magazine has photo blow ups of beauty queens, fashion models, poets, writers, big blow-ups of paintings. And I couldn't find my part in it— you know, a little ego, where I am boy?—and ok, there is a picture of me and so on and I turn the page.

And all the mas, every band, maybe one, sometimes two pictures from a band, has been brought down to the size of a postage stamp on two pages. And that's ok, because it's thirty years of work and it would take up too many pages. So ok, you do a kind of discipline. But the part that really hurt me was Tan Tan and Saga Boy which, let me tell you, revolutionized world notions of what puppetry is about, far less what mas is about. Earl Lovelace passed me one day with my groceries coming round the corner: "Hey Minshall, I have something to tell you. You see that Tan Tan and Saga Boy, Minshall, you don't know what you do there. Black people in this country never see themselves so big." Oh God. Oh Lord. Now those were words from one artist to another to hold to your grave.

I was confounded by the fact that anybody could have the insensitivity, I was confounded that anyone could carry with him through life, into I think his mid-thirties, who loved his country, could yet still carry such a level of self-contempt unknowing to himself, to bring Tan Tan and Saga Boy down to the size of a postage stamp. You don't do that to

---

8   Rubadiri Victor, founder and editor of the magazine *Generation Lion*.

you, you don't do that to your people, you don't do that to the Caribbean. Please.

So you see, it is still only mas.

How many here are practitioners in the mas? Ten maybe? Tony Hall, the playwright, is here. Please, whenever I say playwrights, don't get me wrong. This man has paid his dues to the mas handsomely. Talk about a Robber speech! He and Errol [Seetahal] wrote a Robber speech for a figure called Papa Mas to be played by Errol Jones in a stadium. It was the first stadium where a mas ever played. Long before Barcelona, Atlanta and all those others, we did it ourselves.[9] And it could not have been done without him. [points to Tony Hall] He and Errol wrote the script and everybody, every artist, every actor, every dancer was involved.

Really, in the final analysis, I'm a cog, I'm just a little dot, but I'm a conduit. It's just that my life opened up with a lot of accidents that allowed me to see things a little more clearly than others. And I understand because I too went from Trinidad. I wanted to be a PAINTER!

Now it is time for the two PMs: Prime Minister and Peter Minshall. [laughter] This is a graphic, hard, solid example of Nignorance and Enwhitenment.

So I am in the Prime Minister's office,[10] Pat Ganase[11] next to me, there to explain why you mustn't build a building, glass or any other, in the Savannah, to house the Carnival. The Prime Minister is there in tie, neat. Me just T-shirt and jeans. In White Hall.

"Sir, when people go to village to town to city, they need to take a little of the bush with them. Otherwise they go crazy. Sir, the Savannah is a space, and even though people may not realize it, the Savannah as a space belongs to Port of Spain. The Savannah as a space is spiritually vital to the people of the city, and their island, and the Caribbean. It is the only city—not just in the Caribbean, not just in the Southern

---

9   Papa Mas was the performing narrator of Minshall's *Santimanitay*, a mas presented in T&T's National Stadium on Carnival Monday night, 1989. The Barcelona and Atlanta events referred to are the ceremonies of the Olympic Games in 1992 and 1996, for which Minshall was artistic director and designer.

10   Patrick Manning, Prime Minister 1991-95 and 2001-10.

11   Pat Ganase, expert on the Minshall oeuvre, who has assisted him professionally.

hemisphere, not just in the Americas—it is the only city in the whole world that has in its centre a savannah, a grassland peopled with trees. And on that side the flatlands go to the sea, and right behind it the Northern Range.

"Oh God, what a space, Sir. And don't you ever dare, Sir (I didn't say this then), to so enwhiten yourself as to plant flower gardens on the Savannah. No! Sir, this Savannah has not been touched after forty years of Independence. Sir, imagine, think of it! Like LeRoy Clarke thinks of a canvas.[12] Every inch of it must be perfect and beautiful. Every grass blade: nothing must interrupt its growth.

"And now then, Sir, let us deal with what is on the Savannah. What comes into town, once a year, for the people's joy and entertainment, does its big show and then departs? The circus. It pitches its tent, does its thing, then packs up and leaves. Carnival could do exactly that.

"But Sir, you don't realize it: in Carnival the traditional costumes only started becoming traditional when we became independent. You know why that happened? Because you threw the carnival out. You didn't know what to do with it and you just left it there for corbeaux [Caribbean vultures] to come and pick. And then businessmen took it over. And the big bands got bigger and bigger and bigger. And what we have now—imagine a garden and you don't tend it and these things get bigger and bigger and they grow. But nothing underneath could grow because of the darkness of the covering overhead. Like any gardener would know. So you want to find talent in the carnival? You won't! It's impossible.

"So instead, in the Savannah, you put in a tent, sized for bands of thirty and under, and first prize will be one million dollars. In five years' time the carnival art will be right back on track. You'll see: it needn't be big as a house and be pulled on wheels. It will be art. It will be meticulous. It will deal with life and death. It will be fate. It will be Shakespeare in mas, and everything fine, I promise you. You can encourage your people and have another tent over there, a little smaller ..."

Please, it's too much. My heart bursts.

"Sir, we will do something that all the theatre people of the world have wanted: we will free the audience from that word 'captive.' The whole Savannah is free for the audience to wander from tent to tent. You see you have a pamphlet here: this is happening at three o'clock.

---

12   An abstract impressionist, known as "de Poet", LeRoy Clarke is regarded as the doyen of Trinidad painters.

'Oh God, come children, come, we have to hear the Robber speeches. Don't worry with Minshall, nah. Don't worry with MacFarlane.'[13] Robber speeches at two o'clock in the Savannah in tent number five. The one with all the flags. A million dollars for the best Robber speech! And the poets will stop being laureates and they'll put on big hats and they will come and speak.

"And Sir, the crowning glory (this would have been before they start building the blue igloo[14])—the crowning glory, Sir (and I really can't give you the whole history of pan)—see where the Prince's Building was? That is where you will build the cathedral of a concert hall of shimmering steel. And that will be our skyscraper! Churches have steeples just because steeples are lovely. And this church of pan must have a series of steeples that rivals and surpasses those of Gaudi in Barcelona. And at the bottom of it, a vast rotunda that shall be called 'The Steel Drum'."

I'm a dreamer. Only a madman could come up with Mancrab.[15]

The Prime Minister at the end of this speech said: "Well, Mr. Minshall, I don't know anything about art. Why don't you go and see Calder Hart."

Hart, as it happens, is a man from this country [Canada], very well fed on the goodies of Trinidad.[16] So I went and saw Calder Hart, knowing the battle was already lost, and this plump, middle-aged Canadian sat opposite me. This man—who had never, as I had done, cycled or walked around the Savannah twice a day for eight years as a schoolboy, seeing it in its many seasons, in its many guises, and then come back to do my life's work in the Savannah—this man was telling me what was good for the Savannah and bad for the Savannah and why mas needed a glass coffin in the Savannah in which finally to expire.

---

13   Brian MacFarlane, a commercial designer who began producing mas-bands in 2005 and has won several Band of the Year prizes in the carnival competition.

14   A squat modernist construction of overlapping half-domes, housing the National Academy for the Performing Arts, recently built on the Prince's Building grounds by the Manning government using Chinese design and construction services.

15   The symbol of human greed, empowered by modern technology, in Minshall's 1983 environmental mas, *River*.

16   Calder Hart was chair of the Urban Development Corporation of T&T (UDeCOTT) and other state enterprises. He has since left T&T and the police are investigating allegations of fraud and corruption against him.

And the most tragic thing about enwhitenment is this thing which we little islands take from European—I'm not knocking it— European thoughts and ideas of the past two or three hundred years where anything worthwhile is put in a museum in a glass box. And now we want to take the vigor, the energy, the life, the blood of carnival and put it in a glass box so that it looks like a dead armadillo. And I'm saying, "No, please don't do that."

In the Savannah I just told you about, the big bands would be on the periphery. And the expert designers would design out of the same steel and brass little folding bleachers that go around the Savannah under the shade of the trees. And, dammit, let it be for free. You've got the oil money.

All right. I went to see Calder Hart. And at the end of the meeting I just listened and thought, this is impossible. The die is cast. At the end of the meeting he said: "You know, Patrick Manning is a great leader." [*laughter*] (You don't know the man. You shouldn't laugh.) Patrick Manning is a great leader. And I said, "Why do you say that, Mr. Hart?" And Mr. Hart said to me: "He listens to people."

Now for the closing.

I was asked about three years ago to write an introduction to a book of photographs by Pablo Delano entitled *In Trinidad*.[17] With his permission, I am sharing with you in advance of the publication of the book this fall what I wrote and some of his images. [*as Minshall proceeds to speak, photographs from the book are projected in view of the audience*]

I am a masman. I work in the medium of mas in the masquerade of the Trinidad Carnival. Mas is the living expression of elemental human energy out on the streets in a celebration of life that dates back to ancient times. Mas is living art. Pablo Delano's art is resolutely still-life. It also celebrates life. My work is visceral, pulsing, spontaneous and immediate. His work is contemplative. Yet we see with the same eye. We feel with the same heart. We are both island men and Caribbean.

I have chosen three of my own works in Trinidad not just to establish our common ground but to better see and appreciate his book of pictures.

---

17   The full title is *In Trinidad: Photographs by Pablo Delano*.

These are verbal descriptions of the mas, excerpted from the past. They deal as intimately with the island and its people as do the pictures in this book.

The three works are *River*, *Tapestry* and *The Lost Tribe*.

River was performed in 1983. It consisted of a mile of light, white cotton held aloft on poles, a river of cloth. Under the canopy there was a river of people. The people were all dressed in pure white cotton in apparel that recalled the fashions of their many ancestors. They carried the names of the many rivers on the island. It was one river, one people.

River
1983

A mas in two acts

The cast: Mancrab, Washerwoman, the River People

The story: We first meet Mancrab and Washerwoman at the Carnival preliminaries, which is a sort of prologue or overture.

We can see straightaway that Mancrab is very clever, an accomplished master of technology, full of complicated genius. He is clearly most powerful and dangerous. Yet he is never satisfied or content with himself. Enough is never enough for Mancrab. He always wants more. Washerwoman is just the opposite. She is really quite simple, as her costume shows. Her power is her love for life, which is the simplest thing of all. Her heart is pure and clean and happy, like her lines of washing dancing in the breeze. Washerwoman is the beloved leader of the River People.

On Carnival Monday (Act I) Mancrab embattles Washerwoman. He is eager to take from her the River, which he needs for his own purposes of enrichment, to build his factory on its banks, but he must first defeat her and win over her people's trust. Washerwoman's very strength is in that trust, and it is with that trust and love, in the form of a simple square of white cloth, that she overcomes Mancrab and banishes him from the Savannah.

Washerwoman leads her people in happy celebration before us. The River People, all in white, dance and sing. The River is saved. Its waters run clear and clean as their hearts.

But that night Mancrab develops a clever strategy. He settles quietly by the riverbank, and using his finest chemicals and oils, assisted by his best technicians, he floods the River with a rainbow of extraordinary colour. He stirs the water with glowing promises of profit and luxury for all. The River People are truly amazed. They run to see, and with buckets and calabashes and cups, anything to hold water, they attempt to catch and keep Mancrab's illusory colours, each fighting the other for more. In their haste and greed, they leave Washerwoman unprotected. That very night, Mancrab steals into Washerwoman's mascamp which is no longer surrounded by the force of love.

He kills her.

On Carnival Tuesday (Act II) Mancrab is victorious. The River is his. The waters are polluted. He drags the lifeless body of Washerwoman before us, her lines of washing now blood-stained and borne by others. The rainbow River follows, and the River People. They are wild and frenzied in their dance. They believe themselves the richer for Mancrab's rainbow. They bathe themselves in its colours. In so doing they destroy themselves.

We now live in the age of Mancrab. Twenty-five years later his triumph seems complete. The island races helter-skelter-smelter to self-destruction. Greed and tribal dominance, oil and money, and empty pomposity borne of ignorance and insecurity, have made the island a living surreal nightmare. This was the mas of 2001. The streets became a dark, oil-drenched landscape of lost faceless souls, themselves drenched in glittering, worthless bling. This is Hell.

But the first full page picture in Pablo Delano's book shows Washerwoman rising gloriously from the river. Her spirit is strong. Among the callaloo of people there is love.[18] There is hope. There are riches greater than Mancrab ever imagined.

---

18   Callaloo is also the name of a characteristically mixed Caribbean dish, and the term is used in Trinidad as a metaphor for many different parts, or peoples, mixing together to create a new and harmonious whole.

TAPESTRY
1997
A mas in celebration of Humanity in all its Diversity

TAPESTRY
A mass Celebration of the interconnectedness
of all Mankind.
A Patchwork Quilt of the Many Races and Faces
that Coexist in This Space.

TAPESTRY
draws Threads from the Cloth of Africa, Asia,
Europa and the Americas, weaving
a new Fabric of Multicoloured Hues and Textures.

TAPESTRY
is an Ode to the Peaceful coexistence of all Peoples
and a Tribute to the Emergence of
A New world, A New Tribe, A New Vibe.

TAPESTRY
is based firmly in the understanding that
ALL AH WE IS ONE, brown, yellow, black, white,
same struggle, same fight;
and stresses the ideal of the Unity
of all colours and creeds, working together for the
Good of the Whole.

TAPESTRY
is a Celebration of You, Me, He, She, It, Them, Us,
All ah We!

This book of pictures is the Tapestry. This book is the fingerprint of an island identity. It is the map of an island destiny. It is the mas of life in Trinidad. To contemplate these images is to see ourselves, to play ourselves, to be ourselves. We grope in blind unthinking imitative ignorance towards the future. To contemplate these pictures is to help us find our own way.

The Lost Tribe
1999

There once was an island place that was blessed with many riches. Green mountains, fertile valleys, clear rivers, warm seas. The greatest of its blessings, though, was its people.

They were a people whose ancestors had come from many different places, who had come together to make one tribe, in a new world. They invented new ways of doing things, new ways of dancing and singing, new ways of praising the High Spirit, new ways of celebrating, new ways of travelling through the world. They travelled together toward a wonderful new destiny.

To know the direction in which they must travel, they followed a great map. No one man could have drawn this map. It was a map that had been assembled from the knowledge of all the ancestors of all the people.

But one day, at a time when the travelling had become difficult, the leaders of the different families within the tribe quarreled amongst themselves. In their foolishness, the map was torn into pieces, and the pieces were scattered among the people. Each of the families, looking at its piece, thought that it possessed the whole map.

The island place became a spiritual wilderness. The tribe lost its way.

Until the pieces of the map are put together again, the people will squander their riches. Their destiny will remain distant and obscure. And they will wander aimlessly. The Lost Tribe.

Pablo Delano's book of pictures puts the pieces of the map together again. The book illuminates a vision for Trinidad. It excoriates division. It joins the tribes together between its two covers. It celebrates Washerwoman and her river people, one river, one love, one people. It vanquishes Mancrab. Pablo Delano's camera studies every exquisite thread of the Tapestry with equal ardour and fascination. He joins the threads together and lays the pattern out. We are perhaps too close to ourselves to see ourselves as clearly as he does. Look at the pictures. Look at the beauty and the immense potential of an island people.

I make mas. Pablo Delano makes pictures. I salute his work with these words from Federico Garcia Lorca, which guide me always in my work.

The poem, the song, the picture,
are but water
drawn from the well of the people,
and it must be given back to them
in a cup of beauty,
so they may drink,
and in drinking,
understand themselves.

It is the close. There is a battle on for the soul of my little country. It is truly a war and as far as I am concerned the bad guys are winning. [*Minshall puts on his black hat*] Also from the *New York Times*, an op-ed article on the subject of Karadzic and war's lessons. (Cohen: July 24, 2008) And in the end of his piece, this journalist, Roger Cohen, has the following to say: "I took that away from the war: the indivisibility of integrity and the importance of a single dissenting voice." [*standing ovation*]

2

THE AFRICAN HERITAGE

Interrogating the Roots, Elements, and Crossovers of the Caribbean Carnival: A Case of West African Celebrations

Modesto Mawulolo Amegago

Introduction

In tracing the origin of the carnival, one needs to think of it as a broad set of cultural values and practices. Some societies have celebrations or cultural practices similar to carnival but refer to them with different names. Colonised societies, such as the African Caribbean, continue to use western language and have adopted and applied the word carnival to some of their own traditional celebrations. In such societies, a blending of characteristics of both national and European carnivals has occurred. This is not to deny the fact that the word carnival might have been borrowed, together with the cultural practices, from the West.

Some writers maintain that it was the European version of carnival that was introduced to the Caribbean (Trinidadian 1785) by wealthy, white planters who held fancy-costumed balls. People wore masks, wigs, and beautiful clothing and danced all night long. Errol Hill notes that during the period of the British rule before emancipation of slaves, the carnival in Trinidad and Tobago was an important institution for whites and free coloureds particularly in the towns (Hill 1972, 6-15). Brereton states that before the emancipation of slavery, the carnival in Trinidad "had been an elegant social affair of the [W]hite Creole." This involved the leaders wearing European type masks, street promenading or making house-to-house visits. Music from small bands accompanied them and people played practical jokes on each other (Brereton in Riggio 2004, 53).

Contrary to the claims made by some scholars about the European origins of Caribbean carnival, some Afrocentric scholars and Egyptologists, such as Smart and Nehusi, maintain that the complex ideas and practices that shaped the carnival originated among the Afrikans in Kemet, or Kemit, along the Nile valley of ancient Egypt. These scholars also state that the Africans in Kemet historically had an organic and dynamic relationship with the rest of Africa and their civilization was a specific elaboration on African cultures (Smart and Nehusi 2000, 79).

The Afrocentric scholars claim that Herodotus also made reference to the Greek borrowing of certain cultural practices. According to Smart and Nehusi, these included ceremonial meetings, processions, and processional offerings from the Kamit, or Kamau, or the ancient Egyptians, who were black (2000, 91). They also claim that Greek scholars, such as Socrates, Plato, and Aristotle studied in Kemet. These philosophers returned to Greece where they reinterpreted the fundamental ideas they had absorbed about civilization. These ideas were then passed on to the Romans, who, in turn, reinterpreted and transmitted them to other Europeans (2000, 79).

The Afrocentric scholars also hold that although the cultural transmission was a two way process, it was dominated by the Kemites, who, during their heyday, in almost every respect, "constituted the most advanced power" in Africa and the rest of the world (Smart and Nehusi 2000, 80). They further maintain that periodic migration from the Nile valley led to the spread of cultural ideas and practices throughout Africa. Smart and Nehusi suggest that these customs were interpreted in different ways as ideas were disseminated among people from the various regions. As a result, carnival evolved (80). Egyptologist, Budge, believes that some of the Kemites cultural festivals were in vogue by at least the beginning of the dynasty period, most probably before then, and that the festival tradition may be between 5,200 and 6,700 years old, existing possibly before the beginning of Europe (Smart and Nehusi 2000, 78).

The First Carnival in Kemet

Afrocentric scholars believe that festivals constituted an important part of the lives of ancient Egyptians, having religious, political and social significance (Smart and Nehusi 2000, 81). An example is the Wosorian festival, an agricultural ritual celebrated along the Nile river valley more than a millennia ago. It lasted from about five days to a month and marked the end of one year and the beginning of another. According to Smart and Nehusi, this festival re-enacted the sufferings, triumph and resurrection of Wosir over his brother Setekh (Seth). There were processions of priests and priestesses as well as ordinary people carrying images of gods and goddesses to the accompaniment of instrumental music, singing, and dancing. The festival dramatised the arrival of a boat containing images of gods and goddesses and their followers. A crowd of men representing the foes of Osiris attacked the boat with sticks. And amidst the wailing and lamentation of women beating their breasts, there was a re-enactment of the coming of Osiris from the temple after his death and the departure of his body to his tomb (2000, 83-84).

Smart and Nehusi also document records of the rites of succession and accession of Pharaohs (which Henry Frankfort called "The Mystery Play of the Succession"). These include secret ceremonies restricted to certain initiates, ceremonies relating to the public appearance of Pharaohs, ceremonies of reversion, and offerings involving the wearing of elaborate regalia and masks by religious leaders. It is believed that the theatre of the Ancient Greeks, as well as their sports, such as athletics, boxing, wrestling, archery and stick fighting, were rooted in the Ancient Egyptian carnival, as, it is also suggested, were the Euro-Christian beliefs of the Virgin Birth, the Resurrection and the struggle between good and evil (2000, 81-83).

From Kemet/Egypt to West Africa and the Caribbean

Smart and Nehusi further claim that the distinctive ideas, practices and elements of the Kemet's festival, such as procession, rituals, music and dance, stick fighting, costuming, masks and masquerades, remain vital aspects of many African festivals and it was from West Africa that these ideas and practices were directly introduced to the Caribbean and the Western hemisphere (Smart and Nehusi 2000, 94). These cultural practices manifest in the agricultural rites referred to as first fruit or crop over in America, the Caribbean and Latin American celebrations. Thus, what is now referred to as the carnival in the Caribbean and other African Diaspora settings is celebrated in various forms and under specific names. For example, the Jonkonnu parade (crop over and street procession satirical songs) is held in Jamaica, the Bahamas, and Bermuda; the Kwanza harvest festival is celebrated in North America and the Diaspora; the Mardi Gras in New Orleans and Louisiana, Texas, and Florida; the Candombe in Uruguay; the Juego de los Congos in Panama; and the Reisado or Congada in Brazil (Foster and Schwarz 1995, 21-22). Most of these celebrations re-enact the major events that occurred during the period of enslavement and foreign domination (Adeyinka in Smart and Nehusi, 119).

The Trinidad and Tobago Carnival

One of the world's most popular carnivals is celebrated in Trinidad and Tobago during the month of August (as a three to five-day event). In his essay: "Origins of Rituals and Customs in the Trinidad Carnival: African or European?", Hollis Urban Lester Liverpool "states unequivocally that the Trinidad and Tobago carnival is 'African in character and function and traces it development to Cannes Brulees or Canboulay ceremony'" (Adeyinka in Smart and Nehusi 2000, 127). The Cannes Brulees or Canboulay, which means cane burning, is said to have been created by the Trinidadian-Africans "to celebrate their 'freedom from slavery' in 1838" (Elder in Riggio 2004, 49). The ceremony involves: a re-enactment of the African pageant, midnight procession through the street, satirising the ruling class, beating African drums, performing African type dancing condemned by white moralists as profane, carrying lighted torches, blowing cow horns and conch shells, burlesquing the Europeans' life style (as in Dame Lorraine) and stick fighting on the streets (Elder in Riggio, 49).

The preparation for the carnival may take a year long. It involves brainstorming to generate ideas, selection of themes for the bands, designing of elaborate and colourful costume, the creation of masks and masquerades, calypso songs and steel band rhythms, narratives and dance in mas camps, the construction of Ranchos bamboo huts, or palacio or palay, Orisha temples, (in Columbia, Panama and Trinidad), the selection of the king and queen, and the decoration of performance settings (Adeyinka in Smart and Nehusi 2000, 118). The festival features the Canboulay ritual, which commemorates and praises the Orishas and their ancestors for guiding them through the middle passage to their new location and pays homage to Mother Africa. There is a solemn torchlight procession at midnight on 1st August to usher in the carnival. The torches symbolise the Caribbean People's past bondage and newly found freedom (Adeyinka in Smart and Nehusi, 118-119).

The climax of the celebration occurs during the Monday and Tuesday processions/parades along the main streets. This involves a display of elaborate and colourful costumes, make up, body paint, masks and masquerades, depicting various characters such as the law enforcing agencies, policemen, soldiers, clergy, politicians, slave masters, satirical figures, animals figures, instrumental/steel band music, singing and dancing, costume competition, crowning of the king and queen and feasting/merry making.

In essence, the Pan-Caribbean or Pan-African festival is, according to Adeyinka, a resistance to and re-enactment and commemoration of the

brutalities of slavery, oppression, exploitation, deprivation, rape, alienation and emancipation. The celebration provides a forum and a license
for the down trodden to express their reaction against politicians, social
injustices and scandals of the day (Adeyinka in Smart and Nehusi 2000,
105-129). As Kimani Nehusi observes, it also involves the gay abandon,
serious play, inversion of social order, release of tensions and frustrations
resulting from one's location in society, the symbolic and real presence
of good and evil, old and young, life and death, creation and cosmology
(2000, 77-103). The carnival also serves as catharsis, thus providing a
forum for purifying the mind and body and renewing human spirituality.

Concerning the claims about the Kemite's Origin of the World Carnival

Claims about the Kemite or the Ancient Egyptian origin of the world
carnival may be valid if we maintain that carnival, as a cultural practice,
originated from a single source (being Africa) and if we acknowledge that
there is much empirical evidence to support this belief. Indeed, some
scholars maintain that Africa is the cradle of humankind. Evidence also
exists concerning contact between the Ancient European (Greek and
Romans) and the Egyptians or North Africans, which, no doubt, would
result in intercultural borrowing (as has occurred in this current era).
Also, some of the West African ethnic groups, such as the Yoruba and
the Wolof trace their origins to the Sudan, Ethiopia, or Egypt, but then
a problem arises in that most Egyptians today are Arabs. It is possible
that the boundaries of the Ancient Egypt shifted and, over time, some
of the original settlers of Kemet migrated to other places.

Obviously, certain cultural practices may originate from a single
source and spread to other parts of the world, while some practices
may emerge from multiple sources. It appears, however, that many of
the world cultures/peoples desire to re-enact or celebrate significant
aspects of their life experiences in the form of festivals. Therefore, the
act of re-enactment, celebration, or festival may be regarded as a universal human phenomenon. Of course, any form or re-enactment of festival is shaped by the peoples' particular experiences in place and time.
For example, tropical environments and the summer seasons usually
favour outdoor and practical activities/celebrations involving processions. Also, in societies where communal living is cherished, relatively
larger numbers of people may participate in such celebrations/festivals.
This is the case of many West African and Caribbean societies. One may
witness similar or common cultural elements in the celebrations of the

various peoples around the world, thus pointing to the interconnectedness of all human beings. Nevertheless, claims about the intercultural borrowings and adaptation of ideas and practices may also be valid.

As Smart and Nehusi point out, there is much evidence to support the fact that most of the people living in the Caribbean and African Diaspora originated from the West African towns and villages and brought with them traits of their cultural traditions that have been retained over the years. Such cultural practices are continually reinforced by ideas and practices brought by the new arrivals from the African continent. However, the cultural practices of the Diaspora Africans have also been influenced by the Amerindian, Western and Oriental cultures with which they have come into contact. Nonetheless, one would see common elements in both the Caribbean carnival and many West African celebrations.

In many West African societies, festivals are initiated around major agricultural rites, state divinities, environmental and historical episodes, such as drought, famine, migration, endurance and resistance to political authority. Such festivals are usually great occasions for public re-enactment of the peoples' past and present experiences and values. For example, the Homowo (meaning hooting at hunger) is celebrated annually by the Ga people of Ghana during the month of August to commemorate the victory of their ancestors over great famine and to celebrate good harvest in their land. The celebration involves the arrival of Soobii, Thursday people, at a special location called Mukpono, and their procession contains lots of food, particularly vegetables, to indicate their overcoming the famine; the dressing of twins in white costume and feeding them with festival meal; the marking of doorways with red clay to signify protection against evil spirits; visits of chiefs to stool houses to commemorate the ancestors; a procession of chiefs and people sprinkling Kpoikpoi, the festival meal to door steps and the surrounding area (Nishwamo); and drumming, blowing of trumpet, singing, dancing, eating of the festival meal, merry making on Saturday afternoon, followed by the greeting of relatives, friends, and lovers on Sunday (Fosu 2001, 2-5).

The Bakatue is also celebrated annually by the people of Elmina (in the Central region of Ghana) in June/July during the beginning of the fishing season. This week-long festival is preceded by a ban on fishing (in the Banya lagoon) and drumming for a period of time. The celebration involves a procession through the town amidst drumming, singing, and dancing, canoe racing on the Banya lagoon (located at Elmina) and a durbar of chiefs, involving a display of elaborate paraphernalia (Fosu, 10-11).

The Adae (ketewa) and Ada Kese (resting or resting place) are celebrated by the Ashanti over forty days every fifth year to commemorate their ancestors, offer them gratitude, and solicit their help and guidance. The celebration involves mass cleansing; the sending of royal messengers to towns and sacred locations; and a procession of king and chiefs to the mausoleum (the burial place of the Akan leaders) to offer prayers of prosperity and welfare. It also includes visits to stool houses and temples; ritual prayers; durbar of chiefs and people on Sunday (during which the Asantehene, the king and chiefs sit in state to receive homage from their people); and a display of the golden stool, which is a symbol of political and national unity (Fosu, pp.12-16).

Hogbetsotsoza is another festival celebrated by the Ewes between September and November to commemorate the successful migration of their ancestors from a tyrannical ruler at Notsie, a walled kingdom in the present day Republic of Togo. This festival begins (in September) with mass cleansing, followed by a ban on music and dance for about a month. The festival continues with music and dance performances at Anloga, the state's capital. This involves students' music and dance processions and durbar, featuring youths playing leadership roles such as kings and chiefs, ceremonial leaders, musicians and dancers, prayers, a reconciliation ceremony, communal feasting, a re-enactment of the exodus, a procession and durbar of chiefs, and people and merry making (Kodzo Vordoagu 1994, 1-30; see also Amegago 1988, 1-63).

The Apoo festival is also celebrated annually between March and April by the chiefs and people of Techiman, Nkoranza, and Wenchi traditional area (for about a week) to honour the god Ntoa. According to the people, Ntoa detests wrongdoing and punishes them for any such deeds. Ntoa recommends that during a certain period every year, any ill feelings harboured between citizens should be purged through song. The celebration involves the banning of drumming and weeping for a set period of time. It also includes the decoration of temples with white clay (Nnunsi-tuo), and the symbolic destruction of harmful spirits by the priests and priestesses. Past wars are re-enacted through mock fighting (on Thursday), and prayers are said in commemoration of ancestors and the Apoo carnival (from Saturday to Monday), which involves the procession of chiefs and people amidst drumming, dancing and the singing of Apoo songs of criticism (Fosu, 27-29).

In addition, a festival called Gelede is celebrated annually by the Yoruba of south-western Nigeria and south-eastern Nigeria (between March and May) to honour the mothers for their mystical powers relating to fertility, knowledge of the secret life, and the destructive and surreptitious power Ajé, witchcraft. The festival takes place at market place, which is considered the domain for women and "a metaphor of the world," a place where mortars and spirits continue to interact. The celebration involves the use of elaborate masks, headdresses, men masquerading as women, ritual performances, processions, dancing, singing and the playing of instruments (Drewal and Drewal 1983, 7-13). There are also ceremonial events, such as the installation and enstoolment of chiefs/kings; the celebration of ancestral rites; and the inauguration of new performing groups which involves the designing and display of new and elaborate costumes, masks and masquerades, big umbrellas, geometric figures, carved human figures, flags, music, dance and dramatic processions, re-enactments and rituals/prayers.

Commonalities

The common elements manifested in both the West African festivals and the Pan-Caribbean carnival include the lengthy preparatory period towards the festivals. This includes the designing and featuring of elaborate and colourful costumes. Then there are the rituals/prayers, a procession, rhythmic music, singing and dancing, stilt walking, stick fighting, re-enactment of historical and cultural episodes/values, resistance or reactions to certain environmental conditions, social commentary or criticism, and merrymaking.

Robert Farris Thompson also makes direct symbiotic linkages between these New World festival art forms and their continental African cognates. He identifies the common performance aesthetic principle such as "dominance of a percussive concept of performance; call and response; battles of aesthetic virtuosity between two singers, or two dance groups" (Thompson in Smart and Nehusi 2000, 126). Adeyinka cites Thompson, stating that the principal contributors of these 'popular aesthetic vocabularies' that include 'concepts of parading and processioneering' in the Carnival arts in the Americas are 'notably the Yoruba of Nigeria and Benin, the Bakongo of Congo, Bas-Zaire, and Angola'" (Adeyinka in Smart and Nehusi, 126-127).

Crossovers

Nowadays, the organisers of the carnival in places such as Canada and USA often feature African musicians and dancers or cultural groups in their annual carnival to add more home flavour to the celebrations and reinforce their African connection. A recent arts and cultural festival in the Republic of Benin (April 2008) featured a dance called

Bourian, reported to have been brought by the African returnees from Brazil. This dance depicts the relationship between the Portuguese leaders and the Afro-Brazilian men and women through elaborate costumes, masks and stilts (as revealed in conversation with Abalo in August 2008). In 2007, the Pan-Caribbean style of the carnival was celebrated in Togo. This involved mass procession/parading with moving vehicles through the major streets of Lome with music and dance, stilt walking, a display of colourful costumes, masks and masquerades, prayers/rituals and merrymaking. This all emphasises the continuing contact and exchange of ideas and cultural practices between the Africans at home and in the Diaspora.

In this paper I have elucidated the debates about the origin of the carnival, have discussed the Pan-Caribbean or Pan-African carnival, and considered the commonalities in the Pan-Caribbean carnival and West African festivals. In conclusion, I would like to reiterate that all social groups desire to re-enact or celebrate significant aspects of their experiences. Such celebrations are shaped by the people's environmental, historical, and cultural factors. These celebrations may reveal cultural particularities, similarities and universals and intercultural influences. Attempts to trace the origin of the carnival are worthwhile, for this would enable us to acknowledge or pay tribute to the various sources of origin. Paramount to this endeavour is the sharing of experience. It would draw together the various contributors: victors and victims, enslavers and enslaved, oppressors and oppressed, leaders and the led, and all social groups, regardless of their race, ethnicity, class or gender, to interact, recreate, redress and relearn from such experiences, and live in harmony in recognition of the complex human desires, values, experiences and actions.

Bibliography

Aching, Gerard. 2002. *Masking and Power: Carnival and Popular Culture in the Caribbean*. Minneapolis and London: University of Minnesota Press.

Adeyinka, Olaogun Narmer. 2000. "A Carnival of Resistance, Emancipation, Commemoration, Reconstruction, and Creativity." In *Ah Come back Home: Perspectives on the Trinidad and Tobago Carnival*, eds. Smart and Nehusi, 105-129, Washington D. C. and Port of Spain: Original World Press.

Amegago, Modesto M. K. 1988. *The Role of Misego Dance in Anlo's Migration and the Hogbetsotso Festival*. Diss. University of Ghana.

Brereton, Bridget. 2004. "The Trinidad Carnival in the Late Nineteenth Century." In *Carnival Culture in Action: The Trinidad Experience*, ed. Riggio, 53-63, London: Routledge.

Drewal Henry J. and Margaret T. Dewal. 1983. *Gelede Art and Female Power among the Yoruba*. Bloomington: Indiana University Press.

Elder, J. D. 2004. "Cannes Brulées" In *Carnival Culture in Action: The Trinidad Experience*, ed. Riggio, 48-52, London: Routledge.

Foster, L. and Chris Schwarz. 1995. *Caribana: The Greatest Celebration*. Toronto: Ballantine, 1995.

Fosu, Kwaku Amoako-Atah. 2001. *Festivals of Ghana*. Kumasi: Amok.

Hill, Errol. 1972. *The Trinidad Carnival: Mandate for A National Culture*. Austin: University of Texas Press.

Kodzo-Vordoagu, J. G. 1994. *Anlo Hogbetsotso Festival*. Accra: Domak Press.

Koningsbruggen, Peter Van. 1997. *Trinidad Carnival: A Quest for National Identity*. London: Macmillan Education.

Liverpool, Hollis Urban. 1998. "Origins of Rituals and Customs in the Trinidadian Festival: African or European?" *The Drama Review* 42:3, 24-37.

Remedi, Gustavo. 2004. *Carnival Theatre: Uruguay's Popular Performers and National Culture*. Minneapolis: University of Minnesota Press.

Riggio, Milla Cozart, ed. 2004. *Carnival Culture in Action: The Trinidad Experience*. London: Routledge.

Smart, Ian and Kimani Nehusi, eds. 2000. *Ah Come back Home: Perspectives on the Trinidad and Tobago Carnival*. Washington D. C. and Port of Spain: Original World Press.

Ware Carolyn. E. 2007. *Cajun Women and Mardi Gras: Reading the Rules Backward*. Chicago: The University of Illinois Press.

Web Sources

www.allahwe.org

http://www.carnivalpower.com/history_of_carnival.htm

http://www.randafricanart.com_gelede_mask_snake_andbirds.html

http://www.theafrica.com/magazine/carnival.htm

http://en.wikipedia.org/wiki/carnival

The Transculturation of Yoruba Annual Festivals: The *Día de Reyes* in Colonial Cuba in the Nineteenth Century

Henry Lovejoy

Carnival in Cuba has undergone many historical transformations since the introduction of annual festivals in the Spanish colony. One obvious change was a departure from an annual colonial holiday, *Día de Reyes* (Day of the Kings) held on January 6, to the one celebrated today during the month of February. It is not known when the first *Día de Reyes* was held, but the Spanish presumably introduced it very early on. This annual holy day was originally observed as a *Corpus Christi* procession intended to celebrate the Epiphany or the day the three kings came to visit baby Jesus bearing gifts. As thousands of African people were brought to the island, groups of slaves began to reinterpret the original meaning associated with the *Día de Reyes*. A significant development of this colonial festival, especially in relation to Afro-Cuban history, occurred in 1823 when the colonial government permitted *cabildos de nación*, or African "ethnic" associations based on Spanish *cofradías* (guilds or fraternities), to march with flags during the annual celebration in Havana and other western cities of the island. The abrupt end of the colonial holiday in 1885 can be attributed to a governmental decree on 19 December 1884 (two years before the abolition of slavery) prohibiting, due to public safety, the involvement of *cabildos* in processions.

Those concerned with understanding the history of Afro-Cuban culture continue to analyze the historical importance of the *Día de Reyes*. It was well documented as the one day of the year when African slaves and their descendents could "freely" express themselves beyond the bonds of slavery. The colonial holiday and associated annual festivals in

Cuba today exemplified a theatre of transculturation. Transculturation highlights the work of the great Cuban scholar, Fernando Ortiz, whose detailed studies of African and African-derived cultures during the *Día de Reyes* were a feature in the development of his theories related to cultural change in Cuban society. Transculturation refers to the complex "processes of creolization" defined by Sidney W. Mintz and Richard Price (Mintz and Price 1976).[1] Ortiz applied transculturation to express the multilayered phenomena that have come about in Cuba as a result of the complex transmutations of cultures (1940, 98). Transculturation, following Ortiz expands upon Herskovits' use of acculturation, retention, or survivals to incorporate equally important processes of deculturation. Deculturation can be defined as the antonym of acculturation, referring to the losses or disruption of cultural tendencies or traditions. The history of the *Día de Reyes* provided an example of deculturation because it was first introduced by the Spanish, but, eventually, it was outlawed. The cultural loss occurred in 1885 when a Catholic festival was cancelled because Africanized adaptations of that festival were believed to be unsafe. The result of transculturation, which Ortiz called neoculturation (the formation of new Creole cultures), can be exemplified by a disconnected extension of the *Día de Reyes* reflected in Cuba's Carnival today.

Transculturation and processes of creolization are especially complex concepts in terms of the historical reconstruction of slave communities and understanding identities of Africans and their descendants in the New World. These concepts imply a multifaceted nature of cultural history that does not lend itself to a clear-cut, one-dimensional, or chronological sequence of events. Ortiz, for example, valorised forms of sociality embedded in certain traditions, but he did not root identity in the past. In this context, Ortiz theoretically conceived a historical re-construction of the *Día de Reyes* as a conglomeration of non-linear or non-chronological events whereby new Cuban cultures and identities emerged. However, due to the co-existence of an array of diverse cultures interacting with one another over long periods of time, the history of the annual festival and the formation of new cultures cannot be anything *but* chronological, as Mintz and Price have argued. Essentially, I am applying the concept of transculturation to describe the complex processes of creolization in which new cultural identities in Cuba were forged and to show how that process had to be linear, chronological, and hence, historical.

---

1   See also Richard Price, "On the Miracle of Creolization," *Afro-Atlantic Dialogues: Anthropology in the Diaspora*, Kevin A. Yelvington ed., (Santa Fe: School of American Research, 2006), 113-145.

This paper will specifically deconstruct the history of the *Día de Reyes* from a *Lucumí* perspective.[2] I am arguing that Yoruba identities in colonial Cuba had West African origins, which by the nineteenth century, had already undergone processes of creolization *in* Yorubaland before reaching Cuba. In West Africa, the Yoruba sub-groups such as Oyo, Egba, Egbado, Ijesu, Awori, and Owo, were organized into networks of related villages, towns, and kingdoms. Most towns were headed by an *oba* (king or chief), or *baale* (nobleman or mayor) who was subject to an *oba*'s authority. Most Yoruba sub-groups not only had relative degrees of exposure to one another, but also in other circumstances to Islam and/or Christianity. David H. Brown, a respected anthropologist of African-derived cultures in Cuba, has argued that the *Día de Reyes* had particular meaning to slaves of Yoruba descent in the nineteenth century, no matter what their particular lineage was or what sub-group they came from because it was the "Day of Kings" (2003, 25-62). Special meanings of *Día de Reyes* for communities or groups of slaves of Yoruba descent who were involved in *Lucumí cabildos* and marched during the colonial holiday are abundant and well documented. In essence, this chapter will seek to highlight comparable characteristics and functions of the *oba* in annual festivals in different Yoruba cultural contexts in West Africa in order to discuss the involvement of the *rey* (king) of the *Lucumí cabildo* during the *Día de Reyes* in Cuba.

Annual Festivals in Yorubaland

To a certain degree, annual festivals in Yorubaland were similar, even though different Yoruba sub-groups revered different deities (*òrìsàs*) and practiced different rituals associated with any given festival. Festivals, whether annual or not, were numerous and could occur anytime throughout the year depending on the season, reason, and cultural tradition of each sub-group. In general, Yoruba annual festivals were held in honour of prominent or local *òrìsàs* and were often connected to local founding myths that supported the *oba*'s position within his domain. These traditions praised specific *òrìsà* symbolically attached to a lineage and the particular geographical area. Annual festivals reinforced legends associ-

---

2   In Spanish-speaking colonies the *nación Lucumí* referred to certain groups of people taken from the "Slave Coast" (Togo, Benin, and western Nigeria) and mainly referred to those people we identify as being "Yoruba." See Robin Law, "Ethnicity and the Slave Trade: 'Lucumí' and 'Nago' as Ethnonyms in West Africa," *History in Africa*, Vol. 24 (1997), 205–219.

ated with the king's power over his subjects, his kingdom and his loyalty to an *òrìsà* (Falola and Genova 2005, 7).

Yoruba annual festivals were generally fixed by traditions and organized into yearly cycles, usually related to a harvest. Festivals also included prayers for blessings such as rain and good fortune on the town. Most annual festivals played on an association between sex and agriculture, a day of license in which repressed feelings come to the surface, and according to E.G. Parrinder's Christian viewpoint, could "degenerate too easily into an orgy of lust" (1951, 56). It was believed that fertility gods would help people reproduce children, who were highly valued. It was generally believed that children were the reincarnation of the deceased ancestors of a lineage.

Another major purpose of annual festivals was specifically concerned with the glorification of royalty and was a display of an *oba*'s ancient beaded crown. Typically, it was the *oba*'s duty to ratify the date of any given festival, which could change yearly depending on the date of harvest. The display of his crown was a symbolic demonstration of that power, and also in the case of the Yemoja festival, a way of regenerating the king so that the crown would stay on his head (Apter 1992, 97-98). Unlike other monarchical systems of government that determined kingship by primogeniture, an electoral college of lineage heads in Yoruba towns were usually charged with selecting a member of one of the royal families of the town to be the *oba* or *baale*. The selection of a new *oba* or *baale* was usually confirmed by a priest (*babalawo*) through Ifá divination and took place just before or on the day of an annual festival. Festivals might also celebrate the number of years the *oba* or *baale* had reigned.

The *babalawo*, who worked directly for the *oba*, had a prominent role during every Yoruba festival. The sacrifices he made during the annual celebration were intended to appease or "feed" a number of *òrìsàs*, specifically those associated with the harvest and other fertility gods connected with the upcoming agricultural year and the conception of many new subjects. In the past, sacrifices sometimes involved humans, even though animals were also used. The first sacrifice usually occurred in front of the *oba*'s or *baale*'s palace with a dramatic procession forming at his courtyard.

In Oyo, the *Aláàfin*, or owner of the *àfin* (palace), was sometimes portrayed as a "sacred king" (Law 1970, 64-66). According to oral traditions, the *Aláàfin* was regarded as the re-incarnation of Shango, the god of thunder, and one of the earliest in *Aláàfin* Oyo. Leo Frobenius, a German ethnographer from the early 1900s, wrote:

> He is lightning and thunder, but most importantly the
> element of fire, behind the effigy of a ram: The fire cult of the
> Ram-headed God... ...The most varied assortment of offer-
> ings is laid on his altar on the day of the great festival...
> ...held in the great temple and compounds of all Shango's
> descendents... ...The poor but kill one ram and keep holiday
> for three days; but the rich let the high priest sacrifice a large
> number of these animals, and spread the feast over weeks
> (1968, 169-171).

If Sango was indeed a living human being, genealogical lists at the very best locate his existence somewhere between 1400 and 1500. In accordance with numerous legends and oral traditions, Sango had apparent connections to Islam. For example, his mother was from Nupe, not to mention the obligatory ram sacrifices. At the very least, oral traditions related to Sango indicate that Islam began to transculturate into Oyo culture well before the nineteenth century.

Robin Law has effectively demonstrated how the *Aláàfin* controlled a large administration which carried out political and ceremonial tasks connected to the city of Oyo. Many important officers of this political administration were expected to show devotion to the *òrìṣà* Sango. The Sango cult, just like many other Yoruba cults, was extraordinary for having elaborate rituals, iconography, and specific functions in and outside the kingdom of Oyo. The cult was certainly an important prop of royal power in Oyo, and Sango worship was an identifiable characteristic of people of Oyo descent, especially *babalawos*. The Sango cult had a centralized organization that was closely integrated into Oyo's complex political structure (Law, 1970, 66). Furthermore, the *ajélè* (system of imperial administration) oversaw Oyo's subordinate towns and were sanctified by the Sango cult as extensions of the *Aláàfin*'s kingship (Apter 1992, 24-25).

The *Aláàfin*, due to his political and spiritual leadership, was subject to a number of ritual restrictions, mainly in his confinement to the palace. He only appeared in public at three major annual festivals: the *bèrè*, *mole* and *orun* festivals. According to the Reverend Samuel Johnson, himself of Oyo descent, the *bèrè* festival was the most important festival because it was then that the general public might get a glimpse of the king. The *bèrè* festival took place toward the end of the agricultural year between late-February and early-March.

The *bèrè* festival was Oyo's most renowned annual festival for three main reasons: First, the payment of *bèrè* grass as a form of tribute to the *Aláàfin* was a major feature of the festival. According to Andrew Apter,

whereas the Sango cult sent out the *Alaafin*'s representatives
to supervise vassal kingdoms, and if necessary overrule them,
the *Beere* festival called in local leaders to the capital to pay
tribute to the *Alaafin*, both real, in the form of taxes, and symbolic, in the form of *beere* grass... The act of giving *beere* grass
was a symbolic act of homage which added, both literally and
figuratively, to the strength of the palace (1987, 8).

Second, the festival marked the end of the agricultural year and the
beginning of a new one. As S.O. Babayemi observes:

The ceremonial cutting of grass during the Bere festival is
known as Pakudirin....In another sense, the Pakudirin may
be regarded as marking the end of an agricultural year when
thanks-offering would be presented to Sango, "the Alaafin
in heaven," through the "Alaafin on earth." ...Jelepa, a ceremony in Bere may be regarded as marking the beginning of
the agricultural year. Jelepa is the ritual burning of the bush
(1973, 121-122).

Finally, the festival marked the anniversary of the *Aláàfin*'s reign,
or when a new *Aláàfin* was installed. In terms of idioms of kinship,
power and sovereignty, the *bèrè* festival represented the power of the
king's person as the symbolic embodiment of Sango instead of the
authority of the *Aláàfin* over his subjects.

The *bèrè* festival was described by Hugh Clapperton, a British dip-
lomat who travelled through Oyo in 1826. When Clapperton was in the
capital "Eyeo" on February 22, 1826, he observed a number of people
arriving to pay their annual visit to the king, and the custom of officials
[caboceers] from the different towns to act what he called plays or pan-
tomimes.[3] Clapperton was almost certainly referring to the *bèrè* festival
because it was the time of harvest, and his descriptions of processions
and people paying tribute to the "king" of Oyo was consistent with later
accounts. As Law noted, Clapperton's observations appear to be the earliest documented example of an annual festival in Oyo (1970, 66).

Annual festivals among other Yoruba sub-groups were also important in the transfer of traditions to Cuba and helped explain how Yoruba
annual festivals in Cuba may have transculturated. Unfortunately, few
festivals have been documented in a historical context for this purpose.

---

3   For details, see Jamie Bruce Lockhart and Paul E. Lovejoy, eds. *Hugh
     Clapperton into the Interior of Africa: Records of the Second Expedition
     1825-1827*. Leiden: Brill, 2005.

As Apter has argued, rituals commemorating the "conquest" of Obatala really represent Oyo-centric expansionism and the incorporation of vassal kingdoms, generating an Oyo-centric ritual field resisted by an Ife-centric counter-field that sustained Ife origins as charters and thus histories of independent kingship. These independent kingships, no matter how sovereign they were, still had knowledge of neighboring groups transmitted with deep historical connections via oral traditions that transculturated over time.

The annual *itapa* festival in Ife (for the worship of Obatala) re-enacted the conquest of the old Oba civilization (near Akure in Ekiti) by the Oduduwa group and the dispersal of the children of Oduduwa from Ife to new settlements all over Yorubaland. The *itapa* festival dramatized not only a major migration, but also how Oduduwa defeated Obatala in battle and exiled him from the òrìsà pantheon. Later the vanquished Obatala was readmitted into the pantheon, which this festival came to celebrate. Similarly, Babatunde Agiri has argued that the *itapa* festival commemorated what must have been a long process of conquest, reconciliation and assimilation among the Oba people (1975, 7). In other words the *itapa* festival commemorated a long process of creolization, even though this was not the original intent of the festival.

Annual festivals often narrated in dramatized forms the migration of people to new settlements, the tribulations of that migration, and the struggles of obtaining hegemony in new spaces. For example, the *iden* festival was celebrated by the Idanre, a Yoruba people located in Ondo state at the border between Yoruba and Edo speaking peoples of southern Nigeria. Yomi Akinyeye has described elements of the festival:

> Iden is celebrated at the end of the year, during which it is believed the departed ones are remembered and requested for guidance for the following year. During the procession, the songs are sung by members of the royal family with the Chief leading. After the festival, the songs are forbidden until the next year's festival. This festival centers on the Owa, who represents Olofin, and starts with the sacrifice of a cow by the Owa to his departed ancestors (2007, 90).

The Idanre did not acknowledge Oduduwa as the father of the founder of their town, instead it was Olofin. Songs sung in the *iden* festival told the story of the Olofin's migration from Ile-Ife, their various settlements, and the evolution of their political institutions.

Another cult that must be mentioned, which every Yoruba sub-group has participated in to some degree, was that of *egúngún*, which represented the "collective spirit of the ancestors" (Jackson and Mosadomi, 2005, 152). In every Yoruba town there were specialist *egúngún* priests, and separate *egúngún* festivals, which were usually long and spectacular events. Priests and initiates of important lineages were trained in ancestral communication and funeral rites. They were placed in charge of invoking and bringing out the ancestor spirits in ritually charged situations, especially during the annual festivals. It was their responsibility to compel the living to uphold the ethical standards of past generations. It was believed that *egúngún* spiritually cleansed the community through exaggerated acting/miming to demonstrate both ethical and amoral behavior that occurred since their last visit. Ancestral spirits were personified in masquerade, possession, drumming and dance.

Masks or masquerades were an important element of most Yoruba festivals. Masks and costuming made impersonation in ritual drama possible and they made any character, whether supernatural, human or animal (dead or alive), appear real. Karin Barber has described the *òtìn* festival in Òkukù where a mask with "a fierce wild personality" was brought out during the celebration and behaved like an *egúngún*. The mask was said to be "the husband of the female *òrìsà* Òtìn (who in her own legend was married to the oba of Òtan)" (1981, 736). As Jubril Adesegun Dosumu states, "The Agemo masquerades of the Ijebu appear (annually or occasionally) covered from head to toe with raffia threads and a crown mask with figurines imaging Ijebu history or royal totems" (Dosumu *Orisa*, 119). Dosumu argues that masks in Yoruba culture recreated and preserved the people's precolonial, colonial and postcolonial experiences. Masks carried a variety of meanings that could help illuminate a people's remote and immediate past because they disguised the spirit medium and activated local histories (*itan*) through spirit possession.

Song, music and dance had a prominent place in Yoruba festivals and spiritually charged rituals. The use of call-and-response song, and accompanying dances, were frequently employed to transmit oral traditions, legends and proverbs relevant to the history of an annual festival, migrations, genealogies, or to induce a favorable climate for the upcoming agricultural year. Although musical instruments varied among different Yoruba sub-groups, there were many common ones, such as the use of the *agogo* (bell), which was generally used to keep time. Other instruments had specific uses associated with the *òrìsàs* and *obas*, for example *bàtá* are said to "belong" to Sango and, as I have argued, are connected to the Oyo Empire. Both *bàtá* and *dùndún* drums are classified as "talking drums" because they encode structural properties of Yoruba speech. As William Bascom has observed, "there is a true drum language and the drums actually 'talk,' reproducing the melody and the rhythm of the sentence, and approximating the quality of consonants and vowels by fingering the head with the left hand" (1992). "Talking drums" have an important function in the transmission of oral traditions. Furthermore, the commonality of music, dance and call-and-response songs were found in every Yoruba culture in the Atlantic World and have always been present during every annual festival.

Transculturation of Yoruba Festivals in Cuba

Festivals in Yoruba cultural history have been a major field of research because the veneration of òrìsàs is where many comparisons can be drawn, especially in the Yoruba diaspora. The "Day of Kings" was the perfect setting for the transculturation of enslaved Yoruba òrìsà worshippers within a Catholic Cuban slave society. Furthermore, in Cuba one of the largest and probably most important sugarcane harvests frequently took place at the end of December, coincidentally close to the *Día de Reyes*. Fires were set at the sugarcane harvest to promote new growth, just as they were at *bèrè* festivals in Yorubaland (Fragenills 1976, 100). New slaves arriving from Oyo could have perceived elements of the *bèrè* festival embedded within the Day of the Kings. As sugarcane fields were set on fire could have simulated elements of the *bèrè* festival, such as *jelepa* which symbolized the start of the new agricultural year in Oyo through the burning of the grass. Yet, attempting to comprehend exactly how people of Yoruba descent in Cuba might have perceived the *Día de Reyes* is difficult. In order to provide a *Lucumí* perspective, an analysis of available historical evidence is required to legitimize a chronology related to the process of creolization and provide valuable insight into the reconstruction of Cuba's complex cultural history. This section will examine what the circumstances were like in West Africa in the nineteenth century. It will summarize how many people of Yoruba descent were sold to European merchants on the coast. Lastly, it will outline what Cuban slave society for *Lucumí* slaves was like during the *Día de Reyes*.

The largest migration of Yoruba to Cuba, and indeed to the Americas, coincided with the disintegration of the Oyo Empire. The collapse of Oyo was associated with a Muslim uprising at Ilorin in 1817, the Owu War (c. 1820–1825), and the declaration of Ilorin as an emirate within the Sokoto Caliphate (1823). Those events further coincided or contributed in the destruction of many towns and settlements, such as the abandonment of the capital district of Oyo by 1836. The collapse of the Oyo Empire is central to understanding the complexities of trans-culturation of Yoruba culture in West Africa before heading to Cuba.

The exposure of many Yoruba to Islam as well as Christianity in West Africa is an important point of consideration. As J.D.Y Peel and others have argued, Christianity and Islam were important influences in the development of Yoruba ethnic consciousness (Peel 2000). Returning ex-slaves, many of whom were Christians, propagated this identity in the homeland among those who had not crossed the Atlantic. In terms of *Lucumí* identity formation in Cuba, equivalent forms of transculturation in various cultural zones in West Africa must be considered. These cultural zones not only included the relationship between Yoruba sub-groups, but also broader zones, such as an Afro-European zone along coastal regions and exposure to Islam in the north. In Cuba, therefore, the process of transculturation became more complex as many different Yoruba sub-groups were exposed to one another, as well as many other non-Yoruba cultures from Africa and Europe before being exposed to the diversity of African, European and Creole cultures in Cuba.

As revealed in *The Trans-Atlantic Slave Trade Database*, one of the largest concentrations of people of Yoruba descent put onto slave ships destined for Cuba happened after 1825 (Eltis, Behrendt, Richardson and Klein 2009). Despite British efforts to abolish the transatlantic slave trade in 1807, roughly 96,200 enslaved Yoruba, largely classified as *Lucumí*, left the Bight of Benin for the Hispanic Caribbean between 1801 and 1867; roughly 80,000 to 85,000 arrived in Cuba. Breaking down the migration further, between 1801 and 1825 there were an estimated 5,600 African departures from the Bight of Benin for the Hispanic Caribbean. Thereafter, the number increased dramatically, with an estimated 65,600 Yoruba leaving West Africa for Cuba between 1826 and 1850. From 1851 until the last documented ship arrived in 1867, another 25,000 Yoruba were estimated to have landed. The "Middle Passage" also played an important role in processes of creolization since many Yoruba sub-groups and non-Yoruba groups may have been introduced to one another for the first time aboard slave ships. As Jerome S. Handler has demonstrated, music and dancing were often permitted on slave ships in order to decrease mortality rates (Handler 2009, 9-11). Unfortunately, there is no detailed evidence of specific musical instruments, such as "talking drums." By placing "African" music and dancing aboard slave ships, at the very least, illustrated processes of creolization occurring during the "Middle Passage."

Although a thorough analysis of the figures related to the Yoruba diaspora obtained from *The Trans-Atlantic Slave Trade Database* has proven to be the best and most accurate indication of Yoruba arrivals to date, they cannot be considered absolute. Slave trading records fail to provide any accurate indication of estimates to the specific Yoruba sub-groups leaving West Africa. Those people classified as *Lucumí* may also have included other African ethnic groups as well, such as Fon, the Bariba of Borgu, Hausa, Gwari or Nupe among others. Nevertheless, the figures obtained from the database demonstrate that there was a concentration of Yoruba whose presence can explain the transcultura-tion of *òrìsà* worship in Cuba. As a result of Oyo's collapse many people of Oyo descent went to Cuba, where they attempted to re-establish aspects of the former empire in Cuban slave society. For example, as I have argued elsewhere, *bàtá* drums were especially associated with Oyo because they "belong" to Sango and that their symbolic re-establishment in Cuba represented a degree of Oyo dominance among *Lucumí* communities in Cuba (H. Lovejoy 2009).

The arrival of many Yoruba in Cuba coincided with the change in Spanish colonial policy which permitted *cabildos* more freedom to orga-nize, especially during the *Día de Reyes*. In colonial documentation cited by Ortiz, the highest ranking member of a *cabildo* was called *rey* (king), *capataz* (foreman) or *capitán* (captain). There is insufficient evidence to know what the "king" was called by members of the *Lucumí cabildo*. In Lydia Cabrera's dictionary of *Lucumí* terms, however, there were many words associated with *oba, baale* or *Aláàfin*. *Obá bi* was defined as "name of the son of Changó. King begot by Changó. Born King" (1970). The word *Baá* meant "chief of a town" and *Bale* meant "foreman." *Alafi* was defined as "Changó of Egwadoland." There is insufficient documented evidence to know when the election of the *rey* of a *Lucumí cabildo* hap-pened (although there is evidence for other *cabildos*, which happened on the *Día de Reyes*), if there was an electoral committee or if the deci-sion was confirmed by a *babalawo*. The "king of the *cabildo*," however, enjoyed a considerable amount of power, such as being in charge of the *cabildos* funds and being able to impose fines on his subjects. The "king" was also responsible before colonial authorities for faults and crimes committed by members of his *cabildo* (Ortiz 1992, 1-4).[4]

A hierarchy existed within the *cabildo* with other positions, mainly of ceremonial character, were not well defined. Women formed a part of the *cabildo* and there were elected queens. Another coveted posi-tion within a *cabildo* was the *abanderado* (flag bearer); a post created when flags were used as a symbol of a *cabildo* and displayed publically

---

4   Changó is a transculturated spelling of Sango.

during times when the *cabildo* was allowed to march. Brown states "Historically, *banderas* were time-honored markers of political units, institutions, and regions, as well as religious mutual aid, and occupational societies in the Iberian-Atlantic world." The earliest evidence of Changó's presence, and hence Oyo, in Cuba was displayed on the *Lucumí* flag. It roughly translates to "the Mutual Aid Society of the Lucumi Nation of Santa Bárbara, year of 1820." This *Lucumí cabildo* was also known as Changó-Tedun, meaning "Changó arrives with a roar!" (Brown 2003, 37). *Lucumí cabildos* centered on Changó indicated a symbolic connection to the Oyo Empire because of its connection to Sango and hence the Sango cult.

Slaves of Yoruba descent had begun to worship Changó in Cuba because Santa Barbara was the Catholic Saint who came to represent Sango. Pedro Deschamps Chapeaux stated that "the *Lucumí cabildos* preferred Santa Barbara" (Chapeaux 1968, 50-51). The transculturation of Catholic iconography into òrìsà worship (often referred to as syncretism) and the simultaneous reverence to several òrìsà at once could also be considered part of the creolization process. This process probably began as the first people from Yorubaland were introduced to Christianity and hence before the nineteenth century. Apter argues, however, that òrìsà clustering in Yorubaland undermined the contrast between the one versus multiple òrìsà worship associated with West Africa versus the New World. Regardless, other people who did not identify with Oyo also came to Cuba. Sango was not the only òrìsà worshipped in Cuba as other Yoruba sub-groups contributed to the formation of *Lucumí* culture in Cuba.

Colonial observers intrigued by the *Día de Reyes* often wrote about it. Ortiz transcribed several passages describing the annual procession from nineteenth century sources. I have selected some relevant passages and translated them into English. For example, P. Riesgo described in 1843, "Large groups of *negros* and *negras* crossed through the large city in every direction, to the sound of their drums, dressed ridiculously."[5] Pérez Zamora wrote in 1866, "Over here one sees a false *lucumí* king in the middle of his black phalanx; there a *gangá*; over there another from the *carabalí* nation, etcetera, etc... and all of them sovereign for one

---

5   Originally published in 1925, Ortiz, "La fiesta afrocubanos del Día de Reyes," *Los cabildos y la fiesta afrocubanos del Día de Reyes*, Colleción Fernando Ortiz, (Habana: Editorial de Ciencias Sociales, 1992), 32. Cited as P. Riesgo, "El Día de los Santos Reyes," *La Prensa*, (La Habana: Jan. 6, 1843).

day, singing in monotone and disagreeable sounds in African language, the memories of their people."[6] Ramón Meza wrote in 1891:

> Ever since the break of dawn, one could hear all over the place the monotone rhythm of those big drums... ...Believers abandoned their houses very early in the morning; and they came from the farms near the city... ...Everyone ran to join their respective cabildos, that had for a chief, generally, the most ancient of the tribe or nation to which they belonged... ...At twelve in the afternoon the diversion reached its height. In the streets of Mercaderes, Obispo and O'Reilly there was a procession without interruption... ...The captain of each *cabildo* climbed the stairs of the Palace, and doing the most alive demonstrations of adhesion, received, at least, an ounce of gold as *aguinaldo* (offering)... ...Soon they left from the Palace in order to leave space for others and they went marching, in perfect order, the *congos* and *lucumís* with their large feathered sombreros, stripped blue shirts and red percale pants.[7]

Processions during the *Día de Reyes* were clearly well organized events that ended up at the palace, whereby *cabildo* captains received offerings from the colonial government. Unfortunately, these nineteenth century descriptions did not provide much detail beyond generalized and often inaccurate representations of African and African-derived cultures, such as "dressed ridiculously" and "monotone and disagreeable sounds." Masquerading had a purpose depending on the Yoruba sub-group and music, especially "talking drums," imitated tones of the Yoruba language.

During the *Día de Reyes*, *cabildos* and carnival processions were granted permission to enter inside the city walls, a space usually prohibited to non-domestic slaves. Music, singing and dancing would have been performed as illustrated in the famous nineteenth century artwork by A. Galindo (1837) and Víctor Patricio Landaluze (c. 1880). Much of Ortiz's work on masquerading and costuming was based on that artwork. He called this form of costuming *diabolitos* (little devils), a term taken from colonial documentation. *Diabolitos* were for the most part associated with *Abakuá* groups (largely descendants of Ekpe people from the interior of the Bight of Biafra). However, *diabolitos*

---

6   As cited in Ibid., 33: Pérez Zamora, "El Día de los Reyes en la Habana," *El Abolicionista Español*, Año 2, no.7, (Madrid: Jan. 15, 1866).
7   As cited in Ibid., 26-27: Ramón Meza, *El Hogar*, (La Habana: Jan. 11, 1891).

closely resembled the costuming of *egúngún* and therefore may have been confused not only by colonialists, but also Ortiz.[8]

The *cabildos'* potential for attracting the organization of free blacks and freed slaves posed an ongoing threat to the colonial government. Throughout the 1800s different *cabildo* groups resisted slavery and persisted in rebellious behavior. For example, in Havana in 1835, Juan Prieto, the foreman of the *Cabildo Lucumí* known as Ello y Oyo led an uprising (Bettelheim 1991, 69). La Escalera rebellion (1843-1844) was linked to the *Lucumí cabildo* Changó-Tedun.The potential for rebellion can be identified in colonial documentation related to the involvement of *cabildos* during annual festivals.

Slave laws related to marching during festivals in Cuba were extensive. Slave laws reflected a climate of political opinion even though the treatment of slaves was usually up to the discretion of individual masters. They also provide clues into what degree slaves and free blacks were able to participate in the festival at different points in time. In 1792, Article 36 of the *Bando de Buen Gobierno y Policía* (Proclamation of Good Government and Police) "permitted dances on holidays in the *cabildos de nación*, from 10 until 12 and from 3 until 8 in the evening. Article 38, however, forbade all *Negros de nación* going in the streets with flags or other insignias" (Ortiz, 1992, 11). In 1823, public processions of *cabildos* and *Día de Reyes* celebrations were officially sanctioned and flags were permitted. Again in 1839, a mandate was distributed throughout the island. It stated, "Slave dances with drums could be permitted at fiestas during afternoon hours provided they are supervised by some white person, and no slaves from any other estate attend."[9]

A document from 1841, dated January 5, contested the 1839 mandate, "to not permitting *negros* from going out onto the streets with drums tomorrow" (Ortiz 1992, 12). By 1842, the infamous *Reglamento de esclavos* (Slave Code) was implemented to control the slave population. Of the 260 articles in the code three were related to the *Día de Reyes*. Article 51 was identical to the 1839 document, but made no mention of the clause "that no slaves from other estates attend." Article 87 stated, "Negro *cabildos* should only be held on Sundays and on other days of important

---

8 For further details see David H. Brown, *Santería Enthroned: Art, Ritual, and Innovation in an Afro-Cuban Religion*. Chicago: University of Chicago Press, 2003.

9 Joaquin de Ezpeleta to Gobierno General, Havana, July 23, 1839, Archivo Nacional de Cuba, Havana, Gobierno Superior Civil "Esclavitud," orden 33102, legado 998.

fiestas." Finally, Article 88 declared, "that the Negroes require special permission to march with flags and native costumes. Such marches can be held twice a year, and during daylight hours."[10] The *Reglamento de esclavos* was implemented up until the *Ley de la abolición de la esclavitud* (Law of the abolition of Slavery) was instigated in 1880.

The last time the *Día de Reyes* was celebrated was on January 6, 1884. In 1891, the day commemorating Saint Barbara (Dec. 4), became the official marching day of the *Lucumí cabildo* under the leadership of Joaquín Cádiz. Changing the date of the annual festival to one honoring Saint Barbara, and hence Sango, demonstrated, at the very least, how symbolic elements of Oyo cultural history continued to transculturate in Cuba. Nevertheless, many other Yoruba sub-groups came together and the transculturation of their culture also helped to form new cultural practices.

Conclusion

No doubt, the *Día de Reyes* became one of the most important days for the entire enslaved and colored population in Cuba during most of the nineteenth century. The *Día de Reyes* had special meaning for people of Yoruba descent because it was comparable to most annual festivals in Yorubaland. It was an annual festival commemorating "kings." It took place around a harvest. Fields were burnt. The "king of the *cabildo*" was displayed publically. Dead ancestors could be remembered. And perhaps, the festival provided the opportunity for people to re-enact festivals associated with specific òrìsà and in the process enact the formation of the Yoruba diaspora in Cuba. A presentation of annual festivals has focused on a "symbolic" identification of the Yoruba background entrenched in *Lucumí* culture in Cuba. Regarding closer links to Africa, a focus on annual festivals in Africa, such as bèrè, has yielded a vision symbolically interconnecting Oyo culture with Yoruba-derived culture in Cuba. The specifics of the bèrè festival have long since "deculturated" in Cuba, much like the *Día de Reyes*.

The transculturation of Yoruba festivals was a process of creolization that occurred step by step in a chronological fashion beginning *first* in West Africa and *then* in Cuba. The collapse of the Oyo Empire between 1817 and 1836 was a principal cause of one of the largest peaks

---

10 Comunicación al Gobernador Político y Militar de Matanzas, José Maria de Torres por la Inspección de policía del cuartel de "Fernando" (sic) Séptimo, Matanzas, 5 January 1841, Archivo Historico Matanzas, Fondo Provincial Religioso Africana, expediente 1, legado 1.

of Yoruba arrivals to Cuba. A large influx of Yoruba people, most likely of Oyo descent, arriving in Cuba was reflected in the consolidation of a *cabildo* dedicated to Sango in 1820. As Clapperton observed, *bèrè* festivals had not yet disappeared in Oyo by 1826, while the Catholic *Día de Reyes* was "deculturating." The legalization of *cabildo* processions with flags happened in 1823, 1839 and 1842, which ensured the continuation of *Lucumí* cultural tendencies established from the 1820s and prior. Descriptions of the festival by Riesgo (1843), Zamora (1866) and Meza (1891) and artwork by Galindo (1837) and Landaluze (c. 1880) demonstrated, in very general terms, how Africanized cultural traditions continued to transculturate in Cuba. After the festival was outlawed in 1884, the representation of Sango, and hence Oyo domination, was at this point well-established and the most important festival day for the *Lucumí cabildo* changed to the day which honored Saint Barbara, a.k.a. Sango, in 1891.

Even though Sango, and hence Oyo, played an important role in Cuba, many other *òrìsàs* that were tied symbolically to other Yoruba sub-groups, also came to Cuba. The relationship between Oyo and other Yoruba sub-groups, not to mention Islam (Sango's Nupe mother, obligatory ram sacrifices, the disintegration of Oyo, etc...), demonstrated how Oyo culture had already been transculturating *in* Yorubaland well before the early nineteenth century. Since the late seventeenth century the Bight of Benin was an embarkation point for the transatlantic slave trade and people near the coast were exposed to European contact. The "Middle Passage" extended the process of transculturation, demonstrating that the process was not just an Old or New World occurrence; it involved interaction on the high seas among different Yoruba sub-groups and with other ethnic groups from further inland, such as Hausa, Nupe, Bariba, Gwari, etc... Clearly Oyo was a factor in the cultural phenomenon of the *Día de Reyes* in Cuba, but the extent to which the Oyo were able to reestablish their supremacy in Cuba remains ambiguous. The dominance of Oyo should not overshadow the influence of other Yoruba sub-groups in the process of transculturation.

Works Cited

Agiri, B. A. 1975. "Early Oyo History Reconsidered." *History in Africa*. 2:7.

Akinyeye, Yomi. 2005,"Iden Festival: Historical Reconstruction from Ceremonial Reenactment," in *ORISA: Yoruba Gods and Spiritual Identity in Africa and the Diaspora*, Ed. Toyin Falola and Ann Genova. Trenton, N.J.: Africa World Press.

Apter, Andrew. 1987. "The Historiography of Yoruba Myth and Ritual," *History in Africa*. 14:8.

_____. 1992. *Black Critics and kings: The Hermeneutics of Power in Yoruba Society*. Chicago: University of Chicago Press

Babayemi, S. O. 1973, "Bere Festival in Oyo." *Journal of the Historical Society of Nigeria*. 7:121-122.

Barber, Karin. 1981. "How Man Makes God in West Africa: Yoruba Attitudes Towards the 'Òrìsà.'" Africa: Journal of the International African Institute. 51:3: 730-736.

Bascom, William. 1992. "Drums of the Yoruba of Nigeria." CD liner notes. Washington: Smithsonian Folkways Records. Originally recorded in 1954.

Bettelheim, Judith. 1991. "Negotiations of Power in Carnaval Culture in Santiago de Cuba." *African Arts*. 24:2 (Special Issue): 69.

Cabrera, Lydia. 1970.*Anago: vocabulario lucumi (el yoruba que se habla en Cuba)*. Miami: Cabrera y Rojas.

Chapeaux, Pedro Deschamps. 1968. "Cabildos: Solo para esclavos." *Cuba Revista Mensual*. Jan: 50-51.

Dosumu, Jubril Adesegun. 2005. "Masks and Masques in Yoruba Ritual Festivals," in *ORISA: Yoruba Gods and Spiritual Identity in Africa and the Diaspora*, Ed. Toyin Falola and Ann Genova. Trenton, N.J.: Africa World Press.

Eltis, David, Stephen D. Behrendt, David Richardson, and Herbert Klein, eds. 2009. *The Trans-Atlantic Slave Trade Database*, Online Edition, www.slavevoyages.org.

Falola, Toyin and Ann Genova, eds. 2005. "Introduction," *Òrìsà: Yoruba Gods and Spiritual Identity in Africa and the Diaspora*. Trenton: Africa World Press.

Fraginals, Manuel Moreno. 1976. *The Sugarmill: The Socioeconomic Complex of Sugar in Cuba, 1760-1860*. trans. Cedric Belfrage. New York: Monthly Review Press, 100.

Frobenius, Leo. 1968. The Voice of Africa: Being an Account of the Travels of the German Inner African Exploration Expedition in the Years 1910-1912. vol. 1. London: Benjamin Bloom.

Handler, Jerome S. 2009. "The Middle Passage and Material Culture of Captive Africans," *Slavery and Abolition*, 30,:1:9-11.

Jackson, Joyce Marie and Fehintola Mosadomi. 2005. "Cultural Continuities: Masking Traditions of the Black Mardi Gras Indians and the Yoruba Egunguns," in *ORISA: Yoruba Gods and Spiritual Identity in Africa and the Diaspora*, Ed. Toyin Falola and Ann Genova. Trenton, N.J.: Africa World Press. *Orisa*. 151-156.

Law, Robin. 1970. *The Oyo Empire, c. 1600- c. 1836*, (Oxford: Clarendon Press.

_____. 1997. "Ethnicity and the Slave Trade: 'Lucumí' and 'Nago' as Ethnonyms in West Africa." *History in Africa*. 24: 205–219.

Lovejoy, Henry. 2009. "Drums of Sàngó: Bàtá Drums and the Symbolic Rees-tablishment of Oyo in Colonial Cuba, c. 1817-1867." *Sàngó in Africa and the African Diaspora*, ed. Joel Tishken, Toyin Falola and Akintunde Akinyemi,. Bloomington: Indiana University Press. 447-489.

Mintz, Sidney W. and Richard Price. 1976. *An Anthropological Approach to Afro-American Past: A Caribbean Perspective*. Philadelphia: Institute for the Study of Human Issues.

Ortiz, Fernando. 1940. *Contrapunteo cubano del tabaco y el azúcar (advertencia de sus contrastes agrarios, económicos, históricos y sociales, su etnografía y su transculturación)*. Habana: J. Montero.

_____. 1992. "Los cabildos afrocubanos." *Los cabildos y la fiesta afrocubanos del Día de Reyes*. Colleción Fernando Ortiz. Habana: Editorial de Ciencias Sociales. 1-4.

Parrinder, E. G. 1951. "Ibadan Annual Festival." *Africa: Journal of the International African Institute*. 21:1:56.

Peel, J.D.Y. 2000. *Religious Encounter and the Making of the Yoruba*. Bloomington: Indiana University Press.

The African Heritage in Trinidad's Carnival: From Cultural Resistance to Identity Negotiation in Earl Lovelace's *The Dragon Can't Dance*

Sabrina Ensfelder

First published in 1979 and reissued in 1988, *The Dragon Can't Dance*, a novel by Earl Lovelace, depicts a community in Trinidad preparing for a carnival celebration. Well-known for its famous annual masquerade, Trinidad—with an emphasis here on Calvary Hill—is described by Lovelace as both a place of beauty and one troubled by political and identity struggles. Carnival is an event during which social and cultural tensions are both revealed and negotiated. At the beginning of the novel, Miss Cleothilda sings the unifying motto "All of we is one" as a way of affirming some kind of cultural *union*. The novel, however, progressively depicts and questions the significance and limitations of this motto. The characters fight for cultural and social recognition and struggle to become visible in a multicultural society while, at the same time, attempting to integrate themselves.

The title of the novel calls the reader's attention to questions of cultural heritage, community integration, and national identity. Indeed, if the "dragon" is an integral part of Trinidad masquerade, it also calls to mind Asian origins. The ethnic composition of Trinidad and Tobago makes one question this symbolical choice for the opening of the novel and raises questions about the dance that will not be performed by the dragon. Interestingly, the character chosen by Lovelace for that dance is Aldrick, a young Trinidadian of African descent. This choice enables the reader to consider the presence of African culture in Trinidadian carnival, and then to analyse the process of cultural negotiation in a society made up of various ethnic groups.

The opening pages of the novel lead the reader into a sacred world where carnival is compared to popular religion: costumes, bands, and masqueraders become vestments, holy music and devotees. While portraying the main characters of the parade, the author also presents characteristics that take the reader back to the African origins of carnival. The tent where musicians play steel-band music is compared to a cathedral; calypso tempo becomes a hallelujah humming; and some of the carnival masqueraders are priests, priestesses, or saints, while others are "mounted" (54).[1] The festivities of this carnival plunge the Calvary Hill community back into the solemn atmosphere of masked African ceremonies, echoing those of West Africa. Indeed, by the eighth chapter, Lovelace clearly affirms these African origins placing specific emphasis on the Trinidad carnival's spiritual link with West-African religious ceremony:

> Up on the Hill Carnival Monday morning breaks upon the backs of these thin shacks with no cock's crow, and before the mist clears, little boys, costumed in old dresses, their head tied, holding brooms made from the ribs of coconut palm leaves, blowing whistles... sweeping yards in ritual, heralding the masqueraders' coming, that goes back centuries for its beginnings, back across the Middle passage, back to Mali and to Guinea and Dahomey and Congo, back to Africa when Maskers were sacred and revered, the keepers of the poisons and head of secret societies, and such children went before them, clearing the ground, announcing their coming to the huts before which they would dance and make their terrible cries, affirming for the village, the tribe, warriorhood and femininity, linking the villagers to their ancestors, their Gods, remembered even now, so long after the Crossing, if not in the brain, certainly in the blood. (1998, 112)

Despite the Middle passage, carnival in the Caribbean retains many features of West-African ceremonies, religious or profane—although the majority of ceremonies in West Africa are heavily influenced by religion. The first writings on Trinidadian carnival date back to the end of the eighteenth century and, for the most part, relate to European indoor carnival parades. With the arrival of slaves from West Africa,

---

1   In Caribbean culture, to be mounted means to be possessed by a spirit.

which included such ethnic groups as the Yoruba, Rada, Ibgo, Ibibio, Hausa, Kongo and Mandingo, all with their strong tribal traditions, carnival took a new turn and became a place for cultural resistance. As Lovelace acknowledges, with the passing of time, some of the traditions are now forgotten, but, nonetheless, they still flow through the blood of the Trinidadians. It is, thus, interesting to focus on the African traditions now forgotten by the Trinidadian population.

While it is commonly believed that carnival was brought to the Caribbean by Europeans, a study of the outdoor masquerades suggests the strong influence of West-African street parades that is still detectable today. Such a study reveals that Africans also brought their carnival to the New World. Confusion may have arisen since a comparison of structures and symbolism demonstrates that European and African cultures bear resemblances in areas such as religion and festivals.

In his novel, Lovelace celebrates the sacred connection uniting inhabitants, ancestors, and gods during West-African masquerades, a connection which features strongly in Trinidadian carnival. While colonialism and Christian evangelism left little room for the worship of African deities in new lands, carnival provided an arena in which such religious ceremonies could be reproduced both structurally and symbolically. Just as in West Africa, the Trinidadian carnival route is circular, thereby forming an alliance between the visible and invisible realms, the living and the dead. The costumed, music bands are a distinctive feature of Trinidadian carnival and can be traced back to Nigerian Egungun masquerades in which each family clan wears its own specific colour.[2] Gordon Rohlehr believes that the grouping of African nations in nineteenth-century Trinidad may have influenced the emergence of bands in Carnival: "the various Carnival bands from East Dry River and La Cour Harpe," he argues, "might during the nineteenth century have been partially organised according to the ethnic grouping of immigrants from Africa" (1990, 156).

Religious gatherings would be another lead to corroborate the influence of African culture on the emergence of carnival bands in Trinidad. George Eaton Simpson, whose research on African-derived religions in the Caribbean, especially Trinidad, Jamaica, and Haiti, draws attention to the existence of religious groups in nineteenth century Trinidad

---

2   Egungun masquerade is a masking spectacle in Yoruba culture that honours the spirits of ancestors. See Margaret Drewal Thompson, *Yoruba Ritual, Performers, Play, Agency*, Bloomington: Indiana University Press, 1992.

whose names, form, and function are similar to the names, form, and function adopted later by Trinidad masquerade bands:

> according to all witnesses, the slaves throughout the Island but especially in Maraval, Diego Martin and Carenage (Districts which were chiefly inhabited by the French settlers) had formed themselves into 'Convois' and 'Regiments,' each of which were known by its peculiar appellation. These were for instance the 'Convoi des Sans Peur' or 'Dreadnaught bands,' the 'Convoi de St-George,' the 'Regiment Danois' or 'Danish Regiment' which probably had been formed by slaves of St-Thomas or St. Croix; the 'Regiment Macaque' or 'Monkey Corps' and many others with titles more or less suggestive. Each 'Convoi' or 'Regiment' had its King and Queen, Dauphin and Dauphiness, Princes and Princesses, a Grand Judge, soldiers and alguazils. (Simpson 1970, 14-15)

Those 'Regiments' or 'Convoi' undoubtedly influenced the emergence of music and mask bands, which, in *The Dragon Can't Dance*, are called armies: Red Army, Desperado, Tokyo, Invaders, Casablanca, Rising Sun. These armies function as social groups that provide identity marks, as shown through the character Fisheye, who only seems to be alive in society with his band:

> In this war, in this army, Fisheye at last found the place where he could be a man, where his strength and quickness had meaning and he could feel pride in belonging and purpose to his living, and where he had all the battles he had dreamed of, and more, to fight. While he was with them, Calvary Hill became a name to be respected, began to be spoken of with the same measure of awe with which young men whispered Desperadoes, Rising Sun, Renagades, Red Army, Hell Yard, Tokyo. (Lovelace 1998, 46)

Nineteenth-century Trinidad 'Regiments' and 'Convois' are also very similar to rival religious societies such as Société la Rose and Societé la Marguerite that appeared in nineteenth-century Saint-Lucia. They were, and still are, secret societies organised according to a complex hierarchy, including kings, queens, princes, princesses, as well as judges, policemen, or soldiers. Thus, just as the formation of West-African music-bands influenced the formation of those in Trinidad, so the organisation in terms of structure of these bands in Trinidad may be seen to reflect that of West-African secret societies.

The colourful masks, costumes and artefacts that decorate the carnival route in Trinidad are of African origin. Their significance and symbolism, however, have long since been forgotten or erased from memory by colonial cultural manipulation, which discouraged, or disallowed, any expression of cultural diversity. Nonetheless, many features of African culture survived the colonial regime of Trinidad and prevail in modern carnival:

> there were devils, black men who blackened themselves
> further with black grease to make of their very blackness a
> menace, a threat. They moved along the streets with horns
> on their heads and tridents in their hands. They threatened
> to press their blackened selves against the well dressed spec-
> tators unless they were given money. And there were the jab-
> jab, men in jester costumes, their caps and shoes filled with
> tinkling bells, cracking long whips in the streets....It hit him,
> the red and black and gold and green, the colours and the
> feathers and the satin, and the people's face with that look in
> their eyes, and the smell of cologne and face powder and the
> smell of grease. (Lovelace 1998, 113-114)

Interestingly, many of the objects, masks, or symbols referred to by Lovelace are also observed in carnivals of other Caribbean islands as well as Latin and South American countries. These similarities lay emphasis on common roots, especially African roots, which are sig-nificant when deciphering symbols. Indeed, it is through West-African festivals and ceremonies that clues may be found to interpret the sym-bolism of vegetal or animal representation, the use of colour, and the different masks used in the Trinidadian carnival.

West-African secret societies own sacred instruments for religious ceremonies such as divination objects, vases, whips, sticks, drums, horns and mirrors. The vegetal, of which these elements are composed, is omnipresent in African society because of its virtues. Plants, for instance, are transformed and used in different ways for medicine, as well as in ceremonies for their purgative functions. In ceremonies, whips are used to drive away evil spirits and, in the Caribbean, are used at the beginning of festivals to neutralise evil spirits (Pradel 2000, 103). The horn, carries phallic meaning because it represents fertility and suggests abundance as maskers charge toward their public. For the Yoruba, horns are associated with Shango sacred ram. In terms of representation, these horns relate to the lightning zigzag of the deity; in terms of interpretation, horns allude to Shango sexual energy and fertility. Alternatively, among Kongos, horns mounted on statuettes are used to heal, to denounce sorcerers, or to locate game. In her study on African heritage in Caribbean culture, the ethnologist Lucie Pradel considers that horns in the Caribbean are associated with the Yoruba goddess, Oya, and refer to her fertility (2000, 103).

The feather is another symbol preserved in Caribbean carnivals. They are important ornaments in African masks and headdresses. They symbolise human ability to rise above mundane problems and traverse other realms. They are synonymous with rebirth and spiritual elevation. Last but not least, the African tradition of throwing powder on people's faces and of decorating bodies has apparently survived the Middle Passage. The Ibibio of the Ekpo masqueraders, for instance, are known to cover their entire body with a greasy mixture of palm oil and charcoal to achieve the colour of death, which is similar to the Trinidad "jab molasses" tradition, or the French West-Indies "Neg gwo Siwo."[3]

"It hits him, the red and black and gold and green, the colours and the feathers and the satin," writes Lovelace (1998, 114). In addition to symbolic objects and natural artefacts, colours are important character-istics in Trinidadian carnival. A closer examination of the predominant colours of carnival strongly demonstrates the African religious influ-ences. Colour and fabric designs in West-African culture are linked to deities. In the costumes of Shango's devotees in Nigeria Yoruba culture, it is common to see the predominance of red and white with triangle shaped motifs. In religious ceremonies, practitioners dress in the colours of the orishas,[4] and, due to the anthropomorphic nature of orishas, an intimate contact between believer and deity is thought to be possible. Red is linked to life, fertility, and power in many West-African cultures. In Yoruba religion, it is linked to Shango, the god of lightning, fertility, and sexual and physical power. In Caribbean carnivals, however, red is associated with the devil, partly because for Christians, red is associ-ated with hell. For the most part, however, red denotes fertility and power. Indeed, in West-African festivals such as those found among the Yorubas, fertility is favoured and even encouraged by deities to ensure

---

3   Jab molasses consists of smearing the whole body with grease or mud, red, green or blue paint. They are feared because they threaten the audi-ence of spreading oil or grease on them.

4   Orishas is the name of deities in Afro-Caribbean religions such as Santería in Cuba or Trinidad's Orisha religion. See Margarite Fernandez Olmos and Lizabeth Paravisini-Gebert, *Creole Religions of the Caribbean: An Introduction from Vodou and Santería to Obeah and Espiritismo*. New York: New York University Press, 2003.

stability and reproduction in the community. In Trinidadian carnival, fertility is often implied through sensual dances of the masqueraders (for example, in the novel, Sylvia is compared to an African goddess); sexual allusions are similarly embedded in the songs of Philo, the calypsonian. Or again there is the idea of sacrifice implied by Sylvia's costume: for Sylvia to obtain a costume and participate in the carnival, she is virtually forced into prostitution. As Peter Mason observes, the notion of sacrifice overwhelms Trinidadian carnival and is somewhat predictable because 'playing mas'[5] is to undergo a rite of passage during which many women lose their virginity (1998, 150). Fertility rites, then, are a popular themes, as the high rate of post-carnival pregnancies would suggest, and, thus, form another strong link between the festivals of West-Africa and the carnival in Trinidad.

Why some elements of African origin have survived in Trinidadian carnival where others have not is curious. In part, the reason may be socio-economic. But that such survival has survived, however, is a strong sign of African cultural resistance vis-à-vis the Middle Passage, slavery and colonial brainwashing. There is still much research to do on African heritage in Trinidadian carnival. Current research corroborates the belief that, despite colonial restraint, African slaves have been able to create and shape their culture in a new environment. It would now be interesting to see how cultural heritage has integrated into its environment to produce a new culture that has become progressively multicultural.

Written in 1979, Lovelace's novel raises questions of identity struggle that are still relevant in Trinidad today. Carnival in *The Dragon Can't Dance* is presented as an event that allows gathering and unity, regardless of ethnic origins or social class. The mulatto in Calvary Hill, Miss Cleothilda, sings the unifying motto "All of we is one," implying that during carnival time, social, cultural, and political tensions are ignored for the benefit of enjoyment and unity of the whole community.[6] In a multicultural society, national unity depends on global acceptance and recognition of an ethnic community's cultural contribution. The socio-political harmony resonating from out of Miss Cleothilda's motto found concrete achievement in Trinidad's political history, when, for the first time in Trinidad history, and a few years after the publication of Lovelace's novel, the National Alliance for Reconstruction (N.A.R) political party came to power in Trinidad from 1986 to 1991:

---

5   'Playing mas' means to play in a masquerade.
6   In Trinidad, a mulatto is a person of mixed African and European descent.

In the historic December 1986 elections, NAR served itself up
as the "rainbow party" committed to "one love" in the promise
to replace the African-based PNM with a merging of identities
in an authentic multi-ethnic party. In Robinson, an African
leader was found; in Panday, an Indian leader was recruited;
and in the ranks of the ONR leadership the Mixed Races and
French Creoles had representation. (CRPLC 2004, 28)

This party promoted ethnic unity and used community cultural recognition during its campaign such as music, oral traditions, or street
parades to support its motives. Thus, supporting the idea that identity
negotiation and national identity are possible only through equal recognition and respect of diversity. The party did not stay in power for long,
however, partly as a result of ethnic rivalry, suggesting, as is implied in
the impossible dance of the dragon, that social and political consensus
go beyond cultural recognition.

In many respects, African heritage is celebrated in the novel.
Aldrick, however, the most African character in the story, is thwarted
in his attempts to celebrate both his warrior-hood and ancestry as well
as the social struggle of Africans in Trinidad. Indeed, he is imprisoned
because of his rebellion against the colonial system. His imprisonment
may also be understood as disciplining his need for ancestry remembrance and celebration. Pariag, of East Indian descent, is another character who desires cultural recognition, and yet the whole community
rejects him. Indeed, the label he is associated with, spectator, signifies
his position throughout the carnival. Both Aldrick and Pariag crave
visibility and the community rejects both of them because of this need.

In multicultural societies, negotiating cultural difference is necessary to affirm Cleothilda's motto "All of we is one." Rather than group
his characters into various categories (Aldrick, Sylvia, Fisheyes, or
Philo as the Creoles, or Pariag, the Indian, and Cleothilda the mulatto),
the author gives each character a specific section in the novel. In this
way, Lovelace presents the individual's struggle in society, regardless of
class, ethnicity, or gender. Through carnival, as a microcosm of society,
one can understand how national harmony, regardless of cultural
diversity, is possible. At the same time, otherness has to be recognised
and taken into account if frustration is to be avoided, and—as seen in
the novel—rebellion is absolutely necessary.

The symbolic appropriation of foreign culture to affirm Creole struggle—as shown through Aldrick's appropriation of Asian culture through
the dragon costume—emphasises that otherness. It also demonstrates
respect for others, and acceptance of the new, while, at the same time,

remaining faithful to one's own singularity. National consensus might be possible if the search for power, which is the ultimate aim of personal or community struggle, is progressively replaced by the search for a "body-nation" benefit.[7] Unconvinced by the various post-colonial theories that have emerged on culture, society, and nation, Hommi Bhabha offers a different perspective on nation construction. He focuses more on the concept of 'locality' (more precisely, temporality) of culture:

> The discourse of nationalism is not my main concern. In some ways it is the historical certainty and settled nature of that term against which I am attempting to write of the Western nation as an obscure and ubiquitous form of living the *locality* of culture. This locality is more *around* temporality than about historicity: a form of living that is more complex than 'community'; more symbolic than 'society'; more connotative than 'country'; less patriotic than *patrie*; more rhetorical than the reason of State; more mythological than ideology; less homogeneous than hegemony; less centred than the citizen; more collective than 'the subject'; more psychic than civility; more hybrid in the articulation of cultural differences and identifications than can be represented in any hierarchical or binary structuring of social antagonism. (2006, 200-201)

Bhabha's perspective may be worth considering when dealing with social and cultural construction of a nation, especially when the latter is multicultural, the challenge of globalisation. In stressing the limits of historicism with regard to the nation, Bhabha considers the latter from a social and textual viewpoint. Though interesting because the debate centres here on the "question of the representation of the nation as a temporal process" (204), the danger might be that, again, the discussion on national benefit falls into another form of categorisation:

> What I am attempting to formulate...are the complex strategies of cultural identification and discursive address that function in the name of 'the people' or 'the nation' and make them the immanent subjects of a range of social and literary narratives. My emphasis on the temporal dimension in the inscription of these political entities—that are also potent symbolic and affective sources of cultural identity—serves to

---

7   Our definition of a body-nation sees the latter as a body whose members/ communities combine and coordinate to ensure the functioning of the body, the nation.

displace the historicism that has dominated discussions of
the nation as a cultural force. (Bhabha 201)

Discussing national identity issues and analysing the place of cultural
identity in a society comprised of various cultural groups, opens up the
discussion to the psychological and symbolic functions of carnival. As
Lovelace shows in his novel, through carnival we see a collective culture
emerge and become visible. Simultaneously, cultural diversity must be
affirmed or reaffirmed in a multicultural society, especially if the latter
is born out of colonialism. In a postcolonial context, however, where
every community struggles to achieve cultural and social recognition
and attempts to break with the prevailing heritages of colonisation
(such as acculturation, cultural difference, disparagement, and ethnic
tensions), more stable foundations are necessary for a harmonious construction of nations. Undoubtedly, recognition of heritage is a step in
the process of giving multicultural societies some psychological stability: giving them pride in their past so as to enable a better future.

Works Cited

Bhabha, Homi K. 2006. *The Location of Culture*. London and New York: Routledge.

Lovelace, Earl. 1998. *The Dragon Can't Dance*. London: Faber and Faber.

Mason, Peter. 1998. *Bacchanal! The Carnival Culture of Trinidad*. Philadelphia: Temple University Press.

Pradel, Lucie. 2000. *Dons de Mémoire de l'Afrique à la Caraibe*. Paris:
L'Harmattan..

Premdas, Ralph. 2004. "Elections, identity and the ethnic conflict in the Caribbean: the Trinidad case." *Pouvoirs dans la Caraïbe, identité et politique
dans la Caraïbe insulaire*. Ed. CRPLC. Paris: L'Harmattan.

Rohlehr, Gordon. 1990. *Calypso and Society in Pre-Independence Trinidad*. G.
Rohlehr: Port-of-Spain

Simpson, George Eaton. 1970. *The Religious Cult of the Caribbean: Trinidad,
Jamaica, Haiti*. Rio Piedras: Institute of Caribbean Studies University of
Puerto Rico.

3

❖

CARIBBEAN CARNIVAL

Carnival/Masquerade in Trinidad: Resistance through Performance

Jeff Henry

Introduction

Beginning in the nineteenth century, two festivals were celebrated in Trinidad. One was the European derived 'Carnival,' and the other was the African referred to as 'Masquerade.' These two festivals have completely different histories, origins and meanings. The European carnival is properly archived, documented, and historically profiled. The same cannot be said of the African-influenced masquerade which is passed on by anecdotal stories, newspaper clippings, essays, stories with information garnered by visiting journalists, transient bureaucrats, and elite families, which are filled with misconceptions and misinformation.

This paper is about giving voice to the masquerade by defining aspects of its original meaning and purpose and by examining its spiritual connections to Africa. It will explain the use of masks, the meaning of costume design, the rhythmic structure of the drumming and the music, and the use and importance of language as a means of identification and communication.

Carnival originated in Italy many centuries ago, following the establishment of Christianity by the Emperor Constantine as an official religion. Roman, Greek and Egyptian religions before Christianity worshipped various gods including Bacchus, who lends his name to elements of Carnival, so that today many participants refer to it as a bacchanal.

Many of the festivals associated with these early religious groups were co-opted by the Roman Catholic Church. December 25th became the birth date of Jesus Christ, which followed the Roman convention that celebrated the same date as the birth of Mithras. (Mithras was the god of light from Persia, adopted by the Romans). It was also the same period that many cultures recognized the return of the sun at the winter solstice. Therefore, the roots of the European carnival are deeply embedded in ancient pagan rituals.

This association with pagan materialism and sensuality, the self-indulgence which characterized the early festivals, was brought into the mainstream. It is said that the Catholic Church, disapproving of the disorderliness inherent in the festivals, sought to integrate the carnival with religious observance in order to exert some measure of control. The Roman Emperor Constantine convened the first ecumenical conference of bishops of the Christian Church in the celebrated Council of Nicea in AD 325. Here, it was decreed that January 6th would become the official start of the festivities, ending on Fat Tuesday, and on the next day— Ash Wednesday—begins the forty days of fasting (Lent), in preparation for Easter, which celebrated the resurrection of Christ.

It is commonly believed that the term carnival originated from the Italian *carne*, meat and *vale*, goodbye. There is another school of thought which states that carnival originated from the Latin *carrus navalis*, the ship of fools.

Today, the masquerade in Trinidad is understood to be an impulsive expression of joy and happiness made manifest by outbursts of energy which possesses a life of its own. However, the reality of its genesis was quite different. It is a product of enslavement, exploitation, brutality, subjugation, and indentureship. The enslaved had little social opportunity to spend time together because of long working hours; they were housed in barrack rooms. Although the yards were large, there were many people packed into the limited space with sparse facilities for recreational activities. Despite the distrust, suspicion, and animosity such a vile system entailed, they were able to avoid the negative and inhibitive conditions, and they tried to develop a creative path of resistance. They avoided confrontation and utilized, instead, dramatic presentations hiding their intentions behind words, masks, and movement.

The Emancipation of enslaved Africans in Trinidad took place on August 1st 1838, after which two celebrations existed side by side. The European-style carnival continued to be played out by the French plantation owners, who organized large costumed balls in which celebrants drove from mansion to mansion to display their wonderful costumes. They also organized theatrical presentations and musical evenings.

Many of the African communities produced bands and characters of various types depending on the communities in which they lived. They deoicted in character and in presentational form many of the experiences they endured under slavery and indenture. Many of the characters they created owed their local manifestation to a remembered past handed down from generation to generation via Griots and Elders through costume design, drum rhythms, songs, dance, and street displays. Masquerade was used by the newly freed masses in Trinidad to register their discontent at the realities of their predicament, whether by a subliminal aggression or a satirizing of the pretensions of the plantocracy.

Masquerade in Trinidad derives from the Yoruba tradition of parading through villages in costumes and masks. Some of the costume designs were strongly influenced by the Egungun which represented spirits of the living-dead ancestors. The literal translation of the word Egungun in Yoruba means 'walking dead.' Thus, Egungun is no a masquerade character, but a symbol of a spiritual concept. The Yoruba believed in a life after death. Death is not the end of life. It is only a means whereby the present earthly existence is changed for another. After death, therefore, man passes into a 'life beyond' which is called Ehin-Iwa which means 'After-Life.'

The internationally acclaimed playwright Wole Soyinka states:

> Each person comes to this life, from the world of the unborn, through the 'abyss of transition.' And each will leave again through this archetypical realm, as they make their way to the world of the ancestors." (1976, 26)

Many masqueraders in Trinidad designed costumes to align themselves with the concepts of the Egungun. When bits and pieces of loose cloth and unrelated articles were attached to a costume, it was a sign of the influence of the Egungun. All material used for making costumes was organic or of found substances. However, the Trinidad masquerade, despite its historical attachment to the Egungun, was a local creation which stemmed from the need to protest the condition of their lives and to communicate with others the ways, means, and places to gather without the knowledge of the authorities. The use of a mask was not only to cover the face; every intention was masked, and each word and every movement were devised as a select means of communication.

The Use of Masking

Masks have been used for centuries by a diverse range of cultures. Early humans resorted to magical rituals, which included mask dances to influence the hunt. The quality of this rite stressed the importance of the mask as the catalyst for invoking mysterious forces that mankind sought for practical purposes. The mask transcended culture as a common tool for human spiritual existence that expressed a basic psychological need. However, in many cultures the mask has lost its power as a spiritual tool; in Africa it has retained its eminence. The African continent is one of the few places in the world where masks still play an important role in society. African society is rooted in ancestor worship. Sculptures portray ancestors. Masks represent the spirits of the ancestors as they are the vehicle through which the past and the present communicate. The Egungun is totally masked, the entire persona is submerged. The wearer escapes the self and that part of him of which he is consciously aware. Total masking allows the wearer to escape from the realities of daily life and to create new identities.

These are the memories that could not be obliterated from the minds of the enslaved Africans. In particular, those who experienced the Egungun ceremonies in Africa, and those in Trinidad who, through the storytelling of the Griots and Elders, had these images implanted in their psyches. Sophisticated methods of survival were possible through the ingenuity of the Griots and Elders who posited themselves as links to the past. They told stories, sang songs, and played games; they relied on African oral and dramatic traditions. It demonstrated that the African use of performance is no less valid in recording society's history. It explains the ability of Africans to use their environment to showcase incidents that make up their daily lives. Methods of obfuscation were adapted to deflect the constant vigilance and the lack of privacy imposed upon them. They recognized and compared the existing festival to the masquerade in their homeland and noted how it was manifested differently.

In this cauldron of pretension and denial, one witnessed the supposed illiterate enslaved who, although totally disenfranchised and without rights under the law, devised, burnished, and shaped the masquerade into various formats as a tool to confront the powerful ruling forces. This was not done through violence, but through subversion and deception, by using the tools of performance and presentation.

Traditional mas Characters

The following section will introduce several of these traditional characters in order to explain them and give voice to their struggle.

The Pierrot Grenade

The name is a misnomer. Grenade is a French word for Grenada, but the people of Grenada know very little about the Pierrot Grenade; the name is a Trinidadian fabrication. This was done in order to make a distinction between the lowly immigrants who came from Grenada at the turn of the twentieth century and who participated in the festivities by attempting a similar characterization of the Pierrot, a carnival character, who was elaborately and splendidly attired. They were referred to as Pay-Wo Grenade. Patois (current spelling: Patwa), a derivative of the French language, was the language spoken by most people during that period. Pierrot was pronounced Pay-Wo in Patwa.

The Pay-Wo was a fascinating character born out of the creative imagination of the Grenadian migrant. He was a pseudo-intellectual, full of confidence, who believed that in order to be knowledgeable, a son of the soil does not have to go abroad to Europe to study. He believed in the love of family, community, and environment, and thought that enough to shape and define one's persona. The Pay-Wo was a gardener who recalibrated the English language in a convoluted picturesque type of spelling by syllable. This unique style was a game in which one was taken along a path of clues given in sections and in a seemingly unconnected storyline. However, the message of protest was loud and clear.

It is acknowledged by the older masqueraders and Elders that the Pay-Wo is the true descendant of the Egungun. The Pay-Wo's gown was made up of crocus bags (thick, crudely-threaded bags made of twine used to transport sugar). He further decorated himself with strips of cloth of all varieties, colours, lengths, and sizes. He attached cigarette boxes, milk cans, and biscuit tins to his costume. In some of these cans and tins he deposited pebbles and tiny marbles to create different tones and sounds as he moved. His headgear was made up of paraphernalia such as a cloth or cork hat or a helmet or felt hat, which, in turn, was adorned with sprigs of hibiscus and other pretty flowers surrounded by leaves and grasses. He tied his head with a bright extremely large handkerchief. Under all this head dressing hung an obviously false hair—a grotesque wig made from rope—plainly dyed with no attempt at finery.

From the inception of the masquerade in 1838 up to the early twentieth century, coded symbols were used in costume designs which had special meaning only to the initiated; secret societies were common among the Africans. It was one element of the culture evident in the masquerade which survived the middle passage. As Africans became creolized, many adopted the values of western society and the loyalties and attachments to Motherland Africa were diminished and became frayed at the edges as the younger generation assumed leadership. It is not uncommon for many masqueraders today to use the designs purely for design reasons without any understanding of its spiritual and political significance. African masquerade represents spirits; hence the word jumbi is commonly used.[1]

The Dame Lorraine

While carrying out their domestic duties, the enslaved took note and observed the planters in their private moments. These private moments were indeed informative. They would return to the barracks at the end of the evening and, in a storytelling mode, would portray the ineptitudes and physical grotesqueness of their owners by mocking their behaviour and pretentiousness. They created an ensemble called the *Dame Lorraine*, which included fifteen to twenty characters and was performed in two acts. In the second Act, the African interpretation of satire and parody prevails. The scene changes to a barn and the show is staged in a rustic environment. This is because this is where the Africans believe the elite belong—where the pigs lived, the cows slept, and the chickens roosted. The ballroom has become a barn with none of the finery of the previous scene. A schoolmaster is in charge with a whip, a threatening figure of stern authority who occasionally strikes a guest to keep order.

With much pomp and ceremony, the schoolmaster introduces each guest as they enter. Their names, announced in Patwa, are really a description of their physical deformities, such as Monsieur Gwo Koko (Mr. Large Balls), Madame Gwo Buden (Mrs. Big Belly), (Monsieur Gwo Lolo (Mr Long Penis) Mise Gwo Bunda (Mrs Big Backside) Jaffen Bea, (is a well muscled young man who the planters wife chose for a bedroom mate), Mise Gwo Tete (Madame Big breasts) Nom Kishoe (Scratches a perpetual crotch itch) and many more. It is important to note that the creativity and inventiveness of the masqueraders encompass play, posture, walk, attitude, and gesture. Thus, through physicality, the characters become much richer.

Today, all that is left of Dame Lorraine's parody is a female with a large backside and huge breasts cavorting with an umbrella. In today's theatre parlance, this would be referred to as parody. Enslaved Africans who worked on the estates were taught to dance European dances

---

1   Jumbi is a Kikongo word from West Africa, pronounced nzambi, which means spirit. Spirit is a Caribbean term for ghost.

because African dances and rhythms were thought to be too barbarous. Little did the estate planters 'masters' realize that their erstwhile pupils would change the form into an elaborate and grotesque parody of the way the elites conducted themselves at their stylish balls.

This presentation of parody and mimicry suggests that despite the elite's power, and the fine clothes they wore each day, the Africans knew what lay underneath. They were intimately acquainted with their foibles. The exaggerated physical forms reflected the elites' deformities as perceived by their bondsmen and bondswomen. The show was staged in a rustic environment because this is where the Africans believed the elite belonged, where the pigs lived, the cows slept, and the chickens roosted.

The Devil Dragon

Trinidad is a very religious country. Christianity is a major hegemonic force in the society, and the concept of evil as exemplified by devil figures is an important ingredient not only in the religious life of the people, but in the Christian values that frame one of the most dominant ethos governing society. Thus, it is amazing to many to see on carnival day a band of underworld characters glorifying Satan and his entire entourage. It is said that the men responsible for this band were unbelievers, and they may have resulted from an underground protest directed against the forced Christianization of enslaved Africans.

Imagine early dawn on a masquerade morning. The sun is barely peeping out from behind the clouds. One can hear in the stillness of the dawn, the sounds of bells and horns, and looking through the louvers, one can distinguish in the distance, elegant figures dancing and cavorting playfully. That special, entrancing, tantalizing, but intimidating, group, is the Dragon Band.

The Dragon Band has many characters because it is composed of a community of players who tell a story from beginning to end. Each character has a significant role to play. It was one of the first bands on the streets on the morning of the Masquerade, and the ringing of bells and blowing of horns was the work of the Imps who were at the front of the band announcing their presence on earth.

Imps were roguish characters. Dressed in red from head to toe, they were light on their feet, athletic, and balletic. Wings attached between the shoulder blades responded to every move the Imp made. Their spinal column was pulled straight up, allowing movements to be defined and economical. The essence of the movements is quick, frenetic, and nervous. They made high kicks, sometimes sustaining the leg up in the air for a long period. However, the instruments in their hands dictated the form, shape, and flow of the fundamental function of each Imp.

Leading the band was the Key Imp, who carried a massive key that had many functions. It was used to open the 'Gates of Hell' for the underworld to enter Earth. Another Imp carries a scale, the symbol of justice, in order to scale and weigh the sins committed, which are reported to Satan so that one can be placed in the proper section of Hell. A hierarchy was established in descending order according to the severity of one's deeds. There was the Imp with the Axe who cleared the path, followed by the Imp with the Scythe. Many of us are familiar with this image. He is depicted with a skull mask and black hood, and, in religious paintings, is depicted as 'The Grim Reaper.' He is a symbol of suffering because of famine and plague.

Imps are the blue-collar staff of the underworld; they are absolutely necessary for the infrastructure enabling Hell to function. (Even the Devil needs organization.) For the myth of the Devil and Hell to make sense, it was necessary to create a structure and hierarchy to which humans could relate.

The Pantheon of Evil

Many of the characters in the band are one and the same manifestation of evil. All demonstrate different characteristics, moods, and personas of Satan. Since evil is depicted in many forms, the characters run the gamut from beauty to physical psychological and emotional ugliness. However, on the surface, they are charming and attractive. The person playing each character must understand the subtext, which is the essence of the character, and must portray it in context of costume design complemented by movements to complete the image. The following characters are the Devil incarnate.

The Sun of the Morning is responsible for his own downfall from heaven. He shone brighter than God, so he thought he was better and more powerful.

Bride of Lucifer: Queen of the Band: She is reputed to be the most Satanic and evil character in the Pantheon.

Bookman/Beelzebub: Wearing an extraordinarily large head mask, with an expression dripping with mischief and sensuality, Bookman is an enchanting monster; he carries a large book, with a big pen in hand and an inkwell on his heel. Bookman is Hell's recording secretary. Occasionally, he moves in slow motion. In an ethereal moment, he twirls and dips his pen in the inkwell, points to one of the spectators and calmly writes in his book. The action means the person he points at, or someone close to them, is going to die.

Gentleman Jim: This character is an aristocrat; he appears fragile and vulnerable, dressed in top hat and scissors tail coat; in this form it is said 'he is an illusion.' He makes one believe that Hell is a paradise.

The Prince of Darkness is surly, suspicious, cunning, assertive and belligerent. His movements are short and sharp.

The Caged Beast represents Lucifer in rage. The beast is the guardian of the gate to the entrance of Hell/Earth. He wears a large Dragon Mask. His fingernails are long, pointed, metal claws. From neck, to wrist, to ankles his body is encased in a suit of fish-like scales. Around his waist is a chain with locks, which must be opened with a key, and it is the Key Imp who must approach the Beast to unlock the chains. The inability to control his movements enrages the Beast; he rears up on his hind leg and totters in midair just waiting to pounce on any being that ventures within his space. The fluid movements of attack and retreat and the interplay among the Imps at this moment are fascinating to watch.

Lucifer King of the Band wears a crown and carries a fork wrapped with a serpent. His costumes are of expensive silks, and his jewelry flashy; he dresses elegantly in flannels and silks—a sign of class and nobility for the period. He was a father figure.

According to John Grey (1985) the first reference to the Devil, or Satan, came from these words:

> And The Great Devil Was Cast Out, That Old Serpent Called The Devil And Satan Who Deceives The Whole World (Revelations 12:9)

The influence of these lines from the Bible on the Devil/Dragon mas band in the Trinidad Masquerade are clear. Pioneers of the Devil/ Dragon band read the Old Testament as well as other books and constructed many characters and situations straight out of Revelation 20:1. However, the Dragon band paints a different picture of Hell. In their interpretation for the masquerade, Hell is glamorous, filled with preening, prancing self important demons, who parade their evil selves in a grand display of splendor and joy.

Mikhail Bakhtin's theory of carnival in *Rabelais and his World* provides some explanation as to why such dreaded figures entered the mas, despite the religious nature of the society. Bakhtin's study of carnival tradition covers the European medieval period, but his conclusions are applicable to any culture of Masquerade. Essentially, he believes that a carnival is necessary for the functioning of human existence. Its main function is not only to provide entertainment, but also to turn reality, as it is lived and experienced, upside down.

The Midnight Robber

The Midnight Robber was a character larger than life. He was known for his flamboyance, bombast and grand gestures, coupled with a powerful and an energetic personality. His costume was designed with fringes around the brim of his very large round hat. Fringes ran along his shirt sleeves and pants seams. His cape was also bordered with fringes. Elements of this design were indicative of a belief system which many of the spectators understood.

The Midnight Robber was one of the classic masquerade figures of resistance; his persona was threaded into the culture of the society, so much so, that he continues to live in the hearts and minds of the modern generation. Many do not consciously understand his power and impact on society, yet he lives on.

The Robber was a locally evolved character whose focus and thrust indicated the subversive intention in the people of African descent. In their quest not only for a profile, but for a voice in their developing society, the Robber proved to be an efficient conduit. The bombast and extreme exaggeration conveyed a hidden anger and resistance to authority; in all its manifestations, a contained powerlessness was evident and deeply understood by the spectators. Despite their humble social status, the powerful character enabled them to ascend into unbelievable visions of earthly grandeur. The feet were the centre of energy.

The Robber established a low stance with knees bent, back arched, elbows bent when holding a gun and trigger cocked with fingers at the ready. Never immobile, the Robber's head and neck are on constant alert, surveying the landscape. There is an incessant internal movement induced by a smooth, deep breathing, giving the impression of a close connection with terra firma. This connection, together with a compelling aura, generates an energy that captivates spectators, who, subsequently, fall under the influence of his boasts and bombast. Through speech and movement, the power of the feet become the focus. His signature is his whistle. The sound of his whistle is heard long before he can be seen. He attracts attention by his flamboyant and grand movements. With the combination of sound and movement, the spectators became enthralled and attentive, waiting with bated breath for his pronouncements.

His calling card is: "Stop! Stop! You Mocking Pretender!"

What does he mean by 'mocking pretender'? He accuses all and sundry of being two-faced. We are not what we pretend to be; we are all hypocritical deceptive beings. He (the Robber) is the avenging power whose mighty presence forces us to revaluate the circumstances that dominate our lives.

> Drop your keys and bow your knees,
> and call me the Prince of Darkness, Criminal Master.
> For if I grind my teeth and stamp my feet
> it will cause a disaster. So bow your knees.

Another Robber claims that:

> When I clash my feet together the earth crumble famine
> follow. Wherever I stand grass never grows, sun never shine,
> far more for mankind to go.

The theme of the feet is stated by many Robbers in different ways. The earth in African culture is the source of power, strength, and energy. The feet connect each person to the earth, which is symbolic to the universe. The power of the character is derived from his feet.

The following excerpts from Robber speeches indicate that Robbers align themselves to the supernatural with a surrealistic sense of power over day and night which becomes an overarching theme in many Robber speeches:

> For the day my mother gave birth to me, the sun refused to
> shine, and the wind ceased blowing. Many mothers that day
> gave birth, but to deformed children. Plagues and pestilence
> pestered the cities, atomic eruptions raged in the mountains,
> Philosophers, scientists, professors said the world is come to
> an end, but no, it was me, a monarch was born. Master of all
> I survey, and my right where none could dispute.
>   Cast me in a dungeon. I roam there for forty days and forty
> nights, until I reach that big bank of the Sahara.

There were strong biblical parallels in many Robber speeches. Forty days and forty nights and references to the Sahara desert are related to Christ's experiences in the desert, which the Robber equated with the enslaved Africans crossing the middle passage. The dungeon was darkness, "enslavement." "Let there be light" was a dream of hope for freedom.

Robbers created grandiose names for themselves, conveying images of power and greatness through strength of purpose such as: *Two Gun Crowley, Tombstone, One Shot Burke, and Agent of Death Valley.* They would fight fire with fire. This approach was the Robber's answer to enslavement colonialism and exploitation: "Away down from the vast eyeless regions of the lost centuries came I, invincible, undauntable, impregnable." He represents his family history: they never gave up, never lost hope, and would never be defeated. The family was the community who crossed the middle passage together. He demanded that we fall down on our knees and bow to him. He was an autocrat, he ruled absolutely; he mirrored the behaviour and attitudes of the dominant group. He deflected what he said by making himself appear to be the villain so that the authorities cannot accuse him of plotting against the state. In fact, he boldly accused the plantation 'slave owners' and the colonial authorities of murder and mayhem. He could not do so outright, so he cleverly assumed the role of the tyrant; he spoke openly of atrocities they had committed and laid claim to it as his own. The audience understood his double talk and responded spontaneously to his story.

African theatre is usually performed in public open spaces. The spectators are a vital part of the presentation, and they complete the magic circle by responding to the situation as it unfolds. So, too, in the Trinidad masquerade the Robber, for example, would use his grand movements and his whistle until he was satisfied he had a sufficient audience. He would then establishes a playing area by his gestures. As a masquerade character, he has left his mark on the culture of Trinidad and Tobago. His fullness, sense of self, love of words, and descriptive images of his own importance created a powerful presence with a birth history second to none. When these speech patterns, with all the grandiose manifestations of impossible deeds, are copied by citizens, it is referred to as Robber Talk. Robber talk has a special context. Robber Talk means the opposite of what is said and displayed. It is considered hot air and a personality flaw (bragging), particularly in men.

Conclusion

This essay attempts to explain the many ways in which the newly freed African masses used characters in the masquerade to register their discontent at the realities of their situation. One way of doing this was by creating characters who were subliminally aggressive. This paper also explores the ability of the African to change ordinary daily occurrences into dramatic scenarios in form and presentation. They did not write books or plays but, instead, relied on African oral and dramatic traditions. It demonstrates that the African use of performance is no less valid in recording society's history. It explains the creative use of Africans who used their environment to show case incidents that made up their daily lives. The *Pay Wo* did this through language, The *Midnight Robber* used speech and movement, and *The Devil/Dragon* employed mime, dance, and characterization to create a persona symbolising all the elements of the dramatic form to tell a story. All this creative effort was produced by unschooled performers, who clearly understood the shapes and images they were trying to project and what stories they were trying to convey.

Today, the celebration of carnival/masquerade is romanticized. History has been discarded and mostly forgotten. Carnival is merely colour, revelry, gay abandon, and a period when creative people can showcase their artistic achievements, in design, music song and dance but largely without recourse to history.

Works Cited

Bakhtin, M. 1984. *Rabelais and his World*. Indiana University Press.

Grey, J. 1985. *Near Eastern Mythology*. London. Peter Bedrick Books.

Soyinka, W. 1976. *Myth, Literature and the African World*. Cambridge: Cambridge University Press.

The "Other Half": The Articulation of Carnival in Nineteenth-Century Trinidad

Teruyuki Tsuji

Introduction

The custom of feasting *Shrovetide*—the assumed prototype of Carnival in Trinidad—was introduced by the Spanish and later enriched with *divertissements* brought by French Creoles. During Christmas holidays, Catholic families of the planter class visited each other for dinner or lunch. In the following weeks, they attended concerts and balls. When Ash Wednesday approached, they went on a procession in a line of decorated carriages "accompanied by musicians playing such instruments as the violin, guitar, bandol, mandolin, and chac-chac or maracas" (Carr 1992, 363). In pre-emancipation Trinidad, Carnival was a Catholic festival of the dominant class with European origins—it was not publicly open, spatially or temporally, to people of color.

Emancipation initiated an influx of liberated Africans from the plantations and attracted working-class Africans from nearby British colonies, creating the ghettoes on the eastern outskirts of Port-of-Spain.[1] In the late nineteenth century, Carnival developed into a celebration of the ghetto occupants, who came to be known as *jamettes*—a word from French-Creole *patois* for those who lived outside the diameter of a decent, respectable society. Their coarse "canoe[s] on wheels"

---

1   The population in Port-of-Spain and its adjacent wards, which was 18,980 in 1861, jumped to 23,561 in the succeeding decade, and reached 42,682 (28% of island's total population) by early 1880s (Brereton 1981, 114; Besson 2001, 67).

pushed Catholic nobles' carriages out of the streets (Wood 1986, 246). And tunes of violin, guitar, bandol, and chac-chac were drowned out by their "drumming on the abominably monotonous tum-tum" and "singing accompanied by the simultaneous clapping of the hands" (Besson and Brereton 1992, 356). Placing Carnival in the socio-historical context of nineteenth-century Trinidad and addressing what Richard Price terms the "historical conditions of cultural production," emphasises the implications left unexplained by the theoretical framework of cultural hegemony and its schematic reduction of the population's agency in the formation of Carnival to rationalities and political disguises (2008, 304). Without minimizing the implications of Africans' and Afro-Creoles' individual and collective actions, we can demonstrate that they constituted a constellation of conditions, including demographics and historical events, which shaped unique outcomes in their articulation.

Hyphenation: Separating and Jointing

On the first Emancipation Day, the governor of Trinidad asked his aide if martial law should be declared. The aide replied: "Martial Law! Against whom?"[2] As with other British West-Indian colonies, martial law served as a reminder of the disparity in power and status between social segments. Nevertheless, in Trinidad, the question that the governor's aide posed in the Proclamation of December 29, 1824 was not self-evident:

> In the days of fathers, West Indians, in imitation of their countrymen, in Great Britain, indulged in the barbarous customs of those times and made the holy festival of Christmas one continuous scene of noisy mirth, revelry and inebriety. Martial law was then obviously necessary to control the white population and prevent a total relaxation of military discipline (Besson and Brereton 1992, 121).

Each year the militia was called into service from December 23 to January 8 in Trinidad (Fraser 1891, 53). In Jamaica, for instance, the relaxation of plantation discipline necessitated the call of the militia (Curtin 1955, 27), while in Trinidad, being designed to prevent the elites from being immoral, the period of martial law became a time

---

2   An excerpt from Lieutenant Colonel Copadose's *Six Years in Trinidad*, published in 1845, and reprinted on *Newsday Historical Digest*, August 26, 2001: 4.

during which colonial social bounds were simultaneously re-inscribed and openly transgressed (Osugi 1999, 42).

Masters were called up for service. In a gesture of support, their families attended military parades. Empty estate houses were thrown open to the slaves for a "constant succession of dinners, balls, and suppers" (Fraser 1891, 53). An English planter portrayed the scene on Christmas morning after he was "awoke by salutes of small arms" in 1822:

> At nine o'clock while at breakfast, the whole of the negroes came dressed in the gayest clothes to wish us a Merry Christmas, and a piece of beef and an allowance of flour and raisins was distributed to all of them, with a proportion of rum for the men and wine for the women and children. They then began dancing and the whole house is made free for them for three hours and they are enjoying themselves in the hall etc (De Verteuil 2000, 103–104).

Another English planter was invited to a Christmas party with an invitation sent and written by slaves "in the very same way as if one lady wrote to another" (Carmichael 1833, vol. I, 285):

> We had a cold dinner at three o'clock, that our negroes might have the sole use of our kitchen and oven; which were soon filled with good things. I... found them all well dressed. The prevailing costume was thin muslin, and some had coloured slips on. Shoes were not universal; but many had handsome necklaces and ear-rings. Their head handkerchiefs were gracefully put on; and the whole was managed with an attention to politeness and decorum, that was certainly very creditable. [...] they [...] kept it up until near sun-rise; and danced the next night, as long, and as merrily elsewhere (Carmichael 1833 vol.2, 288-289).

Slaves were not the only ones who transgressed colonial, racial, and cultural boundaries. While they celebrated Christmas in imitation of their masters, planters found pleasure in dancing African dances to the beat of African drums. When so doing, the planters and slaveholders did not play Negroes in a general sense nor did they imitate the house Negro with whom they had closer and frequent daily contact. Instead, they were disguised as *negue jardins* (a French-Creole term for field slaves)—the most distant socioeconomic body—with a costly costume (Hill 1998, 11; Osugi 1999, 41–42). A retired French-Creole planter recalled:

At the time carnival flourished, the elite of society was masked or disguised. The favorite costume of the ladies was the graceful and costly "mulatress" of the period, while gentlemen adopted that of the garden Negro, in Creole, *negue jardin,* or black field slave. At carnival time our mothers and grandmothers have even danced the *belair* to the African drum whose sounds did not offend their dainty ears, and our fathers and grandfathers danced the *bamboula,* the *ghouba,* and the *calinda.* (qtd. in Hill 1972, 11)

French Creoles: Colonized Colonizers

Such an inversion was common among, if not exclusive to, French-Creole landowners, slaveholders, and their slaves. For instance, both of the above-quoted accounts of Christmas day come from the same plantation district, *La Reconnaissance,* which was founded by a group of French-Creole planters. Webster Gillman, the English planter, was determined to keep the custom of Negro festival in light of the "happiest effects resulting from it" when he purchased the plantation from the former French-Creole owner (qtd. in De Verteuil 2000, 103-104). The planter who invited Mrs. Carmichael to the Christmas party "fled from Haiti with his family to save his life and came to Trinidad" after the outbreak of slave revolts in 1791 (99).

The majority of the French-Creole planters in Trinidad were *émigrés* from the Francophone West Indies and, as a result, they became "more attached to the island where they had established themselves, to the island in which they were united by memories and interests, than to [their] mother country" (Besson and Brereton 1992, 52). In his novel *The West Indies and the Spanish Main,* Anthony Trollope highlights the traits of French Creoles in the West Indies:

> [T]he Frenchman ... loves France, or at any rate loves Paris; but his object is to carry his Paris with him; to make a Paris for himself, whether it be in a sugar island among the Antilles, or in a trading town upon the Levant....[T]he Frenchman ... never looks behind him with regret. He does his best to make his new house comfortable. The spot on which he fixes is his home, and so he calls it, and so regards it. But with an Englishman in the West Indies—even with an English Creole—England is always his home (1968 edition, 99).

The "Paris" was an imagined reconstruction, not direct interpretation, of putative French cultural origins; in this remote "island among the Antilles," with limited materials available, the reconstruction involved selective appropriation of bodies, objects, and practices attributed to others according to a colonial racial taxonomy. For example, due to a serious shortage of women, French-Creole men used women of color as sexual partners and often made them concubines (De Verteuil 1987, 12). It was not unusual that colored ladies were asked to fancy-dress balls, where young French-Creole men chose a mistress (Besson and Brereton 1992, 57). Calypso developed as a *divertissement* for the Catholic elite's Carnival celebration from the ability of African slaves to compose and sing extempore under the patronage of French-Creole slaveholders (Cowley 1996, 32).

The British conquest of the island marked a critical juncture. Under Protestant-English rule, *Europeanness* or *Whiteness* became an attribute from which the French Creole could not automatically benefit. To claim and protect this most important status-generative quality, French-Creole elites had to distance themselves from the racial and cultural *otherness* of people of color. French Creoles came to conceal their desire for and sexual union with racial others by obstinately refusing to admit anyone who was actually (or was assumed to be) tainted by Negro blood into their family circle (Brereton 1981, 11). Driven by a craving for and a repulsion of low-others, the French-Creole elite built a unique set of circumstances, wherein they retained intimate, yet separate and hierarchical, relations with them, while carefully restricting it in the domestic sphere:

> The stranger...would hardly ever have penetrated the privacy of the family [...]. the French Creole was private; to survive they had long ago created a world within a world, closely guarded by the tenets of their religion and the retention of the French language and in her mother's household not even the servants were allowed upstairs.... A most exclusive entity, the French Creole family. (Besson and Brereton 1992, 59)

Anglicization: Resistance Polymorphous

Nevertheless, the borrowing, exchange, and appropriations between segregated and stratified colonial subjects came to be enacted in public. On 5 February, 1845, the Trinidad Standard reported what a Carnival was like in the mid-1840s:

> The streets are thronged by parties and individuals in every variety of national and fanciful costume, and in every pos-

83

sible contortion and expression of "the human face divine."
Some are gay and noble—some are as ignoble as rags and
uncouth habiliments can make them. [N]ow companies of
Spanish, Italians, and Brazilians glide along in varied steps
and graceful dance...But what see we now?—goblins and
ghosts, fiends, beasts and frightful birds—wild men—wild
Indians and wilder Africans. (Wood 1986, 244)

The noble and ignoble formed a masquerade; bodies representing low-others, such as a "goblin," "ghost," and "beast," paraded along with respective "friends." According to another record, in the Carnival of 1847, White masqueraders wore black masks alongside Blacks, who wore "white flesh-colored masks" and were "droll in the extreme" (Carr 1992, 363).

The above-cited excerpt from the English-language paper could not help applauding Black masqueraders' "exuberant measures and concentrated force in the fantastic revels" (Wood 1986, 244). In 1845, another English paper praised Carnival's diversity like the culturally relativistic media of today: "[N]ever within our memory has the conduct of all classes of the people been so correct—so free from any sort of offensive demeanour or license, as during the present Carnival" (qtd. in Cowley 1996, 35). Since their arrival in Trinidad, the contempt of the Protestant English was directed less at people of color than at Catholics, who apparently preferred mingling with them to remedying the evils produced by slavery. In 1826, an English administrator wrote to his friend in London, showing his displeasure at Trinidadian Catholics who indulged in feasts with lower-class folks:

> I wish...you had been here in the time of the Carnival; you
> have no idea of the gaiety of the place in that season. Ovid's
> *Metamorphoses* were nothing compared to the changes that
> took place in the persons of the Catholics of Trinidad. High and
> low, rich and poor, learned and unlearned, all found masking
> suits for the Carnival. A party of ladies, having converted
> themselves into a party of brigands, assailed me in my quarters
> and nearly frightened me out of my wits (Pearse 1956, 180).

What struck this English administrator with fear was the "party of ladies" who became reduced, albeit temporarily, to "brigands." The Protestant English always perceived shadows of the Catholic Church and the French Creoles behind the masks worn, in the melodies played, and behind the trenchant satire expressed by the *jamettes*. The perceived imprints of Roman Catholicism and the French Creoles enabled the Protestant English to criticize this "foreign" festival and the *jamettes'* self-indulgence and licentiousness. To take another example, Anglican Reverend Charles Day (1847) describes, closely and repetitively, "primitive" Black masqueraders, suggesting that he was fascinated to some extent with their creative faculty (Pearse 1956, 185). In the same diary, he shows no hesitation in disparaging the Catholic priests who "encourage pandemonium of Carnival under the guise of religion to "keep up their influence over the flock" (Cowley 1996, 40–41).

The policy of colonial administrations toward Carnival became more coercive from the mid-1840s. Prohibitions of the "MASKING in the open streets" during Carnival, once occasional, became routine every year (Cowley 1996, 36–37). In 1849, two ordinances were enacted to authorize the colonial administration to use the constabulary whenever necessary, and to restrict the days of street processions, which previously lasted for weeks, for two days until the dawn of Ash Wednesday (Wood 1986, 245; Cowley 1996, 49). These were surely measures against increasing presence of Black masqueraders in Carnival. Equally notable, however, is that it was in the late 1840s that relations between the Protestant English and the Catholic French-Creole communities grew tense over the 1844 Ecclesiastical Ordinance, which designated the Church of England as the "Established Church" (De Verteuil 1884, 172).[3]

By the late 1850s, French Creoles, both White and Colored, had withdrawn from street processions and the influence of Catholic priests had become insufficient to control the extravagance of Carnival (Wood 1986, 246). Street battles became common; the "stickfighters," representing different masquerade bands, wandered the streets and picked fights. The *jamettes* must have been a public nuisance to the Catholic French-Creole community as well as the Protestant English. The French-Creole elite became a target of mockery as often as their English counterparts. In addition, a mass settlement from neighboring British West Indian colonies at this time rendered the *jamettes* culturally and religiously distant from French Creoles: The *jamettes* were chiefly those who were neither born in Trinidad nor professed Roman Catholicism but Anglicanism (*Census of the Colony of Trinidad* 1891, 18-23).

---

3   The Ecclesiastical Ordinance met strong and persistent resistance from the French-Creole community, causing a substantial reduction of colonial fund allocation to the Catholic Church. They claimed that the Ordinance reflected a biased view toward Roman Catholicism among the members of the Legislative Council, regardless of the fact that Catholics accounted for two-thirds of the total population (*Census of the Colony of Trinidad 1851*, qtd. in De Verteuil, *Trinidad*, 2nd ed. 164).

Despite these facts, upper- and middle-class French Creoles continued themselves to profess the original architects of Carnival, and as a gesture, the Archbishop of Port-of-Spain maintained his custom of driving through the streets for an inspection of Carnival until the end of the 1860s (Wood 1986, 247). The French Creoles also organized the most persistent opposition to the repression of this annual festivity (Cowley 1996, 56). When the constabulary collided with the *jamettes* during the Carnival of 1858, the Archdiocese, backed by the French-Creole community, severely condemned the Governor Keate for his deployment of troops to suppress the clash (Wood 1986, 245).

The post-Emancipation migration divided the colored community in Trinidad into ethnic factions. The traditional French-Creole and Roman Catholic element remained the largest part, but the "English-Negro mixture" became more prominent (Powrie 1956, 229). Facing the Anglicization of the colony, which could cause further degradation of their group worth, the French-Creole Coloreds publicly criticized the colonial administration's repression of the *jamette's* formation of Carnival, in contrast to the English-Protestant, who critiqued Carnival as grotesque paganism. On 25 February 1858, the *Trinidad Sentinel*, a newspaper run by French-Creole Coloreds, denounced the administration's reaction to the clash in 1858 as an example of forced Anglicization:

It is sought, say the advocates of this iniquitous and silly proceeding, to make this Colony English in its manners, habits and customs. The absurdity of this assertion appears upon its face, and requires no keenness of perception to discover it. As well might our ruler desire to make this community English in habits of thought, nay in language, or better still in religion (Cowley 1996, 54–55).

Jamet: The "Other Half"

In Port-of-Spain in 1881, the longstanding discord between the *jamettes* and the constabulary developed into large-scale clashes, which came to be known as the "*Canboulay* riots." *Canboulay* is a derivative of a French-Creole term *Cannes Brulées*, which literally means "burning the canes" (Carr 1992, 364). Fires often occurred in sugar estates. Some planters set fires to clear the pre-planting fields and to rid the pre-harvesting fields of rats. However, buffeted by wind, the fire sometimes spread over canes not yet ready for harvesting (Galloway 1989, 91). When this occurred, slaves were chained and forced to fight the fire while grinding the burned canes before they were spoiled. Their faces and bodies became soot-covered, which made them look pitch-black.

Following Emancipation, Black masqueraders intruded into Carnival processions, often making their already black skin blacker by overlaying it with varnish and molasses (Hill 1972, 24; Osugi 1999, 41). The Reverend Day encountered "gangs of negroes," who were "half-naked" and "bedaubed with a black varnish" and one of whom "had a long chain and padlock attached to his leg" and was occasionally "thrown to the ground and mock-beaten" (qtd. in Carr, 1992, 364). Day thought that this enactment may have reproduced the inhumanity of slavery. L. M. Fraser (1881), a one-time police chief, later saw these "performances" as demonstrations of the causality of slavery, Carnival, and the Canboulay riots (Hill 1972, 23). This assumption has been cited to argue that Carnival was an opportune site for *jamettes* to carry out a strategic reversal of the process of domination in late nineteenth-century Trinidad. However, this emphasis has often overshadowed other important dimensions of the development.

The *jamettes'* quarters, popularly known as "barrack-yards," and those of the upper- and middle-class residents, were hardly isolated from each other. A wide ditch, called "Dry River," physically separated barrack-yards, but bridges established "a communication...with the neighboring districts" of upper- and middle-class residents (De Verteuil 1987, 273). Pearse reconstructs what the "communication" was like:

> [The *jamettes*] were not only constantly confronted with the display of cultural standards of the higher social ranks, and thus aware of their distance from them, but paradoxically closely associated with them, especially through the women who were servants and often the predominant influence in the lives of the children. On the other hand, middle-class men would seek liaisons with the women of—and on the fringes of—the *jamette* world and some of them became patrons of yard bands and even stickmen themselves, or "jacket-men" as they were called on account of their superior class which was suitably marked in their dress (1956, 192).

Later, C. L. R. James's novelette, *Triumph*, written in 1929, described how the socioeconomic life of a barrack-yard was busy with daily traffic of human and symbolic capitals of more affluent neighborhoods. Not isolation but material, psychological, and sexual interdependence characterized the *jamettes'* relations with those outside of barrack-yards. The interaction with the "other half"—how the term *jamette* was occasionally defined (Hill 1972, 24)—provided both sides with materials suitable for ritualistic symbolic inversion and prototypes to mimic. The settlement in a new milieu, from an estate to a barrack-yard, was followed by the adaptation of alternate arche-types for imitation, which were constantly imported from hyphenated others. The matrix of intercultural dialogue changed from plantations to urban quarters; Africans turned from *negue jardins* into *jamettes*. This entailed changing the subjects of imitation during Carnival from landowners and slave drivers to politicians, policemen, entrepreneurs, and highbrows, who were ranked higher but formed the "other half" of their lives:

> [P]racticing for the Carnival, rival singers, Willie, Jean, and Freddie, porter, wharf-man, or loafer in ordinary life, were for that reason ennobled by some such striking sobriquet as The Duke of Normandy or the Lord Invincible, and carried with dignity homage such as young aspirants to literature had paid to Mr. Kipling or Mr. Shaw (Grimshaw 1992, 29).

After Emancipation, liberated Africans flocked to the streets with their bodies and faces covered in molasses and varnish. One theory holds, however, that French-Creole landowners and slaveholders entertained themselves earlier than that by imitating *negue jardins,* whose bodies and faces became pitch-black from working in a sugar estate on fire (Hill 1972, 24). If so, *jamettes* supposedly celebrated their freedom by imitating masters who had imitated them (24).

The colonial authorities became irritated at *jamettes* led by warlike stickfighters, who became more aggressive each year. As nineteenth-century writers suggest, in pre-Emancipation Trinidad, the "[d]uels had been as frequent [among the free class] as they used once to be in Ireland" (Fraser 53). *Jamette* stickmen "walked through the streets pro-claiming themselves champions and looking for some rival with whom to have a fight" (Innes 1932, 12-13) in a sense, imitating white "duelists who [earlier] repeated scuffled in public" (Masse vol. III, 164; Osugi 42). Reflecting historical events and shifts in socioeconomic conditions, sailors and soldiers succeeded stickfighters, and imitation guns, tanks, and fight-ing planes replaced sticks in "mimic warfare" and jacket-men applauded the performers imitating and ridiculing them (Grimshaw 1992, 29).

Instead of a Conclusion

"[C]arnival celebrates temporary liberation from the prevailing truth of the established order; it marks the suspension of all hierar-chical rank, privileges, norms, and prohibition" (Bahktin 1995, 109). Drawing on Bahktin's ode of "carnivalesque," James Scott theorizes that Carnival is a "free zone" where the unprivileged plan the strategic reversal of—and actually challenge—the dominant cultural discourse and order, plying an "undominated" "art of resistance" (1990, 172–82). His valorization of a "novelist (intentional)" form over an "organic" model from Bahktin's doubled hybrid leads Scott to conclude that the subordinate section of Carnival formation intends to win an "ambiguous political victory wrested from elites" (178), and their ritual expression is, in response, political disguises that "conceal their intentions" (182).

Scott takes Le Roy Ladurie's *Carnival in Romans* as the best illustration of the conjunction between Carnival and class-based social revolution. It drew attention to the synthetic relations between the leaders representing two distinct social echelons—aristocracy and peasantry:

> [Class] division did not exclude synthesis. [They] were mortal enemies; still they communed intellectually through a Carnival folklore which constituted their 'code.' They played contradictory roles in the Carnival, but it was the natural element for them both: Despite their rivalry to the death, they were cultural brothers" (1979, 370).

According to Le Roy Ladurie, however, in sixteenth-century Rome, rising class-consciousness turned Carnival into a site of conflict, where the peasantry obtained the ways and means to launch social revolution. As a result, the preexisting shared "code" and interclass "cultural brother[hood]" were disrupted.

In this respect, Carnival in nineteenth-century Trinidad was different. In pre-emancipation Trinidad, Christmas and Carnival holidays placed various cultural objects, practices, and worldviews, which would have otherwise remained isolated, into the same temporal and spatial limits. Customarily enacted in reverse, yet side-by-side within the shared bounds, perceived cultural differences were essentialized as exclusive but formed the "other half" to one another. In Trinidad, emancipation and the rise in class consciousness did not necessarily disrupt such identification and hyphenated cultures. In nineteenth-century Trinidad, assimilation did not mean simply Europeanization and Christianization; it was an asymmetrical process that valorized the English language and Protestant religious values and ethnicity against non-Christian expression *and* Roman Catholic/French-Creole cultural representations. As a result, the Protestant-English stigmatization of Carnival incited polymorphous cultural politics of resistance within and over this terrain and capital. Despite their occasional sympathetic attitude toward *jamettes*, the upper- and middle-class French Creoles never saw their ritual performances and expressions as having the same value the *jamettes* placed upon them; the *jamettes* did not face the constabulary because of their "align[ment] with French sentiments" (Cowley 1996, 32). However, their parallel reification and ideologisation of Carnival against assimilation (i.e. Anglicization) placed the different social echelons in an unintended alliance. As a result, in-betweens of cultural combinations did not turn into a "free zone," where the powerful were necessarily absorbed in retaining their relative position through ideological incorporation, whereas the powerless busily waged a war of resistance with "arts of resistance." Carnival in Trinidad remained an extensive ritual moment wherein separation and integration of the reified ethnic cultural essences were qualified only against each "other."

Works Cited

Bakhtin, Mikhail. 1993. *Rabelais and His World*. Trans. Hélène Iswolsky. Bloomington: Indiana University Press.

Besson, Gerard. 2001. *The Angostura Historical Digest of Trinidad and Tobago*. Trinidad: Paria Publishing & Angostura.

_____. 1992. "Behind the Bridge." *The Book of Trinidad*. Eds. G. Besson and B. Brereton. Trinidad: Paria Publishing.

_____. 1992. "The French Creoles of Trinidad." *The Book of Trinidad*. Eds. G. Besson and B. Brereton. Trinidad: Paria Publishing.

Besson, Gerard, and Bridget Brereton. 1992. *The Book of Trinidad*. Trinidad: Paria Publishing.

Brereton, Bridget. 1981. *A History of Modern Trinidad, 1783–1962*. Exeter (NH): Heinemann.

Carmichael, Ms. A. C. 1961. *Domestic Manners and Social Condition of the White, Coloured and Negro Population of the West Indies*. 1833. 2 vols. London: Whittaker, Treacher, & Co.

Carr, Andrew. 1992. "Old Time Carnival." *The Book of Trinidad*. Ed. G. Besson and B. Brereton. Trinidad: Paria Publishing.

Cowley, J. 1996. *Carnival, Canboulay, and Calypso: Traditions in the Making*. Cambridge, Eng.; NY: Cambridge University Press.

Curtin, Phillip D. 1955. *Two Jamaicans: The Role of Ideas in a Tropical Colony, 1830-1865*. NY: Greenwood Press.

De Verteuil, Anthony. 1987. *Begorrat: A History of Diego Martin, 1784-1884*. Trinidad: Paria Publishing.

_____. 2000.*Great Estates of Trinidad*. Trinidad: Litho Press, 2000.

_____. 1984. *The Years of Revolt: Trinidad 1881-1888*. Trinidad: Paria Publishing.

De Verteuil, Louis A. 1858. *Trinidad: Its Geography, Natural Resources, Administration, Present Condition, and Prospects*. London: Cassell.

_____. 1884. *Trinidad: Its Geography, Natural Resources, Administration, Present Condition, and Prospects* [2nd edition]. London: Cassell.

Fraser, L. M. 1891. *History of Trinidad*. Port-of-Spain, Trinidad: Government Printery.

Galloway, J. H. 1989. *The Sugar Cane Industry: a Historical Geography from Its Origins to 1914*. Cambridge, Eng.; NY: Cambridge University Press.

Grimshaw, Anna. 1992. *The C. L. R. James Reader*. Oxford: Blackwell.

Hill, Errol. 1972. *The Trinidad Carnival: Mandate for a National Theatre*. Austin: University of Texas Press.

Innes, L. O. 1932. "Carnival in the Old Days (from 1858)." *Beacon*, 10 (1932): 12–13.

James, C. L. R. 1992. "Triumph." *The C. L. R. James Reader*. Ed. Anna Grimshaw. Oxford: Blackwell.

Kelshall, Candyce. 1992. "The Story of St. Annes." *The Book of Trinidad*. Eds. G. Besson and B. Brereton. Trinidad: Paria Publishing.

LeRoy Laudurie, Emmanuel. 1979. *Carnival in Romans*. New York: G. Blaziller.

Massé, Armand. 1998. *The Diaries of Abbé Armand Massé, 1878-1883*. Trinidad: S.N.

Osugi, Takashi. 1999. *Mui no creole* (creoleness and alterity). Tokyo: Iwanami Shoten.

Pearse, Andrew. 1956. "Carnival in Nineteenth Century Trinidad." *Caribbean Quarterly* 4. 3&4:175-193.

Powrie, Barbara. 1956. "The Changing Attitude of the Coloured Middle Class Toward Carnival." *Caribbean Quarterly* 4. 3&4 (1956): 224–32.

Price, Richard. 2008. *Travels with Tooy: History, Memory, and the African American Imagination*. Chicago: University of Chicago Press.

Scott, James C. 1990. *Domination and the Arts of Resistance*. New Haven: Yale University Press.

Trinidad. Registrar-General's Dept. *Census of the Colony of Trinidad, 1891*. Port-of-Spain, Trinidad: Government Printery, 1892.

Trollope, Anthony. 1968. *The West Indies and the Spanish Main*. London: F. Cass.

Underhill, Edward B. 1862. *The West Indies: Their Social and Religious Condition*. London: Jackson, Walford, and Hodder.

Wood, Donald. 1986. *Trinidad in Transition: The Years after Slavery*. London, NY: Oxford University Press.

Unpublished Works Cited

Tsuji, Teruyuki. 2006. *Hyphenated Cultures: Ethnicity and Nation in Trinidad*. Diss. Florida International University.

The Mas I Know

Jeffrey Chock

The pages that follow are not meant to summarize the history of Trinidad's Mas. The intention is to recall some aspects of my experience of Canaval, with a special emphasis on the performance aspect in the Mas. Steelband and Calypso, two equally important elements of Canaval are not discussed.

I am a photographer. Most of my work has been done in Trinidad. I have focused my efforts on Festivals, the Dance and the Stage. In my view, Canaval is partnered by the other two. They all have one element in common: Performance. Even as a child, before I understood the concept, I was fascinated, then as now, by its various aspects. Why did people do it? When and how did it come into being? What does it signify? Without being able to articulate or formulate answers to these questions, I set out to satisfy an urge for looking at this behaviour and its meaning.

In Canaval, I say Canaval as my mother and her mother both pronounced the word that way: KANAval (they both spoke the French patois of nineteenth-century Trinidad fluently). I feel I have discovered a rich vein of performance, part of which may not even be evident to the player. Among many interpretations, performance is defined as 'an act or action' or 'a carrying out of something.' At its best, the whole process of involvement in 'the Mas' (as Peter Minshall, a universally known and most revered Mas man and artist, elegantly calls Mas) has some element or destination of performance. From conceptualisation to realisation, it is what drives the process. It is all-pervasive. At its best, performance is the dedication of a piece of work to excellence. It involves attitude, technique, temperament, awareness of the moment, and a striving to transform oneself into the spirit of creation. It requires total concentration and the ability to anticipate any error with an improvisation that does not disturb the flow. To seriously attempt Mas is to dedicate one's being to the idea. Naturally, not everyone is successful in achieving this, but the will to arrive at it, even imperfectly, is to give one's best. For serious masqueraders, the goal is commitment to this excellence.

In the shifting conditions of the streets, the real Canaval stage, one may have to perform at a moment's notice. There are rules and disciplines attached: staying in character is one. Then, again, a fleeting moment of inspiration may trigger it. Form is as essential as instinct. In the Mas, it is always a joy to come across, and an achievement to document.

Mas is played for a variety of reasons. It may be to show one's self off, to have a good time with friends, to get away from the mundane, to try to fulfil a fantasy, to be able to compete within a category, or, overall, to be judged as the best. Some forms of Mas, as is currently popular, require no more than registering with the band of one's choice, showing up on Carnival day and joining in a corporate type of cele-bration. Other forms require months of practice and, in some cases, even an apprenticeship. All those who take part are Mas people. The particularly devoted are dubbed Mas men or, more politically correct, Mas persons. The true Mas men or women are dedicated to the crea-tion they aspire to be. A costume, no matter how splendid, comes alive only when it is displayed or performed well. Thus, the most expensive is not always the best and many an ordinary effort rises above itself when skilfully used. Conditions, environment, temperament, and a host of other factors are responsible for success. One of the most sensi-tive and skilful performers I know plays a Mas called Blue Devil. The costume itself is rudimentary. Andrew Sanoir, known universally as Coutou, plays in the most minimal attire the Mas permits. Heavily smeared in laundry blue mixed with petroleum jelly, the character Blue Devil or Jab, a corruption of Diable, is supposed to terrify and scare people (children love it) by threatening to rub against them unless a little cash is handed over. Many a pretty frock or smart trousers have been ruined through noncompliance. Par of the Jab's choreography or routine involves much rolling on the ground and blowing of fire out of his mouth. Sanoir NEVER touches an onlooker. His appearance always causes a stir. His presence evokes evil and mischief. His antics are as outrageous and they are inventive, and he uses whatever comes to hand to carry out his dastardly and outrageous actions. I once saw him dash into a fish shop, announce himself with silent menace, and grab a five pound shark, yet uncleaned. He began to tear it apart with his teeth. Suddenly he stopped and spat. He had broken his top left incisor on the head of the fish. Without missing a step, he continued his performance.

To this day Coutou smiles a broken smile. Invariably he collects the most money from the audience. Why is this? I once asked:

"Is doing' the right ting at the right time, all de time" he answered.

Mas Memories

Hellyard Barracks Yard: the Setting for Mas camps

I grew up in Belmont in the 1940's and 1950's. At the time, Belmont was an area throbbing with Carnival activity. A large part of its population was the direct descendants of people who may have taken part in the Carnival riots of the 1880's, when the stick-fighting bands resisted the Police effort to prevent them from parading the streets with their sticks, their drums, and their flambeaux. Belmont people would talk about 'the old days' when Carnival was really wild. One would hear the names of illustrious fighters who battled against the Police and rival bands from Belmont or other areas. Belmont was known for its many bands of stick fighters and Wild Indians The former were still to be seen, if not as plentifully as thirty years before.

If memory serves me right, a lane just two doors from our modest house had, perhaps, three Mas camps where groups of six or seven local people, the band members, congregated with their friends. They were males, mainly young novices, under the guidance of a more experienced man. Females setting foot in Mas camps was anathema. The lane is still there, Bedford Lane, and I look nostalgically at the spots where these Mas camps were situated.

Belmont, a small but old community, had hardly any substantial houses. A yard was often common ground between wooden shacks and shared running water and toilet facilities. Thus, such a yard might run into a parallel street or lane, and we children used them as short-cuts to get to places more quickly. Irregular grids of such structures formed blocks. We were forbidden to go further than four blocks away from our homes unless we were in the company of someone older and more responsible. Hard at work but relaxed, the members of these small bands sat around making their costumes: simple feather bonnets and fringed trousers, and, maybe, a wooden knife or tomahawk. War paint would add to the effect on the actual days of Canaval. All this was done in good humour and banter, with talk of what some other band might be 'playing' that season. Sometimes, simple food to be shared during the night was cooked outdoors on an open fire to be accompanied by maybe a drink of rum or beer. Flambeaux, bottles of pitch oil (kerosene or paraffin) with crude wicks provided light. Crude *papier-maché* masks were also fashioned and, in the daytime, put in the sun to dry. What I have described would be fairly generic costumes made by friends for their own use.

At home the conversation often drifted to some aspect of Canaval: Who was the best King, or Senator, the merits of a novel costume, the finest dancer of Mas in different categories, stories of dramas that happened in past productions, failures, band leaders and their methods, but most of all, the coming of this new thing called Pan. My grandmother lived not far from my own home. In her yard, a college boy steel band had installed itself with the family blessing. They called themselves Stromboli. Just around the corner, a grass roots and pioneering outfit called Rising Sun was encamped. I knew some of these fellows and had a friendly relationship with them.

By 1954, my mother's sewing skills and sense of organization had brought her to the attention of Harold Saldenah, an up and coming bandleader with a popular following. "Conquerors of Kishra" was the title of the proposed production. Like the true showman he was, he convinced my mother to make the costumes. He said it would be a sensation and predicted that the band would boast two-hundred members. This had never been heard of before. After some thought, my mother accepted the offer. OUR HOUSE WAS TO BECOME A MAS CAMP. This meant people coming and going, talk of Canaval (which I loved to eavesdrop on), and sundry activity of working out the designs and colour schemes to be prepared. "We Go Kill Them Wid Dat!" were the optimistic cries of the faithful.

As well as his showman ways, Harold Saldenah, popularly known as Sally, was a man of some vision. He was the natural successor to impresarios such as Harry Bassilon and Charlie Savary. These were the two top bandleaders from the late 1930s until after World War II (during which Canaval was suspended). They were men about town and always had a moneymaking idea. The thing about Sally was his faith in his own ideas. I am not sure if any one had given Carnival the twist that Sally made popular. Of course, the huge sailor and military bands had been borrowed from movies. But Sally's masterstroke was to divide the band into sections of players, each section wearing its own design. That way he could divide the band into several people playing the same in identical costumes. He was also meticulous about the colour combinations that he used. One section would be red and gold, another would be peacock blue and silver, then another maybe royal purple and turquoise, and so on. This way, the public had a clear idea of what they were seeing. This was the system for floor members. Then there were characters who had specially designed costumes or an elaboration of a floor-member's garb. Finally, the King and Queen of the band were the most lavish and had hopes of taking the honour of best King or Queen of Canaval. The best Band overall would be declared "Band of the Year," and have bragging rights over the rest until next Canaval, plus a handsome cash prize and trophy.

Before this system was put into place, a bandleader would have sketches of the designs on view at the Mas camp. These were given to prospective members to be made by the tailor or seamstress of their choice (or one recommended), a system not certain to produce the appearance of uniformity within the section. Sally copied costumes straight from publicity pictures of films. Around the same time (approaching the sixties), a number of designer bandleaders used variations of this technique with great success. Lyle Akryll, Bobby Ammon, Wayne Berkeley, and, most significantly, George Bailey are a few that come to mind. Bailey was hailed for his approach, which included bands with themes which the rank and file empathized with: elaborate and innovative

Peter Minshall: *Adoration of Hiroshima*. 1985

renditions of African and tribal costumes showing the dignity of other civilizations. A touch of class and wry humour was evident when among all the African, New Guinean, and Egyptian bands for which he was known, he produced 'Ye Merry England,' complete with horse-drawn coaches and scenes from Coronations, mostly portrayed by people of

African origin. Then, towards the end of the 1970s, a Colossus arose. Peter Minshall appeared, a white Trinidadian, who was trained as a stage designer in London. He had designed individual costumes for his stepsister when still a boy, and a few bands in London for the Notting Hill Carnival, but 'Paradise Lost,' done for the veteran bandleader Stephen Lee Heung in 1976, was his real debut. Minshall expanded on the range of construction techniques and ideas that his London experience had given him. He treated costumes, or groups of them, as pieces of mobile and kinetic sculptures, designing some twenty bands, some of which caused great controversy.

Apart from this monumental accomplishment, he has also designed the opening Ceremony for at least three Olympic games. These innovations introduced the basic features of today's Mas, even though many changes have happened, both in the organization of the bands, the types of costumes and the huge numbers of players in some of the present productions.

Narrie Approo

In the Mas fraternity, one gets to know many people: the real Mas enthusiasts. One sees them, perhaps, three or four times a year. There are the has-beens, the wannabees, and the present frontrunners, full of themselves, as they should be, to help the adrenalin flow. They all converge on the Savannah, Port of Spain's main judging venue, starting with the Preliminaries. Some are there to watch and remember their salad days. The wannabees are mostly helpers attached to the King of a particular band, learning the ropes of big Mas, for that is what it is. Anyone who feels he or she might stand a chance of advancing to the next round, or even the Finals of the National King and Queen Competition, would do absolutely anything to compete. Backstage is the place to be. All sorts of informed and technical Mas talk goes on between the barking of orders, well meant banter, final adjustment and assemblage of costumes, and so on. Then there are the connoisseurs, mainly of placid demeanour. Others are just there for the status (it is a restricted area, a place to be seen), absorbing the vibrations that the occasion produces. Among many of these people, I am sometimes recognized and my opinion asked. After all, I have been watching and photographing these events for thirty years.

I know a man. I have been watching him play Mas since I was a child. He has always given me pleasure, and I seek him out at Canaval. We are friends also outside of the Canaval arena. His name is Narrie

99

Approo. The son of East Indian indentured labourers, he went to school about once every two weeks for a year. From the age of six years, he had to help his mother at home with the most taxing chores. He started gambling when he was seven (his mother sponsored this). He taught himself to read and write through comic books. His handwriting reflects the comic-book style. Cowboy and Indian stories transported the child to another zone. Straight Arrow is his favourite character. "Is all the green an the rivers an' t'ing nuh," he once explained. Soon after his parents arrived from Madras in 1917 to fulfil their indentureship duties, they were posted to an estate (Harmony Hall) in south Trinidad along with other indentured East Indians. Four older siblings are now all dead.

Narrie and Foe

Soon after his birth, his parents decided to move to Port of Spain to start a new life. The young family settled in John-John, an underclass neighbourhood in the hills of East Port of Spain, largely populated by people of African extraction who had settled there after Emancipation.

Narrie Approo (with horned headdress) and tribe

Narrie Approo as Black Indian

There, being close to the city, they expected to find work in a new environment. Narrie grew up without any formal religion, but had a Negro godmother who was a Shango priestess. It was she who introduced him to Mas, although he remembers playing an East-Indian inspired spotted devil with his father at age seven, and sailor Mas one year with USS Oregon, before the days of the steelband.

Narrie Approo is a genius. He, without being aware of it, has made a unique space for himself in the world. His understanding of performance is total. Again, I asked him why he plays Mas (he has been doing it for seventy-five of his eighty-two years): "I is a action man, nuh. Ah like de movements an' t'ing." To see Narrie in street clothes is unremarkable, although he was and is a handsome and dapper man of style. When he dons a costume, the transformation is stunning. He becomes a different person, even without performing.

A rough estimate of the amount of people who play Mas (in costume) each year might be one hundred thousand. Narrie plays the Black Indian, a character portrayed by only about thirty people each year. It is a demanding character to undertake and, thus, is slowly disappearing. It belongs to the family of 'Traditional Characters,' and Black Indian is master of them all. The rich history of Black Indian and its portrayal is not for the timid. There is a 'language' attached to it. Many of the words are either invented or the etymology lost. Yet, Narrie can recite fluently endless passages and explain their meaning in his wide repertoire of evocative sound that is uttered against foes or strangers trespassing upon ground he considers his territory. In all his many characters, his speech and movement are fluent. His Midnight Robber speeches are all self-composed, and his performance is continuous, not spasmodic. Every step he takes, every chant he wails, every opponent he encounters, asserts this. Had Peter Brook or Jacques Lecoq seen him, I feel they would recognise his vast command of performance. There are many Mas men, past and present, who are considered more illustrious than Narrie Approo, yet, for me, he is the quintessence of the true spirit of Canaval, the best Canaval performer I have ever seen.

I have asked Narrie if in the days when crowds gathered to see and hear rival Black Indians perform, before the era of televising the event and, thus, speeding things up, if he ever experienced total unison with Chief Sya Bilbo, his Black Indian name. "Many times," he said. "Ah feel kinda giddy an' shudderin." This, for me is trance, but not being connected to any religious rite, I call it 'secular trance'. At some level, I have seen this in most Mas forms, and certainly in the theatre and on the stage.

Jamettes Today: Pretty Mas

Yet there is another side of Narrie that is important. As a young man, to quote Lou Reed, he walked on the wild side. Narrie was a gambler and cheat (he has shown me some of his techniques). He lived off women without being a tout or a pimp, carried a razor, the weapon of choice in 1940's Trinidad, and was not afraid of a brawl if it came his way. Life was sweet and without cares. He has told me of his habit of

Jamette Behaviour

consulting the death notice columns in newspapers to find any wakes, as there was always gambling at wakes and one did not have to know the deceased to attend. He also loves opera as much as his vast collection of old westerns. I have seen him sing an aria from *Carmen* privately and dressed in full Black Indian regalia. It was surreal.

The Carnaval of the Jamettes

There is a reason for relating all the above. Narrie Approo seems to embody all that I have read about the jammettes of circa 1850 to 1890 in Trinidad. In the urban areas, especially in Port of Spain, two paths were open to those eager to escape the poverty and narrow confines of their lives. The first, heavily promoted by the British Establishment, was respectability. It consisted of improving one's status by means that were open to ordinary people. Training as an office clerk, a teacher or civil servant a craftsman, a small business owner, or tradesman was given official blessing and progress could be made. That path to respectability did much to establish the black and coloured middle class. Indeed, many fine socially- and intellectually-minded persons, brought up by their parents to fill that bill, blossomed. Born in Tobago of slave parents two years after emancipation in 1840, writer J. J. Thomas became a school teacher. By 1868, he had produced a seminal work on Creole grammar, the first book of its kind in the world. He then refuted a book by Oxford professor James Anthony Froude, *The English in the West Indies*, which claimed that the black man was an inferior subspecies of the human being. All this was accomplished at the time of realization that Emancipation was a kind of fool's gold. Inevitably, such a realization created bitter feelings, leaving the black youth of the island without direction or occupation, and making them vulnerable to feelings of a futile existence, thus, inviting lawlessness.

The second path was reputation. One could be known for one's ability to sing, dance, gamble, entertain, show one's sexual prowess, and for one's wit, style, cunning, and fighting power, if one was a man (although many women did not back down from a brawl and there were some women stick-fighters). This was the way of the Jammettes who came to dominate Canaval from the 1860s to the first years of the 1880s. Today the term has come to signify a loose woman and her behaviour, and not the subculture it originally was.

The old-style Jammettes cleaved to their African-rooted modes of expression in spite of all the efforts by the 'better classes' to 'civilize' them. They rejected a society that did not offer them sympathy. They expressed an anger and frustration that was not only embedded in their present, but also in the memory of generations of their ancestors who had been traumatised by the harsh cruelty of the slave system. They did it with bravado and by using their well-known African gift for satire and mimicry. Nowhere were these qualities expressed better than in Canaval. This is not to say that all those attracted by the Jamette way of living were of African origin. At this time, Trinidad's population was already very diverse. People mixed and continued to mix more and more. Narrie Approo's integration in a Black Indian band partly led by a Shango priestess in the 1930s is a good example of that dynamic. In any case, wherever it came from, ridiculing the foibles of well known personalities of the colonial establishment was deeply satisfying for lower-class, non-white people, who, at every turn in their daily life, were reminded of their inferior status. Interestingly some white men, secretly or overtly, had connections with the Jammettes and not all of them 'proper.'

Satire lightened the drudgery of everyday life. Fighting was another way to ward off frustration, and defend one's honour and manhood. Jammettes must not be romanticised. Many of them belonged to neighbourhood gangs, which, as neighbourhood gangs do, behaved brutally. Their battles generated a senseless violence that did not only antagonise the authorities but also frightened their own communities. Battling the Police, as the jammettes did in 1881, was, in fact, a rare occasion. Most of the time rival bands fought between themselves as they did sixty to seventy years later, during the first decades of the steel band movement, and, indeed, as many youths do today. But for all these negative traits, the Jammette Canaval provided people with a foundation to feel free, even those people around them who were scandalized by their extremism.

Following the riots of 1881 and 1883, stick fighting bands and costumes considered obscene at the time were banned from the streets. A movement to 'improve' Canaval developed, promoted by merchants interested in the profits to be made from the festival. That movement was also embraced by progressive members of the black and coloured middle classes, and by some members of the white elite, especially among the French, who were traditionally partial to the festival. Masqueraders responded positively, paving the way for Canaval as we know it. However, the Jammette subculture did not disappear, as the story of Narrie's youth shows. He later took a wife, settled down, and lived a more socially acceptable life. The Jammette way morphed into many forms and features, best demonstrated in our Canaval. The role it played in Mas, calypso, and the birth of the steel band has been largely recognized in the ongoing process of Nation Building.

To much of the youth, the Jammette way of life seemed more attractive and exciting, enticing many who embraced it. But a majority of the people found some compromise between the Jammette side of their personality and their desire for respectability. To some extent, I have the feeling that this still applies in Trinidad today, for, whatever our skin colour or ethnic origins, most of us descend from people who were not part of the elite, and even the privileged among us have been exposed to the collective behavioural climate. The Jammettes may have influenced our national personality more than we care to admit. After all, they did fight for the Festival, which is so beloved and precious to us. It was a mighty blow for freedom.

Policing the 'People's Festival': State Policy and the Trinidad Carnival Complex

Suzanne Burke

The aim of this paper is to measure the performance of state policy against the Trinidad Carnival since the establishment of the National Carnival Commission in 1991. The carnival is the only indigenous festival that has been subject to ongoing state 'policing', even predating the nation's independence in 1962.[1] The use of the word 'policing' employed here draws heavily from the French word *'politique,'* which refers to both politics and policy. In this way, carnival policy is presented as the relationship between policy, politics, and people as contested domains with diverse interests and ideologies. In addition, policy is defined as whatever governments choose to do, or not to do, which covers government action, inaction, decisions, and non decisions, as it implies some deliberate choice between alternatives (Dye 1992, 2).

To evaluate the set of practices, programmes, and narratives that have been used to police Carnival, this paper draws from two evaluative frameworks to obtain a comprehensive view of the impact of the Carnival policy. The first is an assessment of the stated objectives of the National Carnival Commission (NCC) by applying a set of indices, including effectiveness, equity, appropriateness, and responsiveness to measure the outcomes and outputs of the policy developed by Dunn (1994). The second framework examines the role, the choice, and effectiveness of various stakeholder groups involved in shaping carnival policy and draws from Hede's (2007) interpretation of Stakeholder Theory as it pertains to special event management.

---

1   The Carnival Development Committee, established in 1957 was first agency tasked with managing the Trinidad Carnival.

Mapping the Trinidad Carnival Complex – History and Structure

The Trinidad carnival is in the pre-Lenten carnival tradition and consists of three main components, *Mas*, Pan, and Calypso music. *Mas* refers to the Masquerade which is a very sophisticated form of street theatre. It consists of groups of masqueraders who come together in various bands to portray a particular historical or fantastical theme. Pan refers to the steel drums that were invented in Trinidad & Tobago around the 1930's after the traditional forms of music from drums and bamboo were banned by the colonial authorities in the latter part of the nineteenth century. The calypso, or *kaiso*, is a didactic song that employs various literary techniques to tell a story. It usually reflects the socio-political conscience of the society. During Carnival season, calypsonians perform their most recent offerings in tents or concert halls situated throughout the country. One of the more recent sub-genres of this art form is *Soca*, which is usually referred to as party music and enjoys popularity at the fetes and the street parade that bring the season to a close. These three ingredients (*mas*, pan and calypso) constitute the holy triumvirate of the Trinidad's carnival and their presence is generally used to determine the origin of carnival in the Caribbean diaspora. Of the more renowned Carnivals in the Americas, the Trinidad carnival is singular in its ability to replicate itself in diasporic communities throughout North America and Europe. Like Mardi Gras in New Orleans and the Carnival in Rio de Janeiro, Trinidad's festival represents a hybrid of European, African, and Asian customs that came together in the New World, and lays claim to over fifty festivals in the Caribbean diaspora[2] as seen in Table One (Hill 1983, 11)[3].

The main state agency given the task of being responsible for managing the Trinidad Carnival complex is the National Carnival Commission (NCC), formed in 1991. The NCC works along with other state-owned agencies, such as the Tourism Development Company and the Ministry of Arts and Multiculturalism, as well as carnival trade associations including Pan Trinbago, the Trinbagonian Unified Calyp-

---

2   The growth of carnivals in the diaspora can be traced back to the influx of West Indians to the cities of North America and Europe in the 1960's. These carnivals replicated the structure of Trinidad's celebration but also reflected the new ethos of West Indian life in these new environments while accommodating migrants from other parts of the world.

3   Hill, E.—'The History of Calypso Music in Trinidad'.

sonians Organisation, the National Carnival Bandleaders Association, and the National Carnival Development Foundation.

At its inception in 1991, the NCC's main goal was to "maintain the cultural authenticity of the Carnival as a national festival while judiciously optimizing its economic potential." Later, this goal was refined to "make Carnival a viable, national, cultural and commercial enterprise," a dualistic policy approach that seeks to exploit both the intrinsic and instrumental values of carnival that remains to this day (www.ncctt.org/home/index). However, finding a balance between these two seemingly disparate goals has proved to be a challenging mandate. Over time, the emphasis has shifted in favour of the more instrumental value of the festival as evidenced by the current organizational objectives[4]:

1. To provide the necessary managerial and organizational infrastructure for the efficient and effective presentation and marketing of the cultural products of Carnival; and

Table One—Overseas Carnivals in the Caribbean & its Diaspora

UNITED KINGDOM (21)	USA (30)
Acton	Long Island (New York)
Bedford (20,000)	Miami Caribbean Carnival
Birmingham (600,000)	Orlando Carnival
Bliswich	Philadelphia Carnival
Bristol (40,000)	South Jersey Caribbean Carnival
Cardiff	Springfield Carnival (Mass.)
Charivari (Folkstone)	St. Paul's Winter Carnival
Cleethorpes Carnival Parade	Tallahassee
Darby Carnival	Tampa Bay Caribbean Carnival
Devizes Carnival	Tampa Caribbean Carnival
Herne Bay Carnival	Test Carnival (New Jersey)
Jersey Battle of Flowers	Vineland Caribbean Festival
Leeds Mela	Virginia Caribbean Festival
Leeds N.I. Carnival	CANADA (7)
Leicester Caribbean Carnival	Calgary Carifest
Liverpool International Streetfest	Caribana (Toronto)1 million
Luton	Carib Expo (Ottawa)
Newham Africabana	Carifesta (Montreal)
Notting Hill, London (1.2 million)	Caripeg (Winnipeg)

---

4   www.ncctt.org/home/index. Accessed September 14, 2008.

Oxford (20,000)	Edmonton Carnival
Stoke on Trent Carnival	Vancouver Carnival
USA (30)	CARIBBEAN (14)
Atlanta	Anguilla
Baltimore	Antigua
Bayou (New Orleans)	Barbados Crop Over
Boston	Belize Carnival
Brooklyn Labour Day (1.5 million)	British Virgin Islands
Broward County (Miami)	Carricou Carnival
Cambridge (Mass.)	Jamaica Carnival
Caricabela (L.A.)	Mas Dominik (Dominica)
Charleston Carifest (South Carolina)	Mashramani (Guyana)
Chicago Carifete	Montserrat
Dallas Caribbean Festival	Nevis Culturama
DC Carnival (Washington DC)	Spice Mas (Grenada)
De Original Baltimore Carnival	St Kitts Nevis National Carnival
Houston Caribfest	Vincy Mas (St. Vincent)
Jacksonville Beach Carnival (Miami)	EUROPE (2)
Jersey City	Zomercarnaval (Rotterdam)
	Nice

Source: www.caribbeanchoice.com/carnival

2. To establish arrangements for ongoing research, the preservation and permanent display of the annual accumulation of Carnival products created each year by the craftsmen, musicians, composers, and designers of Carnival.

The state works with a complex group of carnival stakeholders both within and outside the islands to activate the festival on an annual basis. Each group has overlapping and competing interests in the festival that include the political, economic, environmental, socio-cultural and touristic impacts. These groups are shown in Table Two.

Table Two: Carnival Stakeholders

PRIMARY	SECONDARY	TERTIARY
Government and selected experts	Citizens	Third sector organisations
Private sector	Returning residents	Employees
Media	Tourists	Volunteers
Special Interest Groups (artists)	Audiences and consumers	
Event promoters, technical support services		

The carnival has always been recognized for how deeply embedded it is in the national economy, and, in 2007, it was estimated that carnival generated approximately $TT 1 billion in revenue.[5] As seen in Figure Two, the Trinidad carnival economy can be divided into two discrete areas: the core and the secondary economy, both of which overflow into the overseas carnival economy. The core economy derives revenue from the key drivers of the sector, namely *mas* and pan music, while the secondary economy includes areas such as tourism and hospitality, transport, and media. Within the core economy, a further subdivision can be used that demarcates the more traditional type of carnival activities from the more commercially oriented activities. This traditional/commercial dichotomy can be loosely framed within the arts versus entertainment paradigm, which finds its historical explanation in the Mardi Gras and Cambouley traditions that shaped the Trinidad Carnival. The Mardi Gras tradition originates from the French Creole planter class and emphasizes pageantry, display, and enjoyment. The Cambouley tradition comes from the African slaves who incorporated their own customs into the festival, and used the carnival as a platform for resistance, identity formation, and release. The tension between the two traditions has always defined the Trinidad Carnival and is discernible to this day.

Table Three: Traditions in the Core Economy

CAMBOULEY TRADITION (ART/CULTURE)	MARDI GRAS TRADITION (ENTERTAINMENT/CULTURAL INDUSTRY)
Traditional Masquerade	Modern Masquerade
Steelband events & manufacture	Brass bands
Calypso tents & related events/shows	Carnival fetes and related events
	Recorded music

The more recent focus on the economic values of the carnival can be considered under the pressing need to find alternative vectors for socio-economic development. This need has become more urgent in the wake of the loss of value added from the traditional drivers of economic development in the region, such sugar and oil as a result of the introduction of Structural Adjustment programmes beginning in the late 1980's. In addition to the economic imperative that guided policy makers at the beginning of the 1990's, there was also an increased politicization of the

---

5   The rate of conversion is $TT6.2 to $US1 (2008).

country's ethnic diversity, following the implosion of the government of national unity that ruled from 1986-1991.[6]

Figure One: Carnival Economics (TT$ 1billion—2007)

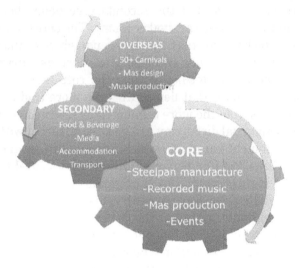

Given these factors, carnival was increasingly used as a platform to solve some of the country's most pressing development problems including:

1. The growing polarization of the country along ethnic, political, and class lines.
2. The need to diversify the economy away from its base in natural gas and oil.
3. The need to find a vehicle to improve brand 'Trinidad & Tobago' in an increasingly globalised world environment.

As such, the Trinidad carnival complex was employed as a solution to the country's larger developmental problems and not as a unit of policy analysis in and of itself.

_____

6   The National Alliance for Reconstruction (NAR) swept to power in 1986, beating the incumbent People's National Movement (PNM) by a 33 to 3 margin. The party represented a coalition of political parties and members from the major ethnic (African and East Indian) groups. However, by the end of the five-year term the party imploded due to the competing interests, the egos of the leaders of the various parties, and a failed coup de etat in 1991. The fall-out from this experiment meant that political coalitions become more difficult to sell to the electorate. As such festivals like the carnival grew in importance as the preferred space to negotiate and promote diversity

Implementation of objectives

The NCC and other institutions of support have employed three main strategies to exploit the intrinsic values of carnival. Firstly, they market it internally as a springboard for national unity, employing the 'all ah we is one' narrative. Secondly, carnival is projected as a safety valve that allows citizens to air their frustrations in an increasingly stressful society. Finally, carnival is promoted as the mecca, or mother, of all carnivals in the Caribbean diaspora, in a home and host country dichotomy. The home (Trinidad) carnival is positioned as the source of creativity and inspiration for those in the host countries, as seen in this excerpt from the Tourism Development Company's website from 2005:

> An explosion of colour, music, revelry, and creativity, Trinidad's Carnival has spawned similar celebrations around the world; but nothing on earth can rival the abandon, euphoria and stunning spectacle of our festival. With its massive masquerade bands, spectacular costumes, pulsating music and unparalleled stamina for partying, Trinidad's Carnival is often described as the greatest show on earth. It is a time for release and everyone is invited to join the party.[7]

In recognition of the intrinsic value of carnival, the NCC attempts to preserve the Cambouley carnival tradition. As such, it seeks to preserve traditional masquerade by training people all over the country in the carnival arts. In the calendar year 2007/2008, fifty-five workshops in fifty-three communities were conducted, resulting in the training of 1375 persons.[8] In addition, expenditure on the regional carnivals has increased from $TT 300,000 in 2002 to $TT 7,000,000 in 2011. The organization has also trained 9,500 persons between 2003 -2010.[9]

However, the resources dedicated to this area of the NCC's mandate is paltry in comparison to the expenditure on other income generating activities, resulting in poor returns for practitioners involved in these exercises. Many who work in this area as volunteers are simply "left to

---

7   www.gotrinidadandtobago.com/trinidad/carnival.php. Accessed on September 8, 2008.
8   Interview with John Cupid of the National Carnival Commission in March 2008 (Port of Spain, Trinidad & Tobago).
9   NCC Chairman speaking at the launch of the regional carnivals in 2007. http://www.trinisoca.com/carnival/2006/2011.html. Accessed December 10, 2008.

the wind" (Cupid, 2008). Meanwhile, the narrative about the cultural importance of the carnival has enjoyed success since most citizens have accepted the notion that carnival acts as a vehicle for social cohesion.[10]

On the other hand, there has been a plethora of strategies to ensure that carnival's instrumental values are realized. To this end, the NCC has positioned carnival within an export-oriented framework to enhance Trinidad's position within the network of overseas carnivals. In this regard, new institutions have been developed to activate this branding of carnival. For instance, the Carnival Institute was developed in 1999 to funnel business activities in the carnival arts, while the Entertainment Industry Development and Export Company (1997) was created as a mechanism to enhance the export thrust of the cultural industries of which Carnival played a major part. More recently, the Trinidad and Tobago Entertainment Company was established to maximize the earning potential of the entertainment sector inclusive of carnival and its related activities.

In this regard, there is a trend to support the expansion of the Trinidad Carnival by encouraging business interests to become more involved in the festivities. Beginning in 2001, businesses were given tax incentives for investing in cultural activities. Importers of carnival material were given exemptions on certain goods. The banking sector also began to offer loans for the carnival season, as a result of the escalating costs of festival participation.

During the period under review, the NCC's mantra turned on 'the bigger is better' theme as evidenced by the expansion in the carnival cycle—from a two-month season to one that currently extends from six to eight months.[11] The Minister of Arts and Multiculturalism during his first year in office exclaimed '*2011 Carnival will be the biggest and best ever hosted in the world. There will be greater emphasis on big events that would see profits at the micro and macro economic levels*'. In 2008, for the first time in its history, carnival masquerade band-launches

---

10   There are some faith-based organisations that have rejected the notion of the carnival as a unifying symbol. Instead, they site the many socio-cultural ills that are associated with the festival including substance abuse and alienation of some social groups.

11   Up until the late 1990's, the carnival cycle lasted three—four months beginning in November and culminating with carnival in February. More recently, the cycle has expanded and begins as early as August of the previous year in order to facilitate the number of commercial activities that now make up the festival.

that normally begin in September, started in July for the 2009 season. The growth of the carnival cycle is primarily to satisfy business interests and profiteering as is evident from the exponential growth in the number and size of carnival events during the last decade. For instance, the more popular events such as Soca Monarch attract participation of between 40,000—50,000 patrons, while big masquerade bands have attracted over 8,000 participants. In this regard, the NCC's expenditure on carnival has grown from $TT 12m in 1996 to $TT 125+m in 2011.

Thus, the NCC has achieved some of its goals, namely in developing the economic benefits of the festival. For instance, according to figures from the Central Statistical Office, there has been an increase in visitors to the carnival, as is shown in Table Two. In this regard, visitor expenditure over the period also increased from $TT 64m in 1987 to $TT 106m in 2006.

Table Three: Visitor Arrivals & Expenditure to Trinidad Carnival

YEAR	VISITOR ARRIVALS	VISITOR EXPENDITURE ($TT M)
1977	20,000	18
1987	23,000	64
1997	27,414	-
2007	43,000	106
2011	60,129	306/visitor per day

Source - CSO

Despite these growth trends, there is still a keen sense among the primary stakeholders that Carnival earnings can be increased further. Thus, they clamour for a more focused marketing strategy. This is especially within the overseas carnival circuit in North American and European markets exclusive of the immigrant enclaves in those countries. For instance, after the positive reaction to Trinidad and Tobago's cultural contingent to the FIFA World Cup 2006 in Germany, there was a feeling that carnival 2007 should have been launched shortly thereafter. The NCC's inability to piggyback on this success caused one bandleader, David Cameroon, to remark:

> The administration is the problem. Carnival should have been launched since August following the World Cup. Carnival was launched on January 12. If we are the mecca of Carnival we have to set the pace (Long 2007, 3).

These stakeholders also call for greater synchronicity within the various public policy domains that govern carnival, such as a regime to curb piracy along with a broadcast quota to increase overall airplay of festival music.

In terms of the equitable distribution of the costs and benefits of this policy approach, there have been winners and losers. Preliminary research shows that enterprises in the secondary carnival economy are reaping more economic benefits than many of those in the core. For instance a survey conducted by this author in 2008 on enterprises in the core and secondary economy showed that the firms in the secondary economy were making as much as 35% of their annual income from carnival activities, whereas enterprises in the core economy that followed the Cambouley tradition were making about 20% of their annual earnings from carnival.[12] For instance, the average steelband earns about 20% of its income from the carnival season, while most calypso tents must obtain government subventions to survive. These findings mirror problems that are faced by many festivals globally, including the carnivals in the diasporic markets, namely one of free-riding by the business sector. In this scenario, the business sector reaps economic benefits from the festival, but contributes little by way of sponsorship or grant funding to the entities that organize and own the event.

However, there are some enterprises in the core carnival sector, namely those following the Mardi Gras tradition, that earn sizeable incomes from the carnival. On average, a big masquerade band hosts between 1500—7000 participants, with the average size of an extra big band fielding around 4000 masqueraders.[13] Calculating the income from costumes, (each costing on average $3,500) sponsorship, and production launches, the average big band can earn upwards of TT$ 12m per season.

---

12 The author conducted a preliminary survey of the carnival economy in February 2008 to ascertain the earnings of firms. Entrepreneurs in the core (mas, pan and music) and secondary economy (new media, décor, and food & beverage) were asked to estimate the percentage of the overall activities and earnings resulting from carnival. Enterprises in the core area estimated that between 20-40% of their activities and income were related to carnival, while enterprises in the secondary economy estimated that between 20-30% of their activities and 30-45% of their income could be attributed to the carnival.

13 According to NCC guidelines there are four categories of bands—An extra big band has over 3000 participants, large has over 1000, medium between 301-1000 and small fewer than 300. There are at least 7 extra large bands, 15 large, and over 30 medium bands.

This figure does not take into account the enterprises that produce bands in the overseas carnival circuit.[14] Thus, there is a further subdivision of winners and losers within the core carnival economy that can be easily positioned within the Mardi Gras versus Cambouley, OR the art versus entertainment paradigm. The art-oriented sectors, such as traditional masquerade, calypso, and steelband, require more public funding to make them commercially successful and their audience is narrow. The more commercial sectors, on the other hand, such as popular music, fetes, and big masquerade bands, have more broad-based appeal, focus on entertainment, and exact greater earnings from the festival.

An analysis of equity as it relates to the public participation in the carnival also reveals a mixed bag. In the pre-NCC era, one of the hallmarks of the Trinidad carnival was the high level of public participation. This feature distinguished Trinidad's Carnival from other carnivals in the New World, namely Mardi Gras in New Orleans and Carnival in Rio de Janeiro, both of which are spectator-driven festivals. However, as the Trinidad carnival has become more commercially-oriented, the growing cost of participation has marginalized many social groups from engaging in festival space. Many among the working classes are unable to participate in the very festival their ancestors played a major part in shaping through decades of struggle with the colonial authorities. By and large, they have been reduced to spectators, and, very often, those of the middle classes have to access commercial bank loans to attend the plethora of events during the carnival season.

The appropriateness of the carnival policy, namely whether the desired outcomes are actually worthy or valuable, also yields an uneven picture. On the positive side, the economisation of the carnival has been successful in some key areas, namely visitor arrivals, foreign exchange earnings, and the multiplier effecting ancillary sectors. However, these successes have undermined the efficacy of another part of the economic mandate, namely employment creation and carnival's authenticity as a marketing tool. In the main, the growth of the carnival has facilitated shifts to off-shore production and sourcing of carnival goods and services. For example, in the big masquerade sector there has been a growing tendency to either source part or import entire costumes from markets in India and China. The band-leaders claim that local labour

---

14 Some enterprises in the masquerade sector produce bands for various carnivals throughout the Caribbean and in the diaspora. Firms such as Genesis, Poison, and Masquerade assist in the production of bands for carnivals in Jamaica, Barbados, Grenada, Toronto, New York and London.

costs are either too high or too unreliable, and have not kept apace with the imperatives of the global festival. This trend has meant that the local artisans who have traditionally produced masquerade costumes are not being employed during the season but more importantly their skills are being lost and are not being passed on to future generations. This off-shore trend is now so pervasive among big bands that in the past two years, some bands have been forced to respond to this criticism in their marketing campaigns by assuring customers that the unique selling position (USP) of their band is that their costumes are locally produced! As such, in an ironic twist of fate, the national festival of Trinidad and Tobago, touted by the NCC as the greatest source of national pride and cultural confidence, is increasingly wearing a 'Made in China' tag. Moreover, it appears that the festival's growth is undermining the key aspects of NCC's mandate, specifically the social inclusion, diversity, and employment creation platforms that are used to promote and justify expenditure on the carnival.

Policy Performance

The preceding analysis has shown that the policy approaches to carnival by the NCC have yielded uneven results and is under-performing in the key areas of Dunn's evaluative framework. In addition, the discussion has revealed that there has not been any revision of the NCC's mandate since its inception in 1991, which reinforces the notion that the carnival policy is in a state of stasis.

The reasons for this stasis are multifaceted. At an operational level, the challenge is related to the deployment of financial, physical, and human resources to plan this annual festival. For example, the timeliness of the subvention that comes from government to the NCC has proven to be an intractable problem with successive governments. The tardiness in the release of funds inevitably affects the NCC's resource deployment to the carnival, resulting in a sub-optimal planning cycle. In this regard, the structure of the NCC generally promotes an uneven decision-making process which, in turn, creates an embedded culture of inaction and slow responsiveness to the needs of the festival. As such, a feeling of learnt helplessness is discernible among some NCC operatives as this quotation from one of managers' illustrates:

> We don't get bothered about planning for Carnival because no matter how much you plan, something always goes wrong, so we just take it easy, Carnival always happens. (Burke 1997, 82-83).

This feeling of carnival always happening has meant that for the past decade the NCC, itself, has become increasingly marginalized from shaping the carnival. In fact, enterprises both in the core and secondary carnival economy launch their events and activities long before the NCC officially launches the carnival. Masquerade bands have also been known to flout NCC rules regarding the parade route on the two days of carnival.

Within the past two years, this resource problem has intensified with the removal of major physical resources, namely the Queen's Park Savannah (QPS), which is the main venue for carnival activities. This fact has made the role and efficacy of the NCC even more fragile and nebulous. In 2011, a new structure was constructed on the site but it still is not adequate to accommodate expansive visions of the festival. The human resource allocation also seems to present some challenges in terms of quantity and quality. In 1996, the NCC only employed sixteen full-time persons to administer the festival, and this figure has not changed dramatically enough to meet carnival's expansion.[15] The situation is exacerbated by the lack of specific training in events and financial management.

The absence of a clearly articulated policy also seems to affect the strategic direction of the organization, sometimes resulting in a lack of consensus between the board and the political directorate in terms of making the festival operational.[16] It is also clear that not all the carnival stakeholders have an equal seat at the table. Two obvious stakeholder groups come to mind, namely the returning resident community who consistently make up over 50% of visitors to the carnival, or the environmental groups who are concerned about some of the negative impacts of the festival on the environment. Due to a lack of clearly articulated strategic vision, the NCC is unable to effectively implement a policy for carnival. This situation is due in large part to a policy conundrum that resides within the two-fold mandate of the organization, namely its intrinsic (socio-political) and instrumental (economic) imperatives. The socio-political component of the mandate aimed at bolstering national pride, celebrating diversity, and maintaining carnival heritage is framed within a traditional cultural policy paradigm that is state-centric, cen-

---

15   The number of persons employed for 2008 was stated as sixty, which include full time permanent, part time contract and part time temporary workers.

16   This lack of consensus became obvious within the last four years resulting in the resignation of the Board Chairman, board members and the General Manager. The board members cited interference from the political directorate.

tralized, institutional-based, and more concerned with the production of carnival goods and services. On the other hand, the economic agenda is framed within a cultural industry policy paradigm where the focus is on the export of goods and services, mobilizing the transnational nature of the festival, extracting earnings, and concerned with the consumption of goods and services, as shown in Figure Three (Pratt, 2005).

Thus far, the government in general and the NCC in particular have been bereft of strategies to reduce or resolve this tension, reinforcing the slow responsiveness of the organization and underscoring the policy stasis. So, by a process of default, the major outcome of the current approach is that carnival is increasingly being left to big business interests, who are more organized and have greater access to economic and political resources. Meanwhile, the social agenda is constantly being neglected.

Concluding Statement

Changing the performance of the NCC policy towards the Trinidad carnival complex is based on developing a new way to police the festival that is dedicated to achieving greater balance between the various traditions cited above. The approach inevitably calls for a widening of the stakeholder groups that will hopefully lead to an expansion of the policy's objectives. These stakeholders will have to return to the first principles of the policy by ascertaining the problems the policy is trying to solve and, subsequently, develop a projected programme of goals, values, and practices that would frame policy action. The triple bottom line (TBL) framework that is currently being applied to festivals and events across the globe might also provide some useful guideposts by addressing the social, economic, and environmental impacts of the festival (Hede, 2007). However, I would add a geo-political component to this framework. Since the Trinidad carnival is transnational in nature, its tourists are largely from the Caribbean overseas community, and it has been the catalyst for the creation of over fifty overseas carnivals in the Caribbean diaspora. This multiple-bottom line strategy (socio-cultural, environmental, economic, and geo-political) would facilitate the inclusion of representatives from the overseas carnivals to widen the group of stakeholders.[17]

---

17 Currently, the National Carnival Bandleaders Association (NCBA), which represents the masquerade community, has a seat on the board of the International Caribbean Carnival Association (ICCA).

Figure Two: Cultural Policy/Cultural Industry Policy tension

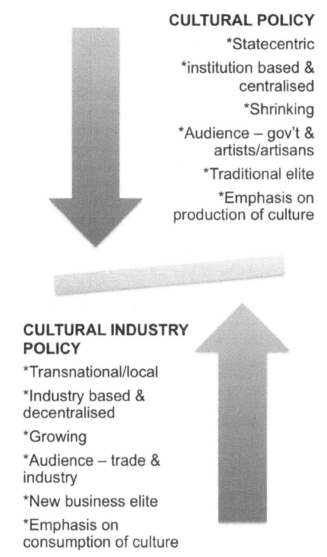

CULTURAL POLICY

*Statecentric

*institution based & centralised

*Shrinking

*Audience – gov't & artists/artisans

*Traditional elite

*Emphasis on production of culture

CULTURAL INDUSTRY POLICY

*Transnational/local

*Industry based & decentralised

*Growing

*Audience – trade & industry

*New business elite

*Emphasis on consumption of culture

The widening of the stakeholder groupings, along with the focus on the multiple bottom line, can alleviate some of the tension that currently exists in the policy field. This shift can encourage greater cooperation among and between the Trinidad carnival and those in the Caribbean diaspora at both the strategic and operational levels. In addition, the continued thrust towards the export of carnival must be positioned within the global debate on trade in cultural goods and services and the various regional and international trade policy initiatives to which

Trinidad and Tobago have acceded in the last five years.[18] For example, the initialing of the Economic Partnership Agreement (EPA) with the European Community in October 2008 has many implications for the Trinidad Carnival complex, which has spawned over twenty carnivals in the United Kingdom alone.

The driving mechanism to force this change can only emanate from increased advocacy among stakeholder groups, who, then, ensure these interests be included in the mix. During carnival 2008, an announcement was made that the NCC was in the process of creating a carnival policy. This can be taken as a tacit admission that the current approaches are not as effective as they should be. However, the announcement of TT$ 2 million prizes for winners of the major competitions in 2011 seems to reinforce the instrumental policy focus of past regimes.

All of these interventions can be encapsulated in the ACT agenda that attempts to frame a more balanced approach to the Trinidad carnival complex (see Table Three). ACT promotes the development of a keener understanding of how carnival stakeholders operate, the improvement of linkages between and within the festivals in the Trinidad carnival complex, and the management of the historical tensions between the Mardi Gras and Cambouley carnival traditions. Given the composition of the new board, the implications of the impending trade agreements for the overseas carnival circuit, and the impact of the global financial crisis on the tourism sector, such intervention by stakeholders is extremely propitious.

Table Three: The ACT Agenda

ADVOCATE for a more balanced approach to develop the Trinidad Carnival complex in keeping with the multiple bottom line approach.
CONDUCT more expansive research on carnival in all areas—socio-cultural, geo-political, economic-touristic and environmental, to increase linkages and opportunities between the carnival traditions.
TARGET specific programmes and projects that encapsulate the values and practices of the multiple bottom line approach.

---

18   These include the Caribbean single market and economy which seeks to make the Caricom Region (except for Haiti and the Bahamas) a free trade zone. The agreement allows for the free travel of artists and cultural services.

Works Cited

Burke, S. 2010. *Policing the Transnational: Cultural Policy Development in the Anglophone Caribbean 1962—2008*. Lampert Academic Publishers, Germany

Burke, S. 1997. *Cultural Industries and Economic Development—The case of the Carnival sector in Trinidad and Tobago*, The Institute of Social Studies: The Hague.

Cupid, John. 2008. Interview with Suzanne Burke, Port of Spain, Trinidad & Tobago.

Dunn, W. 1994. *Public Policy Analysis—An Introduction*. Englewood Cliffs: Prentice Hall.

Dye, T. 1992. *Understanding Public Policy*. Englewood Cliffs: Prentice Hall.

Hede, A. 2007. "Managing Special Events in the New Era of the Triple Bottom Line." *Event Management* 11:13-22.

Hill, E. 1983. *The History of Calypso Music in Trinidad*. St Augustine: University of the West Indies.

Long, S. 2007. "Carnival Inflation's Making Mas." *Trinidad Guardian*. http://legacy.guardian.co.tt/archives/2007-015/bussguardian1.html

National Carnival Commission. www.ncctt.org/home/index.

Pratt, A. 2005. "Cultural Industries and Public Policy: An Oxymoron?" *The Internatinal Journal of Cultural Policy* 11 (1), 31-44.

Trinidad and Tobago Soca, Calypso and Carnival. http://www.trinisoca.com/carnival/2006/2011/html

Trinidad Tourism Development Company. www.gotrinidadandtobago.com/trinidad/carnival.php.

4

❖❖

THE CARNIVAL DIASPORA

Transformation of the *Ékpè* Masquerade in the African Diaspora

$\sim$

Paul E. Lovejoy

The tradition of masquerade in western Africa was historically associated with religious and political institutions that reinforced social
structures and established mechanisms for determining citizenship. In
many cases, masquerades were a component of what anthropologists
and others have called "secret societies," such as *Ékpè* in the interior
of the Bight of Biafra, and *Poro* along the upper Guinea coast. In both
cases, the societies were anything but "secret," since people knew that
these were associations of the most influential men, all of whom were
well known locally. While there were parallel associations of women,
it is important to recognize that the associations discussed here were
confined to men, and specifically to men who had to be initiated and
pay entrance fees. The question of "secrecy" only related to the collective nature of decisions, which protected the individual identities of
members. The secrecy was reinforced through access to encoded knowledge that had to be acquired to achieve membership. Moreover, membership was often graded, much the same as membership in motorcycle
gangs, where being a "full patch" member is different from lower grades,
commanding more respect and access to more of the resources available
to the society. This paper addresses the issue of how secret societies
were transformed in the context of trans-Atlantic slavery through an
examination of the *Ékpè* society of the Bight of Biafra and its colonial
manifestation in Cuba as the *Abakuá* society. A study of the transformation demonstrates how the social and political functions of *Ékpè* and
the legal and economic intent of membership were transformed in Cuba

when the first *Abakuá* lodge was apparently established in 1834 or 1836 (Palmié 2002, 91).[1]

The images, ideology, and secrecy associated with *Ékpè* have been studied for more than one hundred years, and yet crucial features of the history of *Ékpè* and its transformation have been neglected. A reconsideration of *Ékpè* and *Abakuá* suggests an agenda for the study of *Ékpè* in diaspora from a different perspective. An approach from Africa privileges the origins and coterminous development of the institution in Africa, allowing for an analysis of the inevitable changes in diaspora, but recognizing that there were changes in Africa, too. Indeed, an important innovation permitted European ship captains to buy into *Ékpè*, which did not happen before the emergence of Duke Ephraim as the head of the *Ékpè* lodge in Duke Town at Old Calabar (Lovejoy and Richardson 2004). The multiple layers of transformation that prevailed in both Africa and Cuba resulted in a masquerade that had changing significance, depending upon whether it was public and included the participation of women and children, and whether it was connected to authority or to resistance to authority.

As studied in Cuba, the *Abakuá* society is considered to have been introduced only in 1834 or 1836, at least two hundred years after its introduction in the port town of Old Calabar on the Cross River, from where the *Abakuá* chapter in Cuba appears to have derived.[2] Despite

---

1   Palmié cites twentieth century oral traditions and three important historical sources, including Trujillo y Monagas (1882), Roche Monteagudo (1925) and Cabrera (1958), who concur in dating the emergence of *Abakuá* in Cuba to the year 1834 or 1836. See José Trujillo y Monagas, "Los Ñáñigos: Su historia, sus prácticas, su lenguaje," in Carlos Urrutia y Blanco, ed., *Los criminales de Cuba y Don José Trujillo* (Barcelona: Establecimiento Tipográfico de Fidel Giró, 1882), 363-74; Rafael Roche Monteagudo, *La policía y sus mistérios* (Havana: La Moderna Poesía, 1925); and Pedro Deschamps Chapeaux, "Margarito Blanco el 'Ocongo de Ultan'," *Boletín del Instituto de Historia y del Archivo Nacional*, 65 (1964), 97-109.

2   Noah, *Old Calabar*, 29-32; Bruce Connell. 2004. "Efik in Abakuá: Linguistic Evidence for the Formation of a Diaspora Identity," *Contours: Journal of the African Diaspora*; Ivor Miller. 2005. "Cuban Abakuá Chants: Examining New Linguistic and Historical Evidence for the African Diaspora," *African Studies Review*, 48:23-58; and Stephan Palmié. 2009. "Ekpe/Abakuá in Middle Passage," in Andrew Apter and Lauren Derby, eds., *Activating the Past: Historical Memory in the Black Atlantic*. Durham NC: Cambridge Scholars Publishing.

considerable confusion in the literature on Cuba, *Ékpè*, and, hence, *Abakuá* are considered to be Ejagham (variously referred to as Kwa, Qua Igbo, Efut) in origin, but widely dispersed as an institution among Ibibio, including the Efik at Old Calabar, and Igbo, and extending into the hills of Cameroon. The extensive scholarship on *Abakuá* includes the writings of Fernando Ortiz, Enrique Sosa Rodríguez and Lydia Cabrera, and more recently Robert Farris Thompson, Judith Bettelheim, and Ivor Miller.[3] The question of when *Abakuá* was introduced to Cuba does not seem to be in doubt, although Shubi Ishemo has argued that the society may have been present in 1812, if not earlier.[4] However, my purpose here is to examine the implicit transformation that occurred in the transfer. I contend that the political and social functions of *Ékpè* and *Abakuá* were significantly different; in Africa, the society was ultimately a political institution of domination, while in Cuba it was a social institution arising from subordination. The rituals and secret knowledge that are recorded in Cuba certainly derive from *Ékpè* in the interior of the Bight of Biafra, but the full significance of this connection has obscured crucial changes that arose in the context of racialized slavery in Cuba.

---

3   Fernando Ortiz, "La tragedia de los ñáñigos," *Cuadernos Americanos, Mexico*, 52:4 (1950); Lydia Cabrera, *La sociedad secreta Abakuá narrada por viejos adeptos* (Havana: Ediciones C. R., 1958); Lydia Cabrera, *La Lengua Sagrada de los Ñáñigos* (Miami: Colección del Chichereкú en el exilio, 1988); Lydia Cabrera, "Ritual y símbolos de la iniciación en la Sociedad Secreta Abakuá," *Catauro: revista cubana de anropología*, 1:1 (1969), 130-64; Enrique Sosa Rodríguez, *Los Ñáñigos* (Havana: Ediciones Casa de las Américas, 1982); Enrique Sosa Rodríguez, *El Carabali* (Havana: Editorial Letras Cubanas, 1984); Robert Farris Thompson, *Flash of the Spirit: African & Afro-American Art & Philosophy* (New York: Vintage Books, 1983); Judith Bettelheim, ed., *Cuban Festivals: A Century of Afro-Cuban Culture* (Princeton: Markus Weiner, 2001); Ivor Miller, "Cuban Abakuá Chants," 23-58; Miller, "A Secret Society Goes Public: The Relationship Between Abakuá and Cuban Popular Culture," *African Studies Review*, 43:1 (2000), 161-88; Miller, "Cuban Abakuá Participate in the Ekpe Festival, December 19-26, 2004, Cross River State, Nigeria." Also see Palmié, "Ekpe/Abakuá in Middle Passage," and Palmié, *Wizards & Scientists*.

4   For a review, see Shubi L. Ishemo, "From Africa to Cuba: an Historical Analysis of the *Sociedad Secreta Abakuá (Ñáñiguismo)*," *Review of African Political Economy*, 92 (2002), 253-72; and Tato Quiñones, *Ecorie Abakuá* (Havana: Ediciones Unión, 1994), who base their analysis on a critical reading of the earlier work of Sosa and Ortiz.

Bight of Biafra and Interior

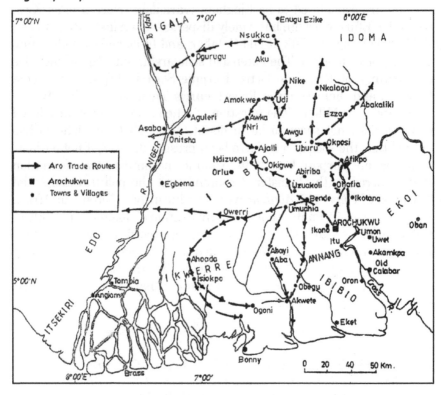

Ékpè in the Interior of the Bight of Biafra

Ékpè, and its derivative *Abakuá*, originate from the Cross River interior. The society has existed for a long time, since well before the first documented records of this region, and, through oral tradition, it seems to have pervaded the interior as far inland as several hundred kilometres by the seventeenth century. The society was found in the eastern Niger delta, at least as far as Bonny, among the Ejagham, Ibibio, and Igbo, and thereby transcended ethnic frontiers. It was an important institution among the Aro merchants who dominated the slave trade of the interior by the middle of the eighteenth century. *Ékpè* was the underpinning political institution that facilitated exchange, marketing, resolution of disputes, and enforcement of contracts over a wide area, and, as such, was the dominant form of social and political organization by the eighteenth century, if not earlier. From a Cuban perspective, therefore, its formal transference in 1834 or 1836 marked a late chapter in the consolidation of *Ékpè* as an effective organization.

There have been simplistic projections of the origins of *Abakuá* that do not take into consideration the complex interaction in the interior of the Bight of Biafra that spread the leopard society to Aro communities, and even to Bonny, in the Niger delta, and, hence, pervaded the traffic in enslaved Africans from this region. There has been some attempt to understand the relationship of the spread of the institution to the slave trade.[5] *Ékpè* proved to be an effective means of structuring exchange and social interaction in the interior of the two principal ports of the Bight of Biafra, Old Calabar and Bonny, and this context requires explication in trying to understand how the society spread to Cuba.

It is essential to have some conception of the geography, linguistics, and ethnography of the region where the *Ékpè* society had been established by the early eighteenth century, more than a century before its introduction into Cuba. As in the study of *Abakuá* in Cuba, there is an extensive scholarship on *Ékpè* in the interior of the Bight of Biafra, and, as in Cuba, much of this the result of anthropological investigation.[6] Moreover, *Ékpè* has attracted the attention of historians, who have attempted to document the origins and distribution of the society over time because of its presence and importance in the interior of Bight of Biafra, especially among the Ibibio, Igbo, Qua-Igbo, and Efik, and its role in governance at Old Calabar, Bonny, Arochukwu, and the Aro network.[7] Among the

---

5   See, for example, Ishemo, "Historical Analysis of the *Sociedad Secreta Abakuá (Ñañiguismo)*," 253-72.

6   In addition to A.K. Hart, *Report of the Enquiry into the Dispute over the Obongship of Calabar* (Enugu: Government Printer, 1964), see P. Amaury Talbot, *The Peoples of Southern Nigeria* (London, 1926), 4 vol.; and Donald Simmons, "An Ethnographic Sketch of the Efik People," in Daryll Forde, ed., *Efik Traders of Old Calabar* (London: Oxford University Press, 1956), 1-26. Also, Daryll Forde and G.I. Jones, *The Ibo and Ibibio-Speaking Peoples of South-Eastern Nigeria* (London: International African Institute, 1950).

7   In addition to Noah, *Old Calabar*, see K.O. Dike, *Trade and Politics in the Niger Delta 1830-1885* (Oxford: Clarendon Press, 1956); A.J.H. Latham, *Old Calabar 1600-1890: The Impact of the International Economy upon a Traditional Society* (Oxford: Oxford University Press, 1973); David Northrup, *Trade without Rulers: Pre-colonial Economic Development in Southeastern Nigeria* (Oxford: Oxford University Press, 1978); Paul E. Lovejoy and David Richardson, "Trust, Pawnship and Atlantic History: The Institutional Foundations of the Old Calabar Slave Trade," *American Historical Review*, 104:2 (1999), 332-55; Lovejoy and Richardson, "The Slave Ports of the Bight of Biafra in the Eighteenth Century," in Carolyn Brown and Paul E. Lovejoy, eds., Repercussion of the Atlantic Slave Trade: The Interior of the Bight of Biafra and the African Diaspora (Trenton, NJ: Africa World Press, 2009).

Ibibio the society was known as Ekpo Nyoho, which was hierarchically ordered, with grades that conferred social status. Some of the grades in Ekpo society were: Akpan Ekpo (senior Ekpo), Eka Ekpo (mother Ekpo), Inyon Ekpo (lame Ekpo), and Ikpe Ekpo (judgment Ekpo).[8] Each village had its lodge and a sacred drum that was similar to the *Ékpè* drum. But since the Ibibio also had an *Ékpè* society, it would be difficult to conclude that *Ékpè* as practised at Calabar, was adapted from the Ibibio Ekpo, though *ékpè* is the Ibibio word for leopard.

According to Missionary Hope Waddell, the government of Calabar "was essentially patriarchal which meant simply that the head of every family governed it independent of every other, by his sole authority" (1970, 313). As Macgregor described the patriarchal system,

> the oldest male of the ruling house was recognized as head of the clan, and all matters affecting the clan was decided by him sitting in council with the free members of it. Age was greatly honoured, but even the youngest member of the council had a right to speak (Hart, 131).

According to British Consul Beecroft, *Ékpè* functioned as the legislative, the executive, as well as the police force in Calabar.[9] Although it may have begun as a religious cult (Hart, par. 148), *Ékpè* had assumed political and economic importance possibly by the sixteenth century. It became a graded society with open membership to men, both bonded and free. As it operated at Old Calabar, at least, only free men who were wealthy could attain the highest grade in the society, and the enslaved male population, if allowed to belong, were confined to the lowest grade. No age requirements appear to have been required for membership, and historically women were not admitted (Hart, par. 150). The governmental duties of *Ékpè* covered a wide range. The merchants of Henshaw Town told George Offor of London that the wards at Old Calabar lived separately, "each under its own laws except in the line of Egbo [*Ékpè*]" and that it was only through *Ékpè* that it was possible "to put in force any law that may exist and to punish offenders" (Noah 1980, citing F.O. 84/1527). Civic duties like cleaning the streets and night-watch were under its command. All heads of families were members of the society. All the important people

8   Percy Amaury Talbot, *Life in Southern Nigeria: The Magic, Beliefs and Customs of the Ibibio Tribe* (New York: Barnes and Noble, 1967 [1923]), 183-192.

9   Consul Beecroft to Viscount Palmerston, October 27, 1851, F.O. 84/858, as cited in Noah, *Old Calabar*, 37.

in a community had to join *Ékpè*. Each community had an *Ékpè* lodge, usually under an Eyamba (head of the society), a title that was assumed until death. The first person to hold the title at Old Calabar is considered to have been Essien Ekpe Oku of Ambo House, Creek Town. *Ékpè* also took responsibility for the funerals of deceased members.

In the case of *Ékpè*, as it functioned at Old Calabar and elsewhere in the interior of the Bight of Biafra, membership was divided into seven grades (sometimes nine, ten and more), the highest levels closed to anyone considered of slave status, whether or not they themselves owned slaves and were wealthy. *Ékpè* was a male institution, and no one was above its authority. It passed laws, the violation of which was usually punishable by death. Membership involved levels of initiation and payment of fees that accrued to the members of the highest grade.[10] According to James Holman, who visited Old Calabar in 1828, only a few years before the society was transferred to Cuba, there were five grades, each requiring an initiation fee that was calculated in the local

10 The literature on secret societies, and specifically *Ékpè* is extensive. For early treatment, see Fitzgerald H.P. Marriot, "The Secret Societies of West Africa," *Journal of the Royal Anthropological Institute*, 29 (1899), 21-27; and F.W. Butt-Thompson, *West African Secret Societies: Their Organisations, Officials, and Teachings* (London: H.F. & G. Witherby, 1929). On *Ékpè* and the related *Okonko* society, see A.K. Hart, *Report of the Enquiry into the Dispute over the Obongship of Calabar* (Enugu: Government Printer, 1964); G.I. Jones, "The Political Organization of Old Calabar," in Darryl Forde, ed., Efik Traders of Old Calabar (London: Oxford University Press, 1956), 135-49; Elliott Leib and Renee Romano, "Reign of the Leopard: Ngbe Ritual," *African Arts*, 7:1 (1984), 48-57; Keith Nicklin, "Un embleme Ejagham de la société Ekpe," *Art Tribal : Bulletin annuel publié par l'Association des Amis du Musée Barbier-Muller* (1991), 3-18; Keith Nicklin and Jill Salmons, "On Ekkpe, Ekpe, Ekpo, Ogbom," *African Arts* 15, 4 (1982): 78-79; Monday Efiongh Noah, *Old Calabar: The City States and The Europeans 1800-1885* (Nigeria: Scholars Press (Nig.) Ltd., 1980); Malcolm Ruel, *Leopards and Leaders: Constitutional Politics among a Cross River People* (London: Tavistock, 1969); Margaret M. Green, "Sayings of the Okonko Society of the Igbo-Speaking People," *Bulletin of the School of Oriental and African Studies*, 21 (1958), 157-73; Ali Bentor, "Aro Ikeji Festival: Toward a Historical Interpretation of a Masquerade Festival" (Ph.D. thesis, Indiana University, 1994); John Boston, "Some Northern Ibo Masquerades," *Journal of the Royal Anthropological Institute*, 90 (1960), 54-65; Paula Ben-Amos and Omoregie Osarenren, "Ekpo Ritual in Avbiama Village," *African Arts*, 2, 4 (1969), 8-13, 79; and U.N. Abalogu, "Ekpe Society in Arochukwu and Bende," *Nigeria Magazine*, 126/127 (1978), 78-97.

currencies, "bars" and "copper rods." These included Abungo (125 bars), Makaira (400 copper rods), Bakimboko (100 bars), and Yampai (850 copper rods, rum, goats, and palm wine) (Holman 1841, 291). In 1846, according to Waddell, there were "ten branches of the various degrees of honour and power," which were later confirmed through investigation in the colonial period (1970, 313).[11] As the diary of Ntiero Duke from the 1780s confirms, these dues were divided among the highest members of the society. According to the entry for February 2, 1785, "about 6 a.m. in aqua Landing with fog morning so I goin to work for my Little Yard[;] after that Duke & all we go to King Egbo for share Egbo moony for 40 men after that we com[e] away" (1956, 80).[12] Membership was open to all who could purchase it, even slaves who were wealthy enough and who "had been made Chief may purchase Egbo, that is, the right to remain in the streets when Ekpe was abroad."[13] But they could not belong to the highest grade, which raises issues of how *Ékpè* was transferred unless it was purchased by free people in Cuba.

Historically, masquerade played an important part in *Ékpè*, as it still does.[14] The *idem ukwo*, the masquerade of *Ékpè*, represented the leopard—*ékpè* in Ibibio means "leopard." The masked and costumed figure traditionally ran through the town or village, manifesting the secrecy and limited access to knowledge that was restricted to the selected few. Masquerades were a central means of display and enforcement in the Bight of Biafra. Except on specified occasions, the mas-

---

11   Also see A.K. Hart, *Report of the Enquiry into the Dispute over the Obong-ship of Calabar* (Enugu: Government Printer, 1964), 157.

12   "About 6 a.m. at Aqua Landing, and a very foggy morning, so I was going to work in my little yard. After that Duke and all of us went to King Ekpe to share the ekpe money for 40 men. After that we came away."

13   Major MacDonald to the Marquis of Salisbury, June 12, 1889, F.O. 84/1940, as cited in Noah, *Old Calabar*.

14   Simon Ottenberg and Linda Knudsen, "Leopard Society Masquerades: Symbolism and Diffusion," *African Arts*, 18:2 (1985), 37-44, 93-95; Bentor, "Aro Ikeji Festival;" Keith Nicklin and Jill Salmons, "Ikem: The History of a Masquerade in Southeast Nigeria," in Sidney Littlefield Kasfir, ed., *West African Masks and Cultural Systems* (Tervuren: Musee Royal d'Afrique Centrale [*Annales, Sciences Humaines*, vol. 126], 1988), 123-52; John Boston, "Some Northern Ibo Masquerades," *Journal of the Royal Anthropological Institute*, 90 (1960), 54-65; and Elliott Leib and Renee Romano, "Reign of the Leopard: Ngbe Ritual," *African Arts*, 7:1 (1984), 48-57. Also see Herbert M. Cole, ed., *I am Not Myself: The Art of African Masquerade* (Los Angeles: Museum of Cultural History, UCLA, 1985).

"Cuban Abakuà Participate in the Ékpè Festival" December 19-26, 2004
(photo: Ivor Miller)

querade was not public in the sense that all members of society could observe the occasions of display and celebration. Women, children and uninitiated slaves were subject to beatings and humiliation if caught during masquerades that were not public. The purpose of the masquerade, unlike in the ceremonial contexts of diaspora, was enforcement. Someone, often possibly a relative, was punished for reasons that might range from suspected adultery to failure to honor a debt. *Ékpè* decrees were prompt and strictly enforced. The society regulated almost every aspect of life, and while sometimes it was assumed that decrees were directed at the lower orders of society, in fact everyone was subject to its decisions.[15] Eyo Honesty I was ruined by *Ékpè* fines in the 1780s,

---

15   See, for example, Macdonald to the Marquis of Salisbury, June 12, 1889, F.O. 84/1940, as cited in Noah, *Old Calabar*, 32.

135

even though he was a member.[16] In 1856, the Presbyterian compound at Duke Town was sealed off by an *Ékpè* decree. According to Reverend Anderson, three men accused in the death of a resident of Duke Town had sought refuge in mission quarters, which prompted a proclamation that no one was to take provisions to the mission, children residing there had to leave, and that nobody could visit the mission, attend school or church. The decrees were announced by the *Idem Ukwo*, the masquerade dressed in a multi-coloured costume who wore a bell around his waist to announce to non-members of the public that they should keep off the streets. Before 1834, according to Holman,

> When a person cannot obtain his due from a debtor, or when an injury has been received, personally or otherwise, the aggrieved party applies to the Duke [Duke Ephraim, who died in 1834] for Ekpe drums; acquainting him at the same time with the nature of his complaint. If the Duke accedes to the demand, the Ekpe assembly immediately meets, and the drums are beat about the town; at first sound of which every woman is obliged to retreat within her dwelling, upon pain of losing her head for disobedience: not until the drum goes round a second time, to show that council is ended, and the Ekpe returned, are they released from their seclusion (1841, 393).

Besides its importance in imposing the punishments of the lodge, the masquerade appeared in public on specific ritualized occasions. The masquerade was displayed at public ceremonies and whenever people from elsewhere attended with the purpose of purchasing membership or acquiring the rights to open a lodge. *Ékpè* was held in awe, especially among those who had not been initiated. In the 1880s, Hugh Goldie described the public manifestation of the masquerade at Old Calabar as a "display of Egbo [*Ékpè*] grandeur," in which

> all the townspeople were allowed to come and witness it. They crowded both sides of the main street from top to bottom and even women, especially excluded on other occasions, and who dare not utter the name of Egbo, as too sacred for their lips, were now spectators.... Egbo runners, disguised with black masks and wild dresses of dried grass and sheep skin, scoured the street in all directions wielding, however, a long rod instead of the terrible cowskin whip. They kept

---

16   E. Aye, *Old Calabar through the Centuries* (Calabar: Hope Waddell Press, 1967), 73.

the centre of the street clear, confining the populace to the covered way on each side. One rash fellow tried to cross, but was so hunted down the whole length of the street by three of these runners, who followed him closely, amidst the laughter of the crowd, till he reached the beach and plunged into the river (1901, 30).

However, when the masquerade appeared suddenly, without warning except for the beat of the *Ékpè* drum and the sound of the bell around the waist of the performer, the purpose was to inflict retribution on anyone deemed guilty of a crime or who had failed to pay a debt, and in the course of retribution, the masquerade could attack anyone in the path. When inflicting justice, the masquerade was not to be seen, at least not by women and children. Both publically and politically, the masquerade constituted a form of ritualized recognition of authority. *Ékpè* had its esoteric language that was conveyed through *nsibidi*, forms of image, body motion and text message that approaches writing. Specifically the development of *nsibidi* as a language of signs was a feature of *Ékpè* secrecy.[17] Knowledge of the script was reserved for the members of the highest grade and could not be divulged to members of junior grades. This specialized knowledge provided the password for recognition, especially to people outside of Calabar society whose membership might be in doubt and within the elite. The *Ékpè* drum announced to people that something was wrong. By beating the drum in a peculiar way, people were alerted to enemy attack, an outbreak of fire, or the summary justice that was to be meted out.

The power of *Ékpè* rested in the ability to enforce collective decisions of the elite, who were supposed to govern in the interests of the community, but this often meant the enforcement of pawning arrangements, notarizing marriage contracts, legalizing use of land, providing access to forests to harvest fruit, and assuring safety at markets and the security of travel to and from market. While there is evidence of arbitrary and brutal action and confrontation, it can be assumed that usually the threat of such enforcement was sufficient to assure

---

17   J.K. MacGregor, "Some Notes on *Nsibidi*," *Journal of the Royal Anthropological Institute of Great Britain and Ireland*, 39 (1909), 209-17; Dayrell Elphinstone, "Some 'Nsibidi' Signs," *Man*, 67 (1910), 112-14; Elphinstone, "Further Notes on 'Nsibidi Signs with their Meanings from the Ikom District, Southern Nigeria," *Journal of the Royal Anthropological Institute of Great Britain and Ireland*, 41 (1911), 521-43; "Nsibidi," Dayrell Elphinstone Mss, Royal Anthropological Institute.

Nisibidi Script of Ékpè and Abakuà

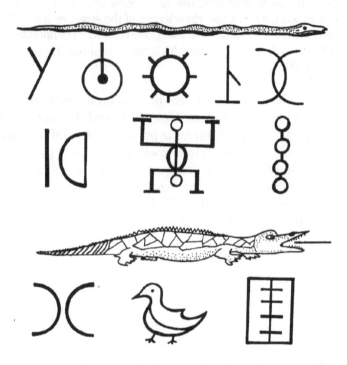

compliance with community norms. In brief, *Ékpè* was central to the governance of society and the interaction through common institutions with adjacent and distant communities who shared an allegiance to a recognizable governing society associated with the leopard.

On the whole, the wealthiest and most powerful merchants dominated the highest grades of *Ékpè* and competed for its principal offices. These men were responsible, among other things, for debt enforcement, having the power to "blow" *ékpè*, that is, punish offenders through summary justice. Membership in *Ékpè* extended to Aro traders, who formed similar closed associations of their own in the interior, known as *Okonko*. Moreover, the Aro controlled the Ibinukpabi oracle at Arochukwu, their capital; the oracle was recognized as the supreme court of appeal for a range of legal issues that pertained to credit and trade, including the protection of merchants and markets, the settlement of sectarian disputes, and the accumulation of slaves through fines and fees levied on litigants. Hence the leading ward houses at Old Calabar participated in a network of overlapping agencies that served to enforce payment of debts and to protect the commercial interests of the export trade in slaves. Similar institutions, related to *Ékpè*, governed society in the region of Cameroon and Gabon. While the relationship among these societies is not clear, their role in trade and protecting insiders from enslavement is clear.

Besides prestige, membership assured a regular income for life. The initiation fees were distributed among members, each receiving according to his rank in the society. In 1787 Ntiero Duke reported that Jimmy Henshaw had to pay "4 Calabar afaws [slaves] to be King Ekpe," indicating that a considerable income could be generated (qtd. in Forde 1956, 59). The following list from Ntiero Duke's diary indicates how much income could be raised, based on transactions of a single day:

Willy Honesty	20 rods and one goat
George Old Town	10 rods
Tom Nonaw	10 rods
Old and New Ekpe	8 rods
Robin and Curcock	5 rods
Guinea Company	
King Ekpe	5 rods
Eyamba	10 rods
Old and New Ekpe	8 rods
Tom Cobham	10 rods
Duke Ephraim	20 rods and one goat
Egbo Young Offiong	25 rods and one goat
Robin John	5 rods
John Ambo	5 rods
Willy Tom	4 rods
Tom Curcock	5 rods
Old and New Ekpe	8 rods
Effar	5 rods
Misimbo	4 rods
King Ambo	20 rods and one goat
Ephraim Aqua	5 rods[18]

---

18   Ntiero Duke, "Diary," in Forde, *Efik Traders*, entry for August 31, 1787.

The surviving sections of the diary of Ntiero Duke of Old Calabar provide evidence of how *Ékpè* operated in the 1780s.[19] While we cannot know if similar procedures were followed in the interior where *Ékpè* was also common, it seems likely, given the nature of the anthropological literature and the circumstantial evidence of the eighteenth century.

As Hope Waddell observed at Old Calabar in the 1840s, only a decade after the introduction of Abakua in Cuba:

> Egbo [*Ékpè*] is a secret association, under the patronage of a supernatural being of that name. A person joining its highest rank pays an entrance fee to every member, which though small to each, amount on the whole to nearly £100, there being about a thousand members. Its mysteries cannot be witnessed except by the initiated, nor divulged under penalty of death (1970, 313).

Earlier, in 1828, Holman reported that a member who belonged to all *Ékpè* grades had to pay a total of 300 bars and 1,250 white copper rods, besides food and drinks (1841, 291). Though the value of the bar and copper often fluctuated, Nicholls noted that in 1805, a copper rod was worth a shilling (Hallett, 207), and Waddell gave a similar value to brass in 1846 (1970, 247). By 1856, when brass rods had replaced copper, the value of the bar was about 3d, with twenty bars being the equivalent of 5s.[20] Even after the currency collapsed to 2/6 in 1864, the income to members was still substantial.[21] The proliferation of *Ékpè* grades and the admission of people who previously had not qualified appear to have been a response to the currency crisis. It appears that the number of *Ékpè* grades increased in response to the declining value of currency. As the cost of admission demonstrates, the principal function of the society was the collection of fees and the enforcement of contracts, not entertainment or religious piety.

---

19   There are at least 29 references to *Ékpè* in the surviving sections of Nteiro Duke's diary for 1785-88, and another dozen references that probably refer to *Ékpè*. See "Diary," in Forde, *Efik Traders*, 27-64. Also see the letter of "Grandy King George King of Old Town Tribe," to Ambrose Lace, January 13, 1773, in Gomer Williams, *History of the Liverpool Privateers* (London: 1897), 543-45.

20   General Report on the Bight of Biafra, F.O. 2/16, as cited in Noah, *Old Calabar*.

21   Burton to Russell, April 15, 1864, F.O. 84/1221, as cited in Noah, *Old Calabar*.

Through control of the initiation fees to the various grades of the society, the leading merchants in the different wards at Old Calabar, and also elsewhere in the interior dominated *Èkpè* and thereby regulated trade, settled disputes, protected pawns, and enforced debt repayment. The collective decisions of the senior *Èkpè* council, whose members were the leading merchants themselves, forced individuals to comply with decrees or suffer the consequences. As Ntiero Duke recorded in his diary on 18 January 1785, "we got all the Ekpe men to go to the Ekpe Bush to make bob [i.e., reach a settlement] about the Egbo Young and Little Otto palaver." Although the cause of the dispute between the two men is not mentioned, a settlement was reached and the two men forced to pay a fine: "Egbo Young paid one goat and 4 rods and Little Otto paid 4 rods" (qtd. in Forde, 1956). Other disputes were settled violently, through murder, as recorded in Ntiero Duke's diary for the 1780s. Virtually all men in Old Calabar had to belong to one of the grades of the society and pay its fees, which in turn were shared among the members of the highest grade of the society, that is, the principal merchants. Ntiero Duke refers to these payments in his diary, and it is reasonable to assume that *Èkpè* lodges acted in the same manner elsewhere.

The terms and practice of this method of governance amounted to a form of private ordering that even involved European ships. *Èkpè* was involved because human pawns were used as security in trade when Old Calabar merchants took goods on credit in anticipation of the delivery of slaves. There was the possibility that if slaves were not delivered on time, masters of ships would sail away with the pawns that had been lodged with them. In short, there were sanctions used against traders who reneged on promises in addition to the judgments of *Èkpè*. According to one report, pawns were often "the sons and daughters of traders," and the latter were "always particularly anxious" about their fate and "seemed much distressed whenever they took up an idea that the ship would sail away with the pawns." (Lovejoy and Richardson, 2004, 22) Concern over the fate of kin was perhaps compounded for Old Calabar merchants by the possibility that pawns might be passed between ships. It is not known if masters needed approval from local traders for such transfers, although in local practice, as far as known, such alterations in pawn-creditor arrangements required the approval of close kin. Old Calabar merchants sought to protect pawns from enslavement by "blowing ekpe" on ship masters who might be tempted to abscond with them; ship's crews were sometimes seized or "panyarred" to force the return of pawns, as well. This potential for arbitrary action was always just below the surface. Until redeemed, British merchants regarded pawns as potential slaves for sale in the Americas, "if their friends refuse, or are not able to redeem them" (Lovejoy and Richardson, 2004, 23). Ship captains were ready to sail with pawns on board, should conditions warrant the risk.

In the letter, Duke Ephraim of Duke Town complained to James Rogers and Sir James Laroche of Bristol that two men had been seized illegally. Ephraim complained that he had been a "very good friend" to the ship *Jupiter*; even so, its master had sailed away with two of his canoemen, both of whom were "free men." Outraged by this, Duke Ephraim threatened to "make Bristol Ship pay for them two" unless they were returned by "Any other Ship or himself." Whether the two canoemen were returned or Duke Ephraim carried out his threat is unknown, but the fact that those illegally taken worked for Duke Ephraim, Duke Town's leading merchant by 1790, is significant. Even when British merchants dealt regularly with Duke Ephraim, as Rogers and Laroche evidently did, the behavior of their agents in the field could undermine trust. Written correspondence did not, however, guarantee that the parties would keep their promises. Keeping promises was perhaps especially problematic for local merchants who were dependent on other parties or events outside their control to meet their obligations. The merchants and their extended families who facilitated the deportation of the enslaved, were not immune to enslavement, as correspondence from the time reveals, such as a letter from Duke Ephraim to Richard Rogers in 1789. There were various ways that members of the literate elite might end up in slavery. For example, people were sometimes simply "panyarred" for some debt or abuse that was being dealt with in a collective fashion.

Ékpè sought to regulate European shipping, serving as a collective means of imposing sanctions, boycotting specific ships, and protecting pawns held on board from being taken to the Americas and sold as slaves. As noted by Ntiero Duke, *Ékpè* would isolate a ship, even if this adversely affected the interests of other merchants. According to the entry in his diary for 26 October 1786:

> so I hear Egbo [*Ékpè*] Run and I com to know I walk up to Egbo Young so wee see Egbo [i.e., the masquerade] com Down & the Egbo men he say Sam Ambo and Georg Cobham brow [blow, i.e. "blow *ékpè*"] for Captain Fairwether so all us family Dam angary about brow [blow] that and wee send to call Captin Fairwether to com ashor and after 3 clock noon wee see Eyo & Ebetim com Down and Eshen Ambo so the want to Sam & Georg Cobham for mak the settle with Captin Fairwether (Forde 1956)

As the diary makes clear, Ntiero Duke was upset that other merchants (Sam Ambo and George Cobham) had imposed *Ékpè* on Captain Fairweather's ship, thereby stopping trade, which could only resume once a settlement had been reached. As is clear from several letters, the reliance on personal contact supplemented the pawning system, guaranteeing a method of recourse through written appeal to known business partners in two of the key ports of the British trade.

Abakuá in Cuba

The surprising dimension of the spread of *Ékpè* to Cuba is that it only happened in 1834 or 1836, a feature of the chronology that has not been appreciated. Clearly, there were many people from the interior of the Bight of Biafra in the Americas well before 1834, and virtually all of these people came from areas where the *Ékpè* society was the dominant institution. Yet *Ékpè* was not transferred until the 1830s, and could only have been transferred after it had been purchased, but from where, under what circumstances, and why not earlier? The institution could only spread through such formal transfer, and in West Africa, those who were enslaved could not hold the highest offices in the society.[22] Hence the interaction between the Bight of Biafra and Cuba somehow changed in the 1830s, or otherwise the institution would have been in evidence before then, which it is not. Hence the question, why did it take so long for the institution to migrate? It is suggested here that the introduction into Cuba was connected in some way to Duke Ephraim, who effectively dominated Old Calabar until 1834 and was associated with other reforms that allowed the expansion of the society in the Bight of Biafra. Why wasn't the society purchased before 1834-36? Ephraim had been instrumental in the transition in which Europeans could buy into the society, something apparently not done before his time. Was the transfer of *Ékpè* to Cuba somehow connected with his death?

Whereas the region was a major source of enslaved Africans, it is important to note that the region was associated with a form of governance institutionalized through *Ékpè*. At Old Calabar and in the interior of the Bight of Biafra and Cameroon, the leopard society of *Ékpè* was the mechanism of political, economic and social governance and social

---

22 William Marwick, *William and Louisa Anderson: A Record of their Life and Work in Jamaica and Old Calabar* (Edinburgh, 1897), 206, letter from Anderson to Rev. A. Elliot, April 18, 1849, "I might mention Iron Bar, a man of considerable wealth, though a slave and unable to purchase the privileges of the Egbo [*Ékpè*] institution. He has many slaves of his own."

control. *Ékpè* was the means through which the male elite controlled the resources and the distribution of women in what sometimes has been described as "stateless" societies, but which also bore similarities to the alternate ordering of economies that can occur when one of the principal products of exchange was in some sense illegal, crossing boundaries of acceptability, whether in drugs, alcohol, prostitutes, or slaves. The function of masquerades in diaspora was important as public ceremony that served to unite communities and impose a new social order under conditions of slavery. Whether in diaspora or in Africa, masquerades revealed authority within the community, but the significance in Africa and diaspora could not have been more different.

In the context of trans-Atlantic slavery, *Ékpè* appears to have been transferred only to Cuba. The size of the population from the Bight of Biafra who were taken into slavery and hence knew about *Ékpè* was substantial because almost all people seem to have come from areas were the society was dominate. Yet, as Table I demonstrates, far more people from the Bight of Biafra went to British America (778,000) than in Spanish America (223,000), including Cuba, with substantial numbers of people from the Bight of Biafra also going to the French Caribbean (116,000) and Brazil (123,000). Virtually all of these people came from areas where *Ékpè* was known and served as the mechanism of governance in areas through which they had passed, either reaching Bonny or Old Calabar, the two principal ports of disembarkation in the eighteenth and nineteenth centuries. Hence the demography of movement reveals that there were many people in the Atlantic world who knew about *Ékpè* well before the 1830s. How is it to be explained that while the overwhelming number of people with such knowledge went to British colonies, *Ékpè* was not to be found there, nor is there evidence in Brazil or the French islands, where sizeable numbers of people from the Bight of Biafra also went. In examining the scale and direction of migration from the Bight of Biafra, therefore, it is clear that most people went to British areas and to a lesser extent the French islands before 1808. In the nineteenth century, the movement was heavily to Cuba and to a slightly lesser extent to Brazil, where *Ékpè* also appears to have been absent. *Ékpè* seems to have been transferred only to Cuba.

As Table II demonstrates, most people from the Bight of Biafra arrived in Cuba in the 1820s and 1830s. About 185,000 people reached Cuba from the Bight of Biafra between 1780 and 1850, but the overwhelming majority, almost 139,000, arrived in the twenty years after 1820. About 126,000 arrived in the fifteen years before the first *Abakuá* was supposedly founded. It should be noted that people who knew about

Table One: Arrivals from the Bight of Biafra in the Americas, 25 year periods

	Europe	North America	British Caribbean	French Caribbean	Dutch Caribbean	Danish Caribbean	Spanish America	Brazil	Africa	Total
1531-1550	0	0	0	0	0	0	1,463	0	0	1,463
1551-1575	0	0	0	0	0	0	1,975	482	0	2,457
1576-1600	58	0	0	0	0	0	2,034	0	0	2,092
1601-1625	0	0	0	0	0	0	2,045	0	0	2,045
1626-1650	0	0	18,735	545	0	0	1,405	5,517	172	26,014
1651-1675	382	1,116	43,634	3,715	6,133	0	3,077	269	922	59,248
1676-1700	0	3,934	31,385	320	2,184	0	1,940	9,212	0	48,976
1701-1725	0	13,476	14,871	3,977	9	124	1,184	18,170	0	51,811
1726-1750	528	28,706	104,115	3,019	0	0	689	8,881	0	145,939
1751-1775	0	12,375	203,521	24,364	683	0	10,389	2,327	29	253,687
1776-1800	0	362	226,178	38,193	1,933	4,552	15,344	6,736	162	293,461
1801-1825	0	4,722	69,757	24,825	9,689	7,220	52,897	53,378	8,492	230,979
1825-1850	0	91	427	17,083	0	4,744	129,078	18,005	30,173	199,601
TOTAL	968	64,782	712,623	116,042	20,631	16,641	223,520	122,617	39,949	1,317,773

Source: Trans-Atlantic Voyage Database

Ékpè were settled in Matanzas, Havana and a few other places, so that those knowledgeable of the society were concentrated exactly where the *Abakuá* lodges were established. The line of transmission appears to have followed the normal method by which the right to establish a lodge was purchased from an existing lodge. Hence the *Ékpè* society appears to have been consciously introduced in 1834 or thereabouts.

The transference of *Ékpè* to the Americas inevitably involved change and transformation, or "transculturation," as Ortiz, who studied the transfer, called the process. Why would Ortiz see this as trans-culturation? In contrast to their functions in western Africa, the masquerades became a mechanism of survival under slavery. Rather than demonstrating continuity with the African past, the transformation of masquerades in diaspora reflected a reversal of functions, from one based on domination to one based on subordination.

Table Two: Arrivals in Cuba from the Bight of Biafra, 1780-1849

1780-1782	0
1783-1785	1,424
1786-1790	4,734
1791-1795	4,164
1796-1800	942
1801-1805	8,684
1806-1810	3,916
1811-1815	6,910
1816-1820	5,175
1821-1825	26,283
1826-1830	53,640
1831-1835	35,984
1836-1840	22,897
1841-1845	1,304
1846-1849	9,132
Totals	185,188

Source: Trans-Atlantic Voyage Database

Ortiz was impressed with the similarities between *Abakuá*, as *Ékpè* was known in Cuba, and practice in West Africa. As in Africa, *Abakuá* was an all male society, involving initiation, and relying on secret traditions and *nsibidi* writing. Other scholars, notably Enrique Sosa, elaborated on the parallels between *Ékpè* and *Abakuá*, and more recently Stephan Palmié and Ivor Miller have attempted to demonstrate the trans-Atlantic dimensions of *Ékpè/Abakuá*.

There is the assumption among scholars who have studied *Abakuá* in Cuba that the connection to *Ékpè* was through Old Calabar. According to Palmié, it is generally accepted that *Ékpè* was introduced to Cuba in 1836, while others suggest 1834. For Palmié, the main change was the shift from an ethnic-based religious society to a pan-ethnic society in Cuba.[23] He argues that *Abakuá* came specifically from Old Calabar, but he does not explain why at that time. Miller also focuses on the Old Calabar connection, but also without discussion of the chronology. There were clearly *cabildo* associated with Calabari and different sub-groups, according to Matt Childs.[24] But the *cabildo* included males and females, and *Ékpè* only allowed men to be initiated. Indeed females were banned from *Ékpè* functions and could not be on the streets when *Ékpè* was being "run," that is, when the masquerade was underway. While the various *cabildo* celebrated the Day of Kings on January 6th, this would not have involved active *Ékpè* participation, unless there was radical change from practice in Africa, where there was a yam festival at harvest time that might correspond to the Day of Kings rather than an association with *Ékpè*. Later, some would attribute an *Ékpè* connection to Aponte in the 1812 rebellion, but while it is clear that "Carabali" were involved in the revolt, there is no proof that *Ékpè* was a factor.[25] About 25,000 people had arrived from Old Calabar between the 1780s and 1812, representing almost thirteen percent of African arrivals. As Childs has demonstrated, these "Carabali," that is, those from the Bight of Biafra, were involved in the Aponte revolt in 1812, but there is no evidence of *Ékpè* or *Abakuá*. If there was no *Ékpè* society in 1812, is it possible that, on reflection among participants, the absence of a secret society was the reason for failure? If *Abakuá* had been in operation, the possibility of a breach in security would have been lessened considerably. It was a woman who is alleged to have betrayed the 1812 rebellion, and *Ékpè* prohibited women from membership and even admission to the lodge.

Palmié accepts the evidence that *Ékpè* was not introduced until 1834 or 1836, but he does not consider whether or not only one of the grades of *Ékpè* was purchased, rather than the society itself. Moreover, the direct connection of *Abakuá* with the *Ékpè* of Old Calabar may be problematic, as Victor Manfredi has argued, because *Ékpè* was institutionalized over

---

23   Palmié, "Ekpe/Abakuá in Middle Passage."
24   Matt D. Childs, *The 1812 Aponte Rebellion in Cuba and the Struggle against Atlantic Slavery* (Chapel Hill NC: University of North Carolina Press, 2006).
25   Childs, *Aponte Rebellion*.

a broad, multi-ethnic region in the interior of the Bight of Biafra and Cameroon.[26] *Ékpè* was particularly prominent at Old Calabar, which at the time was one of the two ports from where virtually all the enslaved came, but any direct link in establishing *Abakuá* in Cuba has not been demonstrated. Moreover, almost twice as many people left the Bight of Biafra from Bonny than from Old Calabar. Certainly, *Ékpè* was the key institution of governance at Old Calabar, and was also found at Bonny, and in much of the interior, both in Igbo country, the broader Ibibio territory of which Old Calabar was a part, extending into the interior of Cameroon. The *Ékpè* leopard society may have come from Old Calabar, but it was through the medium of transient slaves from a broad multi-cultural area, familiar with the institution, who gave support to *Abakuá* in Cuba, not only people from Old Calabar itself, of whom there must have been very few, if any.

The various grades of the society functioned together, and it is clear that slavery did not decapitate the system, even though slaves were barred from the upper grades. The formal purchase of the society for its transfer to Cuba almost certainly involved negotiations that apparently occurred in the 1830s. How were the negotiations conducted? The chronology in itself raises methodological issues. We know that *Ékpè* was functioning as an instrument of government and society for at least two centuries before the first recorded references to *Abakuá* in Cuba. The introduction and spread of *Abakuá* in Cuba has to be placed in the historical context of *Ékpè* in the Bight of Biafra. At the time that *Ékpè* arrived in Cuba, Old Calabar was under the rule of Duke Ephraim, who died in 1834. The adoption of *Ékpè* in Cuba, if the connection with Old Calabar is accepted, was in the process of being transformed during the course of adjustments in the trans-Atlantic slave trade. The establishment of *Abakuá* as a lodge of *Ékpè* in the 1830s coincided with the last phase of trans-Atlantic shipment of enslaved people from the Bight of Biafra, which continued to be a substantial migration until the late 1830s. Hence the spread of *Ékpè* occurred at the end of the migration. *Ékpè* had been the mechanism of enslavement in Africa and the "trans-culturation" that fascinated Ortiz seems to have happened at a crucial point in time in which *Ékpè* was being transformed from an institution of governance to an instrument of resistance.

The society had particular appeal because it was not based on ethnic identification but rather on gender and initiation. In parts of West

---

26   Victor Manfredi, "Philological Perspectives on the Southeastern Nigerian Diaspora," *Contours*, 2:2 (2004), 245-46.

Africa, the ethnic dimension was subordinate to mechanisms of grading allegiance on the basis of age and wealth. As an example, *Ékpè* crossed into several ethnic areas and proved a workable mechanism for crossing ethnic boundaries and local political space. It is perhaps not surprising that *Abakuá* revealed similar tendencies in Cuba. This approach is at odds with what Stephan Palmié has concluded—that *Abakuá* was transformed from an ethnic society to a trans-ethnic society.[27] It was a trans-ethnic society and never an ethnic society. Palmié fails to appreciate that this was exactly the characteristic of *Ékpè* in West Africa. Could *Ékpè* admit "strangers," when and under what conditions? By the nineteenth century, it was certainly the case that people of diverse backgrounds were being allowed to buy into the society. But when did it become permissible to admit "strangers" and how were such people identified?

The recognition of insiders and outsiders, members who paid to be members as opposed to others, was the point of *Ékpè*. During the height of the slave trade era before 1808, Europeans were apparently not allowed to become members. However, by the 1820s and 1830s, European ship captains sometimes joined *Ékpè* as a means of securing payment on debts. Previously, Europeans had not been allowed to join *Ékpè* because *Ékpè* was the principal means of protecting individuals who had been pawned, some of whom were held on slave ships as security against goods advanced on credit.[28] *Ékpè* had nothing to do with ethnicity, nor did *Abakuá*, despite what Palmié argues. It had to do with gender and the ability to relate across ethnic categories, however defined. The fundamental idea in Cuba was that adherence to the observances of *orisa* in no way contradicted involvement in *Ékpè*, even though membership in *Abakuá/Ékpè* was closed to females and affiliation with *orisa* included men and women. Hence the admission of "whites" into the society, which is perceived as a factor in its survival in Cuba, was common to the pattern in West Africa, but only at a certain point in time, which has to be considered as relevant to the transformations in *Abakuá/Ékpè* that were taking place on both sides of the Atlantic.

Anyone could become an initiate of *Abakuá* and *Ékpè*, including Ivor Miller. The cross from Africa to Cuba was more than a movement from Old Calabar, the Cross River, or Cameroon, where the institu-

---

27   Palmié, "Ekpe/Abakuá in Middle Passage."
28   Ivor Miller, "How I went to Calabar and became an Ékpè Ambassador to the Cuban Abakuá brotherhood," *WARA Newsletter* (West African Research Association) (2005), 11-13.

tion was indeed important, and this is the point. It remained a male society, and it could incorporate outsiders, as Miller has demonstrated most recently. British ship captains were being admitted to *Ékpè* in the 1830s and later, although not in the eighteenth century at the height of the British slave trade. The institution was flexible. In the eighteenth century, *Ékpè* upheld debt payments related to trade, which was especially important in the slave trade because a person could be held in pawn against a debt, and, if forced, the pawned individual could be enslaved, that is, could be sold. While there were legal, customary, and familial safeguards against enslavement, the act of pawning exposed individuals to the danger of alienation through slavery. Therefore, *Ékpè* acted in two ways, first to protect those who had been pawned, and second, to assure that debts were honored.[29] In the context of the trans-Atlantic slave trade and relationships with European merchants, pawnship served to provide collateral for goods advanced on credit. It was imperative that there was a distinction between those being protected and those whose interests were securing slaves as fast as possible, and by any means, and consequently, Europeans were not admitted to the councils of *Ékpè*. There was a sharp distinction between Europeans and Africans as long as the object of trade was a stolen commodity, as slaves ultimately were. *Ékpè* kept the community as a "family" in which insiders were expected to abide by the consensus of the male elite. Failure to do so could result in execution, as Ntiero Duke's diary from the 1780s makes clear. And it could mean collective punishment, aimed at anyone associated with the miscreant.

The same tactics could be used to organize dock workers as were used to govern the slave trade. *Ékpè* transformed into *Abakuá* apparently resulted in the transformation of a society that provided governance in Africa to a mode of resistance to slavery and then the emergence of a proto-labour union. Palmié recognized the transformation underway in the introduction of *Ékpè* into Cuba, but confuses the requirements of membership with ethnicity. *Ékpè* was common in the Cross River hinterland, and became the dominant "Mafioso" organization over a vast region. At Old Calabar, control of *Ékpè* was crucial in the emergence of the Efik as a distinct and privileged community of Ibibio, with links to

---

29 On pawnship see Paul E. Lovejoy and David Richardson, "Trust, Pawnship and Atlantic History: The Institutional Foundations of the Old Calabar Slave Trade," *American Historical Review*, 104:2 (1999), 332-55; Lovejoy and Richardson, "The Business of Slaving: Pawnship in Western Africa, c. 1600-1810," *Journal of African History*, 42:1 (2001), 67-89.

Arochukwu and the Igbo interior. Ultimately, by the end of the nine-teenth century, thanks to the missionary activities of Hope Waddell and an alliance with the Old Calabar elite, Efik became recognized as the purest form of Ibibio. The distinction between Efik and Ibibio is histori-cal and confuses any effort to link *Abakuá* with the *Ékpè* at Old Calabar, when it is more likely that *Ékpè* was introduced to Cuba by people from the interior of Old Calabar. The confusion is between the port of embar-kation, the places of origin of the actual victims, and the precise *Ékpè* lodge in the Bight of Biafra that allowed the purchase of a charter.

My own experience with *Ékpè/Abakuá* took me to Nigeria and Cuba, as it did Miller. My experience was different. I did not become an initiate, although willingly might have done so, if invited and depend-ing upon the price. In Calabar, I came too close to an *Ékpè* house with a woman, which bans access or even communication with women. In Cuba, I was introduced to an aged *abakuá* elder in Regla who encour-aged me to ask anything that I wished, which I did, but which led to non compliance because the answer was a secret. And yet I was in a mystical space, being told things no one could know. In Nigeria, I was exposed to the retribution of *Ékpè*. One of our colleagues at a conference on the impact of the slave trade on the interior of the Bight of Biafra became a sacrifice at Arochukwu, mysteriously attacked by a masquer-ade dressed in white at midnight. How did *Ékpè* operate? Whether in Regla, Bende, Arochukwu or Calabar, *Ékpè/Abakuá* has had a presence that can be appreciated.

The sale of enslaved individuals fitted into this pattern of "Mafioso" style governance because the origins of the individuals being bought and sold might have been the result of kidnapping or through morally imposed prohibitions against adultery and the birth of twins. That is, slavery was either the result of the crime of kidnapping or was imposed as punishment for some perceived crime, and, in both cases, result-ing in confiscation. While enslavement could take place through "just wars" and the enslavement of political prisoners or through politically sanctioned slave raiding, the use of enslavement as a punishment for convicted criminals, however defined, and the incidence of kidnapping were characteristic of areas beyond Muslim influence. Thinkers in the Muslim world were concerned about the problems of protecting indi-viduals from wrongful slavery, which was considered wrong in relation to the possible enslavement of free born Muslims, and, in such cases, enslavement and trade were declared illegal. Whereas Muslim govern-ments often attempted to limit kidnapping and the use of enslavement as punishment, the interior of the Bight of Biafra was beyond such influence. There enslavement and the sale of victims became a major feature of economy and society. The forms of governance devolved into alternate mechanisms of social ordering that have been labeled "stateless" but which shared similarities with other Mafioso organizations that operate outside the confines of the state.

Works Cited

Apter, Andrew and Lauren Derby, eds. 2009. *Activating the Past: Historical Memory in the Black Atlantic*. Durham NC: Cambridge Scholars Publishing.

Blanco, Carlos Urrutia y, ed. 1882. *Los criminales de Cuba y Don José Trujillo*. Barcelona: Establecimiento Tipográfico de Fidel Giró.

Chapeaux, Pedro Deschamps. 1964. "Margarito Blanco el 'Ocongo de Ultan.'" *Boletín del Instituto de Historia y del Archivo Nacional*. 65: 97-109.

Connell, Bruce. 2004. "Efik in Abakuá: Linguistic Evidence for the Formation of a Diaspora Identity." *Contours: Journal of the African Diaspora*.

Forde, Daryll ed. 1956. "Ntiero Duke's diary." *Efik Traders of Old Calabar*. London: Oxford University Press.

Goldie, Hugh. 1901. *Calabar and its Mission*. Edinburgh: Oliphant Anderson & Ferrier.

Hallett, Robin (ed). 1964. *Records of the African Association*. London: Thomas Nelson.

Hart, A.K. 1964. *Report of the Enquiry into the Dispute over the Obongship of Calabar*. Enugu: Government Printer.

Holman, James. 1841. *Travels in Medeira, Sierra Leone, Teneriffe, St. Jago, Cape Coast, Fernando Po, Princess Island, etc*. London: Routledge.

Killingray, David, Margarette Lincoln, and Nigel Rigby, eds. 2004. *Maritime Empires*. London: Boydell & Brewer.

Lovejoy, Paul E. and David Richardson. 2004. "Slaves to Palm Oil: Afro-European Commercial Relations in the Bight of Biafra, 1741-1841," in David Killingray, Margarette Lincoln, and Nigel Rigby, eds., *Maritime Empires*. London: Boydell & Brewer.

Noah, Monday Efiongh. 1980. *Old Calabar: The City States and The Europeans 1800-1885*. Nigeria: Scholars Press (Nig.) Ltd.

Palmié, Stephan. 2002. *Wizards & Scientists: Explorations in Afro-Cuban Modernity & Tradition*. Durham: Duke University Press.

Röschenthaler, Ute. 2011. *Purchasing Culture in the Cross River Region of Cameroon and Nigeria*. Trenton, NJ: Africa World Press.

Waddell, Hope M. 1970. *Twenty-Nine Years in the West Indies and Central Africa: A Review of Missionary Work and Adventure, 1829-1858*. London: Cass.

The Power and Pitfalls of Carnival as Cultural Heritage

Philip W. Scher

The world will say: Trinidad and Tobago is a place to visit;
Trinidad and Tobago's Carnival is the most enjoyable Carnival anywhere; and Trinidad and Tobago is a country to
buy things from. From regular goods and services to the full
range of our art, crafts and our cultural skills.
— Trinidad Guardian, June 7, 1994

We would not only be missing the boat, but would find
ourselves totally at sea, if the thinking is that we can only
discuss trade and industry at the level of mechanisation or
energy-based products. Haven't we learned anything from
the morgues that were once proud car-assembly plants?
— Terry Joseph, Trinidad Express Newspaper, October 23, 1997

This essay focuses on the uneasy tension that lies between the commodification of cultural forms such as Carnival in the service of
diversifying the national economy of Trinidad and Tobago and the protection and preservation of culture against cultural appropriation *by
outsiders*. The tension lies, here, as I see it, in the local, official desire to
participate in two different forms of valuation regarding National cultural property. On the one hand, the value of Trinidadian cultural forms
such as Carnival may be and are often seen in light of international economic value. That is, what can selling Carnival bring into the national
coffers? Yet, at the same time, the value of Carnival and its allied arts
of calypso and steelband are seen as having a very different kind of
valuation in which the Carnival arts belong to the nation's patrimony
and are part of a larger struggle for self-determination and identity

formation. Protecting and preserving Carnival and the Carnival arts, then, is fraught with danger and filled with potential: the danger to overprotect and, thus, lose key dynamic elements in the form, and the potential of gaining an important opportunity to maintain important expressive cultural forms for the nation's future.

The recent outpouring of literature on cultural appropriation, while extremely helpful in delineating some very important issues, has, overall, failed to really address the enormous subtleties with regard to the kinds of cultural appropriation that may be out there. Although some attempt to create a typology of cultural appropriations has been made (Ziff and Rao, 1997), I have noticed that the idea of cultural appropriation, as treated in the academic literature, seems to be limited, as a matter of course, to the issue of insiders versus outsiders (Barkan 2007). Very little attention is paid to the diversity of motivations that lie *within* a certain group that claims proprietary rights over a corpus of cultural material. Perhaps the most articulate observers in this regard, such as Rosemary Coombe, have been those scholars who have approached the legal ramifications of cultural appropriation.

Trinidadian cultural forms such as Carnival may be and are often seen in light of international economic value. That is, what can selling Carnival bring to the nation in terms of valuable foreign exchange? Yet at the same time the value of Carnival and its allied arts of calypso and steelband, are seen as belonging to a very different kind of valuation in which the carnival arts belong to the nation's patrimony and are part of a larger struggle for self-determination and identity formation. That is to say, the Carnival has value (albeit contested) as part of the structures of national feeling. One could, I suppose, see the two as cynically intertwined, with the latter serving to act as the former's protector in an unassailable loophole to preserve a kind of cultural monopoly. What I mean is that the marketing of culture by the state would be wholly the province of a particular state, not only against outside appropriation, but also against insider or native incursions into the field of cultural profiteering. As part of the preservation and promotion process, the state would have the exclusive right to decide what culture was, to whom it belonged and in what ways it could be dispensed and administered. These two forms of valuation, then, would be revealed to be, in actuality, just one, predicated on the idea of possessive individualism as it is enshrined in a Western legal and ideological discourse. A recent example of this kind of thinking and action may be found in the recent dispute between Bolivia and Peru, regarding the "ownership" of a festival costume and dance called "La Diablada." Bolivia claims that

"La Diablada" is part of its exclusive national patrimony, and yet the state never fully controls any dimension of the cultural forms found within its borders. This is made even more salient by the enduring fact of the migration of nationals abroad, the penetration of foreign goods and media, and the immigration of peoples.

In this light, I am interested primarily in the state's attempt to commodify and "sell" culture both as a strategy for diversifying the economy and reinforcing claims to national sovereignty. I make no claims that their efforts are totalizing or even particularly effective at times. I take as my starting point the notion of culturalisms: "identity politics mobilized at the level of the nation-state...and almost always [related to] struggles for stronger recognition from existing nation-states or from various transnational bodies" (Appadurai 1996, 15). In the case of the Caribbean, a region shaped by, and ultimately dependent upon, the larger nation-states of Europe and North America, and, now, such transnational organizations as the World Trade Organization, the World Bank, the IMF, and UNESCO among others, culturalisms have long been present in public life as strategies to promote awareness of the nation in one form or another.

This is not to claim that all forms of culture are determined wholly by their status as culturalisms, or that all participants carrying out their daily lives are merely reproducing a kind of top-down mass project in national socialization, but I will demonstrate some fundamental contradictions inherent in such a project. As culture becomes something governments are interested in marketing and selling they analogize cultural forms with other export commodities such as oil, natural gas, or sugar cane. In likening expressive culture to other exportable material goods, state agencies speak of gaining market share, of acquiring brand name recognition, and of finding a niche in the global market of culture and tourism. Yet name branding cultural forms (or as it is often called, nation branding) has some pitfalls. Briefly, there emerges a general tension between preservation and stagnation. State preservation strategies cannot reconcile the dynamic changes that expressive forms undergo to keep them relevant to the population at large (and, therefore, potentially popular) with the volatility that such change implies. That is, radical changes in cultural forms potentially keep them beyond the objectification by (and control of) state agencies.

Preservation strategies

State agencies, or, increasingly, private entities responsible for dealing with "national" cultural forms, are involved with identification research, development, promotion, authentication and evaluation. This general mandate calls for the authentication of expressive cultural forms by "recognized authorities" in appropriate fields such as anthropology and folklore. Anthropologist David Scott critiques such authentication projects because it reproduces a kind of academic authority that has generally served to objectify cultural forms. Indeed, such objectifications are necessary for the commodification process but they run contrary to most contemporary anthropological perspectives on culture (Scott 1991). The conflation of cultural forms with other trade goods creates a strange logic and assumes that both may be treated identically. But the marketing and selling of cultural forms is also intended to do work that the sale of other products cannot do, which is to bring specific attention to the nation itself and, by extension, to its ruling government via the creation of a national identity.

As Ernesto Laclau points out: a nationalist identity promoted by a ruling or dominant group must "show its ability to become a realistic alternative for the organization and management of the community" (1994, 16). In other words, in producing an objectified national culture the state must successfully present itself as the logical and natural administrator of that culture-not as its originator, but as its champion. Eric Williams, the first Prime Minister of Trinidad, sought to distance culture from economics for fear of creating what he considered a humiliating and financially unsound tourist industry. Tourism, he noted early on, would be "harmful to the dignity of our people" if left uncontrolled. Williams' saw tourism as secondary to "promoting the Arts and Culture (especially Drama) as part of the process of nation-building and achieving self-awareness" (1993, 309). For Williams, the role of culture was to build, not to brand, the nation.

Compared to William's position, which stressed nurturing culture to increase the nation's sense of self and to build self-esteem after the passing of colonialism, the current state's attitude reflects a much greater awareness of the importance of external factors (global factors) and a perception of the necessary links between nationalism, culture, and economics. One could see it as a capitulation to neo-colonialism in the sense that it conforms to, and is pursued as, a form of neoliberal economic development. But this may be too harsh. State power, resting, in part, on the ability to foment nationalist sentiment, has responded to the changing conditions in which it finds itself. Thus, although the government, dominated as it is by the middle and upper classes, has always had a stake in influencing the direction of national culture, this concern has recently shifted to place a much greater emphasis on the promotion of culture as commerce, thereby yielding nationalist endea-vours that are in and of themselves economically sound and patriotic (Ramcharitar 2008). This has manifested itself as an interest in the export of culture (Nurse 2000).

Carnival and culture in Trinidad have benefited from Trinidad and Tobago-style Carnivals established by emigrant Trinidadian com-munities all across North America, Canada and the United Kingdom. This has contributed to both the spreading of Carnival as well as to the livelihoods of Carnival creators everywhere. The state has cau-tioned, however, that without some kind of firm, centralized control, Carnival is in danger of being appropriated by the world without proper acknowledgment of its roots in Trinidad. Carnival becomes merely "West Indian" or vaguely Caribbean and this process is abetted because it makes greater political sense in a transnational situation to promote the event as pan-Caribbean (Cohen 1992). In order, then, to effect greater control over the production and distribution of "national culture," the state and associated parties employ a strategy of historical admonition, with the state's version of Carnival narrative serving as a cautionary tale of what can happen if the population, left to its own irresponsible devices, is allowed to carry on bastardizing, forgetting, and transforming a cherished tradition. In this scenario that which is "authentically" Carnival: black, working class, strong masquerade tra-ditions, classic calypso, steelband etc... is held up against the degraded, vulgar, meaningless, elitist Carnival of the present day.

The solution is to increase control over licensing, marketing and promotion of Carnival, to tighten the grip on the development of new Carnivals abroad and, to promote and extend Carnival season within the country of Trinidad itself. The goal, here, is to increase the share of profit and actual participation (i.e., constructing costumes, providing music, or organizing fetes) for interested parties in Trinidad itself. This increase in participation would result from "recognition" by the world that Trinidad is the "Mecca" of Carnival. For example, in the mid 1990s something called the Carnival King and Queen of the World compe-tition, as part of its promotional push, issued a magazine filled with short statements of purpose and historical notes all carrying didactic and programmatic appeals to save the nation by saving its culture. In one article, which was ostensibly an historical description of old time Carnival characters that used to make their appearances on the streets of Port-of-Spain, such as jab jabs and bats and midnight robbers, the author stresses:

> The characters in Trinidad's traditional Carnival are the
> repositories of very important features which distinguish Car-
> nival Trinidad and Tobago style from other Carnivals. They
> add to the uniqueness of the national festivals (sic) which,
> with calypso, pan and above all else, the spirit, create a dif-
> ferentiation of the product as Trinidad and Tobago Carnival
> claims a niche in the world economic market (Cupid 1994: 3)

There is in this statement a clear sense that the preservation of "authentic, traditional carnival" is important for the formation of, or, in a sense,
the continuation of, a unique national cultural form.

The form's uniqueness is important because its difference allows for
immediate recognition and, therefore, easier marketability and control.
At least part of the drive to recapture lost culture evident in this kind of
rhetoric is to preserve what is considered to be the product differentia-
tion or comparative advantage that equals its attraction. Thus there is
the implicit sense that aesthetic appreciation requires a "unique" form,
not merely a form that can be said to be National in quality. It cannot
be any Carnival that is the source of this beauty and popularity, but
specifically a Trinidadian Carnival with specific identifying features
such as the old time Carnival characters. It is for this reason that such
characters are treated as "endangered species" and showcased in a
locked parking lot in front of the Queen's Hall auditorium and not out
on the street. There arises, then, a link between the "mythopoetic meta-
narrative" inherent in the construction of a nationalist culture and the
perpetuation and solidification of the nation's sovereignty as it is realized through effective control over commodity production and exchange.

State and related agencies responsible for the creation of national
cultural commodities are also charged, then, with the creation of
national culture, or perhaps it is vice versa. In any case, the success
of this kind of culture is in part measured by the returns realized from
its sale, both internally as well as globally, where sale is seen not only
as an economic boon, but a marker of recognition. For instance, many
Trinidadian officials claim that Jamaican identity is "stronger" for its
general exposure and overall recognition.

I have been using the term commodity here, following Appadurai
(1986: 13) as that point in the life of a "thing" when its exchangeability
is foregrounded. The state conceives of culture as a collection of things
with attributes that can be exchanged either for money or some form
of symbolic capital (Bourdieu 1984: 291). Yet, by dealing with unsta-
ble public forms the state's attempt to commodify (and, therefore, by
necessity objectify) culture runs into the problem of resistance not to

objectification, per se, but to a fixed understanding of the object and, therefore, to exchangeability. The social uses to which objectified and commodifed cultural forms can be put by others, migrants, or artists, for example, are not necessarily the same uses designed for them. Thus, it is not in resistance to objectification or even in commodification that agency emerges, but in the implementation of those objectified and co-modified cultural forms. This is really where the research begins. I have outlined the theoretical underpinnings of a much larger work that will explore the tensions between artists working in the carnival world who borrow freely from many cultural sources, and the state whose claims to control that creativity take the form of preservation.

Privatizing Nationalism

The chief distinction I would make here between older conceptions of nationalism and newer conceptions influenced profoundly by neoliberal ideology is that in the latter, the measure of the success of nationalism is not to be found exclusively in abstractions, in education, in the spirit of the people, or in the collective consciousness of a "folk," but rather in the way that such feelings of pride or national consciousness are generated in, and measured by, the consumption of national products (along with the recognition of their nationality) by foreigners. The distinction is important. It recognizes that nationalism is located increasingly in products and in economic successes, subordinating an idea of culture to an idea of commerce. This, I maintain, is deeply connected to a neoliberal political economy in the region that emphasizes economic production in areas that are not competitive with other markets (such as bananas, for instance, or "anonymous" commodities such as produce, industrial goods etc). In emphasizing the production of local goods and services, there is, inevitably, an emphasis on the production of region-ally and culturally *specific* goods and services.

Thus, the economic productivity of the region is inevitably stamped with its nationality, its culture, and its location. Therefore, although one can easily point to cultural forms as a measure of nationalism in older cases, in Europe, for example, (how else, after all, outside of a general *geist*, would one indicate national distinctiveness?) there is not the same emphasis on the consumption of these national products as a measure of the strength of a given national identity. In other words, the collection of folktales, songs, stories, costumes, languages, customs, beliefs, and cuisines that mark the endeavours of nineteenth-century nationalists in Europe was not simultaneously conceived as a contri-bution to the economic health of the society. In nineteenth-century

Trinidad, Carnival was a constant worry to the colonial administration as a possible detriment to the economic development of the colony, rather than its greatest asset. Only as culture increasingly becomes a prominent element within the economic strategies of Caribbean countries does nationalist expressive culture take on its newest form as commodity. I have called this the privatization of nationalism, as national identity and consumption of culture become conflated. It is privatized because, even though the state benefits from monitoring the flow of national images and products, it has increasingly pursued private sector strategies of branding and even contracted private agencies to develop its brand identities (Aronczyk 2008).

In examining the ways in which culture and nationalism are discussed in public forums, one gets a fairly clear picture of the relationship that has grown in the public imagination between national culture and international consumption. Especially since that which emerges as national culture and is presented as the essence of the "local" is almost always produced out of a historical relationship between consumer and consumed. In other words, the development of local culture is deeply dependent on the foreign imagination of what the local is. This relationship, of course, is erased in the act of consumption and anything that interferes with it is dismissed or disdained, usually by the consumer. For instance, it is routine that foreign tourists to places such as Trinidad, Jamaica, or Aruba, will comment on the presence of American restaurant chains such as McDonalds, Kentucky Fried Chicken, or Wendy's. They may laugh or act surprised or disdainful, but they will readily acknowledge that these are distinctly the products of American culture. But the idea of the Caribbean as "paradise," the obligatory "steelband" in the hotel lobby, or the ubiquitous images of rastas, parrots, and pirates will often be seen as ample evidence of the truly local, and not as images generated by foreign imaginations placed strategically to indicate to the tourist that they have arrived in the land they were expecting. The tourist then disembarks from the airplane already with a landscape in mind and searches diligently for it until it is found.[1] The issue confronting the Caribbean is to compete within that generic landscape, to further differentiate between landscapes of paradise and insert even more specific locales into the hearts and minds of

---

1   Perhaps if the consuming tourist were not to find any evidence of this foreignness they have traveled to find, they would experience some other kind of "culture shock," an over-abundance of the familiar and no sign of difference. We might have to call this "no-culture shock."

foreign consumers. The current forms of Caribbean nationalism reflect this specific relationship, then, the degree to which an adequate vision of the local has been supplied and consumed while hiding the unbalanced nature of this·construction.

Conclusion:
Sifting History: Selection and maintenance of a viable culture

The promotion of certain Carnival characters, such as those portrayed in Viey La Cou, as well as the systematic forgetting of others (Scher 2007), are now no longer simply due to the kind of puritanical reformation within middle class society so common throughout the latter half of the 19th and into the early twentieth centuries. More than ever the decision to maintain such forms is tied to economic priorities in which culture has grown steadily as a percentage of the GDP. In general, that growing importance of culture makes the host society in a tourist exchange a sort of perpetual performance site. Within those cultural events that are most central to the national economy, the careful selection of historic cultural forms becomes valuable. This change in the ideology of culture is in part spawned by the "marketization" of discreet aspects of social life that are themselves influenced by neoliberal ideology. The example of Trinidad shows a changing attitude towards culture and national identity as "neoliberal" concepts of marketing influence state sponsored cultural projects. The measure of success for these endeavours is now the consumption of the nation's culture, conceived as "product." I have called this "privatizing nationalism." I believe this speaks to a larger issue concerning anthropology and identity in which anthropological notions of culture as constructed ignore both native and local/state conceptions of culture, at least to some degree primordial and immutable, as a sense that is emphasized in the contemporary political economic climate. Anthropology ignores or dismisses the primordialization of culture (the creation of culturalisms) at its peril partly because if it listens, it will recognize in the cultural rhetoric of local preservation its own ancestral voice, and because if it continues to be guided by implicit notions of authenticity it will fail to see an important manifestation of neo-liberalism and power.

Works Cited

Appadurai, Arjun. 1996. *Modernity at Large*. Minneapolis: University of Minnesota Press.

_____. 1986. *The Social Life of Things: Commodities in Cultural Perspective*. Cambridge: Cambridge University Press.

Aronxzyk, Melissa. 2008. Living the Brand: Nationality, Globality and the Identity Strategies of Nation Branding Consultants. *International Journal of Communication* 2: 41-65.

Barkan, Elazar. 2008. "Genes and Burkas: Predicaments of Human Rights and Cultural Property." In *Cultural Heritage and Human Rights*, ed. Helaine Silverman and D. Fairchild Ruggles, 184-200. New York: Springer.

Bourdieu, Pierre. 1984. *Distinction: A Social Critique of the Judgment of Taste*. Cambridge: Harvard University Press.

Cohen, Abner. 1993. *Masquerade Politics*. Berkeley: University of California Press.

Coombe, Rosemary J. 1998. *The Cultural Life of Intellectual Properties*. Durham: Duke University Press.

Cupid, John. 1994. Trinidad Carnival Traditional Characters. 1st Carnival King and Queen of the World Magazine, 1:16–17.

Green, Garth L. 1999. Blasphemy, sacrilege and Moral Degradation in the Trinidad Carnival: The Hallelujah Controversy of 1995, ed John Pulis, 189-214. The Netherlands: Gordon and Breach.

Hill, Errol.1985. Traditional Figures in Carnival Their Preservation, Development and Interpretation. *Caribbean Quarterly* 31(2):14–35.

Laclau, Ernesto.1994. *The Making of Political Identities*. London: Verso.

Nurse, Keith. 2000. The Caribbean Music Industry: The Case for Industrial Policy and Export Promotion. Paper prepared for: Office of Cultural Affairs Inter-American Cultural Program Organization of American States, Washington D.C.

Ramcharitar, Raymond. 2008. Tourist Nationalism in Trinidad and Tobago. In *New Perspectives on Caribbean Tourism*, ed. Marcella Daye, Donna Chambers and Sherma Roberts, 79-93. London: Routledge.

Scher, Philip W. 2002. Copyright Heritage: Preservation, Carnival and the State in Trinidad. *Anthropological Quarterly*, 75(3): 453-484.

_____. 2007. When "Natives" Become Tourists of Themselves: Returning Transnationals and the Carnival in Trinidad and Tobago. In *Trinidad Carnival: The Cultural Politics of a Transnational Festival*. Ed. Garth L. Green and Philip W. Scher, 84-101, Bloomington: Indiana University Press.

Scott, David. 1991. That Event, This Memory: Notes on the Anthropology of African Diasporas in the New World. *Diaspora* 1(3): 261-284.

Sheller, Mimi. 2003. *Consuming the Caribbean*. London: Routledge.

Williams, Eric. 1993. The Chaguaramas Declaration: Perspectives for the New Society. In *Eric Williams Speaks: Essays on Colonialism and Independence*. Ed. Selwyn Cudjoe. Wellesley, MA: Calaloux Publications.

Ziff, Bruce and Pratima Rao (eds.). 1997. *Borrowed Power: Essays on Cultural Appropriation*. New Brunswick: Rutgers University Press.

Too Hip to Hop(e)? Post-Katrina Brass Bands and New Orleans Carnival

Bruce Boyd Raeburn

By wiping out many of the neighborhood-based cultural wetlands that have sustained brass band "second line" parades and related vernacular Carnival activities for more than a century, Hurricane Katrina hit New Orleans brass bands where they live. Although many of these bands are still grappling with the consequences of dislocation in terms of personnel and employment, the city's most innovative brass bands—Hot 8, Soul Rebels, ReBirth—have returned in one form or another and have been coping with the problems of re-situation in a market that has been recovering from disaster. Hurricane Katrina intensified and clarified a number of issues pertaining to cultural dynamics within the brass band community, leaving participants and observers alike to ponder various unanswered questions. How has catastrophe affected the divisions between traditionalists and modernists that existed among (and within) black brass bands prior to the storm? What are the strategies by which brass bands reconfigure themselves in order to meet the shifting functional imperatives that define New Orleans in recovery mode? Does music provide a way back into the culture, or is it now an escape route? Does a discrete "black Mardi Gras" existing outside of the social space reserved for the official Carnival offer a means of catharsis or reveal racial divisions that have been exacerbated by Katrina? Since everyone requires their services during Carnival, can black brass bands serve as a force for amelioration? This essay will explore these questions in examining the commercial, social, and artistic imperatives that currently drive the fortunes of black brass bands in the post-Katrina environment. My aim is not only to provide insight into how New Orleans musicians are coping with disaster but also to illuminate the proactive involvement of scholars who care about the brass band tradition, which I see as equally impressive and important for the future.

I should begin with a disclaimer. Accurate and comprehensive statistical information about the displacement or return of Crescent City musicians and culture-bearers post-Katrina is not currently available, so anecdotal information will have to suffice for the present.[1] Under such circumstances, the "little" picture may tell us what the "big" picture cannot. Fortunately, case studies by incipient ethnomusicologists Jeremy Tolliver of Bethel University and Matt Sakakeeny of Columbia University (now at Tulane), along with the documentary and organizational activities of Stella Baty Landis of Tulane University, reveal the responses of musicians in three of the city's most popular and creative brass bands—the Soul Rebels, ReBirth Brass Band, and Hot 8, respectively—to the post-Katrina environment. In addition, Dr. Michael White, a brass band leader and clarinetist who holds the Rosa and Charles Keller, Jr. Chair in Fine Arts and Humanities at Xavier University, has been extremely candid in sharing his experiences in various articles and in interviews for newspapers and radio. He provides a scholarly perspective couched in the experience of a working musician who lost everything except his talent (and the instruments he took with him) to Katrina. These sources furnish enough historical information and anecdotal opinion to permit some tentative conclusions about how cataclysm has affected the city's festival traditions, including Carnival. The more generalized reports of journalist Larry Blumenfeld, who received support from the Soros Foundation to track the fortunes

---

1   During 2008, the non-profit recovery organization Sweet Home New Orleans (SHNO) has been working to compile a report on musician demographics, based on hard data compiled from questionnaires, which can be found at http://www.sweethomeneworleans.org/wp-contents/2008-csr-post-final.pdf. Basing its survey on client information (approximately 300-400 individuals), SHNO estimates that there were 4,500 musicians, Mardi Gras Indians, and Social Aid & Pleasure Club members living in New Orleans before Katrina impacted the city on August 29, 2005. According to the report, by June 2007 66.6% of these tradition bearers had returned to the city but were experiencing difficulty in finding housing (nearly 50%), had fewer opportunities for paid performance, and were earning less than before Katrina when they did find employment as musicians. SHNO estimates that by August 2008 75% of the musicians have returned to New Orleans, yet problems related to housing and gainful employment persist. Although far from comprehensive, the SHNO report is the best statistical model available as of this writing.

of musicians in New Orleans after the storm, provide another potential frame of reference, but I am more concerned in this essay with what Tolliver, Sakakeeny, Landis, and White are doing because they are closer to the musicians and their work better illustrates the symbiosis between theoretical analysis and praxis-oriented fieldwork.

If there is any doubt about the resiliency of New Orleans musicians or concerns about their commitment to festival traditions in the Crescent City, the information provided in the case studies offered by Tolliver and Sakakeeny should dispel them. Musicians who were forced into exile by Hurricane Katrina were willing to travel vast distances to perform back in New Orleans, thus answering the rhetorical question posed in my title. In fact, despite the interest of the younger generation in melding contemporary hip hop with New Orleans brass band styles, thus setting themselves apart from the tradition, these musicians were not "too hip to hope." What they were hoping for was a chance to get their lives back, but their actions entail broader implications for the survival of the tradition. For example, Tolliver quotes Samuel H. Winston of *Gambit Weekly* in April 2006 regarding the members of the Soul Rebels commuting to New Orleans from their respective exiles in Houston, Texas, and Baton Rouge, Louisiana, for a weekly engagement at Le Bon Temps Roulé, a bar on Magazine Street that did not flood: "Despite what seems like an extremely impractical set of circumstances for the band to continue at Le Bon Temps, they insist on it being necessary" (Tolliver 2007, 39).

Lumar LeBlanc, the band's snare drummer, felt that regaining contact with the band's local audience was imperative, even though the band's promotion strategy prior to Katrina had been built increasingly on national touring: "We've committed ourselves to our fans, and we'll do it as long as we physically can"(Tolliver 2007, 39040). One is tempted to interpret devotion to the local audience as commitment to the preservation of traditional brass band heritage, but in the case of the Soul Rebels, some qualifications are necessary. Well before Katrina, this band was distancing itself from the street context of New Orleans brass band culture in order to market itself more effectively as a hip hop act. Shortly after its founding in the early 1990s, the band released two sets of publicity photographs—one in suits and fedoras, the other in berets, black t-shirts, and camouflage cargo pants, proffering almost contradictory images. In retrospect, it is not difficult to see which side won. On the cover of the August 2006 issue of *OffBeat*, a local music journal, the band insisted that they *not* be portrayed with brass instruments for fear of being typecast as a marching band, a continuation of a policy made evident in the title of their 1998 CD, "No More Parades"(Tolliver 2007, 28, 15). Considering the domination of hip hop artists in the popular music market, from a business standpoint, this strategy makes perfect sense. Yet such strategies do not preclude commitment to restoration of endangered brass band traditions. Even if the band did not wish to be perceived as currently "in" the tradition, there can be little doubt that these musicians were originally "of" it and were committed to its survival while also working to create a hip hop persona. Tolliver's interest in finding vernacular "authenticity" may have influenced his first impression of the Soul Rebels (during his audition) as an amalgam of funk, R & B, hip hop repertoire "with an unmistakable New Orleans brass band feel," which helps to explain why he added that "everyone in the group had committed themselves to bringing New Orleans back, and they saw their music as being the best tool for that task."(Tolliver 2007, 20-21). But he certainly did not mistake the renewed sense of agency and urgency that he witnessed as he tracked the band's subsequent activities. Before Katrina the Soul Rebels were looking for a way out of the community-based brass band world, with its street-oriented jazz funerals and Social Aid & Pleasure Club "second lines." Now they were working their way back in, but on their own terms. Katrina had the effect of breaking down boundaries that had developed within the brass band community, substituting a new spirit of cooperation and mutualism that had previously been lacking.

Indeed, Katrina raised issues concerning the definition and evaluation of the New Orleans brass band heritage for all the bands that returned or commuted; it forced introspection and reflection upon musicians whose loss of all worldly possessions left them only with such intangibles as "tradition" to contemplate. This stripping away has led to some surprises. For almost three decades there has been a rift within the New Orleans brass band community between "modern" and "traditional" approaches to performance practices and repertoire. Dr. Michael White has commented on this phenomenon: "During the middle and late seventies, several new younger brass bands emerged to fill in the community void as traditional groups on the street became rarer and rarer. The ranks of younger players were filled with musicians who rarely interacted with older players and had little, if any, contact with, or 'apprenticeship,' in the authentic traditional New Orleans style. Since a once strong high school band tradition was beginning to decline, fewer younger players had training or development before becoming professional. Characteristic of many younger groups, which grew to dominate the streets by the early eighties, were unison section playing, 'riff tunes,' simplified harmonies, reduced numbers of keys, faster and more prominent rhythms, and smaller groups of about eight musicians. Instrumental shifts were also seen: The clarinet virtually disappeared, and the tuba and drums developed a more dominant role with rhythm and blues overtones. The overall sense of pride, professionalism, and seriousness gradually gave way to street clothes, baseball caps, and tennis shoes. Mixing all the musical elements around them—reggae, rhythm and blues, bebop, free jazz, high school band music, Mardi Gras Indian chants, current radio hits, and television themes—the younger brass bands brought a freshness and creative excitement to the streets that had been missing in the older traditional bands. Commercialism and the generation gap were the underlying causes of the older bands' dwindling repertoires, stagnation of styles, and a lack of new songs in the traditional groups"(White 2001, 89). Although White is a traditionalist who has often been critical of the new wave of younger brass bands, it is clear that he appreciates the spirit that motivates them, if not always the musical results.

Because his residence was only a block away from the London Avenue canal breach, White lost a personal collection of more than 50 vintage instruments, numerous unique interviews with pioneer jazz musicians, a recorded sound collection of more than 4,000 items, and reams of sheet music, including his own compositions in manuscript. He evacuated to Houston to care for his mother and his aunt, but commuted regularly to New Orleans to perform and, eventually, to resume teaching at Xavier, where he continues to reside in a FEMA trailer. Like members of the Soul Rebels, White lost all of his material possessions, except for the few treasured instruments he had taken when he fled. In October 2005, the clarinetist was interviewed by a reporter for the *Times-Picayune* as he attempted to salvage what he could from the debris of his former home. "At this point," White admitted,

> I'm trying to figure out if I can be salvaged. I tried very hard
> to picture what this would be like, but you can't begin to
> imagine. The hard part is that there's a lot of history here
> that can't be replaced. It's all gone. I'm overwhelmed. I
> wouldn't know where to start (Spera 2005, B1)

Elsewhere in the article, however, one gains the impression that the healing had already begun. In Houston he landed a regular "jazz brunch" engagement and wrote "two positive, upbeat songs about a restored New Orleans." In reflecting on the past, White reiterated the message of the "jazz funeral," in which the spirit of the deceased is "cut loose" to enjoy a better life in the great beyond. Death is followed by rebirth. "I have to keep remembering that," he says, "That's what gives us the courage to carry on." (Spera 2005, B1, B3).

Interestingly, even before the disaster, White had begun to move beyond what had been a staunch and seemingly exclusive commitment to traditionalism in his musical activities. As a recipient of an artist-in-residence fellowship at Studio in the Woods in Algiers, Louisiana, in 2004, he had expanded his musical horizons to include hip hop, modern jazz, rhythm and blues, and Caribbean music in the two dozen compositions that appeared on the resulting CD, "Dancing in the Sky." Katrina seems to have reinvigorated both his traditionalism and his interest in experimentation, evident not only in a noticeable intensification in his playing, but also in his willingness to work as a mentor with younger, "new wave" brass bands such as Hot 8.

In the months leading up to Katrina, the word on the street was that Hot 8 had replaced ReBirth as the favorite among Social Aid & Pleasure Clubs, largely because of their creative rearrangement of such popular hits as Marvin Gaye's "Sexual Healing" in the quirky, idiomatic New Orleans brass band style, keeping the song's hooks intact while introducing greater rhythmic and dynamic intensity. Yet despite its success, the band had already experienced a degree of misfortune prior to Katrina that was astounding. The Hot 8 was organized by brass bassist Bennie Pete in 1995. Between 1996 and 2004, the band lost two members as the result of murder: trumpeter Jacob Johnson was found shot "execution style" in his home, and trombone player Joseph "Shotgun Joe" Williams was killed by the police during a traffic stop. In December 2006 the trend continued with the murder of snare drummer Dinneral Shavers by a teenaged assailant attempting to murder Shavers' stepson. The previous April, trumpeter Terrell "Burger" Batiste had been hit by a car while he was attempting to change a flat tire in Atlanta, where the Red Cross had provided an apartment—he lost both legs but continues to perform with Hot 8. To say the least, Pete was coping with morale problems that would have paralyzed most bands, but his response was, instead, to seek new avenues for growth and discovery. He promoted collaboration with Dr. Michael White in order to expose his band members (most of whom had studied music at Southern University in New Orleans) more fully to the traditional brass band heritage, a subject not offered in schools.

For White and Pete, drawing on the symbolic potency of a continuum of brass band jazz performance that had persisted for more than a century was a strategic initiative designed to sustain hope—it was a coping mechanism as well as a mingling of artistic perspectives. Apropos of White's remark about the brass band funeral, Pete told a reporter for National Public Radio at Dinerral Shavers' funeral:

> We feelin' that dirge. We expressin' that dirge to the dead. We feel in our mind he could see this some kind of way, but if he can't, we don't know, but if he could, he gone see I brought my best for him on this morn on this day (NPR 2007).

For a population enervated and dispossessed by disaster, the ability to feel, to get beyond the numbness, is a powerful antidote to despair. The weekly Hot 8 sessions with Dr. Michael White at the Sounds Café in the Faubourg Marigny illustrate how "hope" could enhance and redefine "hipness" in a post-Katrina environment. When queried about the traditional repertoire they were performing with White in February 2007, such songs as "Margie," "By and By," and "The Saints" (which is considered by some to be the ultimate New Orleans cliché), Hot 8 trumpeter Raymond "Dr. Rackle" Williams explained, "We got to play these songs; this is who we are" (*The New Yorker* 2007). Before Katrina, that statement would have been debatable. The trauma wrought by the storm blew away what now seemed in retrospect to be artificial boundaries dividing the brass band community and refocused attention on respect for the tradition as a whole—conceived as a holistic continuum in which every brass band musician could aspire to a place of honor.

Hot 8 had cultivated a primarily local following until they were launched into the national spotlight with their appearance in Spike Lee's HBO documentary, *When the Levees Broke: A Requiem in Four Acts,* in 2006. According to an NPR report, the result was that "a new legion of fans caught onto the band's mix of traditional marching music, hip hop, and R & B" (NPR 2007). Did increased national visibility, and an awareness of the commercial potential of identifying with the heavy promotional machinery that would soon be dedicated to "jump starting" the city's cultural tourism industry, factor into the band's reassessment of traditionalism? A more plausible explanation is the mediation of musicologist Stella Baty Landis. In 2007, she was a visiting instructor in Tulane University's Music Department with an interest in following the career trajectory of Hot 8, and she was also the owner of Sounds Café. In an interview with Chicago Tribune music critic Howard Reich published on February 4, 2007, Landis stated: "What we really need is to make [the artists] who are here, and who feel so strongly about the city, feel comfortable about staying here." Obviously, in making her space available for the Michael White-Hot 8 collaboration, she was willing to become proactive in setting an agenda for sustaining the tradition, and she was not particularly concerned about scholarly detachment or observing stylistic boundaries. Yet even Landis, who was instrumental in organizing "Silence Is Violence," a huge street demonstration to protest the murders of her friends Dinneral Shavers and the filmmaker Helen Hill in January 2007, was not entirely optimistic that New Orleans' traditional culture would survive. She said:

> I feel that the city that existed pre-Katrina is done, and that its culture is not going to suddenly reappear, no matter how hard we fight for it. My hope is very long-term and itself kind of abstract, but it's that the kernel of New Orleans, that essence of New Orleans that is deep in our soul and thick in the air, will give rise to something, eventually, newly wonderful (Reich 2007).

In his recently completed dissertation in ethnomusicology at Columbia University, Matthew Sakakeeny ponders the ways in which traditional tools are being used to create new possibilities for brass band musicians in New Orleans. Sakakeeny tracked several brass band funerals in 2006 and 2007, and focused on how bands such as the New Birth and ReBirth were adapting to the post-Katrina environment. Both of these bands draw their membership primarily from Tremé, a neighborhood just north of the French Quarter that experienced minimal flooding but has nevertheless had its share of problems due to perennial crime, poverty, deteriorating housing stock, and police repression. Tremé is sometimes referred to as "the oldest African American neighborhood in North America," and it was no coincidence that the ring shouts of Place Congo were situated on its periphery (as was Storyville), but its demographic configuration from Reconstruction through the 1920s was in fact ethnically diverse, interspersing Afro-French Creoles, African Americans, Sicilians, Germans, and Hispanics within blocks and creating conditions that were conducive to multicultural exchange. As such, the neighborhood became a crucible for the development of jazz. By 1950, however, Tremé was almost entirely black. The eradication of an Oak-lined public space along Claiborne Avenue to make way for an interstate highway in the 1960s, coupled with the cooptation of more space to build Armstrong Park (intended as a playground for tourists) in the following decade, served as an ominous message from city officials and planners that Tremé and its rich "second line" traditions were considered to be expendable. For brass bands from Tremé, the interstate overpass at Claiborne Avenue and Dumaine Street therefore holds a special significance—it symbolizes the disrespect neighborhood residents have had to endure for decades.

Brass bands such as the New Birth and ReBirth routinely use the overpass as a destination for "second lines" following funerals, and Sakakeeny offers an analysis of this phenomenon based on conversations with the musicians who play in these bands:

> Under the bridge' is what locals call the space below Interstate 10, and every jazz funeral and parade I attended in the downtown district of New Orleans wound its way there. Why? For one [thing], the concrete columns and 'bridge' overhead create an intimate space, enclosing parade participants, maximizing participation and a sense of collectivity. And the concrete creates spectacular acoustics, amplifying and multiplying the participatory sound, creating a sort of 'unplugged' feedback loop; acoustic, but also shockingly loud, and made louder by the musicians playing at peak volume to compete with the sound of cars and trucks whizzing by above (Sakakeeny 2007, 3).

Philip Frazier, the co-founder of the ReBirth Brass Band (currently celebrating its 25th anniversary), commented in an interview from November 2006 on how brass bands conform to the acoustical and spatial possibilities of these asphalt bayous:

> When you get to a certain intersection or a certain street where there's an opening, if the street is really wide, you know that's more dancing room for everybody, you wanna keep everybody upbeat. When you get to a street where it's more closed, and the parade might slow down at a pace, you slow it down 'cause you know everybody's trying to get through that small street...When you get under an overpass, 'cause of the acoustics, you know the band gonna be loud anyway, and the crowd knows that gonna be like some wild, rowdy stuff and you want to get everybody hyped" (cit. Sakakeeny, 10).

Utilizing Steven Feld's concept of "soundscapes," Sakakeeny suggests that the manipulation of people, places, and sounds by brass bands to reclaim expropriated terrain, if only intermittently, encourages cultural unity and coherence within the Tremé community. In so doing, he argues, musicians and their followers convert what Henri Lefebvre calls "abstract space" (a matrix of bureaucratic regulations, such as parade permits, impeding cultural production) into "concrete space" (a site of living culture), which is another way of saying that when brass bands and "second lines" are on the streets of New Orleans, they *own* that space.[2] One can scarcely imagine a better or more literal example of citizens using a "people's art" to "take back the streets" than this.

In a post-Katrina environment, where the neighborhoods that remain viable as "cultural wetlands" are more valuable, and more contested, than ever, such strategies are the primary means to fulfilling the hopes of Stella Landis and others who wish for cultural revival in New Orleans, and the consequences for the future of Carnival citywide are momentous. In *Blues for New Orleans: Mardi Gras and America's Creole Soul* (2006), Roger D. Abrahams, Nick Spitzer, John F. Szwed, and Robert Farris Thompson argue that the renewal of Mardi Gras in February 2006, was an existential benchmark, a turning point, in the quest for recovery of the city's past, and thus its hope for the future. The Carnival these anthropologists were most concerned about was not the establishment version administered by Rex, Endymion, and Bacchus in which "bead count" figures so prominently; it was instead the alternative vernacular celebrations of Mardi Gras Indians, Baby Dolls, Bonesmen, and "second lines" with brass bands that persist against the odds in neighborhoods such as Tremé and Central City. Without this creolized vernacular foundation, New Orleans' vaunted "festival traditions" could probably be recreated anywhere. The fact that Mardi Gras Indians and brass band musicians who were dispersed by Katrina feel the need to commute to New Orleans in order to practice their crafts reveals exactly how dependent such cultural production really is on a discrete urban environment, rooted in a site-specific nexus of community, history, and memory. Tourists may come to *observe* such phenomena, but the culture-bearers *live it*. Brass band musicians have found no contradiction, or shame, in revealing their dedication to these time-honored traditions, despite the careful cultivation of "hip hop" personas designed to generate status and sales in the popular music market, precisely because what Katrina taught them was that there is "no place like home," especially when that home is New Orleans. It is the only environment in which what they do (and who they are) actually makes sense, with or without Carnival, a festival which nevertheless derives its singularity from their creativity. In this case, hope leads inevitably to action. Perhaps even more inspirational is the realization

---

2   See Henri Lefebvre, *Rhythmnanalysis: Space, Time, and Everyday Life*, trans. Stuart Elden and Gerald Moore (New York and London: Continuum, 2004) for elaboration.

that, on this issue, scholars and musicians have found common cause in fighting for a unique cultural patrimony that deserves to continue not only because it is important, but simply because it is fun.

Works Cited

"Drummer's Funeral Underlines New Orleans Violence." 2007. *All Things Considered*. NPR, 6 January.

The New Yorker. 2007. "New Orleans Journal: Café Culture," *The New Yorker* blog. 1 February. http://www.newyorker.com/online/blogs/neworleans-journal/2007/02/caf_culture.html.

Reich, Howard. 2007. "A Culture's Sad Finale? Crisis of Culture in New Orleans." *Chicago Tribune*. 4 February. http://www.chicagotribune.com/news/opinion/chi-0702040293feb04,0,665458.story.

Sakakeeny, Matthew. 2007. "A Sound-Body Politic: Making Claims on Public Space through Sound." Unpublished paper presented at the Society for Ethnomusicology annual conference. Columbus, Ohio. 27 October.

Sakakeeny, Matthew. 2008. "Instruments of Power: New Orleans Brass Bands and the Politics of Performance." Unpublished dissertation, Columbia University, 2007.

Spera, Keith. 2005. "Facing the Music: Valuable Jazz Artifacts Drown in Floodwater," New Orleans *Times-Picayune*. 22 October: B1, B3.

Tolliver, Jeremy. 2007. "'No Place Like Home': A Brass Band in Post-Katrina New Orleans." Thesis, Bethel University.

White, Michael G. 2001. "The New Orleans Brass Band: A Cultural Tradition," in *The Triumph of the Soul: Cultural and Psychological Aspects of African American Music*, ed Ferdinand Jones and Arthur C. Jones. Westport, Connecticut: Praeger. pp.69-96.

Designing for the Diaspora: Images of Africa in Contemporary British Carnival

Lesley Ferris

"Carnival Days"

On days like these we dance like freedom,
Like the freedom we carried in our hearts
When the slave driver was with his whip
When his whip was at our backs,
There is no carnival without us
And without carnival there is no us.
The colours of our stories joyful the eyes
And rhythm wise the body moves.
. . . .
On days like these the elders say
Astronauts can see us dance
Glittering like precious stones
On dis rocking British cultural crown,
When Rio's eyes upon us gaze
And Africans are proud of us
With heads held high we say we are
The carnival, sweet carnival.

(Zephaniah 2001, 45-46)

These excerpts from Benjamin Zephaniah's poem make obvious that carnival in Britain is irrevocably tied to its African past. From the whips of slavery to the contemporary dancing days of carnival when "Africans are proud of us," carnival is acknowledged as an art form of emancipation. As Adela Ruth Tompsett states, "Today's carnival at Notting Hill still bears witness to the historical circumstances of its origins. It is a legacy of the European slave trade and much that charac-terizes Caribbean-derived carnival can be traced back to events, actions and circumstances within colonial history" (2007, 7). In the last decades of the twentieth century, numerous books and essays were published that focused on British colonialism and its repercussions. Yet, very few books mention or reference Notting Hill Carnival—that "legacy of the European slave trade"— as a living, ongoing exemplar of what Laura Chrisman terms a "post-colonial contravention," an annual perfor-mance that uses the streets of London (and other British cities) as a theatre, an arena to stage post-emancipation celebrations (2003, 24). As Tompsett explains, "The road is a commemorative space. Carnival's possession of the street holds in the memory and the psyche the right of a free people to occupy the public thoroughfare" (2005, 46). Yet recent publications, such as *The British Slave Trade and Public Memory* by Elizabeth Kowaleski Wallace, do not mention London's carnival, and if anything is a 'public memory,' what can be more public than over a million people on the streets of London on carnival weekend? The pub-licity blurb on the back cover of Wallace's book asks the following ques-tion, "How does a society bring back to its history a momentous event that has been largely unrecognized in public discourse for nearly two hundred years?" How indeed? This essay looks at one of the ways the memory of that 'momentous event' is resurrected annually in London on the bank holiday in August, the last Monday of the month.

Carnival is acknowledged as both a celebration of emancipation and an art of resistance, and it is through its location on the street that carnival enacts its colonial history. Tompsett continues:

> . . . the processional route at Notting Hill resonates with a particular and pertinent history. It is a microcosm of that macrocosm that is a shared history between colonizer and colonized. From the industrial canal behind Kensal Road and the old factory buildings and working man's club in the north of the area, down to the fine streets of Arundel Gardens, Kensington Park and Westbourne Grove, in the south, with their handsome white stucco fronted houses built with the wealth of the empire, the route reflects every level of empire activity from the making of wealth in plantation and factory to the displaying of it in the grand houses (2005, 49).

While Tompsett's image of the carnival route as an encapsulation of colonial history is crucial to understanding carnival today, so is the importance of carnival design and the artists' many uses of history in their creative endeavors. In particular for this essay, I look at the ways in which London's carnival artists draw on images of Africa to tell their carnival stories, tales of resistance and resilience, visual storytelling that is laced with a sense of history. Paul Gilroy articulates the importance of history in his groundbreaking book *'There Ain't No Black in the Union Jack': The Cultural Politics of Race and Nation*. While Gilroy's focus is on the "exclusionary effects of racism" he offers a fascinating chapter on the contemporary music scene and its diasporic power (1987, 153). Thus reggae, rap, hip-hop, funk and soul become cultural articulations of a black expressive culture, which he says can be "loosely described as the voice of a social movement" (223). For this movement to have agency and affect, however, Gilroy stresses the importance of history: "This reintroduction of history is not a minimal aim. Racism rests on the ability to contain blacks in the present, to repress and to deny the past" (12). Houston Baker explains in the forward to this book that Gilroy offers an impressively "forceful critique of classical historical materialism and [proposes] a new form of racial politics based on African, diasporic expressive culture" (4).

British Caribbean scholar, Stuart Hall, adds another dimension to the importance of Africa's 'diasporic expressive culture' in his essay "Thinking the Diaspora: Home-Thoughts from Abroad." He states,

> The reworking of Africa in the Caribbean weave has been the most powerful and subversive element in our cultural politics in the twentieth century. And its capacity to disrupt the post-independence nationalist 'settlement' is certainly not over. But this is not primarily because we are connected to our African past and heritage by an unbreakable chain across which some singular African culture has flowed unchanged down the generations, but because we have gone about producing 'Africa' again, within the Caribbean narrative. At every juncture—think of Garveyism, Hibbert, Rastafarianism, the new urban popular culture—it has been a matter of interpreting 'Africa', rereading 'Africa', of what 'Africa' could mean to us now, after diaspora (1999, 13).

I am particularly interested in this notion of Hall's. I am interested in his concept of 'reworking Africa' in relation to Caribbean derived carnival, and, in the following, I consider carnival artists in London and the ways in which they 'rework' Africa in their designs. But first, let us continue to consider Hall's views on 'Africa'. For Hall, major social changes in Caribbean as well as creative developments in the arts in the last century "began with or included a 'translation moment' of the re-encounter with Afro-Caribbean traditions." He goes on to explain that while Africa is not a "fixed anthropological point of reference"— indeed, as we know, much appropriation and transformation occurred for both the Africans and the colonial powers—'Africa' is "the signifier, the metaphor, for that dimension of our society and history that has been massively suppressed, systematically dishonoured and endlessly disavowed, and that despite all that has happened, remains so." If, as Hall insists, "race remains, in spite of everything, the guilty secret... the unspeakable trauma in the Caribbean. It is 'Africa' that has made it 'speakable'"(1999, 14). So, by 'speaking' through carnival with images of 'Africa,' carnival artists in effect find a means to excavate "alternative histories to those imposed by colonial rule and the raw materials for reworking in new and distinctive cultural patterns and forms." And Hall characterizes this reworking as a "process of cultural translation" (13).

While today images of 'Africa' serve as inspiration for a variety of carnival artists, it was not always the case. So it is worth looking at a key figure representing Hall's concept of 'cultural translation.' In Trinidad, in the early part of the 20th century, some carnivalists "used rags, paint, and spears to portray an image of a miserable, uncivilized past" (Kerrigan and Laughlin 2004). This carnival masquerade, sometimes referred to as 'traditional African masquerade', evoked and commented on the pre-emancipation era. Such depictions had an obvious political edge and 'in-your-face' finger pointing at the colonial authorities on the island. But in the middle of the last century, such images went through a significant transformation with the celebrated carnival artist George Bailey (1935-1970), known as the African King.

At age twenty-two years, Bailey, in his second year as a designer, created "Back to Africa," considered by some to be the most celebrated band in the history of modern carnival in Trinidad. It won Band of Year award in 1957, and with "this single presentation Bailey changed popular perceptions of Africa, history and carnival"(Kerrigan and Laughlin 2004). This band broke with tradition---Bailey meticulously researched the regal heritage of African dress. Prior to his intervention, or 'cultural translation' to use Hall's term, spectators at Trinidad's carnival did not believe any African Mas could match the glory and splendour of the Roman and Greek themes which were so popular in the early twentieth century. Bailey's design was a "watershed moment, both for Carnival and for Trinidad society" (Kerrigan and Laughlin 2004). His work is crucial to understanding the importance of Africa in Caribbean carnival's history and its connection to London's Notting Hill Carnival.

A London-based carnival artist that makes this link to Bailey is Carl Gabriel. Born in Trinidad, Gabriel came to London in 1964. He trained as a sheet-metal worker and began to get involved in London's Notting Hill Carnival. The first street events took place in the mid-1960's, and the first two costume bands, designed by Trinidadians Lawrence Noel and Peter Minshall, went on the road in 1973. Gabriel started to photograph London's early carnival, was active as a steel pan player, and soon began to design costumes. He created his own Mas band, Misty Carnival Club, in 1993. When Carl began bending wire, a traditional method of creating shapes to give costumes height and three-dimensional form, he focused his work on 'tribal art,' a term he uses to describe his work that is inspired by art created by native peoples. His most recent work was motivated by the artwork of new world Native Americans, but his early work was strongly connected to Africa. In an interview he describes how his "grandparents were into Shango,[1] that they knew about and made connections to the African gods" (Gabriel 2007, 24). Gabriel describes this influence as crucial to his work in carnival. His grandparents' beliefs were a 'legacy' that he embraced. (See Figure 1)

Gabriel recounts a telling story. He describes some elder Mas makers visiting his workshop. As they watched him bending wire, they told him that he reminded them of George Bailey. He was embarrassed to admit that he did not know who Bailey was and later learned that he was a carnival pioneer, that "Bailey changed the way African mas was played." Once Gabriel realized the significance of Bailey's work, he explained:

> I felt that Bailey was sort of living in me, because the same thing that he went through, I'm going through now. To be able to have the opportunity to create carnival art, to know there is a history and a clear connection to the past through my family and the amazing George Bailey, this was a powerful revelation to me. I am not exactly sure how to talk about this; I can't find the right words (Tompsett 2007, 23-26).

While finding the right words is difficult, Gabriel does know how to 'talk about this,' but his talking is not with spoken language. His talking is with his hands as he shapes wire into magnificent large-scale creations such as "Ritual Dancer" (1999) and "Steel Pan Player" (2006).

---

1   Shango is one of the principal gods of Yoruban culture in West Africa. The religion is called Orisha, but is also referred to by the name of Shango.

Figure 1: "The Spirit", designed by Carl Gabriel, was part of the design for Spirits of Our Ancestors (1999) for Notting Hill Carnival. This design evokes Shango, one of the principal gods of Yoruban culture in West Africa. Shango is the god of thunder, drums and dance, and was, and continues to be, an important presence in the Caribbean today. (Photo: A. R. Tompsett)

Wire-bending is a foundation to the artistry of Trinidadian carnival.[2] Today, however, many carnival elders fear its artistic usefulness is

---

2   For a discussion of the importance of wire-bending in Trinidad and Tobago, see The Heritage Library of the National Library of Trinidad and Tobago.

fading away and being replaced by lighter and more resilient fibreglass. The advantage of wire is that it provides more exactitude and detail to the shape of a costume. And Gabriel, who is considered the leading practitioner of wire-bending in Britain today, insists on maintaining this tradition. "I believe that in every piece of work I do there is a kind of offering, an acknowledgement, there is a part of the work that is saying 'thank you'" (Gabriel 2007, 24).

Another carnival artist who finds inspiration in her imagined idea of Africa is Clary Salandy, the co-founder of Mahogany Arts Ltd., a Mas camp located in Harlesden in North West London. Harlesden is the centre of the London Borough of Brent's large Afro-Caribbean community, and Salandy is committed to working with local youth and a range of young adults in her carnival workshop. Local volunteers execute Salandy's designs under her artistic guidance and expertise. Unlike the majority of Mas camps in London, Mahogany stays open all year, catering to a range and variety of carnival design commissions. The centrepiece of Mahogany's work is the design created and executed for Notting Hill Carnival.

Salandy's artistic vision is indelibly linked to her Trinidadian heritage. She states,

> I feel the ancestral pull. Before I was in this world, people were making carnival and they made me who I am today. We have to respect this and I start from this standpoint: that people died for this. We are paying tribute to the past (Ferris 2005).

Salandy explains the impact that reading Errol Hill's book *The Trinidad Carnival: A Mandate for a National Theatre* had on her. Hill's groundbreaking work, first published in 1972 and reissued in 1997, was one of the first scholarly works to articulate the troubled history of Trinidad's carnival while also celebrating its revolutionary nature. As he states:

> [C]arnival had become a symbol of freedom for the broad mass of the population and not merely a season for frivolous enjoyment. It had a ritualistic significance, rooted in the experience of slavery and in the celebration of freedom from slavery. In this sense, carnival was no longer a European-inspired nature festival. Adopted by the Trinidad people it became a deeply meaningful anniversary of deliverance from the most hateful form of human bondage. The people would not be intimidated; they would observe carnival in the manner they deemed most appropriate (Hill 1997, 21).

For Salandy, carnival is a 'symbol of freedom', a celebration of emancipation, a "statement that we are here now, in this place and time, and we are not where we were in 1834" (Ferris 2005).[3]

The history of carnival is central to Salandy's work, and she sees as part of her mission as a carnival artist to pass on this history to her local community. Since 2000, Salandy has designed four Mas bands that feature aspects of Africa within a larger frame of allegorical themes or stories of resistance and celebration. These include *Carnival Messiah* (2000), *A Touch of Africa* (2001), *The Afro-Asian Experience* (2004), and *Freedom Song* (2007). *Carnival Messiah* took Handel's *Messiah* and retold it through Caribbean-derived carnival. A focus of the work was drawing attention to four twentieth-century century figures that Salandy identified as contemporary examples of a messiah. These included Nelson Mandela, Ghandi, Martin Luther King, Jr., and Mother Theresa. Silk-screened images of their familiar faces appeared in a variety of ways in her design. A key emblem of Africa that Salandy used in this work is the African shield. She explains the importance of this image:

> I love using the shield because it is a symbol of Africa. It's a symbol for war and I feel that in some ways I am a contemporary warrior. I'm holding on to this culture, protecting it, taking it forward and badgering the police as we go through and use the roads. In *Carnival Messiah* I called them 'shields of honour', they were lightweight, made from silk, and the face of Mandela was printed on the front in red. They looked fantastic. The dancers who carried the shields wore costumes based on the Shango religion. The Shango women with the shields in red and white (and red is the colour of Shango) brought a strong sense of African spirituality to the work (Salandy 2007, 32-33).

In *A Touch of Africa*, Salandy, like Gabriel, drew directly from African tribal art for her inspiration. She designed a sixteen foot high, triple headed costume that used the Luba-style African mask from Ghana as its source. (See Figure 2) With *The Afro-Asian Experience*, she created a variety of African and Asian animals such as giraffes, lions, elephants and zebras that delighted the carnival crowds. *Freedom Song* commemorated the bi-centenary (1807) of the abolition of the British slave trade and used a range of African tribal signs embedded in many of the costumes.

---

3   1834 is the year of the emancipation of slaves in Trinidad and Tobago.

Figure 2: Clary Salandy, designer for Mahogany Arts, designed A Touch of Africa for Notting Hill Carnival (2001). Salandy is known for her development of the use of plastizote, a plastic foam material, to create sculptured-like effects that are lightweight for the player. These large pieces are often complicated in their structure, which is engineered by Michael Ramdeen and the Mahogany team. (Photo: Lesley Ferris)

A central and well-acknowledged characteristic of carnival is its ability to transform the everyday into something out of this world. Indeed, carnival could be considered the quintessential 'translation moment' evoked by Stuart Hall, in terms of utilizing images of Africa in designs and concepts, but transformation occurs on multiple fronts. Carnival transforms the streets of Notting Hill from urban, grubby thoroughfares to vibrant avenues of colour, shapes, and forms moving and pulsating to a contagious, all encompassing musical beat. Salandy's costume art uses kinetic transformation as a crucial element of her artistic arsenal. Her experiments with shape, volume, texture are nothing without the player. As Tompsett explains,

> [A] mas, or masquerade, is in itself neither a character nor a costume, but the combination of the two, given life by the player on the road. A costume is only a costume until the player plays mas (Tompsett 2005, 49).

Another aspect of transformation is Salandy's ability to develop community involvement. Such participation changes the many people who work with her—young, middle aged, and elderly—from every day existence, to being part of a larger artistic achievement. Her iconic use of African images and symbols in her work can be seen to articulate the relationship (one that can perhaps be described as hybrid interplay) between these designs and the community members who perform in her costumes on carnival day. Salandy views this involvement as a two-way street. She appreciates that her designs in their scale and number can only be realized as a result of collective practice, and that in return, the people who work with her are able to take part in a significant creative process, a moment of cultural translation. While such a collective artistic strategy is not new, Salandy plans her designs to take advantage of the skills and abilities of her community collaborators. This method, in which the small (a painted feather, a sequin) gradually transforms into something large (the completed costume), is perhaps a mirror image of carnival itself, in which the event only takes shape when all the Mas players assemble and take over the road.

This creative process, both the microcosm of Salandy's work and macrocosm of the day of carnival itself, can be considered a concrete example of Gilroy's notion: "Black culture is actively made and re-made" (Gilroy 1987, 154). Carnival's remaking is its annual happening, the mere fact of its existence and its very survival depends on that 'translation-moment', its encounter with 'Africa'. Carnival is an art form of the present, but instead of repressing and denying the past, it celebrates it and brings a remembrance of history into the here and now. To return to Zephaniah's poetic tribute: "There is no carnival without us/And without carnival there is no us" (2001, 45).

Works Cited

Chrisman, Laura. 2003. *Postcolonial Interventions: Cultural Readings of Race, Imperialism, and Transnationalism*. Manchester: Manchester University Press.

Gabriel, Carl. 2007. "The Interview," *Midnight Robbers: The Artists of Notting Hill Carnival*, Lesley Ferris and Adela Ruth Tompsett, co-editors. London: Carnival Exhibition Group (22-27).

Gilroy, Paul. 1987. *"There Ain't No Black in the Union Jack": The Cultural Politics of Race and Nation*. Chicago: University of Chicago Press.

Hall, Stuart. 1999. "Thinking Through the Diaspora: Home-Thoughts from Abroad," *Small Axe: A Caribbean Journal of Criticism*. Kingston: UWI Press. 6 (September):1-18.

Hill, Errol. 1997. *The Trinidad Carnival: Mandate for a National Theatre*. London: New Beacon Books.

Kerrigan, Dylan and Nicholas Laughlin. (2004) "The Monarch: George Bailey, 1935-1970", *Caribbean Beat* No. 65, January/February 2004. www.meppublishers.com/online/caribbeanbeat/archive/index.php?pid=6001&id=cb65-1-44.

Salandy, Clary. 2007. "The Interview," *Midnight Robbers: The Artists of Notting Hill Carnival*, Lesley Ferris and Adela Ruth Tompsett, co-editors. London: Carnival Exhibition Group. (28-33).

Tompsett, Adela Ruth. 2005. "'London is the Place for Me': Performance and Identity in Notting Hill Carnival", *Theatre History Studies* 25 (June): 43-60.

_____. 2007. "Notting Hill Carnival: Heritage and Art." *Midnight Robbers: The Artists of Notting Hill Carnival*, Lesley Ferris and Adela Ruth Tompsett, co-editors. London: Carnival Exhibition Group (7-15).

Wallace, Elizabeth Kowaleski. 2006. *The British Slave Trade and Public Memory*. New York: University of Columbia Press.

Zephaniah, Benjamin. 2001. *Too Black, Too Strong*. Tarset (Northumberland): Bloodaxe Books.

Unpublished Interview

Ferris, Lesley. 2005. Clary Salandy.

Shadowland and Ecological Protest in Carnival/Caribana

Leida and Jerry Englar

This is a short story of our design, building and performing efforts in Caribana from 1974-2008.

Jerry and Leida moved to Toronto Island in 1974. The Community lies a seven-minute ferry ride from the city of Toronto. The community co-exits in a park on an island where personal automobiles are not allowed. The municipal government at the time was determined to destroy what remained of a historic community and convert the land to park in particular a golf course. The fight to save island homes from demolition was revving up.

The community did lots of campaigning, sign making and attending meetings. We became very active, both politically and artistically. We finally realized that using our artistic abilities had great power. We just needed to work together and tell our story in a compelling a way to an uninformed public.

In 1980 Welfare State International, a theatre company from the UK lived and worked in our community to create "The Tempest" for the International Theatre Festival. Out of that was created a community percussion band; (de rigeur for any community); and the awakening of the Island artistic spirit and the inspiration to use Art as a tool politically.

In 1984, Toronto's Sesquicentennial year, there was lots of cultural stimulus to Celebrate the City.

Jerry and Leida joined Brad Harley, Kathleen Doody, Sarah Miller, and Whitney Smith to create Shadowland. We now had a vehicle we could use to help the community political committees and use our art to express our frustrations and visions for the future. The History of the Toronto Island community leading up to the political tensions and imminent threat of demolition became central to our communication objectives. With the help of Maggie and Boris Howarth of Welfare State International we created a thinly veiled piece of political theatre, called, Island Follies.

Through Maggie and Boris we learned a model for creating large outdoor theatre with a community. One hundred fifty people were involved, we got lots of attention from press and the public and learned to inspire and help our community to survive and prosper.

Shadowland became a community based theatre company, and with its love of environment, meager finances, mandated respect for community, and the 3 R's (reduce, re-use, and recycle) became serious objectives as we dove into dumpsters and investigated disposal yards searching out materials for various creations.

In 1985, we were approached by Deanne Taylor of Video Cabaret with a suggestion that we enter a masquerade band into Caribana that year. Deanne had been to Trinidad and Tobago with City TV to send live coverage of Carnival to Torontonians. There she met Peter Minshall and Christopher Pinheiro. Having seen Island Follies with its large structures, costumes and use of political satire to tell a story visually, Deanne thought the Caribana Parade was a perfect place to showcase our Art.

Shadowland become the "first Canadian–rooted" band; welcomed into the community of Caribana and Carnival in Toronto. They hoped we would, "learn to dance and make music as they had". That's when our community street band got its' name, The Arythumics, or white people with no rhythm. We were welcomed as long as we respected the Art of Carnival, a Primary Art Form. The Art was larger than life, had a huge audience, and it was celebratory, uplifting. Real street theatre; theatre with moving walls and an infinite ceiling.

With the help of Christopher Pinheiro, Alison Brown (a great kiddies band leader soon to become Peter Minshall's Queen of Carnival), Claude, from "The Cloth" in Port of Spain, Jenny Lee (long –time carnival pan promoter) and Shadowland we created Island to Island, a visual portrayal of our Island community that moved down the street in splendid procession.

In keeping with our mandate we had a percussion street band (sailors with boater hats, the Arythmics), a Queen that celebrated our lake, land, and sky, with a Pollution Train to make note of our polluted water. Cardboard boxes as House Hats, and wave costumes with skeletal fish, head pieces all describing our beautiful island community and environment. Our respect for Mother nature created a demand that our band be "fossil-fuel free". Bicycle carts, decked out as our support vehicles, carried fruit and water for the street performers as well as storage for musical instrument cases and covered areas to provide shade from our sometimes very hot August temperatures.

Inspired by the Steel pan carts, Jerry built a band cart that held our "engine room", a drum kit, brake drums and various drums hung of the side. In true Carnival spirit the cart was pushed by various people. The cart also became a large ship or a One Love heart float.

We learned the "Mas Camp" model of working with community members young and old to create a story. We worked in a tent, in the community, and people of all skill levels, sculpted, sewed, cooked, bought costumes and learned to "play their Mas" during dance rehearsals or "Mas Camp Therapy".

Story telling led us to choose traditional Mas as the style to express ourselves within the Carnival Art form. The roots of Carnival lay in the revolution of Emancipation and the French tradition of celebration days, where people were encouraged to make fun of the boss. The characters of Dame Lorraine, Jamette, Jab Jab, Pierrot Grenade, Midnight Robber, Moko Jumbie, Sailor, allowed us to have fun using historical characters to deliver our messages. The Art form was an easy fit as all we were doing was moving the large–scale, outdoor theatrical performances, which we enjoyed in Island Follies, to the street.

1986 saw 11 of us at Carnival in Trinidad working, building three major individuals for Peter Minshall's "Rat Race". We had made it to the "Indy 500 of Street Theatre". We found a culture that treated its Carnival artists with great respect, a culture that worshipped their calypso singers, singing about the politics of life, Trinidad, and the world. We discovered Mas Camps, Steel Drum bands, J'ouvert, Midnight Mas, and Pan yards. In other words an amazing culture rich in the arts of music, dance, costume, and fun. We learned that the music drives the costumes, drives the Mas, giving it energy, we learned how to build large costumes for the people who played the Kings and Queens of the band, most of all we learned how to have fun and play our Mas. A cathartic moment happened during Rat Race in which we were characterized as Money Popes carrying a 15ft long, articulated, MONEY Rat through the streets of Port of Spain. As we came off the stage people yelled, "go back to South Africa, go back to South Africa, (remember Apartheid still lived). We suddenly realized we had "played" our Mas and it had touched our audience.

Island to Island was formed as an artist exchange programme between Shadowland and their associated artists and the Mas of Peter Minshall, our mentor, in Trinidad and Tobago. Two Islands, Two cultures, One Art.

From 1985-2002 we worked with Shadowland and many artists, Canadian, Trinidadian, Tobagonian, and our First Nations creating great pieces of celebratory theatre, in Canada, Trinidad, Tobago, Manitoulin Island, Big Cove in New Brunswick, and productions along the Grand River in Ontario. Within the parade structure we pushed the envelope physically and politically. We built a 5-storey "puppet-tree" of bamboo, wire, and cloth for Trees 'R' Us, to honour the Temeagami Anishnabes's fight to preserve their lands and forest.

A Toronto Island-style J'ouvert was created in 1988. A Fire Parade that wanders through the community. Kathleen Doody learned the art of lantern making and each year people of all ages created their own lanterns and brought them to the parade with the Arythumics providing the acoustic accompaniment.

1988 was a bench-mark year for us with our participation in the Popular summit, a peoples' protest of the G-7. Carnival-style we took to the street with our effigies, costumes, percussion and stilt walkers. The Art kept the energy during the mass arrests and police threats. Wow.

The Island Mas Band, celebrating 'For the Birds', tied for fifth place. Sixty hand stenciled Loon wings, a stilt walker (as the king) Great Blue Heron, night herons, and even a Flamingo, the Arythmics the proverbial oiseau de merde. (Our small percussion band had a protest put against us for not being 'traditional' enough). The band "Down to Earth" had a 400 square foot ground cloth that covered the stadium stage and a telescoping earthworm that rose to 10 meters. The worm appeared again that year in Torontos' first, First Night celebrations. Shadowland worked with the city that year to bring this arts celebration to the city. Carnival appeared on Toronto streets in sub-zero weather.

Each year, a new story and another character and theme that separated us from what we were seeing as 'Interchangable Mas'. There were no other bands like us. The people loved us. "Island—Island", they would cry.

Once the judges were asked why we didn't win and they told us we didn't spend enough money; this we found humorous because we were a small band of artists that didn't have much money and made things from the trash. The next band HAD to be titled 'Money Talks'. We created our own money and made fashion out of it. An exact replica of a large sound truck was carried by the character "Mas Murderer", built using island made bicycle carts. Our King was called "Hey Big Spender" and the Queen was "Big Money Honey"! Caribana didn't find it funny even though people were throwing money at us. In competition, we were out of the money. The next year it was 'Bare Bones', a basic Mud Mas with each player painted red, yellow, or green.

1995 saw the rise of a repressive government in Ontario and Shadowland's artists made a concerted effort to ridicule it. With the band 'Purge a Tory', Shadowland was put out of the money in competition. We were so surprised by this because what we had learned in Traditional Mas in Trinidad, such work was appreciated by the people but not by the judges. In the year 2000, we did "H2-Oh-Oh", making note of and commemorating the deaths that had occurred in the nearby community of Walkerton from tainted water. The government's de-regulation policy was responsible. By 2001, we were screamed at by one of the provincial members who was a judge at the time, to get off the stage, as the black masked sailors of the band, "Ontario for $ale" and their 8 meter long Arythumic percussion brigantine performed a die-in as a midnight robber talked his talk and told the story of provincial corruption. Wow!

In 1989, the great First Nation actor Gary Farmer was our king in Trees 'R" Us. That year, we were invited to the Open Border Celebration commemorating a 1791 treaty between First Nations and the governments of the U.S. and Canada. We raised and lowered this five-story tree at every major vehicle intersection from Niagara Falls, New York to Niagara Falls, Canada. All by "hand" and bicycle cart. Requiring a team of nine, coordinated to raise, lower, and transport this totem to each site along the procession with the Arythumics providing the "driving sound".

Our Carnival /Caribana work taught us the power of large outdoor celebratory parades. For years before Shadowland's Carnival/ Caribana experiences we were part of peace demonstrations, Save Island Homes, and other protests, always feeling like an impotent person shuffling down the street, listening to too many speeches. Then we learned Carnival. Taking over the street, making joyful music, telling stories and having fun while honouring and celebrating life. Cathartic. In Tobago we were called "Carnival Missionaries".

Jerry has said, "participating in Carnival is like a primal scream". The event may be a small local celebration or taking back the streets or jumping up in Carnival but, play your Mas, and when the day is over you can feel the wind blow through your skull. It gives one a great peace of mind. A clarity that refreshes your soul, and lets you get ready for next years celebration.

Jerry and Leida were graciously invited to participate in a conference at York University "Carnival, A People's Art and Taking Back the Streets". We sat on a panel with Charles Roach and Lyndon Phillip. Charles Roach, a much respected elder in Toronto, talked about "Shaping Caribana: How outside forces alter Carnival in Toronto". We learned that a conscious decision was made by the Caribana executive in 1967 to create only Pretty Mas. They felt the Traditional Mas would be misunderstood. Lyndon Phillips expanded on the times, 1967 a year of great hope but lots of racism. We were humbled to discover the reason behind the reluctance of Caribana bands to do political Mas. We also felt proud that we had carried on a tradition. It explained why the real Carnival people loved it, and why the judges could not accept it. Our being a "banned Band" came clear. It is our hope that in these times of change and tolerance that our Carnival community can bring back some their traditions.

The carnival work led us down many paths over the years. Brad Harley left to work with Bread and Puppet and brought back the art of Stilt Walking. Shadowland and Rick/Simon have passed this art onto hundreds of people; once they learn, they pass it on. Swizzle Stick Theatre with Christopher Pinheiro was born from this.

Alice Norton joined Shadowland and brought with her peace activism and connection to the Mic Ma'community of Big Cove, New Brunswick.

The Lysistrata Project was born and produced in the Toronto Island community and at the Wikwemigong, First Nation on Manitoulin Island. The great tree had its final performance and resting place there. In Big Cove an elder told their creation story which became the focus of the work.

First Nation people respect and honour art. We learned that "work with the kids and the people will come". An important lesson was that every community has many stories and this Carnival/Mas art form lets the community tell the tales. Our First nation work led to Buffalo Jump, a celebration on National Aboriginal day

Kathleen Doody continued the Fire Parade, celebrating 20 years last year. She continues to build and teach the making magnificent paper mache lanterns while being a busy Graphic Artist.

Sarah Miller continues her career as general manager of Canadian Environmental Law Association and sits on Shadowland's board.

Whitney Smith continues his Musical and Theatre career.

Brad Harley and his partner Anne Barber continue to operate Shadowland Theatre Inc. bringing Carnival to the Ashkenaz festival, and teaching stilt walking and theatre arts everywhere

Jerry and Leida continue their work for the local community as members of the Toronto Waterfront group, CommunityAir working to close the Toronto City Centre Airport located on Toronto Island. We have just finished our 100th Friday Night vigil, where we played our

Mas, drumming, singing, inspiring and telling a story about waterfront communities under siege. We work with the Misssissaugas of the New Credit First Nation on their land claim. All this done in Carnival style. We also do Critical Mass bicycle rides once a month to bring respect to our Air.

We leave you with a wish, that you grab a shaker or whistle, bang a bottle, put on make up, a costume, free up and feel the power of Celebrating with your community and taking your place on your Streets.

Many Stories, Many Memories

What follows is a Chronological History of Shadowland's Caribana/ Carnival Work

1984	Island to Island -Caribana	
1985	Rat Race - Trinidad	
1986	Water blues for the Late Great Lakes-	
1987	Stone Wars Apocalypso	
1988	Blue nose Band: first large out-door play since Island Follies, Popular Summit, Bread and Puppet brings stiltwalkers	
1989	Trees 'r Us, Open Border	
1990	For the Birds	(Lysistrata I)
1991	Down to Earth	(Lysistrata II)
1992	Our Power Open Border	Grand River
1993	Money Talks River of Fire I	
1994	Bare Bones River of Fire II	
1995	Witch Island	
1996	Star Tribes	
1997	Boycott year	
1998	Purge-a-Tory	banned
1999	It's High Time	Cultural Clowns
2000	H2O-oh	
2001	Ontario For $ail	
2002	One Love Many 'Arts	
2003-2008	Our Blue Devils appear everywhere	

Building the Carnival Arts in Western Canada—The Cariwest Experiment

Donna Coombs-Montrose

Introduction

Edmonton is home to the traditional celebration of carnival arts. The contemporary celebration includes costumes, drama, street dancing, music, street theatre, theatrical and musical performances, singing. The practices imported with Caribbean and other immigrants from diasporic communities, exist in locations where immigrants of a slave/colonial or secular history reside. The 'freed slaves,' in continuing their African traditions combined with imposed religious practices of the colonial masters, have created a New World culture of 'carnival'. Centuries of tradition have fused carnival at the navel of Caribbean and Latin migrants, celebrated annually in every community, every culture, different languages and every nation. New World immigrants from Caribbean and Latin regions, migrating to North America, Europe, and other locations have traveled with their carnival traditions in their souls, in their psyche.

Edmonton is one such location in North America where immigrants have continued and developed the Caribbean carnival art forms. As part of this development, Cariwest, the driving force behind Edmonton's carnival management, has sought to share, to educate, and tutor a new unrelated strata of practitioners in the carnival arts. The first stage of this developmental plan is the academic experiment. In collaboration with the province's University of Alberta, a course is developed for teaching at post-secondary level, taught by some of North America's leading experts in costume development and construction. This paper seeks to report on this process and evaluate the experiment's results.

Background

Cariwest is a non-profit, community based organization registered in Edmonton, Alberta, which sponsors a Caribbean Arts Festival and annually programmes events in the Caribbean/Canadian community. In 2009, Cariwest celebrates its 25th year of consistent activity, recognition, and celebration of Caribbean carnival arts in all their indigenous and professional forms.

The organization was created by a diaspora community, recent arrivants from the Caribbean region in search of support for cultural, social experiences, and heritage. Edmonton, Alberta—the home of Cariwest and its parent organization, Western Carnival Development Association, mirrored the Caribbean arrivants of Toronto and similarly comprised students, domestic servants, new immigrants, workers, and a sprinkling of entrepreneurs. In addition, Alberta attracted scores of experienced oil, natural gas and other workers in heavy industry for work in Alberta's thriving oil patch. As the need for social, cultural, and economic support grew within this nascent community, modest businesses and organizations formed to fill the vacuum. The community's actual carnival-style celebrations began in the 1960s with the participation of university students in campus and public events. But Cariwest was not formed until 1984, as representative of the Caribana of western Canada, a summer 'carnival' that would celebrate and support the culture of Caribbean diasporic citizens, share the food and heritage with new friends and communities, and recognize the achievements of West Indians in Alberta, Canada.

With an objective of building the carnival arts in Edmonton and Alberta, and enhancing Cariwest summer festival, Cariwest developed a Vision Statement that proposed: "To position CARIWEST as a hallmark festival of Caribbean carnival artistic excellence, that excites all peoples, includes all peoples, and generates belonging, pride, and economic benefits for the citizens of the City of Edmonton." The aim of Cariwest is to promote a vibrant Caribbean cultural custom called Carnival. This allows Canadians of all cultural and ethnic backgrounds to share and participate in the 'freedom of expression' manifested in the art forms of Carnival: Mas' (costume design) Steel band, and other Caribbean Music, Creative Dance, and Street Theatre.

Edmonton, Alberta is called the City of Champions and Festival City. There is a festival hosted in Edmonton every single weekend from late Spring to early Fall. Cariwest, the Caribbean Arts Festival stands head and shoulders above our peers for the most attractive parade in the City of Edmonton, its spectacular costumes and artistic productions, its festive Caribbean musical rhythms, and its live music bands and steel band music. For twenty-four years Cariwest has developed and nurtured the best in mas, the best in pan, and the best in kaiso, in western Canada. It has consistently attracted participants to western Canada from Calgary, Fort MacMurray, Seattle/Vancouver, Surrey BC, Burnaby BC, Winnipeg (Manitoba), and other surrounding places and is supported by visitors from Toronto, Seattle, New York, Miami and the Caribbean.

In 2001, the country hosted the World Games in Edmonton. Cariwest was able to feature prominently in several events attached to the World Games, while playing host to the one-hundred-strong-member Jonkanoo Band of the Bahamas, which joined the street parade that year. Similar events have had the support and participation of Cariwest.

Yet despite these innovations, we plateaued out; we had begun to stagnate. Our self-analysis showed that:

a] the City was not attracting new populations of people with Caribbean carnival traditions or origins in any significant quantities.
b] migration outward and death had depleted the population
c] gen-nex was not as interested in the culture of their Caribbean parents
d] many other festivals had developed to compete for the attention of mainstream Canadians etc.

These realities have forced us to re-strategize. As we move towards our 25th anniversary, we have conceived a development plan to sustain our growth and increase participation and interest in the creation of the carnival art forms, with expansion into new communities, institutions, and interest groups, or among new fraternal partners. We saw a critical need for more mas, more understanding and appreciation of mas, more people involved in the creation of bands and, therefore, a community program was needed to support these projections. As a conduit for creating mas, we would offer a credit course at a post-secondary institution; we would hold workshops.

Within this framework, the First International Mas Workshops were hosted at the University of Alberta in Edmonton, Alberta from May 19 to June 11, 2008. In an effort to build a stronger base, we strategically pursued mainstream Canadians, their organizations, their businesses, academics and students of different disciplines, including fine arts, drama, anthropology, engineering, physical education, music and dance, tertiary institutions, and community groups.

Cariwest contracted Geraldo Vieira Snr., engineer and veteran craftsman extraordinaire, and Greta Pitres, Caribbean regional mas craftsman to lead the facilitation team for the workshops. Vieira has won the Trinidad and Tobago competition on nine separate occasions, and has led mas workshops in Toronto, Germany, and throughout the Caribbean. Vieira and Pitres were flown in from Trinidad and Tobago specifically for the workshops, and supported locally by Osmond Edwards Snr., veteran mas producer and winner of Canadian regional competitions on numerous occasions. The facilitators assembled were the best available in mas creation.

The public workshops were housed first at the University of Alberta's Fine Arts and then at the Faculty of Education (Secondary Education) with support from the Faculty of Human Ecology.

For the past twenty-four years, Cariwest's core programming has included mas(querade), steelpan and calypso. The Friday Night Costume Extravaganza or the King and Queen Show has been a featured event, structured around showcasing the larger, elaborately embellished pieces of costumes, designed and built according to themes and involving expert workmanship and creativity. The Kings and Queens would be featured in the Cariwest Saturday Street Parade, the Centrepiece of the festival in a dancing procession along Jasper Avenue, witnessed by thousands of Edmontonians and visitors to our city.

Goals of the Course and Workshops

With the staging of its first International Mas Workshops, Cariwest sought to achieve the following:
- Develop Edmonton as the western center for the carnival arts in Canada
- Include diverse communities in Calgary, Winnipeg, Vancouver, Burnaby, BC, Fort MacMurray, Grand Prairie, and other surrounding places
- Further develop the skills of local and regional artists and costume builders
- Improve Cariwest's place of recognition among the craft-producing and Festival communities of Alberta
- Enhance the fundamental skills of public members involved in mas' production

- Develop a business plan that would allow sections of the community to derive cultural, economic and social benefit on a continuing basis
- Create partnerships with public educational and post-secondary institutions, and with other community organizations
- Establish learning/teaching (for credit) opportunities for tertiary level students through programmes such as the Community Service Learning (CSL) at the University of Alberta

Invitations to Workshops

With this focus in mind, invitations were extended to:

Community Special Interest Cultural Organizations City and Provincial Representatives	Edmonton Community Leagues Media, Art & Design Exposed (MADE) Professional Arts Alliance of Edmonton (PACE), FAVA—Film & Video Arts Society, Visual Arts Alberta Association (VAAA), Alberta College of Art & Design of Calgary, AMAAS—Alberta Media Arts Alliance Society, Theatre Alberta
Schools with Arts and Drama Programs	Louis St. Laurent Junior/Senior High School, Grant MacEwan College, Victoria School of Performing Arts, M. E. Lazerte High School, J. Percy Page High School and University of Alberta— Human Ecology, Department of Fine Arts and Faculty of Education (Secondary Education), as well as Kings University
Fraternal Festivals and their Representatives	Edmonton Folk Music Festival, Works Arts and Design, Fringe Festival, Giuseppe Albi, Northern Alberta International Children's Festival, Dragon Boat Festival, Pride Festival, Capital Ex and International Street Performers Festival

Fraternal Organizations	Jamaican National Association of Alberta, Congress of Canadians of African and Caribbean Heritage, Trinidad & Tobago Cultural Association of Edmonton, Hummingbird Society of Edmonton, Trinidad & Tobago Organettes of Calgary, Barbados-Canadian Association of Edmonton Trinidad & Tobago Cultural Assocation of Calgary, Sykotikmas of Calgary, West Indian Steel Orchestra of Fort MacMurray, Ozzie George Steel Orchestra of Calgary, Politic Live of Edmonton, Trincan Steel Orchestra of Edmonton, Tn'T Boys of Edmonton, Robert Norman & Friends of Burnaby, British Columbia.

Workshop Syllabus

The syllabus(ambitious) prepared for the workshops covered the principles of harness construction, the selection and sourcing of suitable materials and equipment, engineering and construction of a basic large costume for male or female, fundamentals of unaided carriage of a costume, and budgeting, storage, and transportation.

Flexibility and Innovation in Creating 'Mas'

During the period of negotiations with Messrs Vieira and Pitres, from Fall 2007 through Winter 2008, it became very obvious that the limited days and daytime period of the workshops would only achieve limited results. The workshops needed to be reconceptualized for any reasonable goals, or production outcomes to be achieved. Cariwest, therefore, produced a plan to create a prototype costume, one that would serve as an education tool from which a manual would be created, for future construction of a king or queen costume.

The organization, therefore, conceived of a mas band which would demonstrate that any product, theme, or snippet of history topic can be the subject of "mas," and as a tribute to the Province of Alberta, called its mas band:

Cariwest... Alberta Best.

This masquerade band would contain some of Alberta's best known symbols:

Wheat,

Alberta Rose,

Tar Sands,

Prehistoric creatures (Drumheller)

Canola Flowers and

the People of Alberta in all their diversity.

Mr. Vieira considered these symbols and made a determination that 'wheat' would be the subject, the focus, the specificity of our workshops. The prototype queen costume created is named: "Sweet Wheat, a symbol of Alberta, its farmlands, its staple, its history, and its people. This fabulous creation of a queen, resplendent in green and gold, was constructed with fifty-nine parts, twenty-one bees, four-hundred wheat pods, measures sixteen feet tall and twenty four feet wide, and weighs seventy five pounds. As per the rules in the masquerade industry, it cannot be mechanized, but must be carried by the queen of wheat, the individual whose costume it is.

Report

It should be clarified that it requires many months and thousands of laborious hours for the creation of one of these costumes. In true industrial Alberta spirit, we set ourselves the task of constructing this prototype within the extended period of the workshop. Of course, this agenda required us to work until 1am and 2am many days, as is custom in 'carnival' communities when production is approaching its final stages.

We had turned the University of Alberta's teachers' training facility into a Mas Camp, a place where mas is created and constructed, a social and cultural center that brings masqueraders and mas makers together. We were not satisfied to simply absorb a few rudimentary skills for making mas. In the minds of some workshop participants, the creation of a harness was not sufficient proof to justify this vitally important experience. No! We were reaching for the ultimate goal of creating a magnificent costume from start to finish. And, thus, "Sweet Wheat" was born. It is comprised of sixty detachable parts, and includes four-hundred gigantic wheat pods of green and gold, decorated with wheat flora and fauna, with twenty-one gigantic bees embellishing the wheat content. "Sweet Wheat" measures 16 feet high, is 24 feet wide and 14 feet in depth.

Between May 19 and June 11, fifty-one attendees participated in Western Canada's First International Mas Costume Construction Workshop, proudly sponsored by Cariwest, Edmonton Arts Council and TransAlta. Registrants and volunteers contributed 7,000 hours to the creation of the prototype Queen costume, affectionately called "Sweet Wheat." The product of the classroom/workshop experience had its first public viewing and performance at the Cariwest Costume Extravaganza on August 8, 2008. It was loudly and proudly applauded by 63,000 spectators who lined Edmonton's route on Saturday August 9, 2008 for the annual Cariwest parade. As a testimony to its impact, Albertans, particularly from farming and rural communities, have complimented Cariwest on and strongly identified with the concept of this provincial tribute in masquerade. Cariwest was then invited to display this community achievement at the Edmonton International Airport, where "Sweet Wheat" stood in tribute from August of 2008 until February 2009!

This experiment was considered extremely successful, having achieved its major goals: in particular, building academia in community through costume construction; creating an appreciation for the contributions to Canada's cultural landscape; recognition of the heritage of our diaspora community, including our youth; and developing or enhancing the skills of a new group of Canadian artisans.

Plans are currently underway for the Spring/Summer 2009 Costume Construction credit courses offered through the Faculty of Education at the University of Alberta

5

❖❖

STEELPAN AND CARNIVAL

Why They Play Pan: Steel Band Communities in the GTA

Karen Cyrus

The steel pan, a musical icon of the carnival diaspora, has penetrated far beyond its original ethnic confines to countries such as Poland, Switzerland and China. Though its presence in Canada is most visible at events such as Caribana, amateur and semi-professional steel bands may be heard and seen at smaller street festivals in and around the Greater Toronto Area (GTA) throughout the year. This paper examines the significance of music making for amateur steel bands in the GTA. First, I will describe the social context of these bands and the various tenets of the steel band community in the GTA. Secondly, I will present the theoretical framework that guided my analysis of data, namely, the concepts of community (Ansdell 2004; Buber 2002) and the meaning of music (Rice 2001; Small 1998). I will then discuss the social roles that these bands strive to fulfill as they make music within their respective communities. In addition, I hope to acknowledge and create awareness of the significance of music making for the people that maintain an aural remnant of the carnival season throughout the year.

Context and fieldwork

Toronto and the GTA are often described as a mosaic of diverse cultures with each ethnic group celebrating its culture throughout the year in order to maintain a sense of identity with its homeland. Although the steel pan has been embraced by several nations, I found that in Toronto and the GTA, the steel pan was played mainly by persons of West Indian background, with the exception of steel bands in public schools and at York University, where the members in the pan group were more culturally diverse. As an avid fan of steel band, but a newcomer to Toronto, I was curious to know the extent to which pan was played in the GTA. I set on a trail to find the places and spaces where this instrument was played through searches on the Internet, several cold calls, and referrals from one location to the next. This investigation carried me to many diverse places and spaces in the GTA including schools, a church, and a seniors' recreational center. I spoke to members of the bands, organizers, and, in some instances, I merely observed the groups.

The steel bands in Toronto and the GTA may be placed in two broad groups, amateur bands and semi-professional bands. The main signifier of the semi-professional band is that they usually have a performing name like 'Afro Pan' or 'Pan Fantasy,' and they focus on performing at yearly festivals such as Caribana. On the other hand, amateur groups are known by the name of the organization or institution with which they are affiliated or sponsored, such as a school, community center, or church. There are also solo pan players from the semi-professional bands who are hired to play for functions throughout the year.

Other members of the steel band community include arrangers, teachers, mentors, tuners, organizers and fans. The arranger composes scores for the professional and amateur bands. The mentors or master teachers train aspiring teachers. Another crucial member of this community occupies an ancillary position; that is the tuner. The tuner tunes the steel pans and is especially vital to the amateur group as beginner pannists are likely to beat the pan out of tune frequently. Organizers are the liaison between a sponsoring organization or hosting institution and the amateur band. The organizer hires the teachers to train the band, coordinates group activities, and performs other administrative duties pertinent to the band. Finally, there is the audience, the fans of steel pan music. Steel pan fans, though great admirers of the music, often have no desire to play the instrument. The rationale behind this is that if they join a band, they are limited to the repertoire that their band plays for the season. However, if they are not a part of a group, they can visit other bands and sample different repertoires to their heart's content.

Spaces and Places of Pan

After nine months of visiting and observing several steel bands I was impressed by two elements: the demographic profiles of the pan groups, and the ways in which the band members spoke about their musical activity. The first group that I observed was in the music department at York University: a steel band that is a performance course called

Caribbean Ensemble. Learning to play pan is a year long course for credit and the students, who are mostly young adults, perform mainly within the university community.

Searches on the Internet resulted in websites which were mostly defunct; one call, however, produced a live voice, the leader of a semi-professional steel band in Toronto.[1] He graciously allowed me to sit in on their practices and to accompany him to one of the many classes that he teaches in six public schools across Toronto. Another article from the Internet mentioned a female pan player and the location where she learned to play pan, a church in Scarborough. I visited this church and interviewed the organizer of the band.

This steel band is in a church in Toronto

A call back from my initial plethora of cold calls based on Internet links resulted in an impromptu phone interview with the leader of another semi-professional group and the director of a music school for steel pan in Toronto. Visits with this group were insightful as the students, mainly older adults, were very eager to share their reasons for wanting to learn to play pan at a later stage in life. A referral from one of the students at this school led me to a very elderly pan teacher in Oakville, who also trained other teachers and tuned pans. Another referral led to a group of seniors in Halton, whose members were also quite enthusiastic about playing pan.

I encountered pan players and steel bands in other spaces and places in the GTA. I attended a function at the Jamaica Canadian Association, where the music was provided by a pan soloist. Here, I was able to observe the response of the audience to the music and speak to the

---

1   A very informative website is: http://www.panonthenet.com/world/canada/bands_listing.htm

pannist when he took a break from playing. Also, at the annual Santa Claus parade in the GTA, a steel band on a float carries the sound of pan down Yonge Street. This teacher and his students have played pan in the parade every year since 2001.

A steel band on a float in a Santa Claus parade in the GTA

The meaning of music

Christopher Small advocates that music is primarily "something that people do" (Small 1998, 2, 8); the "people" are all who contribute to the creation and performance of music, including those who listen or respond to it. In Small's definition, music is a verb: *"to music is to take part, in any capacity, in a musical performance, whether by performing, by listening, by rehearsing or practicing, by providing material for performance (what is called composing), or by dancing"* (9). Small proposes that music-making, which he calls *musicking,* results in the formation of relationships or associations between people, that is the creation of community (3).

Small examines the public scope of music-making. Timothy Rice, however, explores the metaphoric significance of *musicking.* Rice argues that music, or a musical activity, may be functioning as an art — a text or object; an emotional expression — "the surface manifestation of inner emotions," such as happiness, rage, nostalgia, sorrow or contentment; a social behaviour — a demonstration of the establishment of a type of relationship, such as intimacy; or commodity — a commercial item (Rice 2001, 24). Rice purports that these conceptualizations about the function and purpose of music, the metaphors, are always present whenever people gather to make music (24). Rice also states that sometimes more than one metaphor is at play in music-making as each person may have a different reason why he or she is taking part in the activity. Perceiving the metaphors is important as they help us to understand the actions of people and these metaphors can be based on what people say about the musical activity.

Based on my observations at the practices and performances of steel bands around the GTA, there is usually an objective for the group coming together that is indicative of a dominant metaphor or set of metaphors. Therefore, I have grouped Rice's metaphors under two broad headings: *process* metaphors — music as an emotional expression and music as social behaviour; and *product* metaphors — music as art and music as commodity. I will refer to process metaphors to indicate those instances when the main objective of music making is an emotional expression or social behaviour. On the other hand, product metaphors indicates those instances when the main objective of music-making is attaining (listening, playing, creating, or purchasing) a quantity or quality of music.

The difference between process and product metaphors is most apparent in the question that many irate teachers have asked a distracted and chatty class: "Are we here to talk to our friends or to play/listen/learn this music?" When a steel band or any music venture is organized as a way for people to spend time together, the answer to the irate teacher is "we're here to talk to our friends!" and the objective of the venture is achieved when the persons come together. Conversely, product metaphors are dominant when the objective of the music-making venture is the perpetuation of the music, and the answer to the teacher is: "We're here for the music...we can socialize afterwards."

The following are two other examples that demonstrate the preeminence of one type of metaphor. Auxiliary members of staff at a college decided to start a pan group for fun, relaxation, and another way to spend time together. Metaphors such as emotional expression (nostalgia, by some) and music as art or commodity (by the teacher) were present. The objective of this venture, however, was the process: music as social behaviour, as the formation of the group demonstrated a solidarity with its members and a desire to spend time with each other. In another instance, students in a school joined the band to increase their skill in playing pan. For most of the term, students played together by necessity, relationships remained surface, and few friends were made in this group; the focus was learning to play the instrument and obtaining a passing grade for playing. While other metaphors may have been present, the dominant emphasis of this venture was the product—music as art or commodity—as the purpose for the class, and joining the group was the acquisition of a skill, not the kindling of relationships.

Types of communities

The idea that making music, *musicking*, creates community is in tangent with the fluid notion of community as described by Martin Buber: "community is where community happens" (Buber 2002, 37). Indeed there are four types of communities that have been exposited in anthropology and sociology: communities of place, communities of hope, communities of circumstance, and communities of interest (Ansdell 2004, 77). A community of place consists of persons who share the same space; they belong to the same community because of proximity or geography; here, community is associated with a location. In communities of hope or utopia, persons come together because they share the same utopian values, which may also be religious. A community of circumstance refers to persons who are together because they are in the same institution because of incarceration, hospitalization, or schooling. Communities of interest refer to persons who come together because of a similarity in identity which may be based on gender, age, culture, or a shared craft.

In my own fieldwork, I have noticed that when a community decided to engage in a short or long term music-making venture, such as a steel band, it resulted in the formation of a community within a pre-existing community. Additionally, I noticed that there were two types of communities likely to be formed based on music-making: a community of hope that focuses on the process of music-making, or a community of interest that focuses on the product of music-making; this is demonstrated in the diagram on the opposite page.

In a community that emphasizes process, the focus is the welfare of the people; music-making is subservient to the community and is used for social therapy and/or political action. On the other hand, in a community that emphasizes product, the concern is the perpetuation and preservation of the object or skill, such as fan clubs and performing ensembles. Here, the focus is likely to be on the quality and quantity of the music. Thus, the community is subservient to the music.

Observations

I will describe three of my encounters with the steel band community to demonstrate how process or product metaphors were manifested. I will also list some similarities between bands that had the same type of metaphors.

A COMMUNITY WITHIN A COMMUNITY

Community
of hope

Community of
circumstance

Community
of place

Community
of interest

Music Making Ventures
creates

community

that focuses
on one or
a combination of

Hope: building community and
social awareness

Interest: making music

The focus is on the process of music
making; the music is subservient to
the community.

Metaphors:

- music as a social behaviour
- music as an emotional expression

Types of activities:

- mobilization for political action
- social therapy

The focus is on the product of music
making; the community is subservient to the music

Metaphors:

- music as an art
- music as a commodity

Types of activities:

- fan clubs
- amateur and professional ensembles
- schools

Product metaphor: music as art

I observed a semi-professional steel band which consisted of a group of culturally diverse young adults, former students of a particular school. The room was filled with pictures showing their tours abroad, and certificates showing prizes won at various competitions. At the time of my visit, the band was practicing an original arrangement composed by their teacher/captain. The practice time was intense and focused on 'getting it right.' The emphasis of the musical activity was more on the product (the quality of the music) than the process of being together. However, after the practice, some of the band members seemed happy to share time with their alumni. The cohesiveness of the group suggested that though their musical activity was art, there were also some social behaviours associated with their meeting, possibly to relive the fellowship of their past association, within a community of circumstance.

Process metaphor: music as social behaviour

A church in Toronto formed a steel band as an outreach program. The band members and organizers shared the same cultural identity. The repertoire of the band was based on religious hymns and cantatas, which supported religious observances and festivals of their faith. Their music activity may be classified as social behaviour, because playing in the band signaled an interest in the music ministry and a possible entrance into the church community. The musical activity may also be considered an emotional expression of nostalgia, because the band members and, mostly diasporic, congregation reconstructed the environment of their native home.

Combination: commodity, art and emotional expression

I observed a pan soloist at a function attended by mainly West Indian guests. The soloist used backing tracks as an accompaniment for his playing, which included "Lady in Red," "Three Little Birds," and "Guantanamera." The audience swayed and swooned during his performance. The pan player was hired to play for the function, therefore his performance was a service and the music, a commodity. The music was also an art symbol for the hostess (who wanted to use it to create a Caribbean ambience); and for those who basked in nostalgia, listening to the music was an emotional expression.

Comparisons

Through observation, I noted the following:

The bands whose focus was the product of music-making (as an art or commodity) had a membership that was culturally diverse. These were the semi-professional bands and steel band classes within a school.

The bands whose focus was on the process had a membership that was homogenous in some way; they shared a similar identity, whether age or cultural background. This is to be expected because amateur steel bands usually operate within another type of community that 'hosts' or sponsors the band. For amateur bands, music making was usually a social behaviour such as social therapy, social cohesion within the group and, at times, outreach to build the community membership. The music performed by these communities was simpler with a repertoire suited to the occasion, season, or interest of the hosting community.

The attitudes of the teachers also differed, based on the dominant metaphor of the band. When the emphasis was the product—music as art—the band captain/teacher was more intense in teaching. Conversely, teachers of the amateur bands were less intense. The teachers recognised that a light atmosphere was primary to the community's objective and welfare. As one teacher commented: "I don't shout, I just let them take their time, because they come together to have fun." The attitude of the teacher was that the music was subservient to the community. To ensure sufficient progress in learning to play the instrument, that teacher provided the members with learning aides for further practise at home.

The musical metaphor also affected how I, as a researcher, interacted with each type of community. If the band came together to create music as an art or commodity, I felt that I needed to be as invisible as possible so as not to disturb the flow of the practise. If, however, they came together to create music as a social behaviour, I was expected to at some level to take part in the activity, by playing along with the group and supporting their public performances.

The members of amateur 'process' groups were generally more interested in talking about why they were playing steel pan and their experience with the music 'back home' than with the skill of playing. They were also highly sensitive about my note taking while they performed, as, unfortunately, they believed their playing was being assessed. On the other hand, the members of the 'product' groups did not seem to notice that I was among them.

Conclusion

The number of steel bands in Toronto and the GTA is apparent from the yearly competition 'Pan Alive,' which is part of the Caribana Festival. I visited eight groups over a period of nine months, and there were still bands that I did not manage to see. However, the time that I spent observing these steel bands was insightful, and what I learnt about the types of communities and the metaphors at work have helped me to understand a variety of behaviours that I have witnessed in other musical spaces. These principles may also be useful for persons who teach, or intend to teach, amateur steel bands.

Works Cited

Ansdell, Gary. 2004, "Rethinking music and community: theoretical perspectives in support of community music therapy." In *Community Music Therapy*. Mercedes Pavlicevic and Gary Ansdell eds. London: Jessica Kingsley. 65-88.

Buber, Martin. 2002 (1948). *Between man and man*. Translated by Roland Gregor-Smith. New York: Routledge.

Rice, Timothy. 2001. "Reflections on Music and Meaning: metaphor, signification and control in the Bulgarian case." *British Journal of Ethnomusicology* 10.1: 19-38.

Small, Christopher. 1998. *Musicking: The meanings of performing and listening*. Hanover: University Press of New England.

Pan-Around-Neck Steel Band Tradition, The London Notting Hill Carnival, and the Concept of Community Cohesion in the UK

Lionel McCalman

For over four decades, the pan-around-neck traditional steelbands have placed themselves as the cornerstone in the Notting Hill Carnival. Bands like The Russell Henderson Steel Band, Nostalgia Steel Band, and The Tony Charles Steel Band forged ahead an agenda that politically mobilised the UK Caribbean people to embrace the systematic dynamics of this cultural art-form. In this paper I will argue that the pan-around-neck genre is a particular inclusive vehicle to promote community cohesion, as it includes all the elements for intra-cultural bonding. I will also argue that the old-fashioned conveyance is not just reassuring, but its ability to intrigue audiences and to entertain humans in streets, matches its pulling power to the many (culturally diverse) people who embrace it.

The Notting Hill Carnival, predominantly a Caribbean styled festival celebrates the diversity and the blends of history through an 'island' perspective, a poly-ethnic fair with undercurrents of self-volition and contradictions. To some, it encompasses 'bonds of slavery'. Naipaul (1989), cited in Nixon (1991) conveyed a disdain for the Caribbean carnival expression, calling it "a version of the lunacy that kept the slave alive". This is probably a minority view, as many commentators, (Cohen 1993) (Barnes 2000) were more concerned with delving into the socio-cultural, political and power dynamics of carnival. This paper will set out, firstly, to examine the cultural history of the Notting Hill Carnival, and the Pan-around-neck steel band tradition, through an extensive analytical literature, exploring the issues of carnival and the steel pan, and how it adds to the pervasiveness of policy discourse around community cohesion and integration. Secondly, I will explore the relationship between the Notting Hill Carnival and the pan-around-neck steel band, as one of carnival's enduring disciplines.

The pan-around-neck steel band is a marching band that encompasses a creative vision within different cultural components. It is employed in regional festivals, wedding celebrations, protest marches, funeral processions, corporate functions, workshops and carnivals.

Reviewing Trinidad Carnival's contribution to popular culture, Ho identifies the distortions of "...the enterprise of empire building in the past and nation building in the present, precisely because of its ability to articulate emotions and its capacity to connect us to a wider world" (Ho 2000, 3). No less obvious, a glaring omission of these claims is the carnival as an avenue for personal expressions of social rebellion. From its origin in the carnival, it generated considerable controversy as a highly charged political event—invoking anarchy and challenging the status quo through its focus on the collective power struggle (Cohen 1980) and the development or otherwise of working-class consciousness (Russell 1993). The cultural landscape of 1960s Britain could be characterised by increased immigration from the Caribbean, some class/ social resentment from some aspects of the white working class, which correlated significantly with pride of one's own cultural capital. Within this paradigm, each sub-cultural group within the Caribbean community, took it upon themselves to organise around a single carnival discipline, mapping out their own interpretations of these, and rehabilitating the image of African and Caribbean societies, both in the eyes of Caribbean and non-Caribbean people.

The most enduring characteristic of the Notting Hill carnival is its conservatism in sticking with the established form. The disciplines, Costume (mass bands), Calypso, Steel bands, Soca sound systems (both mobile and static) made up the strands of influence within carnival culture. But is this culture a direct result of the African heritage? And does the evidence lead to a culture brought over in the Middle Passage and preserved—maybe modified in religion, folklore, satire, social commentary, or even in political and economic forms?

In the Caribbean, there is a time honoured tradition that when it comes to established forms of cultural practices, musical expression, folklore, etc, community identity demands that respect is due. Tracing an African cultural origin, from the drum, to Tamboo Bamboo, then onto the steel pan—the consensus is—pan goes back to its African roots, to Shango and the African Orisha (gods)—and the drum rhythm that evokes them (Grant 1999, 2). More recently, with an increasing understanding of scientific knowledge, the influences of globalisation and the 'psychological' state on the utilization of educational knowledge, traditions are sometimes forgotten and abandoned. Some practices, e.g. the pan-around-neck steel band tradition seems to be neglected, or even relegated to pasture-land, and to the traditionalists, this conjures up all kinds of emotions that are too deep for words. *We stand by our tradition.*

The established practice of clinging to the past can be immensely reassuring, as 'traditions' involve continuity with the past, rather than just the restoration of a given practice, after a break. As Terry (1995) explains,

> It sees the past extending unnoticed into the present—and projects a naive viewpoint: The more deeply a tradition is rooted in the subconscious, the more listeners perceive change as destructive rather than evolutionary. What had previously appeared to them as self-evident truths, to be taken for granted, is suddenly being challenged by a new set of norms (Terry 1995, pp. 30).

Another paradigm explained by Terry, is that of 'Restoration' which seeks to renew contract with a tradition. This presupposes that the tradition was broken, and a link is now being sought which would restore the glories of the past and redeem the present situation. This, attempt at a restoration, the author contends, brings with it 'an aura of sentimentality'. The presence of a third phase—which the author conceptualizes as 'conservatism', sets out to preserve existing traditions. The starting point of this investigation was to test the validity of the 'Pan-around-neck' steel band tradition by seeing how the subsequent course of this tradition has impacted on other European cultures, i.e. Swiss and German steel bands, who have developed a special affinity to this art-form, and are part of a radical movement to preserve it, having themselves been introduced to the 'pan-around-neck' tradition by Trinidadian musicians. The paper, appropriately titled, *We stand by our tradition* surveys the cordial landscape of the steel band in Carnival, and contends that this disowning of the past by Caribbean pan players, could result in a cultural sensation of severance.

Western musical traditions are seen as the standard from which others are judged. However, we must ask to what extent we are justified in applying Western concepts and methodologies of historical-social musical investigation in other cultural contexts. The steel pan musical genre was previously seen as an inversion of this trend since it is Trinidad's gift to the Western world. The Notting Hill Carnival is Europe's biggest street festival and brings its own 'new immigrant perspective' to contemporary British life (Ferris 2005), (Thompsett 2005).

Crowley in an attempt at an explanation of the origins of carnival, contends that, "... the street parade, the masks, effigy-burning, the transvestitism, the political and social satire, even the throwing of water, flower, powder, ... dates back to the Classical world. Huge horse-drawn floats representing ships were reported in early Medieval Spain" (1999, 218). One might argue he has not gone back far enough, and that the characteristics he refers to could be found in Ancient Africa, where carnival originated (Nehusi 2000). He demonstrates that in the earliest known records from the Nile Valley, there were festivals, which displayed all the elements of carnival. These practices were taken to Europe and Europeans added their own dynamics to these festivals. In an age which values African Culture more highly than before, Crowley's opinions might seem a bit out of touch with reality, and indeed some might even view his comments as an example of intellectual imperialism.

Too much has being made of our carnival's connections to Western traditions. Steel Bands are now referred to as 'Steel Orchestras' and in every pan competition, the classical rendition finds itself alongside the perquisite 'soca' and 'calypso' selections. The steel orchestras are seen as 'progressive', as they convey something larger about the shift in Caribbean's consciousness towards the literary minded professional listener, and away from the 'un-refined' culture of working people. As Caribbean people seek to extend their own way of life to encompass others, it would seem to me, in contrast with that of the Western tradition than seek to bring all others under its existing boundaries.

History of the Steel Band in Europe

The Genesis

The history of the steel pan is the story of 'man's ingenuity in trying to get beauty out of something that is absolutely waste product' (Noel 1998, 25). The waste product being referred to here is the oil drum which was available in abundant quantities in Trinidad and Tobago, after the Second World War. Around 1945, local craftsmen began to experiment with these abandoned fuel drums that seemed to be everywhere on the island, and the resulting product was the steel pan. This instrument soon replaced the Tamboo Bamboo as the musical instrument of choice in the annual carnival held every year on 1st August (Emancipation Day). This was the most important celebration as it commemorated the liberation of the black slaves from chattel slavery in 1833. Due to the British colonial administration's suspicions of the islanders' motives, Tamboo Bamboo was suppressed by the island's police force, and this paved the way for the emergence of this innovation, the steel pan (Stuempfle 1995). The origins of the pan lie in the quest for rhythm (Ho 2000), and the technology went through many experimental phases; namely, dustbins, biscuit tins, petrol cans, etc, before the oil drum became the main raw material for pan manufacturing, and the steel band was born.

The steel pan came to Britain in 1951, with TASPO, The Trinidad all Steel Percussion Orchestra, the first steel band to leave the Caribbean and tour the European continent. The twelve musicians (pioneers of this musical genre) arrived in London in time for the Festival of Britain, and the band was well received by the British population. Considering that this was only six years after the invention of the instrument, it is a testament to the rapid progress that was made through the sharing of ideas, co-operation and technological innovation of the early pioneers.

Insights into the development of musical forms, patterns and ideas can be obtained by anthropological research, enabling us to see how individuals and communities have co-operated to develop new ideas parallel with, or diametrically away from the prevailing wisdom of the day, allowing us to test our assumptions about the developmental processes at work. Rennie (1999) pointed out that every time an idea emerged, other pan men would pick it up—experiment with it and improve on it, and the resulting technique would itself be picked up by others who would in turn carry out further improvements to the existing structures and forms. The steel pan is therefore not the work of a single individual but the resulting product of an entire pan community.

In the United Kingdom, TASPO's legacy was a symbolic appreciation of the Caribbean's musical expression through the steel pan, not only for its mockery of the classical tradition, but also for the way it converted derogatory stereotypes into attributes of power (Dudley 2002). Russell Henderson and Sterling Betancourt formed the first steelband in 1952, The Russ Henderson Steel Band (later to be renamed Nostalgia Steel Band), was the only steelband to take part in the first Notting

Hill Carnival (1965). The carnival begun with the pan-around-neck tradition—the most pervasive symbol of decadence within the colonies, and a symbol of rebellion against the long established colonial power. Its introduction into the United Kingdom made it the ideal art form for all festivals and carnivals, as well as high society balls at Cambridge/Oxford Universities and at Buckingham Palace. In carnivals and festivals, musicians and spectators mingled together and many on-lookers joined the procession, participating through the beating of iron (metal beating) or other such implements of percussion. Sterling Betancourt is also accredited with introducing the steelband to Switzerland which was instrumental in the spread of the steel band movement in Europe. All the earlier steel bands were mobile units with options for static performances. The instruments were made from carefully selected drums and stood the test of time. As Achong (1999) pointed out:

> With regards to steel quality, today's drums do not compare favourable with older drums of the 1960s and 1970s. Recycled material? The fact is, the present drums are made to meet the minimum needs of the manufacturers and users. Pan-making is not one of those needs. When pans were invented, the drums carried heavy crude oil. Now one finds drums made to carry Vaseline and light oils being used for pans. They are made of soft thin steel that dent and deform easily. These drums were made as disposal items that would biodegrade quickly in dumps. Can they be expected to make quality, long lasting pans? (Achong 1999, pp4).

While the steel band is experiencing an up-turn in schools and communities, the pan-around-neck steel band tradition is certainly in decline in the United Kingdom. It is a practice or style of playing the steel pan which involves carrying the full weight of the instrument, either around the necks of musicians, or supported from the shoulders. The single pan instruments are usually suspended by straps from four areas, which forms a harness allows the panist to play her/his instrument with both hands. A pan-around-neck steel band is a single pan ensemble and, with the exception of the tenor/soprano pans and the second pans, the instruments are usually not fully chromatic. This method first became acceptable practice in the early 1950s, after it was introduced by Villaroel, a pan player from Tunapuna. As reported by Rennie (1999):

> before TASPO departed to Britain, the tenor men then, held
> the pan on their laps with one hand, and played with the free

hand until one Villaroel, from the Tunapuna/ Tacarigua area came and exhibited to them the use of straps around the neck and the two stick dexterity that it facilitated (1999, 3).

The pan-around-neck tradition became very popular in the steel pan fraternity, and the innovation was described as …'within days everyone was on to it and …. It was widespread, … almost nationwide' (Rennie 1999, p.4). However, it has long been overtaken by new experimentation, new inputs of technology, new ideas and scientific advancement, that few of today's maestros and virtuoso-players seem interested in. Today, in the United Kingdom, The Nostalgia Steel Band is probably the only remaining traditional pan-around-neck steel band that is wholly dedicated to the preservation of this art form. *We stand by our tradition.*

By the mid 1960s, newer London steel bands started to emerge; Melody Makers, Blue Notes, Bay 57, Tropicana, Max Cherrie and the Cherrie Pickers, The Tony Charles Steel Band. Most of the musicians in the emerging bands were Trinidadians. In 1961 The Dixieland Steel Band (the 'white College Boys' band'), was making history back in Trinidad. This band still is the only steel band to win all the four sections of the music festival, i.e. The Zone Finals, Quarter Finals, Semi-Finals and Finals, in the home of the steel band, Trinidad and Tobago. As a reward for their achievement, they were offered the opportunity to come to England to perform over the Whitsun Bank Holiday weekend, 1961. Many of the touring Dixieland musicians made the UK (London in particular) their home and continued playing the steel pan as professional musicians on the gig scene (La Rose and McCalman 2003). Miguel Baradas, Fred Toussaint, Curtis Pierre, Trevor Cumberbatch, Peter Joseph and Russell Valdez were among the celebrated musicians to join the Caribbean Diaspora in the UK. Other Trinidadian bands toured the UK, e.g. The Pan-Am North Stars Steel Orchestra, and the number of musicians joining the diaspora grew. Besides the growth of the steel band movement in London, there were also positive signs in Coventry, Birmingham, Manchester, Bath and Leeds. The steel bands that emerged there could match the quality of the London bands, namely, Metronome, Ebony Steel Orchestra, Paddington Youth (later renamed the London All Stars Steel Band). Mangrove steel orchestra emerged from a very small pan-around-neck steel band to become a power-house in the British steelband fraternity. Mangrove is also a costume (mass) band with its brilliant workings of creative themes and aesthetic expressions—and boasts a very large fan-base in the carnival scene.

The multiplicity of carnivals in the UK required an injection of Caribbean music and this led to smaller pan-around-neck steel bands making their mark on the scene. At the early Notting Hill Carnivals, many of the Trinidadian musicians now resident in the UK, would turn out for one of the two pan-around-neck steel bands, namely, Nostalgia Steel Band and Tony Charles Steel Band. In the case of Nostalgia Steel Band, they would turn up with their instruments, and treat the carnival as a jam session. Most would learn the arranged carnival tunes during the long procession (not having attended the practice sessions) and most saw the event as a bonding session with friends. Practice sessions before the carnival became necessary, in an attempt to maximize innovation and creativity. Though the rhythms became more complex and the chord progression added new dimensions to the music, the players treated the event as a relaxed social event, to drop in and out as they pleased. The more change was introduced; the more things remained the same.

As the members of Nostalgia Steel Band in the 1980s and 1990s were largely gig-men, Carnival day was always predictable. It was not uncommon for the steel band to return to the pan-yard, after the carnival procession, with only half of the musicians that started out along the carnival route; the others having left the band during the procession. Every one understood the situation. They had left to fulfil an obligation to a client. After all, they had to earn their crust, and carnival days were no exception.

The demise of the pan-around-neck tradition

A number of factors mitigate against the pan-around-neck tradition.

(1) The first is the belief that the steel pan sounds better on stands than they do around the torso of the individual. If sound is the determining factor, then this is probably a very understanding reaction against the genre. However, this is not always true. It is without doubt a different sound that traditional bands have, but the quality and texture of the pans also have a lot to do with it.

(2) Second, many believe that the pressure of carrying this additional burden (the weight of the steel pan) is not worth it, when the end product is taken into consideration. A pan-around-neck steel band is limited in its musical range, being a 'single-pan band'. Double-instruments cannot be used as such, so that the full range of the steel pan instruments cannot be achieved. It is true that a conventional steel band

with its triple Chellos, double tenors/ seconds and guitar pans have a different tonal quality—as is factored into the steel pan manufacturing process. A clearly distinguishing factor is the fact that conventional instruments are heavier, having been made by drums that are thicker-gauged. Most traditional steel bands are more careful to acquire lighter (thinner-gauged) drums as the players need to carry these drums for lengthy periods/ long distances.

(3) Many pan observers and commentators believe that people do not want to go back to pan-around-neck steel bands because they see this as harping back to the past. Progress involves increasing efficiency, faster rhythms, louder steel pans, and more complex arrangements; ingredients that are not always evident in pan-around-neck bands.

(4) There are more females playing the steel pan today than ever before. Taking this factor into consideration, the pan-around-neck tradition may not be an attractive musical journey for women and girls.

A Narrative on Pan

I have been a member of a traditional steel band for over twenty years. My first contact with a pan-around-neck steel band was at the carnival (Mashramani) celebrations in Guyana, as a boy of seven or eight. We would stand by the street corners and watch the bands as they played their way through the procession. There were steel bands on trucks, playing their music from the high platforms that this allows. There were bands on racks, pulled along by a well drilled team of efficient pushers and supporters. The pans were suspended from the racks—with three feet of walking space for each musician. This allowed the children (and spectators) to get close enough to see the players display their skills at ground level. However the metal racks did present a boundary and the bands were, to put it mildly, very regimental. Then there were the pan-around-neck bands which, in my opinion—were the real attraction within the parades. We, the audience could stand shoulder to shoulder with the players, and we were not prevented in any way from touching them, looking at them as they played. A few of the players even allowed selected children to 'have a go' on their instruments, an open gesture that would not be seen anywhere else within the steel pan fraternity.

We had what I would describe as a musical environment at home. None of my parents were musically trained but there was always singing, and musical activity in our home. We were encouraged to play a musical instrument, and of my four other siblings, only one is not

225

today actively involved as a performing musician. Three of us are pan musicians and a fourth sibling is a late convert to the genre.

The Notting Hill Carnival; Steel Band and Community Cohesion

In 2005, The Notting Hill Carnival was adopted as an 'Icon of England... and Englishness' and now holds a central position alongside other icons... such as the flag of St. George; Hadrian's Wall; Pride and Prejudice; Blackpool Tower; The Globe theatre; Cricket; .... and the mini-skirt. Popular culture aside, it is clear that recognition is not given for its strategic role in popular culture in the UK. The Notting Hill Carnival contributes up to £93m each year to London's economy and supports the equivalent of 3,000 full-time jobs. 1.16 million people who attend Carnival spend a total of £45m over three days (Nindi 2005). The Carnival, as well as being a powerful symbol of 'community', is also a unique brand of modern carnival aestheticism that resonates across the world.

It is widely accepted that community cohesion, as a concept today, provides the impetus for interaction (Gilson and Dewpoy 2000, 213) and explains the power of communities to operate and develop in accord together than in warfare. It is strongly connected to concepts of equality and diversity, a sense of closeness, affection, love, and social bond at the level of interaction. For these reasons, "... community cohesion then, becomes established on the basis of trying to create shared experiences and values, rather than continuing to entrench separation and to recognise and reinforce differences" (Cantle 2005, 11). However, the debate around community cohesion has become more entranced as opposing sides debate its capacity to connect us to a wider and more globalised and hegemonic world.

One argument—put forward by detractors claim that: "the whole trust of community cohesion represents the death of multiculturalism—of any acceptance of cultural pluralism and a lurch back to the 'assimilationism' of the early 1960s, which assumes that immigrants must abandon their distinctive ethnic cultures to become British" (Kundani 2000, cited in Tomas 2007, 436).

In exploring the relationship between carnival and community cohesion, it is essential to identify the communities that support it, within competing racial, ethnic and class loyalties.

Over 40% of Londoners in the 2001 census were not white British.

The increase in this component of the population is set to continue, making London one of the most diverse cities on the planet.

With a disposal wealth on over £32billion in the UK our ethnic minority communities are becoming an ever increasing market.

Mixed raced relationships are now so common place (1 in 10 children in Britain now live in such households) that one prediction is that some ethnic groups, particularly Caribbean, will virtually disappear (Burton, Nandi & Platt, 2008).

Community cohesion (a new government concept within race relations), asked a number of questions and came up with clear answers. 'What would it take for all groups in our society to have a vested interest in each other'? 'How can we assist the process in getting people to get on with each other, and therefore—develop a shared common identity'? 'Is our society being fragmented by people not mixing outside their groups'? (Worley 2005, 2). Consequently, the idea of a 'common vision and a sense of belonging' seem to be the main tenant of the policy. Can the Notting Hill carnival through its shared cultured participation deliver within the different social segments? Philips (2005) seems to think so, as he argues for attention to be re-routed from social class division to cultural and ethnic action. Is the steel band an inclusive genre?

At the last audit of cultural groups within Nostalgia Steel Band, it was discovered that there were more than 17 nationalities within the membership of the steel band. The nationalities are British, Columbian, Spanish, Serbian, Trinidadian, Dominican, St Lucian, Guyanese, Irish, German, Gambian, Libyan, Jamaican, Swiss, Nigerian, Cameroonian, Dutch and Grenada. This shared musical interest promotes strong ties and common respect within the community. The band is proud of its intra-culturalism, reflected in its costumes, its music and its carnival themes. As one member explained...

"We are black, we are brown, we are white, we are beige. We are the colours of the rainbow". (Interview)

Narrative of discovery

I was at the Notting Hill carnival 25 years ago when I encountered a pan-around-neck steel band slowly drifting down the carnival route with the rhythmic traditional sound of calypso on pan. This was Nostalgia Steel Band. I remember that most of the male pan players were elderly Caribbean men with a splintering of young white female players, which, to my mind was quite unusual. I later came to realise that all the females were Swiss, and that the leader of the band, Sterling Betancourt, was their teacher. I followed the band for about one hour and a half, then became convinced that this is what I wanted to do. I wanted to play in a pan-around-neck steel band. I asked a member how I could join the band and he gave me a business card. After the carnival, I called the number and was invited to their weekly rehearsals. I became a member of the steel band and a convert to the pan-around-neck steel pan tradition.

With new ideas, developments and progress in the manufacturing and tuning of the steel pan, pan-around-neck steel bands are very rare within the steel band gene as a whole. Pan-around-neck steel bands, though limited in their range contained an element of contact with the people. They could engage with the musicians, walk with the musicians, talk and interact (dance even) with the musicians, drink rum with the musicians and even join in (iron beaters, drummers, and maracas-shakers) when the band is out on the road. No one is excluded. It is a misconception, when seeking to disentangle the meaning of the 'concept of change', to accept that all change is, by its nature, 'progress', resulting from the application of such change. As McCarthy (1984) pointed out;

> "The theory of social evolution, by virtue of its location of historical change in an evolutionary framework—enables us to see history itself as a learning process. Whilst the development of technological knowledge and production capacity is often viewed in this light, it must be noted that the history of morality, politics and social organisation can no longer be regarded as mere change—but as part of the historical process. In summary, the theory of social evolution uses a teleological account of history to provide both a narrative-theoretical basis for the analysis of the present, and an interest in the future" (1984, 269-271).

If one wishes to lift the debate to a philosophical plane it may appear that to lose this traditional art form is to abandon the life and soul of the genre. If social evolution is at work, it appears that much of the confusion associated with the concepts of 'change' and 'progress' is distorted, the extent that one tends to conceive of it in a realist manner. Conventional steel bands may be louder, more sophisticated and—to a larger degree—more technically advanced than traditional pan-around-neck steel bands, but, should one progress at the expense of the other? To understand the meaning of change is to accept that it takes its meaning from the function it performs within the community. *We must stand by our tradition.*

Conclusion

Music and art offers an exciting chance for engaging the public through celebration, weather it be carnivals and festivals such as the Cultural Olympiad. By recognising that multi-ethnic London more and more diverse, The City of London, The Arts Council England and the Greater London Council must also recognise the enormous wealth of Caribbean community cultures. We need to work hard, to ensure that the pan-around-neck steel band has a place in the cultural strategy for The London 2012 Olympics, the Cultural Olympiad, and other major / national events. Communities have the potential to be a resource for understanding socially related issues such as carnival, religion, language and expressions of cultural and musical solidarity. There is no single question which would provide the insight into the pan-around-neck steel pan tradition, but, in conclusion, I would like to advance seven modest proposals for moving the genre forward.

Seven Modest Proposals

1. Examine our own ethical code(s) as a collective, working together and helping each other: What are we doing for the pan-around-neck art form; strengthening the awareness of carnival as an art-form and strengthening the critical debate? (There is a need to be a lot more aware of what is going on in the political carnival arena).

2. Review existing statements on 'community cohesion': Do they stand up to their promises of 'equality of opportunity'?

3. Identify what strategies we should employ to ensure that ALL carnival traditions survive, and that pan-around-bands get adequate levels of support within the carnival fraternity.

4. Plan collaboration to share resources for inter-culturality

5. Seek representation on the Carnival Trust as Board Members in our own right. Insist that we are consulted (represented even) on the panel that assesses bands.

6. Encourage training exercises for the art form, similar to the exchanges between Nostalgia Steel Band and PanKultur (Dortmund), and The Coventry Steel Pan Academy—underpinning an ethical professionalism.

7. Support collective action: the carnival administration must re-examine its obligations.

Works Cited

Achong, A (1999) *The Theory of the Steel pan and Pan Making Technology*, Department of Physics, University of the West Indies, St Augustine, Trinidad.

Aho, W (1987) "Steel Band Music in Trinidad and Tobago; The Creation of a People's Music"; *Latin American Music Review;* vol. 8, no. 1, pp 26-58

Barnes; N (2000) B"ody talk; Notes on Women and Spectacle in Contemporary Trinidad Carnival"; *Small Axe*; 7ᵗʰ March 2000; pp. 93-105

Burton, J, Nanda, A and Platt, L (2008) "Who are the UK's minority ethnic groups? Issues of Identification and measurement in a longitudinal study"; Institute for Social and Economic Research; University of Essex.

Cantle, T (2005) *Community Cohesion*, Basingstoke, and New York; Palgrave, Macmillian

Cohen, A (1980) "Drama and Politics of a London Carnival"; *Man, New Series;* vol. 15; no. 1; pp. 65-87

Cohen, A (1993) *Masquerade Politics: Explorations of the Structure of Urban Cultural Movements*; Berkeley, The University of California Press

Crowley, D (1999) "Carnivals, Carnival and Civilization; or How to make a living without actually working"; *Western Folklore*, 58, Summer/ Fall; pp. 213-222

Dudley, S (2002) "Dropping the Bomb: Steelband Performance and Meaning in 1960s Trinidad"; *Ethnomusicology*; vol. 46; no.1, (Winter 2002); pp. 135-164

Dudley, S (2001) "Ray Holman and the Changing Role of the Steel Band, 1957-1972"; *Latin American Music Review*; vol. 22; no.2; pp.183-198

Ferris, L (2005) "On the Streets of Notting Hill; Carnival as/ is Theatre"; *Theatre History Studies*; 25, June 2005; pp. 61-76

Gilson, S & Depoy, E (2000) "Multiculturalism and Disability; a Critical Perspective"; *Disability and Society*; vol. 15; Issue 2; pp. 207-218

Grant, C (1999) *Ring of Steel: Pan Sound and Symbol*; London and Basingstoke; Macmillan Education.

Hegel, G.W.F (1927) "Lectures on the Philosophy of World History, in Terry, P (1995) Accommodating the history of music within the National Curriculum"; *British Journal of Music Education*; Vol. 12, 1995; pp. 29-43.

Ho, C.G.T. (2000) "Popular Culture and the Aestheticization of Politics; Hegemonic Struggles and Post Colonialism Nationalism in the Trinidad Carnival"; *Transforming Anthropology*; vol. 9, no.1, pp. 3-18

La Rose, M and McCalman, L (2003) *The Gerald Forsyth Story. The Lifetime Journey of a Pan Legend in the Steelband Movement*. London, Caribbean Arts and Musical Expression Publications.

McCarthy, T (1984) *The Critical Theory of Jurgen Habermas*. Cambridge, Polity Press.

Nehusi, K (2000) "The Origins of Carnival: Notes From a Preliminary Investigation", in Ian Isidore Smart and Kimani Nehusi (eds.) *Ah Come Back Home: Perspectives On The Trinidad and Tobago Carnival.* Original World Press: Washington, D.C. and Port of Spain, 2000.

Nindi, P (2005) "The Arts Strategy, 2005"; Presentation given to the Carnival Committee; The Arts Council, England

Noel, T (1989) "A Tale from Trinidad; The Rise of the Pan"; *Music Teacher,* Vol. 68, No. 7, pp. 25.

Nixon, R (1991) "V.S. Naipaul, Post Colonial Mandarin, Transition Under Review"; *Transition*; No. 52; pp. 100-113, Indiana University Press, on behalf of the W.E.B. Du Bois Institution.

Phillips, Terry. Speech to The Commission for Racial Equality cit. commentary on BBC News, Thursday, 22 September 2005.

Rennie, B (1999) "Lies and Distortion of Pan, Out of Hell Yard", www.trinisoca.com/steelpan/pan99.html

Russell; D (1993) "The 'Social History' of Popular Music: A label with a cause"; *Popular Music* (1993) vol. 12/2, pp. 139-154

Stuempfle, S (1995) *The Steelband Movement; The Forging of a National Art in Trinidad and Tobago.* Jamaica, University of the West Indies Press

Terry, P (1995) "Accommodating the history of music within the National Curriculum"; *British Journal of Music Education*; Vol. 12, 1995; pp. 29-43.

Thomas, p (2007) "'Anti-Racism'?, Understandings of 'community cohesion' held by Youth Workers"; *Journal of Social Policy*, vol. 36; Issue 3; pp.435-455

Tompsett, A.R. (2005) "London is the Place for Me; Performance and Identity in the Notting Hill Carnival"; *Theatre History Studies*; 25; June; 2005, pp.43-60

Worley, C (2005) "'It's not about race. It's about the community'. New Labour and Community Cohesion"; *Journal of Critical Social Policy*; vol. 25, (4), pp.483-496

Nostalgia Steel Band and the Impact of "Pan-round-Neck" at Street Carnivals in Europe[1]

Haroun Shah

Introduction; *"Pan-round-neck"*

This chapter presents an account of the *pan-round-neck* tradition in UK carnivals based on the views of the supporters of this art form. It focuses largely on the Notting Hill carnival, and the experiences of young people who are themselves pan players in Nostalgia Steelband. The performers account a pattern of the collective experiences of past and present practices and the journey this traditional *pan-around-the-neck* (referred to as *pan-round'neck* in Trinidad) steelband has made. The story is hardly new, but it provides important further evidence of the contribution that this genre makes—through ethnographic narrative—to the carnival culture.

The replacement of the traditional tamboo bamboo and other percussion instruments by steelpans in Trinidad carnivals during the

---

1   This article is a composite of several papers presented at the Carnival Conference in York University, and of the work of Nostalgia over the years. The following band members: Marvin Barbe, Daniel Bessong, Evangelica Brumant, Christine Davis, Adriana Flórez, Raul Gomez, Ivan R. Gonzalez, Hazel Joseph, Yoko Kimura, Louise Shah, Camille Shah, Chloe Mann, Olivia Raven, Jenny Webb, as well as Lionel McCalman, actively participated at the conference by playing at the opening ceremony and were authors/co-authors of 6 papers presented. Following the preparation of this chapter, Nostalgia Steel band was selected to play for the Opening Ceremony of the Olympics 2012 in London.

1940s was due in part to the durability and mobility of the instruments. All steelpans, from a tenor (soprano) to a low base drum, were carried around the neck of the musician during the two-day carnival pageant. In the ensuing decades, as the repertoire expanded and new boundaries were explored, each specialised pan grew into multiple pans to accommodate the vast range of notes now demanded on the tuners. The steelband grew into an orchestra spanning more than 10 octaves from the tenor pan to the 6 and later 12 pan-base sets. By the late 1950s, the *pan-round-neck*[2] tradition gave way to a highly complex racking system to facilitate the ever increasing number of pans now played by each panist. This was later followed by movement to the "big truck", now common place at carnivals globally. The outcome is not only a distancing of the musicians from the street participants but also the replacement of traditional steelpans by powerful sound systems—the latter being cheaper, simpler and louder and driven by commercial interest. However, the *pan-round-neck* tradition has doggedly survived the years outside Trinidad in relatively modest but discernible pockets in England, Switzerland, Germany and now spreading to the Far East.

Since its inception, Nostalgia Steelband has never deviated from its responsibility to persevere with this tradition; playing at many varied events throughout the UK and Europe, actively teaching and developing programmes in numerous schools and universities, helping to start up new steelbands, holding workshops to promote this art form, and organising and participating in steelband conferences. In 2009, Nostalgia had a membership of over 50 steel pan players, representing the major cultures in Inner London. Information on dedicated *pan-round-neck* steelbands are poorly documented and difficult to delineate from hybrid, single pan bands or even conventional steelbands. This paper uses Nostalgia as a model for retaining and developing this tradition, tenaciously linking to other parts of Europe to help retain critical mass at major events such as London's Notting Hill carnival and, even demonstrating its impact at political events to support a more peaceful and greener world. However, the authors acknowledge the immense work being done, particularly in Switzerland, by *pan-round-neck* bands such as Bollito Misto and Sandflöö,

---

2   A steelpan cannot sit directly on the floor but must be suspended to prevent the sound being dampened. Hence the first steelband players carried their steelpans strapped around their necks. Nearly all current bands hang their steelpans on metal racks for performances. For events such as carnivals, they are carried on trucks or floats.

two formidable pioneering bands in the city of Zürich and the huge impact, originality and contribution of Pan Kultur in Dortmund, Germany.

Nostalgia and its Impact on 'pan-round-neck'

Nostalgia Steelband's roots date back to 1951 when its eminent founders, Sterling Betancourt MBE and Russell Henderson[3] MBE arrived in England with ten other members of the legendary TASPO (Trinidad All Steel Percussion Orchestra) to play at the Festival of Britain. Following their return, Sterling and Russell stayed back in England and, in 1952, made their first recording and then went on to form the Russell Henderson Steelband, the first home-grown steelband in Britain. They played at numerous venues and appeared on radio and television. In 1963, they played for a Children's Neighbourhood Carnival in London's Notting Hill area as a *pan-round-neck* band and, during the party, they drifted onto the streets of Notting Hill. Some spectators joined the procession while others gasped at 'this audacious act', which they assumed was a political demonstration. This was the birth of the world's renown Notting Hill carnival and some of the musicians who took part in this event went on to become famous bandleaders and arrangers of several new bands. The Russell Henderson band subsequently changed its name twice before the name Nostalgia Steelband was proposed by Philmore Davidson in 1969.

For over 50 years, Nostalgia's members have almost single-handedly promoted and maintained the *pan-round-neck* tradition in England despite the immense logistical problems. For example, the notes of each steelpan must be condensed onto a single pan for mobility while still retaining the high quality, purity, rich tones, and colourful rhythms that are now expected of steelbands (Dennis 1971, 23; Imbert 1977, 11; Ressing 1996, 26). The key element of *pan-round*-neck is the freedom and mobility given to the panists. This in turn enables pan playing to be more visible and accessible during street carnivals, breaking down the mystery and, allowing audiences to intermingle and freely participate. Nostalgia is therefore called upon to perform at a variety of events. For example, a poignant moment was the wild excitement created in the closing hours of 1999, when the mobility of *pan-round-neck* steelband music enabled the huge enthusiastic crowds to join in a carnival procession along London's Embankment. Nostalgia later went on to usher in the millennium at the opening of the celebrated Millennium Dome in Greenwich, London.

---

3   Russell Henderson, a pianist, had just arrived in England but was not as member of TASPO.

The multicultural dynamics of Nostalgia Steelband as seen for example during the Notting Hill Carnival. Here, there are members of Pan Kultur (Germany) and several groups from Switzerland in 2004. The band placed 2nd in the 'Best Band on the Road' competition playing with costumes and music portraying the distressing tale of 'Ole Black Jo' and playing the same theme music.

A few names in the front include: (from Switzerland), Yves Maino (bass guitar), Monika Nicoletti-Tung (directly behind Yves), 'Sterling Angels (immediately behind); from Germany: Martin Buschmann, (back of the Angels) several Nostalgia members, (to Martin's right). Front right: Eckhard Schulz (player and tuner, Pan Kultur); Sterling Betancourt (extreme right and front) - leader and arranger, Nostalgia Steelband in 2004).

Sowing the Seeds of the *Pan-round-neck* tradition in the UK

"Steelband music is today used all over the world to bring better cultural understanding and appreciation of music" (Wilkins and Rose 2006, Stuempfle, 1995, 112). Since the majority of Nostalgia's current members are school and university teachers, the band has been instrumental also in promoting many cultural and academic activities and organised the first steelband conference in Europe in 2006. Members have held on steadfastly to the *'pan-round-neck'* tradition and have taken this method of playing into many London schools (McCalman 2010, 126). One of the most successful of these is at the Performance Arts and Media Centre in west London. This is a joint venture driven by the author Marvin Barbe (with assistance from Olivia Raven and Ivan Gonzalez), and led to the establishment of The Paddington Arts Youth Steelband. Nostalgia provides the musical instruments and tuition to Paddington Arts voluntarily while, in turn, the students join Nostalgia for *pan-round-neck* performances. In another project, Christine Davis is leading the introduction of *pan-round-neck* at Hay Lane School (North London); a school which caters for children with severe disabilities. Nostalgia Steelband has made an immense contribution to the musical life of this school by providing steelpans, tuition, and joint performances. A parallel study at Rokesly Infants' School, by Hazel Joseph, has resulted in structured programmes that adhere closely to the Government's Department of Education's National Curriculum guidelines, which are laid down in sequential "Key Stages" (McCalman 2003, 48). Olivia Raven is a full-time music teacher at the Chiswick Community School, but also teaches steelpan from junior to senior levels, using a mixture of conventional and traditional steelpan methods. Progress has been rapid and concerts, assemblies, and various events both within and outside the school stimulate interest and lead to pupils joining Nostalgia and other steelbands. Projects in south London, by Adriana Flórez, helps children to develop musicianship using the Kodaly method, while Raul Gomez, a peripatetic music teacher (and arranger for Nostalgia), also runs a large number of steelpan workshops and community projects in several South London schools. As a formally trained drummer and percussionist, his method of teaching has a strong rhythmic and harmonic focus. Many tutors including some of Nostalgia's teachers, whose roots are not linked to the Caribbean, inevitably introduce their own cultural influences, which help to shape the style and diversity of each steelband. Nostalgia members have tutored and made its steelpans available to the Shern Hall Youth Gospel Choir. The result has been a rapid development of Shern Hall Methodist Youth Steelband, which performs as *pan-round-neck* both independently and together with Nostalgia.

Nostalgia Steelband leaving its pan yard and led by the children on carnival day for the streets of Notting Hill carnival at mid-day. The band members will carry their pans around their necks and play all day arriving back at the pan yard between 11-12 midnight. This is done on two consecutive days. and music portraying the distressing tale of 'Ole Black Jo' and playing the same theme music.

Laila Shah (left corner of the flag) has played in every carnival with the band from 1 year old to her current age of 10 in 2008. In 2010, she made her debut by playing with Nostalgia Steelband at the Notting Hill carnival.

The development of established steelbands in London is therefore derived from the conscientious and pioneering work undertaken in various schools in London (La Rose and McCalman, 2003:13). This is an immense resource which this art form must nurture and strive to continually improve. Notwithstanding the many varied methods employed by tutors, steelbands continue to grow and are represented at all major cultural events in modern British life. In less than sixty years, this incredible instrument has permeated the fabric of this society and is now an essential part of the cultural heritage of London.

Outside London Projects: *Pan-round-neck* and a new Steelpan Academy in the heart of the British Midlands

Diana Hancox, an invited speaker at Nostalgia's Steelband conference in 2006, addressed the issue of "Increasing pan provision and its status in Schools and Communities" (Hancox 2006, n.p.). One of the main outcomes of this conference was the need to develop a steelpan grading system on a par with that established years ago for classical instruments. Nostalgia and Diana's group began work on various joint projects. Following several meetings, her colleague Jacqueline Roberts of SV2G focused on developing a grading system, while Diana began plans for the successful establishment of a Steelpan Academy. Nostalgia Steelband worked closely with the group to develop the Midlands *pan-round-neck* steelband, helping to preserve this part of pan history and culture outside London. The band is now playing regularly on its own in the Midlands; it also joins with Nostalgia at Notting Hill Carnival. Projects such as this are being endorsed by Nostalgia to continue to promote the tradition of *pan-round-neck*.

Making inroads into Bridgwater's Four-hundred-year-old Carnival

Bridgwater's West Country Carnival coincides with the British Bonfire night (5th November) and can be traced back to 1605. Like so many events around 5th November, it dates back to Robert Parsons' and colleagues (Catholics, which included the "guy," Guy Fawkes) attempt to blow up the Protestant British Houses of Parliament during the reign of James I. The original Bridgwater celebrations, which celebrated this failed attempt, consisted of a large bonfire in the Cornhill. A large wooden boat was built and over one hundred tar barrels were added together with any inflammable material to create a spectacular bonfire that could been seen for miles. Effigies or "guys" representing the gunpowder plot instigators were added to the fire by local groups of people known as gangs. It is believed that these gangs started the trend towards a procession, as they paraded their guys towards the bonfire. Over the years, the tradition continued and the annual celebrations became more and more elaborate, involving costumes and music, until the main feature of the event became a large carnival procession. Local people who dressed-up and took part in the event were known as "Masqueraders" or "Features"—terms still used today to describe the participants of the parade.

The key elements of this event have been retained, and today the picturesque historic Somerset town of Bridgwater is home annually to a magnificent spectacle of lights, costumes, and music, which is regarded as the largest illuminated parade in the world (Hocking 2005). Despite the near zero temperatures at this time of the year, from 2003, Nostalgia Steelband players have been proudly carrying their pans around their necks through this three-mile-carnival route (lasting between three to four hours), cheered on by some 150,000 spectators who line both sides of the route. Many of these spectators attend in order to see this mesmerising display of colour, sound, and movement, but few would have seen or heard steelpan music before. The impact of this music, as the only steelband in the carnival, can be seen by the curious and excited expressions on their faces. This has proved so popular that Nostalgia has been requested to join the carnival each year. To add to the electric atmosphere and build up for the evening parade, numerous events are showcased during the day.

From London to Europe, *Pan-round-neck* marches on: Developments in Germany and Switzerland

Switzerland

Despite the small number of West Indians living in Switzerland prior to the 1980s, it was one of the first European countries to have adopted, developed, and vigorously promote steelpan. It now competes at the highest level in competitions such as the "World Steelband Music Festival" in Trinidad. With over one-hundred-and-fifty steelpans listed on websites, the country is recognised internationally as one of the leading proponents of steelpan. Most are concentrated in Zürich, Aargau, Thurgau, and Bern with the latter dating back to the early 1970s. Zürich's two best known *pan-round-neck* bands, Sandflöö and Bollito Misto are nearly thirty years old. Nostalgia invited Sandflöö to play with them at Notting Hill Carnival in 1987. In 1995 they jointly participated in the Panorama competition and delighted audiences and players alike with their dexterity and competence.

Nostalgia has had very fruitful collaborations with many Swiss steelbands, particularly Nostalgia's former panist and arranger Paul Francis, director of "Funland Serenaders," Bern. Members have joined Nostalgia for many years to participate in the Notting Hill carnival and vice versa. Nostalgia has been privileged to have many proficient players, such as Junior Gill, Tamla Batra, Rudy Smith, Yves Maino, and many others, who join the band annually to participate in many activities in London.

Nostalgia has forged links with many Swiss steelbands through their former leader Sterling Betancourt, which has resulted in some intriguing outcomes. For example, while playing with Sandflöö during the Zürich carnival of 1989, Elisabeth Pfafflin was inspired to form a new band, the "Jolly Jumpers." The band was eventually dissolved in 1995, giving way to a new dynamic off-shoot, known as "Sterling's Angels." This took root in 1999 and, under Karen Stark's leadership, continues to be very successful. The "Angels" are a dedicated *pan-round-neck* band and have played alongside Nostalgia Steelband for many years in many carnivals, particularly the Notting Hill Carnival. They have had a huge impact both in Switzerland and London and, being a young all-girl band, have been inspirational for many young panists (Joseph 2004, 26-7).

With so many activities occurring in Switzerland and the desire of the Swiss to maintain contact with developments in Trinidad, London and elsewhere, a global network was necessary. They took the initiative and, before long, www.Pan-jumbie.com, the brain child of Monika Nicoletti-Tung, met these needs. This website swiftly became a household name for steelband enthusiasts around the globe. For over twenty years, Monika, an accomplished steelpan player, has joined with Nostalgia to play in London and various parts of Europe. The success of this website and its many varied aspects was eloquently presented by Monika at the Steelpan Conference of 2006 (Nicoletti-Tung 2006, n.p.). Other websites followed, such as panonthenet.com, panpodium.com, and pantrinbago.co.tt, which, while successful, are not as popular as Pan-jumbie.com which reported 136,582 hits in December 2008.

Germany–Dortmund and Hamburg

For centuries, Germany has had carnivals in cities such as Cologne, Hamburg, and Berlin, but the appearance of steelband music has been relatively recent. Among the *pan-round-neck* bands, the "Bäng Bäng Marchingband," Pankultur (www.pan-kultur.de) has been inspirational in its drive to make Dortmund, in Germany's industrial heartland, the hub of this Caribbean art form. Other bands include "Walking Steel" (www.panworld.de), a professional small *pan-round-neck* band that was founded in 2000. There are also two all-girl *pan-round-neck* bands: "Ladypan," that was formed in 2006, and the well-known "Pans' n Roses," whose members have played with Pankultur and Nostalgia Steelband at the Notting Hill carnival for many years.

In Dortmund the foundation of an exhilarating and inspirational carnival is being carefully nurtured from its roots. Since 2000, PanKultur has joined forces with Nostalgia to play at Notting Hill carnival. In 2005,

Nostalgia teamed up with PanKultur's 'Bäng Bäng Marchingband' to participate in an interesting experiment which, it is hoped, will eventually become a major street carnival. Some thirty panists led a carnival parade through the tiny cobbled streets of the city and into the market place, thereby taking this music into the heart of the city. Very curious and astonished onlookers, most of whom had not seen a steelband before, lined the streets and waved on the pan players. This was followed by a number of events, including "Caribbean Night," which featured a live *pan-round-neck* show as well as larger steel orchestras from various parts of Europe.

The band dates back to 1995 when professional musicians Jürgen Lesker, Martin Buschmann, and tuner Eckhard Schulz founded the Steeldrum Association, Pan-Kultur e.V. in Dortmund. Schulz, who had been engaged with steel drum production since 1979, provided the instruments for the small orchestra. Using novel teaching methods, Lesker and Buschmann began holding workshops and found that they could teach a group of fifteen to twenty people to play music together in a remarkably short time (Buschmann 2006, n.p.). They founded the first steelpan orchestra, a traditional *pan-round-neck* band and steel orchestra, "Paninos," for children between the ages of seven to ten. These three groups began preparing for their first concerts after playing together for just half a year. This attracted new people to join Pan-Kultur e.V. and, in 1999, Pan-Kultur e.V. and E.C.S Steeldrums" moved together into a single panyard. Schulz began producing the "ECS Kiddrum" with eight tones for music lessons for children from three years and up. They then developed the "Teacher Steelpan," based upon the "kiddrum," with 13 tones with a reciprocal diatonic tone order and a range from C1 to F2 as well as F sharp1 and B flat1. Right from inception, this reciprocal ascending format promotes the use of both hands. Additionally, there were two musical advantages: the principle of traditional music notation and the basic harmonic functions became extremely clear.

The multifaceted approach of PanKultur serves to highlight the strong foundation established in Dortmund and provides an excellent model for any aspiring steelband. The facilities at Dortmund are exceptional and include all stages of steelpan manufacture and tuning, small and large teaching and practice rooms, and a café and bar. Steelpan is professionally taught and many members and teachers have become accomplished musicians. The band has a very warm and welcoming spirit and teams up with some of the best known steelbands in Europe. Their vision to establish a grand Caribbean carnival in Dortmund will not only materialise but, in a few years, will turn this city into one of the leading centres for steelband music in Europe.

University-based Steelband Conferences

The First European International Conference on Steelpan: "Steelband Music and Education in the 21st Century; Projecting a Vision of the Future through Global Experiences," University of East London.

The First European Steelband Conference in 2006, which was conceived and ran by Nostalgia Steelband, served as a focal point for many enthusiasts to meet. Held at the impressive Docklands Campus of the University of East London, the conference brought together representatives from the UK and various parts of the world. Some of the themes covered by the various presenters included: Pan in education, Pan and global networking, and experiences of particular countries, such as the UK, Trinidad, Germany, Canada, Japan and France. Throughout the meeting, the obvious lack of standards and uniformity of instruments across the globe was mentioned repeatedly. Thus, a major outcome of this meeting, proposed and accepted by all, was that a national accreditation system (similar to those for other classical instruments) should be established for steelpan musicians in the UK. At a 2007 conference on steel pan held at the Bucks New University in High Wycombe, England, a similar debate engaged many sections of the steel pan community.

Outlook: the development of *Pan-round-neck* in distant lands

Japan, a model for the future... Japan represents the opposite frontier of the world for Trinidadians both in distance and culture, yet for the last twenty years, many Japanese enthusiasts have visited Trinidad to study and participate in carnival. The Japanese have begun to import steelpans, learning to play and, also, manufacture their own instruments. As early as 1957, Southern Symphony steelband performed in Japan (Gerald Forsythe, per com, to Yoko Kimura 30th August 2006), which may have been one of the incentives for what was to follow. Over the last five years, Nostalgia has collaborated with Nagoya University to document these developments. One of the authors of this chapter (Yoko Kimura) joins Nostalgia annually as a member of the band for the Notting Hill carnival and was an invited keynote speaker on the subject at its conference in 2006 (Kimura 2006, n.p., Kimura 2009). Much of the information documented here is from research undertaken at Nagoya University and work published by Tomita (2005).

The Japanese Steelband 'Fantastics' playing at the Kobe Festival in May, 2006. The band was established in 2001 following a large earthquake in which the city of Kobe bore considerable devastation and misery. Steelband music was used to help uplift the melancholy spirits of local people during this terrible ordeal.

Steelbands in Japan have developed differently from those in Britain and the Caribbean. In 1961, steelpan was introduced to Japan by a Japanese entertainer, who was living in U.S. In the 1970s, steelbands from Trinidad went to the Osaka Expo and the Marine Expo in Okinawa. Some Japanese artists were so enthralled by this new sound that they started to include steelpan music in their repertoire. In the 1990s, Renegades, Pamberi, and Caribbean Magic visited Japan from Trinidad. Many Japanese were so excited by this new musical sound that several went over to Trinidad to witness it first hand. On their return, they established steelbands and taught individuals how to play steelpans. Akihiro Ishiguro, who visited Trinidad on several occasions, then founded 'Tokai Trio' and, later, a steelband called 'Pansonide' in Nagoya in 1999. Ryo Sonobe travelled to Trinidad and underwent intensive training to become a professional steelpan player. He was the only Japanese at the time who could tune steelpans, which he did at his studio. At a private high school near Yokohama, he taught students how to make and play a steelpan. Sonobe soon became well known in the area and was invited to tune and make steelpans in Taiwan and Hong Kong.

The Sea Gaia Ocean Resort opened in Miyazaki in 1993, and Michael Robinson, a Trinidadian, was invited to play there. He taught lessons in steelpan and, in 1995, founded a steelband. He greatly influenced the development of steelbands in Japan. By this time the first steel orchestra 'Sukiyaki Orchestra' was established in a remote town in Toyama. By 1997, the orchestra was sufficiently confident to join the Trinidad Carnival. This event was considered so ground-breaking that it was broadcasted on NHK TV. By the end of the millennium, steelbands had become so established in Japan that in 2002, one-hundred-and-fifty steelpan players from all over the country gathered for a steelband festival in Yokohama. This event was promoted by Kiyoshi Kawashima, a product manager from the Nonaka Trading Company, which imported steelpans from Trinidad. The company had its own steel orchestra and provided the pan yard and instruments. Members were advanced students of the Pan Village Steelpan School, where Yuki Murakami was the director. He was also director of *Fantastics* from Kobe. Interestingly, this band was founded in 2001 to rejuvenate a town in Kobe after the Hanshin and Awaji Earthquake. The leader, Kenji Akashi, with the help of a local authority, performed at a steelband concert with an audience of hundred people. As steelbands continue to grow in Japan and the history of this instrument and its culture are understood, the Japanese will continue the tradition, as this is a country that does not overlook its roots. Hybrid steelbands can now be seen in Japan, where part of the steelband plays on a conventional truck while other members of the band play *pan-round-neck* (Figure 3). It is clear that this art form is now well established in Japan, and this will serve as a sound base from which steelbands will disseminate their knowledge to other parts of the Far East.

Summary and Conclusions

During the latter half of the twentieth century, the large influx of migrants from the Caribbean to England brought over some of the most talented musicians, including calypsonians such as the legendary Lord Kitchener and the Mighty Terror. Because of greater opportunities, cities such as London, Birmingham, and Manchester were the main recipients of these people. Thus, when steelband music began to take root, it drew on the talent of these musicians, along with those who were already domiciled, and, inadvertently, began sowing the seeds of this twentieth-century wonder, which at that time was largely obscure. Despite the many obstacles and lack of support, however, persistence of the founder pioneers won through. But not even the most optimistic ever envisioned the spectacle that was to unfold in the years to come, leading to the commencement of London's Notting Hill carnival. This soon became centre-stage for steelbands, drawing millions of people and becoming the world's largest two-day Caribbean carnival. Nostalgia, by virtue of its *pan-round-neck* mobility, its location in the heart of the Notting Hill carnival route, and the versatility of its members has, over the years, acted as a magnet for steelpan players from Europe and around the globe (Figures 1 and 2). Groups from Switzerland and Germany have consistently teamed up with Nostalgia to ensure the continued presence of *pan-round-neck* at the Notting Hill carnival. And while competing against the vast superiority of the big bands on trucks, Nostalgia has managed to place within the first top eight bands for the "best playing band on the road" every year since the inception of this astonishing event. It is a real tribute to its pioneers, Russell Henderson MBE and Sterling Betancourt MBE that after nearly sixty years since their arrival in England, the *pan-round-neck* tradition has not only survived, but has been taken by its members to many London schools, universities, and community centres to secure its future, while still actively promoting it at major events in the UK and Europe. During the last ten years, the British Association of Steelbands has produced a unique magazine, *Pan Podium*. Many of the events in Europe and, indeed, the world are carefully researched, summarised, and vividly told by its editor, Robbie Joseph. It is a tribute to the tireless and diligent work of this editor that many steelband events, including *pan-round-neck,* are reported and circulated globally.

In 2006, Nostalgia organised the first Steelband conference in Europe—possibly, the first ever globally. It was the only Steelband present at the 2008 conference at York University, raising all its own funding to take the band there to perform and present five papers on it projects in London schools and the University of East London (Shah, 2009, 8-9). The broad scope of the 2008 conference at York University provided the inspiration for Nostalgia's 3rd International Conference on steelpan which was held on 23-24th October 2010 at the University of East London's Stratford Campus. The conference entitled 'Integrating The Three Elements of Carnival, Steelpan, Calypso and Mass' was a huge success and was reported in Pan Podium (Issue 22, Spring 2011, pp.18-19) by Louise C.F. Shah entitled " The 3rd International Conference of Steelpan 2010".

Plans are now being drawn up for the 4th meeting scheduled for 26—28th October 2012 and will incorporate the extraordinary progress that has been made in establishing graded examinations with the world renowned ABRSM (Associated Board of the Royal Schools of Music, founded in 1889).

In the meantime Nostalgia Steelband has been selected to participate in the opening ceremony of the London Olympics 2012 and has also accepted an invitation to play for the Jamaican contingent upon arrival in London prior to the games. In both case, the mobility offered by the 'pan-round-neck' was perhaps a key factor for selection.

Works Cited

Buschmann, B. (2006) "Teaching methods for the steelpan." Proceedings of The First European International Conference on Steelpan; Steelband Music and Education in the 21st Century; Projecting a Vision of the Future through Global Experiences'. 30-31st August, 2006. (University of East London).

Dennis, R, A. (1971). "A Preliminary Investigation of the Manufacture and Performance of a Tenor Steelpan." *West Indian Journal of Engineering*, vol. 3, No. 1, pp 32-71

Hancox, D. (2006). "Increasing pan provision and its status in schools and communities." Proceedings of The First European International Conference on Steelpan; Steelband Music and Education in the 21st Century; Projecting a Vision of the Future through Global Experiences. 30-31st August 2006. (University of East London).

Hocking, C. (2005). The story of Bridgwater Carnival from 1880 to 2005, The Bridgwater Education Press; Somerset.

Imbert, C. (1977). *Investigation of Commercial Production Techniques of Steelpan Instruments; Project No. E-SBR-73-5-1*. Caribbean Industrial Research Institute (CARIRI): Tunapuna Post Office, Trinidad.

Joseph, R. (2004). "Sterling's Angels; playing heavenly music." *Pan Podium*. Ed. R. Joseph. Issue 10; Winter (2004-2005) pp. 26-27.

Kimura, Y. (2006). "The steelband perspective in Japan and the Far East." Proceedings of The First European International Conference on Steelpan; Steelband Music and Education in the 21st Century; Projecting a Vision of the Future through Global Experiences. 30-31st August 2006. (University of East London).

Kimura, Y. (2009). An Urban Anthropological Study of the Notting Hill Carnival: Focusing on Masquerade Parades, Steelpan Music and calypsos", (PhD thesis). Graduate School of Letters, Nagoya University. Japan.

La Rose, M and McCalman, L. (2001). *The Gerald Forsyth Story: The Lifetime Journey of a Pan Legend in the Steelband Movement*. London: Caribbean Arts and Musical Expression Publications.

McCalman, L. (2003). "Steelband in schools: the instructor Dependency Model Vs the Teacher Transferency Model." *New Era in Education*. vol. 84, No. 2, pp 42-50

McCalman, L (2010) Drumming Up Enthusiasm; Using Steel Pans with Adults and Children with Special Educational Needs. In Ang, Trushell and Walker (eds) *Learning and Teaching in the Metropolis*; Rodopi Press, Amsterdam and New York

Nicoletti-Tung, M. (2006). "The power of the medium: development of a global database and website." Proceedings of The First European International Conference on Steelpan; Steelband Music and Education in the 21st Century; Projecting a Vision of the Future through Global Experiences.. 30-31st August 2006. (University of East London).

Rossing, T, Hampton, D & Hansen, U (1996) Music From Oil Drums; The Acoustics of the Steel Pan; Physics Today; (March 1996), 24-29.

Shah, Haroun. (2009). "Nostalgia Steelband Triumphs in Toronto." *Pan Podium*. Ed. R. Joseph. Issue 18; pp. 8-9.

Stuempfle, Stephen. (1995). *The Steelband Movement; The Forging of a National Art in Trinidad and Tobago*. Philadephia: University of Pennsylvania Press, 1995.

Tomita A. (2005). *Fete and Violence; The cultural politics of steelpan and carnival*. Tokyo: Ninomiya-Shoten.

Wilkins, V and La Rose, M. (2006). *The History of the Steel band*. Northwood: Tamarind.

6

✣ ✣

CALYPSO AND CARNIVAL

The Political Calypso–A Sociolinguistic Process in Conflict Transformation

Everard Phillips

Introduction

This paper takes a look at the language of Calypsos that offers commentary on the social, political, and economic issues within the Republic of Trinidad and Tobago. It discusses how, by doing so, these calypsos function as a medium generating a level of social interaction, which ultimately drives Trinbagonians to think about the prevailing social, political, and economic issues. It argues that by so doing, this subset of calypsos generates a level of social interaction that subsequently enables Trinbagonians to gain understanding, derive meaning, and construct their knowledge of the prevailing situations. Furthermore, it suggests that by doing so, 'Trinbagonians' are able to interpret their lived experiences in a way that subsequently permits them to affect their socio-economic and/or political behaviour, thereby resolving their locally occurring conflicts.

Arguing from that position automatically leads to questions being raised to determine what tools, skills, and processes are used by calypsonians to resolve disputes. This approach ultimately leads to establishing the paradigm of conflict resolution to which such a process subscribes.

In setting out to address these issues, this paper inevitably embraces some of the arguments regarding the rhetoric of performance communication through the medium of the calypso, facilitated by calypsonians, as they engage in a process of reframing. Hence, this paper offers an insight into the tools, skills, and processes used by the calypsonians who offer commentary in this way.

Theoretical Background

This paper is bedded in an understanding of the difference between action and motion. In considering a stone rolling down a hill, this freefalling movement of the stone is considered to be in motion. If, on the other hand, someone takes the stone and throws it, this activity is considered to be action.

This paper is therefore set against the backdrop of Kenneth Burke's concept of "Language as Symbolic Action." The approach exemplifies a theory of language, a philosophy based on the theory, and methods of analysis that are based on the theory and the philosophy. This process is known as "Dramatism" (Burke 1966). As such, this way of looking at language invites an opportunity to move beyond seeing words as labels to help in the categorisation and identification of objects, but rather words, more specifically in this case, the words of the political calypsos become actions. These actions, which manifest as the lyrics of Political Calypsos, now become offers of descriptions of situations.

Interrelationship of formal, informal and non formal systems

In examining the overall development of conflict management and dispute resolution, I need to acknowledge that, traditionally, in the field of Legal Anthropology, studies in the field of conflict, up until now, have been divided into **Formal** and **Informal** approaches to resolving disputes. It is important to understand that while the Formal approaches to dispute resolution relate to the processes within the legal system, as manifest in court proceedings, the informal relate to processes such as Mediation, Negotiation and Arbitration.

Traditionally, in the established informal approaches to resolving disputes, mediation is seen as an intervention of a neutral third party at the request of the parties in dispute. This third party assists the disputants to find their own way out of the dispute through equity and consensus.

Helping the disputing parties to arrive at a mutually acceptable solution to their conflict in this way, the mediator engages a step-by-step process in which agreement and disagreement are carefully explored, relevant information is collated and shared, while options and proposals are discussed as the interests of each party are presented and clarified. Hence, the mediator conducts a form of facilitated negotiation between the parties, helping them to resolve a presented dispute. A key feature of this approach holds that the decision-making power and responsibility for the outcome of the dispute remains squarely with the parties, while the mediator manages the process. Under these circumstances, the mediator has no authority to suggest one or other solutions, but, rather, facilitates a discussion which, hopefully, raises the awareness of the disputing parties to the consequences and implications of the various outcomes being discussed.

In expanding on the duality of the formal and non formal methods of dispute resolution, this paper adds a third strand to the field of Alternative Dispute Resolution (ADR) which it labels: "**Non-Formal**".

While the role of the political calypsonians as an agent of the process of "Conflict Transformation" cannot be mapped exactly on that of the mediator, there are aspects of the two approaches that mirror each other. In this article, I have described the calypsonians as liminal-servants who, using a narrative that encompasses artistic form, very much like the mediator, are not empowered to impose a solution. Rather, in this non-formal approach to transforming conflict, the calypsonians, like the mediator, seek to raise the awareness of their audiences (i.e. one party to the conflict) regarding the issues. By so doing, calypsonians empower their audiences so that they may then recognize their options to take the appropriate action to craft a solution to their prevailing circumstances.

Hence, both mediators and political calypsonians use the same strategies, inviting the parties to think critically about the issues and possible solutions, with the opportunities for action remaining exclusively in the domain of the parties. While both mediator and political calypsonians stimulate discussion and debate with regard to the presenting issues, for the mediator, this function is fulfilled in a mediation room, while for the calypsonians, the venue is either the Calypso Tents or the Dimanche Gras show.

These linguistic actions of the political calypsonian can be seen to fall centrally into the domain of "political theatre," where in the setting of the Calypso Tent, these calypsonians engage in a process of raising the awareness of their audiences in relation to the relevant pathologies. It is this non-formal approach which subscribes to the concept of "Conflict Transformation" (Bush and Folger 1994).

Conflict Transformation

In this text, I have assumed the meaning of the term "Conflict Transformation," as used by Bush and Folger in their ground breaking and seminal work entitled: *The Promise of Mediation: Responding to Conflict through Empowerment and Recognition*, as this more accurate describes the processes engaged in by the subset of political calypsonians in Trinidad and Tobago.

It would be incorrect and inappropriate not to recognise that conflict is an intrinsic part of life in any community, including Trinidad and Tobago. Isenhart and Spangl contend that conflict is "a vital social function where tensions are released and new communal norms are established or refined...Conflicts forces parties to deal with deeper issues and thus serve as a constructive social process" (2000, 9). In reality, conflict is always lurking, it does not really go away; in other words, conflicts cannot really be resolved but they can be managed. Conflict offers an opportunity to learn, to make choices that result form that learning, and to choose to change the way we view a specific set of circumstances or a situation, and, subsequently, take action in the direction of that changed view. So the goal of this transformational process is to enable audiences "to move beyond solutions to transforming relationships. The transformational mediator attempts to influence interaction patterns, change how the partners talk about themselves and each other," (2000, 10).

Hence, the conflicts that occur, of which calypsonians sing, are not necessarily and always resolved. Frequently though, through listening to these calypsos audiences are empowered. They begin to recognise, to think, to reflect and discuss the issues being presented by the calypsonians. It is this process of "Empowerment and Recognition," as discussed by Bush and Folger (1994), which I contend can lead individuals within an audience to identify the options they have that can make an impact, thereby bringing about a constructive change or the process of "Conflict Transformation."

This notion of transformation that I am advancing sees the idea of peace as being intrinsically connected with that of social justice, right relationships, and human rights, within a social structure. This is quite in opposition to what is customarily referred to as "conflict resolution" wherein one party may feel co-opted to succumb, for the sake of either making or maintaining peace. Solutions do not necessarily show up as resolution, and what could be seen as resolution of conflict can in many settings actually perpetuate the inequality or injustice that initially generated the dispute. In the final analysis it is helpful to reflect on Bush and Folger's summary of the value of this Transformational approach. They contend:

The strongest reason for believing that the Transformational Story should guide mediation is the story's underlying premise: that the goal of transformation—that is, engendering moral growth towards both strength and compassion— should take precedence over the other goals mediation can be used to obtain, even though these other goals are themselves important. It makes sense to see transformation as the most important goal of mediation, both because of the nature of the goal itself and because of the mediator's special capacity to achieve it (1994, 28-29).

The development of legal processes in the New World

As with many other colonised countries, in Trinidad, the very practice of colonialism propagated the imperial power's metropolitan legal system throughout the territory, imposing it as the formal dispute resolution process to be used in resolutions of conflict. However, it needs to be understood that there were significant differences occurring between the available structures for resolving conflict in the territories of the "New World," when compared to those available in the African continent or the India sub-continent.

These differences resulted from the fact that imperialism within the African continent, like the Indian sub-continent, was imposed on a people who were already well established in their own homeland, having their own operational socio-cultural systems which included well recognized methods for resolving their conflict. The emergent dispute resolution system in these societies, was a form of legal pluralism where, a hegemonic colonial power shaped the formation of a **formal** dispute resolution processes, while the parallel, local, **informal** system continued to coexist. For reasons embedded in the complexity of the social, political and/or economic matrix that drove developments in Trinidad, this structure was not mirrored.

Hitherto being supplanted in Trinidad, this composite group of Africans from different social groups, now arriving as enslaved people, had been used to a variety of socio-cultural systems that ranged from chiefdoms to acephalous societies. In their new Caribbean homeland, the Africans collectively became an amalgamation of disorientated, disempowered, bemused people, from a range of different tribal systems, having neither a sense of community, nor continuity, nor a common language with which to communicate.

Newly arrived in Trinidad, these totally disorientated people found themselves in submissive bondage, with their primary drive being survival. Within these complex dynamics of subordination and struggle, the Africans, although numerically superior, were not of the mindset that allowed them to entertain either the idea of implementing a unified dispute resolution system, or the resurrection of one with which any of them had previously been accustomed. On the other hand, for their part, the migrant Europeans now residing in Trinidad already had their own imported formalised dispute resolution system which became the *de facto* system for the application of justice.

The 1797 change in imperial governance from Spanish to English, supplanting Hispanic law with British law, engendered accompanying tensions within the Trinidad community. This further impeded the capacity of the enslaved African people to form an integral, informal structure for the resolution of conflict among either themselves or between themselves and their slave masters. The absence in Trinidad of the type of formal/informal legal pluralism that existed in Africa and the Indian sub-continent was sustained for some considerable time as is apparent from the writings of Herskovits, which appeared much later.

Writing in 1947 in relation to the microcosm of the *Trinidad Village* of Toco, Herskovits and Herskovits, comment that most of the villagers, being born elsewhere, had no long, common, local tradition to be upheld, or that required the support of the people in their old ways. Herskovits and Herskovits' research identified that in those early days in Trinidad, the procedure for the resolution of disputes was a process that was conducted through a Court system that was entirely of European origin, (1947). For my part, research into pre-20th-century Trinidad has not revealed any **informal** system of dispute resolution existing in the island that corresponds to those available in either Continental African or the Indian sub-continent.

Quite apart from this, the 50's, 60's and 70's temporarily gave rise to an informal system of resolution wherein respected members of the community (Priests, Head-Teachers, the Post Master/Mistress, and the Village Police Officer) assumed an informal role of peacemaker in local disputes. Within the last 10 years, Trinidadians and Tobagonians have grown in their awareness of the potential of Alternative Dispute Resolution (ADR), with a corresponding increase in commitment to the mediation process. Currently, various national and private bodies, following a North American model of mediation, offer certain types of conflicting parties the opportunity to **informally** resolving their disputes.

Legal Anthropology

Turning to the wider area of legal anthropology, we see the release of Bronislaw Malinowski's study at the end of the first quarter of the 20th Century (*Crime and Custom in Savage Society*), heralding in a significant epoch in modern legal anthropological studies. However, this approach so skewed the understanding of the entire spectrum of the dispute resolution processes that were engaged in at this local level, that it further distorted aspects of the theoretical development that might otherwise have been available. This occurrence was a consequence of the fact that these early studies produced a static analysis that did not take into account the interactions between the formal and informal systems, neither did they consider the implications of the asymmetric power imbalance between these processes, particularly with regard to the importance and impact of the imperial models.

The 70's saw the field of dispute resolution continuing to evolve and grow in a significant way. During this period, Nader and Todd produced a pioneering florescence of studies of village law, using a choice-making model of action, a focus on local places, and a processual mode of analysis of disputes, hence, producing a framework typology for dispute processing (1978). Correspondingly, this inspired other legal ethnographic research, into socio-cultural frameworks in various locations around the world, and as a consequence, provided rich descriptions of the local significance of these contexts.

The literature of the 70's and 80's shows an awareness of the need to regard not just the localised, informal, rational, choice-making models of behaviour, but the formal as well. Some researchers, Snyder (1981) and Chanock (1985), criticised the micro-level approach to the study of disputing, with Starr & Collier (1989), generating an expanded framework of dispute analysis incorporating historical, temporal, and the world system.

In recognition of the link between methods of dispute resolution and culture, and particularly relevant to the approach taken in this paper, is Clifford Geertz's expressed view that law is a type of social abstraction that is driven by culture and imagination and is designed to regulate social life (1983). Geertz argues that there is a direct relationship and correspondence between law on the one hand and myth, ritual, ideology, art, or classification systems focused on structures of meaning, especially on the symbols, and systems of symbols, through which such structures are formed, communicated, and imposed (1983, 182).

The field of dispute processing has evolved considerably over the last forty years or so, with legal anthropologists defining and redefining this evolving domain to embrace socio-cultural systems. As Turner (1957), Gluckman (1955), and Bohannan (1957), state, the processual model of law, of which dispute processing forms part, developed quite significantly in the 1950s, and built upon Malinowski's action oriented functionalism. This approach was supported by comprehensive case analysis. The establishment of this model of dispute processing launched a significant challenge to the existing rule-centred approach. However, the 1970's saw legal scholars attempting to produce a synthesised model that bridged both the rule centred and the processual models.

The 1980's saw legal anthropologists developing a concern for meaning and power, hence drawing from the theoretical orientations of different disciplines, producing enriched and expanded theoretical frameworks that provided a bridge between aspects of the social sciences and law (Comaroff and Roberts 1981; Starr and Collier 1989; Abu-Lughod 1990; Comaroff 1985; Comaroff and Comaroff 1991; Scott 1985). These newer innovations sought to combine the areas of dispute processes in a social context, with notions of how legal institutions and actors create and transform meaning within the context of their particular cultural framework.

This work from the colonial and post-colonial worlds was taken up from the late 1970's, and drawn upon in the process of the renovation of metropolitan legal systems. The ensuing shift in orientation from *formal* to *informal* processes for resolving disputes has been accompanied both in metropolitan centres and in the post-colonial world with new understandings of theories of dominance and resistance, (Abu-Lughod 1990).

The objective of this paper, recording as it does the experience of the ethnographic research that I essentially completed as part of my study, is to illuminate key processes that underlie a different, yet complementary, approach to the resolution of disputes, as applicable to Trinidad and Tobago's local, temporal context. In doing so, I am adding a set of intellectual tools that enable us to recognise the *Language of Calypso as "Symbolic Action" In Resolving Conflict in Trinidad and Tobago*.

My approach, set as it is against the backdrop of the discussions around ideological conditions of anthropology and the implications of these conditions for its discourse, enables a vision primarily of calypsonians, and secondarily their audiences, as social actors, both engaging in and demonstrating their potential for human action or agency within a *Matrix of Domination[1]* (Collins 1990). It invites an understanding of how calypsonians, through the medium of the Calypso, influence the social creation, maintenance, and alteration of structure in their process of articulating an *inequality problematic[2]* in the localised situation of Trinidad and Tobago.

This being the case, using an interpretive framework, I define a *Non-Formal* approach to the resolution of structural conflict within Trinidad, thus taking us somewhere new. In doing so, I extend the duality of resolution processes earlier identified, taking quite a different line from previous researchers of the Calypso Art-Form. Hence, this work unveils a third strand, adding intellectual tools that offer an understanding of aspects of the Calypso art-form, which show it as a *Non-Formal* approach to transforming conflict. Viewed from this perspective, the calypsonian functions as a *liminal servant* using, in part, a Trinidadian language, the vocabulary of which reveals the various ideas encoded in the restricted terminology, used to represent the daily challenges that some Trinidadians and Tobagonians face.

I need, here, to highlight that the ideologies discussed in this work reflect the Trinidad situation wherein there exists radical class inequalities within the system. This, in turn, generates clear forms of socio-political and economic conflict that, correspondingly, have been accompanied by attempts by some governments to exercise control on calypsonians through censorship. In using the term *Non-Formal*, I am, therefore, referring to a process wherein the Calypso functions as a facilitator in a dialectic that is attempting to resolve contradictions or oppositions, as perceived by the calypsonians, in either the socio-political or economic domains of Trinidad and Tobago.

Functioning as a *liminal-servant*, the calypsonian has a sense of immediacy of purpose, offering the audience verbal symbols as part of an artistic rite, which is a response to pathologically prevailing issues.

---

1   *Matrix of Domination* refers to the dynamic interaction of the combination: race, class and colour. It addresses the disempowered effect of the interactive and reinforcing process that exists between these attributes, not as individual attributes in themselves, but only in relation to the interaction between the various attributes as these affect and influence inequality.

2   *Inequality problematic:* In using this term I am referring to the Calypsonians' attempt to articulate the pertinent issues that arise from the *Matrix of Domination,*(as it applies to the Trinidad situation), as they operationalise an approach that necessarily addresses the issues within this Matrix.

In a forthcoming book entitled: *The Political Calypso: A Sociolinguistic Process in Transforming Conflict,* I demonstrate how the audience become co-celebrants in a learning process that is characterised by their committed participation and involvement in "the act," thereby creating a truly deep, meaningful, and edifying learning experience for them.

Using this particular approach to dispute processes, this paper is based on the recognition of how, in relation to the events occurring within a Calypso Tent, the rules for this particular approach to dispute processes are negotiated, and, simultaneously, with the social life within the Calypso Tent, is governed by normative repertoires that involve the manipulation by the calypsonians, of the rules of performance, in order to bring about increased consciousness. My approach builds on other authors' such as Benda-Beckmann (1988) and Roberts (1979), who, lending their weight to an informal approach, argue that the rules governing localised conflict behaviour are not internally consistent codes of action analogous to Western written law, but can, instead, be negotiable, internally contradictory repertoires that are applied with discretion.

Hence, my approach to the anthropology of dispute resolution offers a cultural analysis that identifies how the local institution of the Calypso Tent and its actors create meaning. I identify the impact of this meaning on the surrounding social relationships, and the effect of the cultural framework of the Calypso Tent on the nature of the processes of conflict transformation itself. I recognise a parallel between my work and that of Comaroff & Roberts (1981, 18-19), who, in their work on dispute processes within Tswana society of Africa, examined the cultural logic of the localised dispute processes. Other authors, Schapera (1955) and Dikobe (2003), contend that there are striking similarities between Calypso and Tswana songs of derision in which grievances are articulated.

African music genres and performance styles

Based on her research into the American traditions of black music, Maultsby (1991) argues that the established musical traditions of the slaves derived from their African heritage and that over the years and, certainly, after Emancipation, these customs evolved in response to the local demands and the circumstances of the environment. Maultsby argues that under these conditions of enslavement, "each generation of slaves and freeborn blacks created new musical genres and performance styles" (Maultsby 1991, 185). Although Maultsby's conceptual framework for the musical genres and performance styles of African-American music does not expressly mention calypso, there is no doubt that the experiences of the enslaved African in America were similar to those enslaved Africans who were sent to the Caribbean. Therefore, it seems reasonable to surmise that were this framework to be rewritten to include all the musical genres within the Diaspora, depending on the slant of any given calypso, collectively they would all fall under the general heading of "African American Secular Traditions." Depending on the theme of the calypso, it would then be grouped under either of the two headings of categories that she attributes to having emerged during the 1960s: "Work Songs, Field Calls And Protest Songs" or "Game Songs and Social Songs."

In her discussion on the role of African American musical forms, and the aspects of these that have been retained in "formal and informal settings," Maultsby recognises the fundamental concept underlying music performance in African and African-derived cultures (1991, 187). She contends that "music-making is a participatory group activity that serves to unite black people into a cohesive group for a common purpose" (187). In this paper I contend that for our purpose in Trinidad, the function that the political calypso serves is the transformation of the conflicts that occur in the society.

Linking stage drama and social drama

That there is a close relationship between the calypsos of any particular time and the events leading-up to that calypso season is beyond doubt. A classic illustration of this fact may be seen in the chronology of events immediately below and the list of calypsos that track those events.

Some Key Events in Trinidad and Tobago

1981 - George Chambers becomes prime minister following the death of Eric Williams.

1986 - The national alliance for reconstruction headed by Arthur Robinson wins the general election.

1990 - Over 100 Islamist radicals blow up the police HQ, seize the parliament building and hold Robinson & other officials hostage in an abortive coup attempt.

1991 - Patrick Manning becomes prime minister after his PNM party wins the general election.

1995 - The Indian-based United National Congress (UNC) and NAR form a coalition with Basdeo Panday as prime minister.

Calypsos That Track Political Events

1986: Sinking Ship—Gypsy (A protest at the existing government)

1987: One Love—Sparrow (A welcome to the newly formed amalgamated party)

1989: Chauffeur Wanted—Chalkdust (An expression of abject dissatisfaction with the new PM)

1991: Say ah prayer (for Abu Baka)—Cro Cro (Advocating a balanced view of the coup)

1991: Still the best—Cro Cro (Satirical post coup commentary)

Form: Tools and skills used in calypso art

As part of the process of influence and persuasion, the calypsonian exercises his/her ability as an artificer adept in the art of navigating along a spectrum of meanings ranging from standard English to colloquial dialectic. Using various types of wordplay, the calypsonian successfully and skilfully manoeuvres within this spectrum, demonstrating a degree of sensitivity to each of the attributes of an active triadic co-existing relationship that engages the audience, their encompassing social world, and the performer. Focusing on this intersection, allows the establishment of a dramatic structure for the process of addressing the prevailing dispute. This approach acknowledges the difference between the lived-in world of the audience, the encompassing social universe, and the liminal world of the performing calypsonians, as s/he mediates the tensions between the social world and the lived-in-world.

Tracking some key events in Trinidad and Tobago and juxtaposing them with the calypsos of the era provides a practical appreciation of the relationship between stage dramas and social drama. This opens an opportunity to understand Burke's analysis of the relationship between 'language' and 'reality.' This paper, therefore, now looks briefly at both the context and content of calypsos that offer commentary on the socio-political and economic issues within Trinidad and Tobago, as these calypsos articulate the 'inequality problematic' and mediate the struggle in the competing class structure of the nation. To further guide our understanding of this non-formal process, it is necessary to address both the function and form of calypsos and to explore political and sociological issues as they are addressed through the language of calypso art-form.

This approach requires an exploration of the mechanisms that underpin the concept of 'dramatism' as it manifests in the calypso art form. I posit that calypsonians use reframing in the process of raising consciousness as they engage in transforming conflict. For this purpose, Hall defines reframing as a process where a speaker takes a frame-of-reference so that it looks new or different (1998, 230). Hall argues that when reframing an event or idea, the content or context of a situation is presented from a different point of view so that it invites a different meaning.

Form: Stage drama versus social drama

As discussed earlier, the lyrics of the Trinidad calypsos mirror the country's pertinent issues. In relation to the disputes that inevitably occur within the social world of the people of the islands, the calypso is uniquely poised to prize open a window to the understanding of motives, as we try to grasp the lyrics therein. Thus, this concept brings an awareness of the relationships between: language *of* motives (i.e. the structure of the language), motives *in* language (i.e. the intentions of the calypsonians) and language *as* motive (the relationship between these two).

The use of reframing is central to the calypsonians' role in the process of conflict transformation, as it helps their audiences to see alternative perspectives. When reframing, calypsonians can change the conceptual and/or emotional setting of a set of experiences, placing the experiences in another frame that fits equally well facts of the same concrete situation. Through this process, the calypsonians change the entire meaning of the circumstances, thereby enabling a new and different vision of the situation.

Frames and masks

I have already stated that calypsonians, singing on the social and political issues occurring in Trinbago, enable their audiences to take an alternative perspective, thereby helping their development of a social construction of reality. The following section of the paper looks at the processes that calypsonians employ in achieving this outcome.

The necessary fieldwork for this study showed the extensive use of frames and masks by calypsonians as they endeavoured to effectively deliver their messages to their audiences. Used as a tool in this way, reframing permitted one idea or object to be thought of as fitting into a different category. Hence calypsonians abundantly use metaphor, metonym, and polysemy. While metaphors establish a relative relationship between two different fields, mapping from one domain of experience on to another, by contrast, in metonym, the mapping is within the same domain. On the other hand, the use of polysemy enables multiple meanings of the same expressed view to be effective. Hence, this can be seen as a stage in the interpretation of expression that goes beyond that of *double entendre*.

The work of Bateson (1972) and Goffman (1974) form a backdrop for this study. Hale has further grounded this area of work and, as an academic and practitioner in the field of ADR, has taken a perspective on frames which uses the Burkean epistemology as a touchstone. Embracing the concept of Dramatism, she shows how a practitioner in the field of conflict resolution can reframe a given situation.

Using frames, Calypsonians plausibly juxtapose principles and pragmatics, exposing the inconsistencies of Caribbean experiences. Rohlehr refers to this process as "oscillation between geographical and situational opposites" as a way of shaping, not only the Caribbean aesthetic, but the social and psychic experiences of the dispute (1985, 2). In doing so, Hale argues that in conflict, individuals can find themselves in one of the problematic drama fames. She contends there are a number of different types of frames that can be placed into two fundamental categories. These she identifies as the problematic frame and the hopeful frame. (Hale 1998, 149-156). While the former does not necessarily help resolution, the latter more frequently does. Using these techniques, the calypsonian's artistic use of linguistic form deploys a nebulous haze that invites multiple meanings and interpretations of the lyrics of a calypso, The mediator Robert Benjamin calls this process the "creation of dissonance in thinking" (1995, 7-8).

I refer to calypsos that engage this process of polysemy as having 'lamina lyrics'. Much like an onion, these calypsos have a number of different levels of meaning, concealed one beneath the other. Achieving this phenomenon, calypsonians use frames and masks that manifest in calypsos as metaphor, metonym, polysemy irony, and satire. While a number of calypsonians repeatedly use these techniques, I will illustrate its use by focusing on the lyrics of Ras Shorty I's admirable demonstration of the use of metaphor and reframing devices as occurring in the chorus of "Watch out My Children":

> *Watch out my children*
> *Watch out my children, yeh*
> *It have a fella called Lucifer with a bag a white powder*
> *And he doh want to powder yuh face*
> *But to bring shame and disgrace to the human race*

Nowhere in this calypso does Shorty reveal the names of any of the drug lords but, through the use of the imagery, of frames, we are able, in this indigenous, non-formal conflict transformation mechanism, to see that Lucifer represents the drug lords, while white powder represents illegal drugs.

The process of language as 'Symbolic Action' is further illustrated by the words of the calypsonians: In the Calypso Tent, Sugar Aloes introduces the audience to the calypso "My Observation." This calypso is a critical observation of the due processes of law within The Republic of Trinidad and Tobago.

The following calypso lyrics further illustrate the points made in this paper:

(In the example below, I have emboldened some of Aloes' words to draw specific attention to the way in which he uses language. The words that are in the shaded area, emboldened and in brackets, are my focus and explanations of the conflict transformation resolution process as displayed by this rendition of the calypso.)

While appearing in the "Review" calypso tent in 2004, Sugar Aloes, upon entering the stage, introduces his calypso to the audience thus:

"Al yuh enjoying the show?"

"Al yuh missing anybody? Neither we, Tasha fall-in for Denyse, Super fall-in for, what he name ...Bomber. We have Steve Sealy falling in for DeFosto. And we could go on and on, right? But give yourself a round of applause for supporting a tent that had exist for 43 years and still going strong. And we ent care what no body say, if after 43 years for the first time we ask for a little help, we well deserve it."

"All yuh reading about is Revue get [$]85 million, two days before that, they say that Chutney get [$]280 Million, nobody ent talking about that."

"Ah think dat is more than wat we get ent?" [demonstration of getting the audience to think critically about this situation]
[He then neutralises the situation with these words]
"Ahhhh but doh bother with that, every brook have to get a little water ....do bother with that."

"Ah want to do something here, ah breaking it down slow so that all yuh could understand what a saying because if ah do it fast the thing does go over alyuh head, and al yuh doesn't understand, but this is reality, this one ent name face reality enh, not me!" [demonstration of Aloes' direct communication with the cognitive ability of the audience].

"Dis one is called 'My Observation' and **ah go bring back some things for all yuh to remember to**" [example of Aloe's engaging the audience in the important process of re-cognition or recognition] "Le'we go"

Lyrics of My Observation By Sugar Aloes

I made ah serious observation, couple years ago
And my findings really disturb me, I want yuh to know
Every time we hold a criminal in high society
By the time the matter reach the courts
They get away Scott-free
Whether it's a priest, a lawyer, or a politician
It seems like the wheels of justice greased with corruption
I find we should check out the system, cause *listen my friend*
It looks like the UNC no more law than the PNM

Cause Gopeesingh, get away Scott-free
And Bill Chaitan, they never charge he
If a **poor black man** did commit that crime and boast
All now so he in jail getting he ass roast
But Gypsy, get away Scott-free
Galbaransingh, he free already
Once the UNC put their lawyers on the trail
None ah dem doesn' make no jail

Verse 4
See if all yuh remember this one (Aloes spoken words to the audience)
Police found some coke and a missile, in a water tank
Town say that they must charge the fella, I'm telling you frank
With that kind of evidence in hand, so the critics say
As a big UNC minister, he can't get away
I was even hearing talks you may not believe me
People say he control the two gangs in Lavantille

> PNM supports plan that day, Panday start to ball
> Investigation was stopped,
> As yuh know the man wasn't charged at all.
>
> Lewis Gomez, get away Scott free
> And Sadq Baskh, they never charge he
> If the police did find all that Coke by Cro Cro
> The midget would be making jail until he grow
> But Richardson, get away Scott-free
> Brian Kuei Tung, he free already
> Once they have Carl Hudson-Philip jamming the tail
> None ah dem doesn't make a jail

In the Calypso above, Aloes uses appropriate language to challenge the audience to identify the ridiculousness of our legal system. He draws on their memory of key events that illustrate the state of the legal processes in the country. He aids them to recognise the disparity in how the wealthy and powerful are regarded and how the 'poor black man' is treated. The request is to "check out the system" because we need to listen, to heed the signals of the demise both of and within the society.

Conclusion

Traditionally, established informal approaches to resolving dispute mediation is seen as an intervention of a neutral third party, at the request of the parties in dispute. This third party assists the disputants to find their own way out of the dispute through equity and consensus. As shown earlier, in helping the disputing parties to arrive at a mutually acceptable solution, the mediator engages in a step-by-step process during which agreements and disagreements are aired, relevant information is collated and shared, and options and proposals are discussed in the interest of each party. Hence, the mediator conducts a form of facilitated negotiation between the parties, helping them to resolve a presenting dispute, while the decision-making power and responsibility for the outcome remain squarely with the parties. Under these circumstances, the mediator has no authority to suggest, one or other solutions, but, rather, facilitates a discussion which, hopefully, raises the awareness of the disputing parties to the consequences and implications of the various outcomes being discussed.

While the role of the political calypsonians as an agent of conflict transformation cannot be mapped exactly on that of the mediator, there are aspects of the two approaches that mirror each other. In this article, I have described the calypsonians as a liminal-servant who, using a narrative that encompasses artistic form, is not, unlike the mediator, empowered to impose a solution. Rather, in this non-formal approach to transforming conflict, the calypsonians, like the mediator, seek to raise the awareness of the audience (as parties to the conflict) regarding the issues, and thereby empowering them to take the appropriate action in crafting a solution to their problem.

Hence, both mediators and political calypsonians use the same strategies as they invite the parties to think critically about the issues and possible solutions, while leaving the required action in the exclusive domains of the parties. Both mediator and political calypsonians stimulate discussion and debate concerning the issues. For the mediator, this function is fulfilled in a mediation room, while, for the calypsonians, the venue is either the Calypso Tents or the Dimanche Gras show. The activities of the political calypsonians fall into the domain of political theatre as they engage in a non-formal approach to transforming conflict.

In the final analysis, the efforts of political calypsonians can be recognized as a non-formal approach to conflicts transformation within the community of Trinidad and Tobago. This approach empowers an audience to recognize the issues and, subsequently, decide what action is needed for resolution. While this process of empowerment and recognition has occurred many times within Trinidad and Tobago, the most recent and significant example of this was witnessed in the chain of events surrounding the 1990 coup and other political perturbations in The Republic of Trinidad and Tobago.

Works Cited

Abu-Lughod, L. 1990. "The Romance of Resistance: Tracing Transformations of Power Through Bedouin Women." *American Ethnologist*, 17:14=56.

Bateson, G. 1972. *Steps to an Ecology of Mind*. New York: Ballantine.

Benda-Beckmann, F. von et al. eds. 1988. *Between Kinship and the State: Social Security and the Law in Developing Countries*. Dordrecht: Foris.

Benjamin, R. D. 1995. "The Constructive Uses of Deception: Skills, Strategies and Techniques of the Folkloric Trickster Figure an their Application by Mediators." *Mediation Quarterly*, 13: 3-17.

Bohannan, P. 1957. *Justice and Judgement Among the Tiv*. Oxford: Oxford University Press (for the International African Institute).

Burke, K. 1966. *Language as Symbolic Action: Essays on Life, Literature and Method*. Berkeley: University of California Press.

Bush, B. and Folger, J. 1994. *The Promise of Mediation: Responding to Conflict Through Empowerment and Recognition*. San Francisco: Josey-Bass.

Chanock, M. 1985. *Law Custom and Social Order: The Colonial Experience in Malawi and Zambia*. Cambridge: Cambridge University Press.

Collins, P.H. 1990. *Black Feminist Thought: Knowledge, Consciousness and Politics Of Empowerment*. New York: Allen & Unwin.

Comaroff, J. L., & Roberts, S. 1981. *Rules and Processes: The Cultural Logic of Dispute in an African Context*. Chicago: University Chicago Press.

Comaroff, J. 1985. *Body of Power: Spirit of Resistance: Culture and History of a South African People*. Chicago: University Chicago Press.

Geertz, C. 1983. *Local Knowledge: Fact and Law in a Comparative Perspective*. New York: Basic Books.

Gluckman, M. 1955. *The Judicial Process Among the Barotse of Northern Rhodesia*. Manchester: Manchester University Press.

Goffman, E. 1974. *Frame Analysis*, New York: Harper & Row.

Gulliver, P.H. 1978. *Cross-Examinations: Essays in Memory of Max Gluckman*. Leiden: Brill.

Hale, K. 1998. "The language of Cooperation: Negotiation Frames." *Mediation Quarterly* 16:147-162.

Hall, M. 1998. *The Secrets of Magic*, Carmarthen: Crown House.

Herskovits, M. J. and Herskovits, F. S. 1947. *Trinidad Village*. New York: Knofp.

Isenhart, Myra Warren and Spangle, Michael. 2000. *Collaborative Approaches to Resolving Conflict*. Thousand Oaks, CA: Sage Publications.

Maultsby, P. 1991. "Afrcanisms in African-American Music." *Africanisms in American Culture*. Ed. Joseph Holloway. Bloomington: Indiana University Press.

Moore, E., P. 1985. *Conflict and Compromise: Justice in an Indian Village*. Lanham, MD: University Press America.

Nader, L., and Todd, H. F. 1978. *The Disputing Process—Law in Ten Societies*. New York: Columbia University Press.

Roberts, S. 1979. *Order and Dispute: An Introduction To Legal Anthropology*. New York: St. Martin's Press.

Rohlehr, G. 1985. "The Problem of the Problem of Form: the Idea of an Aesthetic Continuum and Aesthetic Code-switching in West Indian Literature." *Caribbean Quarterly*, 31(March):1-52.

Schapera, I. 1955. *A Handbook of Tswana Law and Custom*. London: Cass.

Snyder, F. G. 1981. "Anthropology, Dispute Processes, and Law: a Critical Introduction" *British Journal of Law & Society*. 8:141-80.

Starr, J., & Collier, J. F., eds. 1989. *History and Power in the Study of Law: New Directions in Legal Anthropology*. Ithaca, N.Y.: Cornel University Press.

Turner, V. 1957. *Schism and Continuity in an African Society*. Manchester: Manchester University Press (for the Rhodes-Livingstone Institute).

Wood, D. 1968. *Trinidad in Transition: the Years After Slavery*. London: Oxford University Press.

Unpublished Dissertation

Dikobe, M. 2003. "Doing She Own Thing: Gender, Performance and Subversion in Trinidad Calypso." PhD Thesis, University of California Berkeley.

Sir Lancelot: Taking Calypso from Carnival to Nightclubs, Hollywood, and the World

Ray Funk

Trinidad Carnival remains one of the richest, cultural, and artistic events that any country of its size has ever produced, and one has only to see Carnivals such as Toronto's Caribana, with its strong roots in Trinidad Carnival, to understand that. Particularly fascinating is how Carnival has been adapted to suit the various cultural, social and political forces in different parts of the world. Certain carnival forms that have come out of Trinidad, such as those closely associated with calypso and steelpan music, have been interpreted in a variety of ways around the world.

Sir Lancelot (Lancelot Pinard) was key to spreading calypso around the world. His life story, and his success, though little remembered today, is one that reflects the true nature and versatility of calypso. And his career exemplifies the ways in which calypso music spread to become recognized as the sound of the Caribbean Diaspora throughout the world, as well as becoming integrated with the new media of contemporary society.

His popularity is reflective of his skills as a calypsonian, those that are intrinsic to the art form itself. They not only brought him success as a performer in nightclubs and a recording artist—the primary media of other calypsonians who lived in the USA or indeed in Trinidad in the late Thirties—but also in the new media emerging at the time: radio, movies, and, later, television. He also knew how to be a showman, and attract sponsors. Indeed he was one of the first to take calypso to Europe and, in the 1960s, to put together a tour of Asia involving both pan and limbo dancing. His career shows how a Trinidad song style that told the local news and scandals on street corners, rum shops and in tents during the Carnival Season, came to be associated with the Caribbean tourism industry.

Sir Lancelot was the first person from Trinidad to have a significant career as an actor and performer in Hollywood. His movie career stretched over fifteen years. It began with a brief appearance singing a verse as a backup singer in *Two Yanks in Trinidad* (1942), included a brief scene in *To Have and Have Not* (1945) with Humphrey Bogart, and ended with his appearance as Scipio, the pirate, in the swashbuckling biography of John Lafitte, *The Buccaneer* (1958) with Anthony Quinn and Yul Brynner. In all, he appeared on camera in a dozen films as well as doing voice-overs and soundtrack work in two or three others.

Sir Lancelot also worked in radio and television, had a lengthy recording career, and performed in many different countries—a considerable career for a man who had never even trained for a career as a calypso singer or an actor. As a black actor in Hollywood in the 1940s and 1950s, he was often assigned minor parts as servants, but, in whatever role he was given, he was able to stand out. He used his ability to extemporize calypso creating roles that enabled him to perform songs that were integral to the plots of several of his films. Sir Lancelot was also the first calypsonian to target white America. Until this time, all West Indian calypsonians and entertainers performed first for a Trinidadian audience, then for a generalized West Indian audience, then for an African-American, and then for a white American audience. Sir Lancelot represents the first entertainer whose primary audience was the last group. He also brought calypso to the movies.

Lancelot Pinard grew up in Cumuto, Trinidad, one of seventeen children from an upper-middle class family. His father, Donald Pinard, was a Government railway official. His education included studies in German lieder and the Italian operatic arts. He worked for a while as a pharmacist at the Bonanza Drug Store in Port of Spain and then went to New York officially to study medicine, but really to follow his girl friend. He did not pursue his studies for long. A guest at a party of Trinidadians, Sir Lancelot, who had been asked unexpectedly to sing a bit of German lieder, was later asked by the band leader providing entertainment if he would sing a calypso. And even though he had never sung a calypso in public before, he so impressed the bandleader Gerald Clark that he was quickly invited to join the band and soon appeared with them at the famous Village Vanguard. Shortly after that, he recorded two numbers with Clark's band on the Varsity Record label. I t was then that he adopted the name Sir Lancelot. One of those records is distinctive: a calypso about Edgar G Hoover, the head of the

FBI. Sirens provided a dramatic effect that brought the listener right into the song. This wasn't the usual song about Trinidad politics; it was, instead, about American politics. Nor was it focused on the life of Caribbean expatriates, like Wilmoth Houdini, who, at roughly the same time, recorded a series of 78s for an album called *Harlem through Calypso Eyes*. Sir Lancelot was looking for a more universal theme, a theme that would have far more popular appeal.

Now these were the war years and Sir Lancelot sang certain songs in support of the American war effort. These were songs such as "Defenders of Stalingrad" as well as songs that, in a few years would be recognized as expressing a leftist view. He wrote a political calypso for the 1948 Progressive Party candidate, Henry Wallace, and recorded for a leftist record label that focused on anti-war issues. But these started with a song based on a speech that the then vice-president, Henry Wallace, made on May 8, 1942. Wallace delivered his most famous speech, known by the catchphrase "Century of the Common Man," to the Free World Association in New York City. This speech, grounded in Christian references, laid out an egalitarian vision of the future that was more socialist than either Roosevelt or Churchill contemplated. Shortly after, Wallace was blackballed for speaking out on the treatment of African Americans; and Roosevelt decided not to have him as a running mate in the next election.

During the race riots in Detroit in 1943, Wallace declared that the nation could not "fight to crush Nazi brutality abroad and condone race riots at home." Without ever mentioning Wallace by name, Sir Lancelot espoused a political line that was far from mainstream. While it might be what we expect from Calypsonians today, it was certainly not for those out to make a popular career abroad. He also got involved with "People's Song," a musicians' union combining folk music with the labor movement that had been formed in New York, led by Pete Seeger and Alan Lomax. While Lomax was presenting his famous "Calypso at Midnight" concert at Town Hall in New York, Sir Lancelot participated in a Los Angeles concert called "I Hear America Singing" in October of 1946. A prime mover for "People's Song" on the West Coast started a record label for "People's Song" artists. Their first release was Sir Lancelot singing "Walk in Peace" and "Atomic Energy". Boots Casetta—a writer for the *Daily People's World*, as well as the initiator of Charter Records, issued a two 78s-album of his songs for them. He chose Sir Lancelot partly for his sales potential, "not only will he do good stuff from a political/social standpoint but maybe commercially with this guy" (Cohen 2002, 48). While Sir Lancelot could have just focused on concerts and recordings, he was in the right place at the right time to be the first calypsonian to have a role in a Hollywood film.

Film

After about a year working in Greenwich Village, Sir Lancelot joined the Trinidad composer, pianist, and ex-film owner/manager Lionel Belasco in a cross-country tour of Catholic Church organizations. The tour ended in Los Angeles and that chance occurrence changed his life. He gave concerts at the Wilshire Ebell Theatre that sparked interest in the Hollywood film community, and he was soon summoned from New York for a small film role. It was a low budget 1942 Columbia Pictures patriotic film comedy, *Two Yanks in Trinidad*, starring Pat O'Brien and Janet Blair. The plot involves a set of rival criminals who join the army and are stationed in Trinidad. While Trinidad did have at that time an important American military base, the film was not shot in Trinidad, but in California. The only authentic Trinidadian element in the film was the inclusion of Sir Lancelot and his two musical companions. Sir Lancelot and the two other musicians (one who was Lionel Belasco in his only film appearance), appear in one scene and can be seen seated at the front of a white dance band, with maracas and a cuatro, during the film's first musical number. Janet Blair sings the song "Trinidad" and Sir Lancelot performs the third verse of the song. His appearance on screen is less than a minute, and he is not identified in the credits. Perhaps his appearance was a result of being one of the few Trinidad performers who had performed in LA at the time. But his appearance in that film led to him being discovered and brought him bigger roles.

His next film was a high budget Paramount musical, *Happy Go Lucky* (1942), starring Dick Powell and Mary Martin, about a cigarette girl who chases a millionaire to a Caribbean island. Sir Lancelot is prominently featured leading a band singing "Ugly Woman" by the Roaring Lion (Raphael de Leon). This was the greatest public exposure of a real calypso in a blockbuster Hollywood film. Lion himself was very proud that his composition was used in a feature film. It had been recorded in 1934 on Lion's first trip to New York and was one of the best known of all calypsos in America. As a result of the film, it went on to become an even better known calypso and, amazingly, in the 1960s. it was a top ten rhythm and blues hit for Jimmy Soul called "If You Wanta Be Happy".

Lancelot's other selection was a song written specifically for the movie, "Sing a Tropical Song" by Frank Loesser and Jimmy McHugh.

It became a hit for the Andrews Sisters. However, the chorus featured lines that would regrettably haunt calypso in the US for decades.

> Upon the isle I'm from which we come
> We have a national characteristic
> Which is very strong
> Because we put the accent upon a wrong syllable
> And we sing a tropical song

This business of putting the accent on the wrong syllable was a reductionist view of calypso rhythms. The Andrews Sisters recorded this song before they had a hit with the best-known number by Lord Invader (Rupert Westmore Grant) "Rum and Coca Cola." They had recorded "Sing a Tropical Song" a few months earlier on April 4, 1944. This song was indeed already a minor hit, reaching 24 on the Billboard charts for the week of July 8, 1944. The group was also featured singing it in their fourteenth film, *Her Lucky Night* (Universal, 1944) and recorded it for V-disc for military radio shows. Indeed, it was as a result of the success of that song that may have led them to seek out "Rum and Coca Cola."

After *Happy Go Lucky*, Sir Lancelot appeared in three of the seven low budget psychological horror films produced by legendary producer Val Lewton for the cash-strapped RKO studios. According to Lancelot, in these he isn't just a singer whose performance is presented, but in all three he had speaking roles. His high lilting voice and precise diction made him attractive to the director, Jacques Tourneur. The first, *I Walked With the Zombies* (1943), went on to become a cult classic in the United States. Tourneur called the film "Jane Eyre set in the tropics" (Cripps 1993, 94).

Sir Lancelot played the calypso singer and sang a calypso "Shame and Scandal for the Family" that he specifically wrote for the film based on an earlier Trinidad calypso about a scandal. Tourneur in an interview stated: "Whenever we were having a dramatic scene somewhere in the street at night he would go by singing and he was observing this drama going on and telling us, just like the old Greet tragedies. This gave a wonderful *poesie* to the film....We used him as a Greek chorus, wandering in seven or eight times and explaining the plot." (Fujiwara 1998, 91)

In the film *Betsy*, a Canadian nurse, comes to the Caribbean country, St. Sebastian, to take care of the sick wife of the rich plantation owner, Mr. Holland. Sir Lancelot provides a background to the story in a scene in the market and prepares the audience for the events that are to unfold. He sings:

There was a family that lived on the isle
Of St. Sebastian a long, long while
The head of the family was Harlin man
And his younger brother Rand
Ah woe ah me, shame and scandal for the family.

The Harlin man kept in a tower
A wife as pretty as a big white flower
She saw his brother and she stole his heart
And that's when the badness and the trouble start
Ah, **woe** is me, shame and scandal for the family.

His performance not only helps set the mood of the film but his songs provide a commentary for the events that are to unfold and advance the plot. Sir Lancelot, thus, uses calypso in its classic storytelling role to discuss in song current topical and often controversial events.

Tourneur scholar Chris Fujiwara offers a detailed commentary into the complex way this song operates in the film:

> Over the course of the sequence, the way the film presents the singer changes. Initially, we perceive him in his public role as an entertainer, albeit one who expresses a complex function, since he belongs to the post slavery entertainer tradition of Black Americans and brings out the subversive dimension of this tradition, appropriating and subtly mocking classical culture in his litany of "the world's greatest heroes" ... and indiscreetly recounting the "shame and sorrow" of the whites who are his social superiors. After the singer becomes aware of Wesley's presence (his rebuke to another musician for failing to warn him of this shows, by the way, that he was unaware of Wesley's presence, precluding the possibility that he was deliberately taunting Wesley) his statement of his intention to apologize is humorously florid and consciously ironic: "Apologize, that's what I'll do. Creep in like a little fox and warm myself in his heart." This mode prepares us to see his actual apology as the performance of another role—the contrite servant—and not as an expression of his true nature (Fujiwara 1998, 91-2).

While Fujiwara's analysis is perceptive of the complex use that Tourneur makes of Sir Lancelot in a single scene, he fails to understand that the role Lancelot performs is not a reflection of African-American traditions, but the specific heritage of calypso singers—who, throughout the Thirties, had been noted in Trinidad for singing about the scandals of the upper crust in town. Indeed, Lancelot's song is an adaptation of a specific calypso from the mid-1930s.

The apology results in an explanation of what was clearly understood in Trinidad as the role of the calypsonian. After a bow, Lancelot says:

> I've come to apologize. Just an old song I picked up somewhere. Don't know who did make it up. The singers on this island they tattletale on anybody. Believe me Mr. Rand I would not have sung that song if I would have known you were with a lady.

Wesley continues to drink until the scene fast forwards to the evening when we see Wesley passed out, head down on the table, while Lancelot enters singing a last verse that portends the dark future ahead.

> The wife and the brother they want to go
> But the Harlan man he tell them no
> The wife fall down and the evil came
> And it burned her mind in the fever flame.
> Ah woe ah me, shame and sorrow for the family
>
> Her eyes are empty and she cannot talk
> And a nurse come
> And now you must see that my song is sung
> Ah woe ah me, shame and sorrow for the family
> Ah woe ah me, shame and sorrow for the family

This time Lancelot's appearance is more sinister. His face is often in shadows, while Wesley lies passed out in the forefront, and he now foretells the future rather than the past: predicting exactly what will occur in the film.

Sir Lancelot's performance was helped by the fact that Tourneur treated black people with respect in his films. While Sir Lancelot did perform in many films that had stereotypical plots and characters he:

> exuded a warm, laughing confidence that was not threatening to the white male Americans upon which his career depended. He was assertive without being aggressive, and he could play stereotyped roles, as the best of the tragic African-American performers were forced to do, with humor and grace (Hill 1993, 191).

The Trinidad public was aware of this film, as the manager of the Victory calypso tent in Trinidad, M. H. Khan, advertised the event in the 1943 Victory calypsos booklet:

> Calypso in the Movies now! Another scoop for RKO Radio Pictures with the Super startling story of Secret Zombies in an Island in the Caribbean—I WALKED WITH A ZOMBIE set to Voo Doo [sic] Drums and Calypsoes, by a Local Calypsonian" (Rohlehr 1990, 151).

The producer Val Lewton, pleased with Sir Lancelot's performance, cast him in *The Ghost Ship* (1943), a psychological thriller about a merchant marine ship, whose psychotic captain terrorizes a new third mate. Sir Lancelot appears as one of the members of the crew, Billy Radd, and he is heard singing brief snatches of a few songs during the course of the movie as well as having a few brief speaking scenes.

In the last of the three films he made with Val Lewton *Curse of the Cat People* (1944), Sir Lancelot appears as the house servant Edward. The part was originally written as a middle-aged New England motherly person, but Lewton was so pleased with the performances of Sir Lancelot in the earlier films they had made together that the part was rewritten. While his singing role is minimised—he only sings a piece of one folk song—his acting time is increased. His role is indeed significant as he appears throughout the film and he has a speaking part in a number of scenes.

While he may be acting the part of a servant, he portrays the role with sensitivity. The critic James Agee called it "one of the most unpretentiously sympathetic, intelligent, anti-traditional, and individualized Negro characters" he had seen in a movie (Fugiwara 1998, 92). In addition, once again, Sir Lancelot's character has an important function in providing key information in the film, and, as Thomas Cripps notes, his performance provides a "colorful, amusing, and different way of presenting expository information" (Cripps 1993, 94).

Sir Lancelot appeared as a performer in another zombie film, the comedy thriller *Zombies on Broadway* (1945) directed by Gordon Douglas and starring Bela Lugosi. In the film, press agents seek a real zombie for the opening of a new nightclub on Broadway. Sir Lancelot performs his usual role as a calypsonian and is distinctive, appearing in his trademark white hat and suit with his clear slightly high-pitched singing voice. In the film, he performs a song that once again warns of the terror and evil that is to come. He sings the same melody from his calypso "Shame and Scandal for the Family" that he used so effectively in *I Walked with the Zombies*. But In this song he first welcomes the visitors to a tropical island of their dreams, with coconut palms and banana trees, and warns:

> But the visitors would not so happy be
> If they could see what is behind the tree
> They could see this isle of evil men
> But if they wait till the full moon come
> They shine on the hands of the voodoo drum
> The chance to leave may come too late
> And blood on the ground will meet their fate

The most important film Sir Lancelot appeared in was the celebrated 1944 Howard Hawks film *To Have and Have Not* with Humphrey Bogart and Lauren Bacall. It is his best known appearance, and he has a small speaking part on screen with Humphrey Bogart. The film is adapted from a novel by Ernest Hemingway and is typical of the adventure film genre set in exotic locations. Sir Lancelot appears as Horatio, a respectable boat-hand to Humphrey Bogart's character Harry Morgan, who runs a charter fishing boat. Sir Lancelot appears in only one scene putting bait on the line while they are out fishing. A customer objects to Horatio's presence, apparently a racial attack, but Bogart comes to his defense arguing that he is an important part of the crew.

Radio

Sir Lancelot was appearing regularly on film and recordings, and was based in Los Angeles. No doubt, this led to his series of appearances on syndicated radio shows. Again, the details are far from complete. He was a guest on a couple of episodes of a progressive series called *Hello, Americans*, featuring Orson Welles as narrator, and supported the war effort in presenting the distinctive aspects of the other American countries involved in the fight against the Nazis. He appears to have been a regular guest on numerous shows during the 1940s and 1950s that originated in LA.

When I interviewed him in the late 1980s, he noted that his popularity on the radio related to his extempore ability. As anyone who goes to Trinidad today for Carnival can tell you, one of the greatest events of the season is the competition for "extempo champ," in which artists like Gypsy, Black Sage, Lady Africa, and Lingo are among the current masters. The ability to compose lyrics on any subject at the drop of a hat always been a prized skill. In Trinidad, as well as singing your own compositions, it is one of the marks of a "calypsonian," and not just a calypso singer. A recent calypso by Contender (Mark "Contender" John) noted "You can't buy an extempo" (2009).

Sir Lancelot was proud of his extempo skill and noted that it was particularly useful in his radio career because he was able to create a commercial on the spot for the show's sponsor, whether it was Elgin watches or the Hacienda Hotel. In a memoir, his manager Irwin Parnes writes:

> He was engaged to sing Ford automobile commercials for 26 weeks on the Dianh Shore national NBC radio show. I was told his fan mail exceeded Dinah's. Lance sang commercials for Elgin watches, Washington apples, Standard Oil, etc. (Parmes 1998, 78).

His skill singing radio commercials also gained him one of his film 'appearances,' although he never 'appears' on screen. His voice is heard in *Eve Knew Her Apples* (1945), where Ann Miller is driving along in a car and Sir Lancelot's voice is heard singing the radio commercial for the fictitious Vitamin Flakes breakfast cereal:

> I am the calypso singer here to tell
> About vitamin flakes
> They give you vigor, vim and vitality
> And built your Rome in Italy

International Touring

During the war years, Sir Lancelot became the best known calypsonian in the United States. This was through his records, movies, and radio. At the same time, he was also touring. And newspaper reports from the war years suggest that he was not only giving concerts in cities, but also performing in colleges. These articles suggest that he was billed as much as a lecturer on the art of this—to Americans—strange form of music, as he was a performer.

In 1945, following the success of his films and the winding down of the war, Sir Lancelot toured the Caribbean and visited Trinidad. The *Trinidad Guardian* of March 24, 1945 reported that he had attracted "mammoth audiences" in St Thomas. After appearing in Jamaica, The *Jamaica Gleaner* also reported that he sang a new calypso entitled "Jamaican Man" at his local concerts. Again, we see Sir Lancelot realising that as a Trini coming to Jamaica, he could create a local themed song as a good hook to bring in the crowds.

On another level, it was one of his songs that enabled Lancelot to tour both the Caribbean and South America. Although "Pan American Way" was not written at the request of Pan Am, once the management heard it, they went wild. As his manager related in an autobiography:

> The Pan Am publicity department in Miami flipped when they heard this eulogy and purchased 500 albums. I informed their director, Roger Wolin that Sir Lancelot would be willing to sing this song all over the Caribbean Islands, Central and South America, and Mexico if they provided us with two free first class open tickets. One month later, we received the requested air tickets from someone in Cuba (Parmes 1988, 78-9).

It was a different time then for airlines. When I interviewed him, Lance remembered that he would get out his guitar and serenade the passengers and aircrew. From Puerto Rico to Trinidad, on to Guyana, then to Caracas, Venezuela, and ending in Mexico City, they undertook a unique three-and-a-half-month barnstorming tour.

Return to Films

The same *Trinidad Guardian* article (March 24, 1945), also reported that Sir Lancelot was optimistic about his future as an actor and for the success of black films:

> Pinard, who expects to take up acting seriously on his return to the United States expressed the belief recently that there is a future for the serious Negro actor on the screen and that the American movie public would react in the same manner to good Negro pictures as theatre-goers have reacted to Paul Robeson's performance in Othello.

But his film career was far from consistent, and his next film was the low budget *Linda Be Good* (1947), a light comedy set in a nightclub in which Sir Lancelot appeared as himself on screen, singing two of his own compositions: "Old Woman With a Rolling Pin" and "Young Girls of Today." In both, he is accompanied by a large Latin band.

More importantly, Sir Lancelot next performed a dramatic role as a prisoner in the major studio release, *Brute Force* (1947). Six violent convicts, led by Burt Lancaster, revolt against a sadistic warden and try to escape. While Sir Lancelot has a small role, it is, nonetheless, significant in that he appears throughout the film. He recounts, in song, what had happened previously in the film. While performing a role similar to that of the fool in a Shakespearean play, it was, nevertheless, a respected character able to move through all levels of the prison society and comment on what was going on. Not since *I Walked with the Zombie* had his skills as a calypsonian been so integrated into a film.

His last film for almost a decade was *Romance on the High Seas* (1948), directed by Michael Curtiz. This was Doris Day's first feature film. Sir Lancelot was hired to sing a pop calypso, "Run Run Run"—a reworking of the calypso classic "Ugly Women." However, Sir Lancelot did not get the chance to perform the song himself. Instead, it was sung by the film's male lead Jack Carson. Sir Lancelot was relegated to a brief exchange with Carson discussing the "tropical" way to pronounce the word "woman" with the stress on the second syllable, as well as introducing the song. All Lancelot was given to do for the rest of the film was to accompany the lead actor with his guitar. Years later, he still expressed his frustration at this turn of events. In a sense, Sir Lancelot was suddenly returned to the sort of minimal supporting role—the servant—he had in his very first film *Two Yanks in Trinidad*. Perhaps this contributed to his withdrawal from a film career for several years.

At this point, Sir Lancelot left the United States and spent a lengthy period traveling and performing in Europe. This was also the period of McCarthyism, and Sir Lancelot had clearly aligned himself with left wing causes. He was foreign born and, likely, subject to deportation. Whatever the reason, at the end of the 1940s, Sir Lancelot moved to Europe. There, he worked as a calypso singer and nightclub artist before returning to the United States in 1956 to find a calypso craze fuelled by Harry Belafonte's million-selling "Calypso" album.

While continuing with his successful career as a calypso singer, Sir Lancelot appeared in two more films. He appears at the beginning of the low budget science fiction thriller, *The Unknown Terror* (1957) and sings a calypso foretelling the danger that the adventurers will face on a jungle expedition in search of lost explorers. The song warns about a confrontation with a horrible creature. As in *I Walked with a Zombie*, his presence is not a merely a diversion for entertainment, but a device to provide commentary and information critical to the film as well as help advance the plot. Lancelot's last film role was in *The Buccaneer* (1958) starring Yul Brynner. He had a small non-singing part as Scipio, the pirate in the historical romance based on the life of the pirate John Lafitte, who fought with the American navy against the British in 1812.

Again, here was a transformation of a calypso singer to a mainstream Hollywood actor, albeit playing only small roles. However, if you look over his long career in film, including his major and minor films, no other Trinidadian, to my knowledge, has had such a substantial career before or since.

Television

As Sir Lancelot's film career was coming to an end, he turned to that newest media of the time, television. It is not clear how many television appearances he made. The details for television in the 1950s are fairly sketchy but at least a few survive and are known.

His earliest confirmed television appearance is *The Lux Video Theatre*, a 1950 television series. In one of the programmes, in 1957, he acted in a television adaptation of Hemingway's *To Have and Have Not* with screenplay by William Faulkner. Sir Lancelot was one of two actors to appear in both this version and in the well-known film by Howard Hawks. He is no longer the boat-hand Horatio. He is listed in the credits as Bartender, yet he serves no drinks and is seen in two early scenes singing in the bar. In both scenes he plays the role of a singing troubadour with a guitar, providing atmosphere for the opening scenes of the production.

Sir Lancelot also did a voice-over for a 1958 episode of the popular television comedy *Father Knows Best* called "Calypso Bud." In this episode, Bud, the teenage son in the family, gets a set of bongo drums which he learns to play to impress a girl at school. The drums come with a record giving drum instructions using Sir Lancelot's voice. His last known television appearance was playing "Man" in the "Howard's New Life," a 1967 episode of *The Andy Griffin Show*, where Howard throws caution to the wind and moves to a Caribbean island for a short while.

While doing these early television appearances, Sir Lancelot seems to have missed a unique opportunity to have been immortalized as the author and/or singer for the theme song for the show *Gilligan's Island*. The original plan was to use him but there was not enough time to reach him, and he was never used (Schwartz 1994, 33). However, in a sense this is lucky for us. If this had happened, then it is likely that his rich legacy of work would have been eclipsed by this one theme song.

Travel to Asia

Sir Lancelot spent most of the 1960s performing abroad. He was especially popular in Asia and was based in Hong Kong for two years.

As far as I have been able to document, this is one of the earliest Asian residency of any Trinidad Carnival artists. Promotional material for this period shows that he toured with steel drums and featured a limbo dancer. In 1969, he visited his homeland, Trinidad, where he had a religious experience prompting him to compose and record a number of religious calypsos, as well as promoting earlier religious calypsos he had produced. He retired as a performer in the early 1970s and rarely performed thereafter. Although in 1984, he did perform for two sold out shows at the McCabe"s Guitar Show, backed by such celebrated musicians as Van Dyke Parks and Ry Cooder.

Sir Lancelot died in California in 2001, spending the last years of his life in a nursing home. Don Hill credits him as having

> translated calypso for American tastes, and they learnt his
> calypso and mimicked it. No Trinidadian had more influence
> on the form of the 1950s calypso boom in the United States
> than Sir Lancelot (Hill 1993, 192).

His career is proof that he was what in Trinidad would be acknowledged as a true, true calypsonian who extempored his calypso composing and singing adapting to a number of new media—he was the first, or one of the first, calypsonians to break into film, radio, and television. In many ways, he single-handedly brought calypso around the world.

Works Cited

Cohen, Ronald D. 2002. *Rainbow Quest: The Folk Music Revival and American Society, 1940-1970*. Amherst: University of Massachusetts Press.

Cripps, Thomas. 1993. *Making Movies Black: the Hollywood message movie from World War II to the civil rights era*. Oxford: Oxford University Press.

Fujiwara, Chris. 1998. *Jacques Tourneur: The Cinema of Nightfall*. New York: McFarland & Company.

Hill, Donald R. 1993. *Calypso Calaloo: Early Carnival Music in Trinidad*. Gainesville: University of Florida Press.

Parnes, Joy. 1988. *Irwin Parnes takes the "bull by the horns."* Benson, Ariz: World University Press.

Rohlehr, Gordon. 1990. *Calypso & Society in pre-independence Trinidad*. Trinidad: G. Rohlehr.

Schwartz, Sherwood. 1994. *Inside Gilligan's Island*. London: St. Martin's Press.

7

❧❧

DESIGNING AND
PRODUCING CARNIVAL

Artists Who Dare:
Contemporary Carnival Designers

Loyce L. Arthur

I've long been intrigued by carnival costume design. Over the years I have become more and more fascinated by the work of carnival designers around the world and the variety of ways that they choose to express themselves. Contemporary carnival design is a fusion of performing arts, fine arts, and carnival arts traditions, old and new. Yet it is also a unique discipline and carnival designers can do what other artist cannot. They dare to gather thousands together, clothed in splendor, to bring history to life. With their art they challenge beliefs and assumptions or tell stories of worlds as small as a neighborhood and as large as a country. Contemporary carnival is street theater and street art. Designers are performance artists who dare and they don't shy away from using canvases and stages as large as their imaginations will allow.

The question is why do they dare? From what I can tell (and there is still quite a lot that I need to do to find the answer to this question), but, from what I can tell so far carnival designers today draw on what has gone before, re-shaping it to fit the demands of the contemporary world. They have a modern sense of place, a strong desire to serve their communities, whether their work is seen on the main streets of Port of Spain, Trinidad, Toronto, Canada, or Rotterdam, Netherlands. Carnival design is a multi-faceted art form and designers are sculptors of steel, fiberglass, and cloth as well as choreographers and performance artist. Carnival designers dare to set out to create moving, living statements of community values and beliefs rather than let carnival costume arts devolve into just a parade of random color and sound. The daring work of Peter Minshall, Clary Salandy, Michael Ramdeen, and Christopher

Pinheiro who are all highly inventive, dedicated, and original artists, is particularly impressive. Examples of their work will be cited throughout this essay. They are all particularly gifted designers who have a drive to protect and preserve the legacy of the past, while pushing the creative boundaries to carry carnival design into the future.

I have found that author Robert Farris Thompson eloquently provides insight into both the fundamental core elements of carnival display rooted in traditional African arts as well as the way contemporary artists draw on this past to re-shape the present. In *African Art in Motion*, Thompson explains that visibility is a highly important characteristic of African art/dance/music—three forms in one, impossible to separate one from the others—certainly a very familiar carnival concept. Thompson writes:

> The aliveness of the concept among the Igbo of southeastern Nigeria is apparent in the need, in this society, to be 'transparent' or 'open' in one's actions. Visibility, in the sense of aesthetic clarity, governs the thought of artists among the Chokwe of Angola... "danced sculpture"—(means) the sculpture is removed from the secrecy or relative privacy of the shrine or grove and restored to the public view...Compare the Yoruba proverb: 'if the secret is beat upon the drum, that secret will be revealed in the dance.' This is also the basic premise among the Ndembu of Central Africa, where it is believed that what is clearly seen can be accepted as valid grounds for knowledge (105).

Thompson's characteristics of African art also can be useful in understanding *carnival brilliance* (my emphasis). He describes the notion of luminosity and brilliance as a function of African art. He says, "The Yoruba maintain that some forms of artistic motion positively shine, a belief that perhaps continuing, in change, within the Yoruba barrios of Bahia where it is believed that vanished, shining drums produce more brilliant tones than drums without varnish or shining surfaces" (Thompson 108). It gives one a new appreciation of sequins! From the beginning carnival has been an outdoor event, with a few exceptions, and carnival designers have used the space to their advantage, whether this means incorporating organic materials into their costumes or using materials that look spectacular in sunlight or at night depending on the time of day of the event.

In the book *Caribbean Festival Arts*, Thompson, John Nunley, and Judith Bettleheim make an excellent case for the links between African aesthetics and carnival traditions that are seen in contemporary carnival designs. Thompson's uses the term, "high-affect aesthetic" to describe a common principal that governs the aesthetic sources that historically shaped carnival —early European, African, and Asian arts and culture.

Nunley and Bettleheim continue with a statement on the impact of contemporary carnival creations:

> While this quality—of a high-affect aesthetic, is enhanced by the modern technology of an urban environment it's source is really the individuals desire to stand out in a crowd. Wherever large buildings, the sounds of automobiles, machinery, and people all compete with the costumes and music, high-affect aesthetics result (36).

A description follows of a 20-ft jellyfish costume in the 1985 Caribana event, whose mylar-skinned surface reflected the mirrored glass windows of buildings on University Ave, Toronto, "literally reducing and absorbing them onto the costume" (1998, 36).

Implicit in the statement above is the notion that the designer of this costume incorporates the surroundings into the design. This implies that contemporary carnival designers dare to challenge the streets, skyscrapers, and urban environments by creating fantastic kinetic objects. They are not daunted by competing elements, rather, they use them to enhance their work.

Peter Minshall is the grand master of carnival danced sculptures and high-affect aesthetics. The now famous Mancrab industrial machine in *River* 1983 masterfully commanded the stage when he first appeared and provoked gasps from viewers when his towering polluted canopy was dyed red as he danced. The undulating shapes and forms in *RED* 1998 filled the streets of Port of Spain with brilliant color providing a feast for the eyes, more spectacular than any static city facade. Minshall's carnival designs are always full of life and bring to life Trinidadian history as well as contemporary concerns. His creations pay homage to his mentors Carlisle Chang and George Bailey, among others, who were highly instrumental in making carnival arts more visible and more viable as an art form. His art always shows his deep commitment to all facets of Trinidad's rich culture and is rooted in African, Asian, and European aesthetic traditions. Minshall's creative performances embody the African idea of the interrelationship between the kind of sculpture and movement that Thompson describes. He calls his designs kinetic sculptures, dancing mobiles, or walking sculptures.

About his own work Minshall himself is quoted as saying, "It's a whole incredible kinetic form...it is not mechanical. It is alive" (1998, 106).

Christopher Pineiro's designs of fourteen-foot zebras, giraffes, and other imaginative characters for Swizzlestick Theatre and Caribana in Toronto are particularly striking when they play with and against the sky or skyscrapers. Based on the African masks, Moko Jumbies transformed into carnival jumbies, these stilt dancers are a beautiful fusion of traditions past and present that enliven contemporary cityscapes. In addition to the scale of the costumes, Pineiro makes wonderful use of striking colors to catch the eye coupled with materials that move with the dancer, enhancing the grace of the figures.

Clary Salandy and Michael Ramdeen are a team of carnival designers whose works are deeply imbedded in a variety of world traditions and they create high affect art that makes the invisible visible in the streets of London, UK. One of the things Salandy often talks about is the need to create design elements that are seen by spectators in the front AND the back of the crowd as well as anyone in upper story windows along the route of the performance. She has commented a number of times that movement is a critical factor in her work. Salandy and Ramdeen's designs for their band Mahogany are based on the long tradition of Trinidad design. Their creations are dynamic sculptures that move to soca rhythms that Salandy hand-selects to compliment the work. Their highly imaginative and socially relevant presentations set monochromatic London streets awash in vibrant color and capture the imagination of viewers to the delight of all.

But, as with African artists, visibility is not an arbitrary, frivolous motivation for carnival designers. No, there is a deeper purpose beyond street entertainment. Trinidadian designers in particular are adamant that carnival is the process of "playing mas" rather than just walking or dancing in the streets in costumes. The word "mas" is short for masquerade but means so much more. Geraldine Connor & Max Farrar provide insight into this purpose in their essay on carnival in the UK in the book *Culture and Action*. They state:

> Refusing the racial assumptions of Imperial British culture, carnival has appropriated and reformulated European aesthetics, combining them with African traditions, and created a new cultural space as a tool for liberation (2004, 260).

Ruth Tompsett, a London scholar and carnival archivist, gives us the fundamental elements that carnival designers use to accomplish

Minaret from Mosaic, 2006

Yellow and orange were used to represent the tension that is felt by London's Muslim community—the heat of anger. Performed by Tony Morgan (with permission from Clary Salandy)

their daring feats of breath-taking splendor. She writes, "Carnival art is capable of both visual spectacle and detailed narrative, of communal sharing and intense personal experience, of bringing history into the present and creating fearful beauty" (Ferris and Tompsett 14).

She further explains that carnival imagery can be far more than harmless or pretty, saying:

> ...the aesthetic function of carnivals arts is everywhere evident in the design and creation of Mas. As in the disposition of jewels in an elaborate brooch or of fireworks in a large-scale display, the carnival artist seeks to create impact, to delight or terrify, to covey meaning through his/her choice and use of color, size, dimension, shape, and texture, overall effect and close-up detail; the designer will give attention to

the visual impact of how the Mas looks when it moves (Ferris and Tompsett 14).

Richard Schechner in conversation with Minshall and Milla Cozart Riggio in the book *Culture in Action* states clearly that "(Carnival) is ritual definitely...It's a kind of religious service. A celebration certainly, but a playing out of belief also. To put it in Clifford Geertz's words, the carnival is a story Trinidadians tell themselves " (cit. Schechner, 2004, 121).

Contemporary carnival designers are energized by the opportunities presented by playing mas in urban settings, but it is an ongoing fight to have their work seen, understood, and appreciated. Officials, afraid of public disturbances, constantly seek to limit carnival routes and confine activities behind barriers and fences. Drunken revelers just out for a good time, as scantily dressed as possible, have no interest in "playing mas" and helping to present a designer's vision. However, I would like to posit that contemporary ideas of radical street art can help carnival artists to gain the respect that they deserve. Modern art, modern street performance, modern forms of political protest, all come together in contemporary carnival aesthetics. Modernity has produced some of the most exciting and innovative art in the world, including the carnival arts. In her article, "Street Scenes," Eleanor Heartney remarks that modernity is tied indissolubly to the streets. She is discussing the work of the artist, Dennis Adams, who constructs what she calls, subversive public sculpture and social sculpture in public spaces that are unexpectedly free urban environments—or rather spaces that he feels he has the freedom to make his own and make a statement because it is public space. She goes on to say:

> Poets, painters, architects and social theorists have alternately celebrated and reviled the transformation of the city from a loose collection of neighborhoods and semi-Independent enclaves into a complex organism whose lifeblood flows through arteries of its roadways or, as more recent imagery would have it, onto a field of intersecting forces. None, however, would deny that the moving chaos of the street is the quintessential modern experience. This has led to a redefinition of social space (1989, 230).

As Milla Cozart Riggio states in *Culture in Action*, "the essence of carnival remains its inherent capacity to appropriate spaces and transgress boundaries in order to manifest and celebrate aspects of human community." Like Heartney she categorizes efforts to dominate and appropriate space as a modern idea. She further states that carnival participants consciously or un-consciously affirm their right to the streets to celebrate black life and black culture, through carnival, the "aesthetic equivalent of social protest" (24).

Contemporary aesthetics allow several subversive art forms to flourish, such as grafitti with which some young people transform their drab environments and combat urban sprawl and decay. They too proclaim "we are here we will not be ignored!" as they scrawl their names across every surface.

Other similarities exist between grafitti and carnival arts besides a similar purpose. Carnival design has grown beyond basic costuming and grafitti artists transform scrawls into city mural projects, giving communities a visual voice. Murals in cities around the world, like the work of carnival designers, celebrate community values and speak against societal ills of every kind. Betty Merken comments that mural art

> is a visible symbol of a commitment to the development of an urban aesthetic. The benefits of an artistically enriched public environment are numerous and far reaching. Murals more than any other art forms, bring into focus the dynamic between artists and their communities...the images effect us all (1988, 10).

In addition to sharing a kinship with artists and sculptors past and present, carnival designers rank amongst the finest performance artists of their times. Minshall, Salandy, and Pinheiro all have backgrounds in theater that gives them a unique perspective on the effect of shapes, forms, and bodies in space in order to tell dynamic stories. Their work is not merely decorative, but reflects community beliefs, values, and aspirations. They produce massive costume pieces that take up physical space or they costume thousands of participants in the same color and/ or with similar contours and shapes and forms, creating a tsunami of frenetic energy that sweeps along everything in its path. Each sees carnival mas as street theater with a purpose. Carnival designers choose a myriad of themes to illustrate, including the Middle Passage, the Caribbean diaspora, and the struggle to hold on to community and self in an increasingly mechanized, artificial society. And it is there on the streets for all the world to see and share.

Minshall is highly adept at employing narrative and dramatic symbolic associations to tell epic stories on an epic scale. The very best example of this is the incomparable *River* trilogy that took viewers through a tale of life, death, and rebirth while warning of the dangers of industrial pollution and loss of cultural identity in Trinidad. This work and others like it embody a synergy between ritual, theater, carnival masking, and kinetic sculpture. For him mas *is* theater. (Nunley 1998, 108)

In creating mas, Minshall and others seek to honor and respect carnival's ritual, cultural, and aesthetic heritage, particularly in a time when outside social and political forces threaten carnival traditions. As Minshall states, when considering the relationship between carnival and theater:

> Here's a little island (Trinidad) that needs catharsis like anybody anywhere else. We don't have the resources or the audiences for a Broadway season or a West End. But we have the same needs. So what do we do? Carnival. That it goes back to the most ancient times, that it is a celebration of life—is almost neither here nor there. What matters is that we are here now, and we have this festival of the arts...it's our Broadway (Riggio 2004, 121).

Errol Hill, of course, was one of the first scholars to put forth the idea of carnival as dramatic ritual or theater. Lesley Ferris, Ruth Tompsett, Milla Cozart Riggio and others have also written extensively about the subject. As with modernity in the fine arts, modernity in the performing arts has led to brilliant expressions of contemporary life, including carnival.

A theater and performance background gives carnival artists like Salandy and Minshall methodology and techniques to express the ideas in an immediate, visceral way. As with the visual arts traditions, Salandy, Minshall, and Pinherio are also part of the long history of street performers who through their work are able to draw attention to issues that people might wish to ignore.

Author Bim Mason clarifies the relationship between performance, dramatic intention, and visual representation on a grand scale. In his book, *Street Theatre & Other Outdoor Performance*, Mason describes the ways that street performers present their work. In order to reach and educate ordinary people street performers use visual images or symbols that are suggestive of larger ideas to reinforce firmly held beliefs or to persuade spectators to view the world around them differently (1992, 68-69). Mason also explains that in order to get their point across quickly and effectively, before an audience member may be distracted by bustling city life, street performers use popular forms and mediums, such as music and bold images to tell mini-stories in which complex issues are reduced to good vs. evil, nature vs. technology, or oppressors and the oppressed.

Togetherness, from Freedom Song, 2007.

To mark the 100th anniversary of the end of the British slave trade, the section represents the balance and interconnection that is needed between black and white to bring about true freedom. The triangular shapes are the abstracted forms of happy free people with their arms in the air. Salandy says, "When black and white are in harmony with each other we can change the world for good. President Obama is the proof." (with permission from Clary Salandy)

Some participants may leave carnival with ringing ears because they stood too close to the giant sound trucks but the size of the sound coupled with the size of the visual elements means that carnival cannot be denied by onlookers. There is no denying carnival and there is no denying the people clothed in fabulous creations who may feel marginalized and ghettoized by day-to-day occurances and play mas to mitigate the circumstances of their lives. Mason explains the creative shift that must occur this way:

> ...there is a difference between the mere use of spectacular effects and their use in a dramatic way. Choreographing large numbers of people on and offstage can be very impressive in itself. Military parades are a demonstration of organizational ability, discipline and, by implication, power" (1992, 124-25).

As Minshall emphatically states again and again, carnival is mas. Carnival designers who are playing mas and producing designs that are more than costumes are creating a kind of performance that goes beyond the ordinary and the mundane.

In tracing the history of political street performance, Mason refers to the history of European carnival in the Middle Ages as an early form of subversive and provocative street performance that allowed individuals with no authority to indirectly challenge the hegemony of church and state. According to the majority of Caribbean carnival scholars, carnival continued to be a subversive event after it was brought to the Atlantic region by European planter classes. It became an avenue of protest first for slaves, then for post-Emancipation lower-class blacks, and eventually for twentieth-century national independence movement supporters as well as present-day grassroots political activists.

As much as contemporary carnival artists are shaped by modern art aesthetics, they are also shaped by social activism and political protest, often in the form of mas and street performance. Caribbean immigrants are no longer content to stay in their neighborhoods; artists are eager to take on new ways of seeing and expression. Performances are no longer confined to theaters: Carnival designers dare to take their messages and views of the world, both positive and negative, to the streets. Mason declares,

> the shared response of a vast crowd (to a street performance) is a powerful uniting force...It is not dissimilar to the tribal cry, the gaining of strength and security through a display of unity (1992, 213).

Furthermore Mason postulates, forms of communication—film, TV, the internet have put distance between people. He heartily endorses those artists who take on the role of bringing people together for live communal experiences on the smaller scale of a neighborhood or on, perhaps more importantly, a larger global scale. He states:

Outdoor theatre is gradually being seen as one of the best types of cultural exchange; its emphasis on visual rather than verbal communication eases language problems and is therefore more universal in its appeal...it can make direct cultural interaction possible if it uses audience participation. By transcending language and other cultural differences it looks forward to creative contact between ordinary human beings all over the world. (213)

Carnival designers relish this role. Wherever there are Caribbean people there is some form of carnival to mark their presence, and carnival designers to mix together old and new artistic traditions to reflect the cultural landscapes that they are now a part of, be it in Europe, the United States, India, or South Africa. The designers not only engage the crowds of spectators in their creative visions, they also costume hundreds to thousands of participants who plan all year for the one to three days that they can play mas. Designers are fully aware of the importance of the relationship that they must build with every member of their individual bands. Bringing the dancing sculptures to life, telling the stories, and sharing in the wealth of cultural expression cannot take place without the participants/performers. There is frenzied ritualized joy when music, dance, images, narrative, and committed performances all come together in the mas.

Yes, carnival artists dare a great deal. Yet they face disdain for and dismissal of their work. Salandy remarks that during her defense of her degree in college, her work was called kitsch, a word that still angers her but inspires her to always try to change popular perceptions. She is optimistic that things are changing. An appreciation of carnival aesthetics is slowly coming about. There is a lot to do to give these artists the recognition they deserve. I expect to continue my investigations to give carnival design its due as an innovative, original, and extremely vital contemporary art form that is more than just an opportunity to make "pretty costumes."

Works Cited

Connor, Geraldine and Farrar, Max. 2004. "Carnival in Leeds and London: making New Black British Subjectives," p 225—269, *Carnival: Culture in Action—The Trinidad Experience*. Milla Cozart Riggio, Ed. New York and London: Routledge.

Ferris, Lesley and Tompsett, Adela Ruth. 2007. "Midnight Robber: The Artists of Notting Hill Carnival." *Midnight Robbers: The Artists of Notting Hill Carnival*. London: Carnival Exhibition Group.

Heartney, Eleanor. "Street scenes: Dealing With Historical Events or Social Themes, Dennis Adams Constructs Subversive Public Sculpture." *Art in America*. April 1989, v.77, p.230-237.

Mason, Bim. 1992. *Street Theatre and Other Outdoor Performance*. New York and London: Routledge,

Merken, Betty and Merken, Stefan. 1988. *Wall Art: Megamurals and Supergraphics*. Philadelphia: Running.

Nunley, John and Bettleheim, Judith. 1998.*Caribbean Festival Arts: Each and Every Bit of Difference*. Washington: University of Washington Press.

Riggio, Milla Cozart. 2004. "Time Out Or Time In? The Urban Dialectic of Carnival." p 13—30. *Carnival: Culture in Action—The Trinidad Experience*. Milla Cozart Riggio, Ed. New York and London: Routledge.

Schechner, Richard and Riggio, Milla Cozart. 2004. "Peter Minshall: A Voice To Add To the Song of the Universe—An Interview by Richard Schechner and Milla Cozart Riggio, p 109—128, *Carnival: Culture in Action—The Trinidad Experience*. Milla Cozart Riggio, Ed. New York and London: Routledge.

Thompson, Robert Farris. 1979. *African Art in Motion*. California: Univ of California Press.

Jouvay Popular Theatre Process [JPTP]: Finding the Interior

Tony Hall

> A sense of unity is more important to us than an absolutely rigorous logic, and a sense of unity with our own past seems of particular importance.
>
> (Bill Nichols, *Ideology and Image*, 1981)

While growing up in San Fernando, Trinidad, I could see the stress cracks of eternal worry developing on my father's dark and dignified face as he disciplined my brother and me. The simplest of situations became a matter of life and death. I used to think that as a person, all of my natural instincts and impulses could not be that wrong. There must be some system or strategy or approach to living that belonged to us, that was indigenous to us, that resided comfortably in our genes, which would allow the five year old, who is still attached to him or herself, to be. Later, I realized this could take the form of Bob Marley's or The Shadow's "rolling stream."

Over my teenage years, I slowly became aware that I was being forced through a formal system of upbringing that was an attempt to detach me completely from my instinctive self. I was being programmed to end up between being diminished and detached from an objective inner-self and a cultivated and contrived, manufactured outer personality or ego. In *Caribbean Man in Time and Space*, Kamau Brathwaite makes a case for focusing on the inner processes engendered by the plantation encounter rather than on those that were enforced upon us, and Wilson Harris talks about exploiting our *"sleeping resources"* (1999, 152). Our history had been expunged from the pages of the record books. We had to look to what we had done instinctively in the new land.

As an adult, I felt the need to find an organizing principle emanating from my people in their social, psychic, and physical environment. When I was younger, I wished I were part of some tribe where people performed rites and rituals that directly intensified their consciousness of everything that touched their lives, everything that existed in their world. I think my theatre practise has been about that life-long search—fifty-five years of exploring.

I had always wanted to be part of a strong, entrenched system of traditions and rites, which would underscore what I was, where I was from, who I am, and guide where I was going. It is probably this atavistic tendency for tribalism—*the identity of belonging*—the urge in all of us to belong, which rules so much of our electoral politics in the English speaking Caribbean. In my youth, I suppose I was looking for something solid, something inherent in my tribe against which to rebel.

The truth is that we do practise rites and rituals with a fierce intensity. All people, whether they acknowledge it or not, must engage in this practice, or else they cease to exist, or go crazy, or both. However, it is the ambivalence about our immediate historical experience that has led to my search. This 'in-betweenity' may be the true place of our consciousness. It is certainly the place of our awareness. And, as Lloyd Best argues in his essay, *Making Mas with Possibility—Five Hundred Years Later*, "perhaps the conundrum is unravelled if we regard the consistent falling between as the core activity" (1999, n.p.). An entrenched process of detachment, of viewing self as 'other,' is also part of the new-world consciousness, the make-up of the Creole, the Dougla, the Mestizo, the Meti. Therefore, if we look at the Caribbean experience and are able to arrive at this new place, we will be able to encounter a people who went through a unique experience. It is an experience that can only be deciphered if we observe closely through the lens that has been shaped by survival strategies and systems created instinctively by these people in their environment. As Best questions:

> How could we, on that account alone (the fact that we were brought out 'to serve the purpose of business and capital, to guarantee them a supply of labour'), not have been entrepreneurs in human development, innovating and creating anew in the mere act of survival? (1999, n.p.)

This Caribbean existence of slipping between multiple identities (playing *mas*) may be a cross-cultural (Wilson Harris), inter-cultural (Wole Soyinka) sensibility that can be seen as an aid in negotiating tribal conflicts. We can become professional 'negotiators' worldwide.

What, therefore, is the event, or sequence of events, in the Caribbean historical experience that energizes and liberates the human spirit? Is there a single event that defines the sensibilities of entrepreneurs in human development? Is there an event that claims a place for self in such a way as to incorporate the entire experience while looking to a free and uninhibited future? The only phenomenon I can find is the liberation of Haiti, the process of the Haitian revolution and their gaining of independence. In activities fraught with the frailty of humanity, war, rebellion, bloodshed, deception, duplicity, and crafty negotiations, Haiti gained freedom from European colonialism and became the first, free, black society in the western hemisphere.

Haiti set me off on a particular track. It led me to looking at emancipation itself—the post-emancipation era in which certain established pre-emancipation traditions were continued and new traditions initiated let us say, from 1834 to about 1946, in Trinidad. It begins with the 1834-38 so-called 'apprenticeship' to emancipation through the systems and strategies of the ensuing riots: Camboulay Riots in 1881; Hosay Riots in 1884; the establishment of Emancipation Celebrations in 1888; the Water Riots in 1903; and reaching right up to the conflicts which established the first trade unions in 1937; the publishing of *Black Jacobins* in 1938; and, later, the invention of pan and the gaining of adult suffrage by 1946. In Trinidad, this 'corridor of time' represents a definitive period during which significant cornerstones in Caribbean civilization were laid. It is the time when the place Columbus called 'Trinidad' was mentally claimed by the 'people,' on the streets. And the ramifications of these events were felt in some of the other Caribbean territories as they, too, were creating themselves through their own efforts.

It is important to note that the annual Emancipation Day Celebrations, initiated on August 1, 1888, were changed in 1927, by the colonial authorities, to Columbus or Discovery Day Celebrations. This put restrictions on some of the masking that had begun to develop on Emancipation Day, and forced former slaves to slip stream to the pre-Lenten Roman Catholic carnival that, up until then, existed as a mainly French Creole carnival. Thus, all the energy of the Emancipation Celebrations had nowhere else to go but into the Roman Catholic carnival with its traditions of *jouvay*, Shrove Tuesday, and last lap.

Thus, it became obvious that the organizing principle I had been searching for was 'emancipation.' That is the foundation, the opening (*L'Ouverture*). (*Toussaint Louverture*, translated literally '*all saints awakening*.') This was a '*jouvay*' experience, an awakening. From then on, anytime I am lost, unable to figure out where I am, or what to do, or where I am going, all I have to do is to meditate on the word 'emancipation' and my awareness deepens into a new consciousness of 'seeing freedom and bearing witness to freedom,' the essence of 'emancipation'. This liberates my spirit once again and fills me with a clarity of mind such as the founders of Haiti, or the batonniers in the little conflicts of the Camboulay Riots and the Hosay Riots, experienced—even if that clarity always proves to be temporary.

Emancipation, here, is based on the belief that the state of emancipation is achieved in two very broad stages. The first stage is the historic liberation from chattel slavery by the African peoples of the new world. The second stage is an awakening to a spiritual transcendence of the mundane, physical, everyday existence of the illusion of the ego and its relationship to the oppressive authority and tyranny of the organized nation state. And *jouvay*, the name given to the opening 'ritual of the sunrise' at the dawn of the Caribbean Carnival, is carried as an enduring metaphor for the beginning or awakening of a distinct and unique human consciousness of fluid and authentic individuality, as opposed to static and commercial individualism. Today, we concern ourselves with the second stage. Today, we engage in the unavoidable life struggle with this seemingly impossible and somewhat improbable second stage.

When I began my search I looked at the kaiso, the calypso, that folk language of the double entendre, 'saying one thing and conveying so much else.' I noticed that, as indicated by Professor Gordon Rohlehr in his many books on the calypso, the art form stands tall on pillars firmly planted in similar traditions of emancipation. For example, when the Mighty Sparrow wanted to defend himself against a gun charge with intent to wound, in 1960, he sang a song called *Ten to One is Murder*. In his seminal *Trinidad Carnival: Mandate for a National Theatre*, the late Professor Errol Hill says that Sparrow sang this calypso in court, in self-defence (1972, 70-71). A modern calypso composed and sung in the idiom of the calinda stick-fight chant (a call and response technique) in self-defence.

Sparrow sings:

Well they playing bad
They have me feeling sad
Well they playing beast
Why they run for police

Ten criminals attack me outside of Mirama
  Ten to one is murder
Way down Henry Street by H G M Walker

Ten to one is murder
About ten in the night on the fifth of October
Ten to one is murder
They say how I push their girl from Grenada
Ten to one is murder
Well the leader of the gang was hot like a pepper
Ten to one is murder
And every man in the gang had a white handled razor
Ten to one is murder
Well ah back back till I nearly fall in the gutter
Ten to one is murder
Just imagine my position not a police in the area.

(Mighty Sparrow 1963, 37).

Here, Sparrow gets the chorus to sing his defence. In typical calypso tradition, he does not say it directly. And even though, as Keith Q. Warner says, it may have been 'mere creation for the sake of defense," this is not art hanging on a neutral wall, like a painting in a museum or an art gallery, a play in the safe confines of a darkened theatre, or a calypso in the appropriate tent (1988, 148). This is a warrior in the gayelle of a post-colonial courtroom in 1960, reaching back to Camboulay warrior-hood to go forward to defend himself and keep his freedom. He is invoking the spirit of the emancipation battoniers by using the system of creativity they invented. He is calling up the energy of the originators of the calinda of his ancestry to liberate himself. Once I saw that, I experienced another awakening, another dawn, another *jouvay*, that incredible ritual of the sunrise that opens the Caribbean carnival. *Jouvay* is an incredible awakening. Every Carnival Monday morning, year after year, *jouvay* brings us out of the darkness before dawn, the portal of the natural mystic of that magic hour, and awakens within us a new consciousness of the mystery of our selves and our community.

In the Trinidadian Creole language of the late nineteenth and early twentieth centuries, the word *jouvay* means daybreak. It comes from the French *jour ouvert*, or *j'ouvert*, meaning: the day opens. If we move carefully from the French to the Creole, we discover the telling of a creation story. So, in keeping with J. J. Thomas, whose important book *The Theory and Practice of Creole Grammar* was published in 1869 (we are well within our emancipation 'corridor of time' here), we will go with the word *'jouvay'*, spelt *j-o-u-v-a-y*. Using the *jouvay* experience as an all abiding Caribbean metaphor of awakening to self and community, without which no Caribbean carnival can happen, I am forced to conclude that Sparrow's composition and song recital of *Ten to One Is Murder,* is a *jouvay* process.

Jouvay Process is a perception. *Jouvay* Process can be seen as a meditation on an awakening, which manifests when elements of the creative impulses or principles embedded in the secret, subterranean, strategies of the emancipation traditions are invoked, mused on, or instinctively called up.

Jouvay Process happens because we are designed by, and steeped in, the rites and rituals of emancipation traditions.

Jouvay Process is the awakening of the "sleeping resources" about which Wilson Harris writes. These *'resources'* are cultural, ecological and of the "unfinished genesis of the imagination," to use the words of Harris' own title (1999).

Jouvay Process is a system of secret codes in the practical day-to-day creative way of life which emerges out of these manifestations.

As a theatre practitioner, I was inspired to come up with a performance model for a *Jouvay* Process workshop. This had to be a framework to convert the instinctive, creative, and imaginative elements of *Jouvay* Process from secret awareness to strategic, consolidated consciousness, in both the artist and the people of the community, through use of the imagination and through using the notion of emancipation as a never-ending transcendental cycle of creativity.

Jouvay Process is a natural, life-awakening process, a dynamic of spontaneous popular culture, into which an instinctive intervention is frequently made to realize communal art and make an art project. In this way, it is possible to codify *Jouvay* Process.

'The Antilles: Fragments of Epic memory', The Nobel Lecture
> The stripped man is driven back to that self-astonishing, elemental force, his mind. That is the basis of the Antillean experience, this shipwreck of fragments, these echoes, these partially remembered customs, and they are not decayed but strong (Walcott 1992, 3).

Jouvay Popular Theatre Process—JPTP

The workshop framework or performance model is what I call *Jouvay* Popular Theatre Process—JPTP. It is the *Jouvay* Process workshop. JPTP is an interventionist performance/production model for seeing art works happen. It is a framework for personal or group development, or for training artists to deepen their craft, and their consciousness, in direct relation to everything around them.

If we look at the term *Jouvay* Popular Theatre Process, we observe that two words, Popular and Theatre have been stuck in between *Jouvay* and Process. Popular Theatre, here, is making an intervention. *Jouvay* Process represents a dynamic, instinctive, and, by now, systemic process that is really a popular culture of survival. Indeed, as times change, *Jouvay* Process will manifest new variations for our survival. However, once we are aware of *Jouvay* Process and its functions, we become curious. We want to meditate on it long and hard in the hope of a better understanding of ourselves, of our community, and of our changing places in the world. Eventually, there may be ways for us to apply the process ourselves. Before we can probe deeper, we must witness and undergo a lengthy study of *Jouvay* Process. Only then can we gain an instinctive understanding and delve deeper into the process.

JPTP is conceived as a prompt to start your own conscious meditation on *Jouvay* Process. In a sense, it sets you on your own journey or facilitates the journey that you might have already embarked upon. So, what is Popular Theatre? Popular Theatre is a dramatic process that emphasizes a series of creative exercises. These exercises take the participants into an imaginative exploration of their own popular culture, deepening their own consciousness in the context of their social, political, psychic, psychological, philosophical, and physical environment.

Theorist Michael Etherton argues that the words 'popular' and 'theatre' form a dialectic with each other. Popular means participation. Theatre means art. (1982, passim). Etherton believes that the more one participates in this activity, the better the art. But, the more one participates, the deeper the politics also, so, the better the art, the more articulated the politics. Through this stratagem, we can consolidate in our selves the full, creative, and imaginative energy of the emancipation traditions set down by our ancestors. In this way, JPTP can activate the liberating power of our emancipation ancestry and, through self-knowledge, lead to sophisticated personal and group action. Thus, as Derek Walcott said to J. P. White in a 1990 interview, "the temperament and the spirit of the poet would enter the spirit of politics" (1996, 160).

Some Elements of JPTP:

1. The Gatkha Calinda School—the school in the emancipation traditions.
2. The Gayelle System—a curriculum of 'dance & fight' in the school.

3. Traditional Mas, Folk and Religious Character Manifestations —archetypes as guides and guardians.
4. Emancipation: Cycle of Creativity—the continuing circle of transcendence.

1. The Gathka Calinda School–the school in the emancipation traditions

If we expand on the mandate of the second stage of a transcendental emancipation, creative and meditative elements embedded in the emancipation traditions can be brought together under what I call The Gatkha Calinda School. This is founded on the stick-fight traditions of gatkha, the martial art used by devotees in the 1884 Hosay Riots, and calinda, the martial art used by batonniers in the 1881 Camboulay Riots. This martial arts foundation of the emancipation traditions, The Gatkha Calinda School, can be seen as traditional forms of play, combat, prayer, music, dance, meditation, games and drama. In addition, this school of martial arts also believes that through these traditions are platforms and locations for building approaches to self-development through performance. The Gatkha Calinda School, in its many rituals, secular and religious, can stretch into social, political, psychological and philosophical academies of meditation. From these, the theatre practitioner can create development exercises for any season.

One of the major academies to consider is the calinda itself; this stick-fight of the pre-emancipation Camboulay festival was a precursor to, and greatly influenced what later became the Trinidad Carnival. According to a formulation by Louis McWilliams, the calinda can unfold in a sequence of activities or stages. I call this sequence The Gayelle System.

The Hosay Riots of 1884, like the Camboulay Riots of 1881, happened on the island of Trinidad. The Muharram Massacre, the Hosay Massacre, or the Jahaji Massacre are all names used for the Hosay Riots. There occurred an uprising in which Shia Islamic devotees to the prophet's grandson Imam Husain, and other non-Islamic indentured labourers (including a ringleader, Sookhoo, a Hindu) brought to the island from India in 1845, were fired upon (including unarmed women and children). The massacre was a result of their defying colonial authorities in their attempt to preserve their right to form public processions along the street carrying tadjas in commemoration of Al-Husain.

The indentured labourers brought gatkha and the tassa drum (a war drum) with them. These became integral to their Hosay protests. As the poet and historian Ken Parmasad was wont to remark, African Camboulay warriors, who had won some concessions a few years earlier from

Governor Freeling to continue celebrating their Camboulay, journeyed from Port of Spain to San Fernando to appear on the streets in solidarity with the Hosay warriors. Interestingly, some believe that the word Hosay is a Creole pronunciation of Husain. Whether this is true or not, it should be recognised that an inter-cultural reality began in this period.

The practise of gatkha in the Trinidad Hosay context should be codified (we have started with the calinda) as part of the martial arts foundation element in The Gatkha Calinda School of JPTP.

2. The Gayelle System—a curriculum of 'dance & fight' in the school.

The Gayelle System studies different approaches to finding, using, and mastering appropriate weapons of 'Dance & Fight'. Narrie Approu, the legendary traditional masquerader in the Trinidad Carnival, succinctly describes *mas* as 'Dance & Fight.' Through deep and intense meditation, calinda can take students of this martial art to varying levels of expertise which are identified by different colours of head ties, red, green, yellow, blue, black, white to indicate levels of mastery attained

3. Traditional Mass, Folk and Religious Character Manifestations— archetypes as guides and guardians.

In seeking a drama process, or better yet, processes, in the emancipation traditions, I was naturally drawn to the *mas*, the traditional *mas*, which thrived energetically and totally dominated the Trinidad Carnival till about the 1950's. I came across many characters with sophisticated narratives for physical performance, monologues, dialogues, dance, and ceremonial dramas. They ranged from the Midnight Robber to the Baby Doll, from Police and Thief to Nurse and Doctor, the Belair Dance drama, the Burrokeet ceremony, from Pierrot to Pierrot Grenade, from Aboriginal Indian Masquerade, that foundation of traditional *mas*, in all its variations, to the Dame Lorraine plays in the yard. Characters from the Dame Lorraine plays came onto the streets and created the burlesque of early *jouvay*. But, for me, the most interesting elements of traditional *mas* were not the drama and the characters. I was more interested in knowing who the people were who created these characters, and why did they play them? Why did the same person play the same character, or set of characters, year in year out? Why did certain families play variations on a specific masquerade their entire lives—in some cases, passing on the legacy from generation to generation? What were these people who were called *jamette*—below the diameter of the social order—really about?

There appears to be an acute sense of 'nowness' about the sensibility of the *jamette* culture. There are many stories about people of carnival mentality who spent their last money on *mas* costumes, ignoring their rent and school-books for their children, much to the chagrin of the respectable middle class. In my youth, I even knew a man in San Fernando, Nasco, who would build the crown of his Indian costume in such a way that he could not get it out of his house. He would have to break down the house to get his masterpiece out onto the road. Every year, this caused his family, who performed with him in full costume, great wailing and gnashing of teeth in their yard. It seems the *jamettes* of the immediate post-emancipation period lived in the immediate present of time and space. For them, playing *mas* emphasized the present, the here and now, for in *mas* they could be themselves as well as playing various characters in simultaneous time and space. The playing of *mas* removed them from an immediate wretched past and from a future for which they could not even imagine any privileges. This left them only in the present, a time and place in which they could transform themselves through the performance of *mas*. But it appears to have given them empowerment through a kind of mindlessness. Playing mas, then, became a meditation, a Zen experience in space and time: Zen *Jouvay*. Only young people of this sensibility could have invented the pan. But that belongs to another chapter in the book.

My search eventually led me to elements of the West African masquerade where I discovered similarities in the mas. Simple things such as not being permitted to unmask the person or say the masquerader's name, even if you know who is behind the mask, exist in both the Trinidad mas and the African masquerade. In the African masquerade, the person under the mask becomes sacred; the whole masquerade is a mechanism through which the spirit enters the person. Certain maskers embody the same spirit for their entire lives. Indeed, they serve a function in their communities. In dancing that spirit, they may warn of impending danger to the community, or, more simply, scare little children into obedience. It becomes their own masquerade. Many of the maskers belong to a secret order. These secret orders are mainly male enclaves. Some researchers consider them a way of consolidating male energy and power to maintain the established order in the community. The African masquerade system has many functions. Particularly striking is the power of pure masquerading—something I had become aware of while growing up in the Trinidad Carnival. But until recently, I had never realized that what we called *mas* was the Caribbean version of the older sacred West African masquerade form.

I then turned my attention to the older practitioners who were still playing *mas* in Trinidad. They all had a deep affinity for the characters they played over and over again with subtle variations. And there was a relationship between what they played and their everyday lives. For example, in the 1950s, the leader of a group of dockworkers in Port of Spain would play some kind of a king in the carnival. They had some profound personal connection in their everyday lives to how the individual characters functioned in performance. Furthermore, they designed and made their costumes themselves. This, they insisted, was the tradition. This led me further to understand something fundamental about the characters. I began to understand how the spirit possession of African masquerade, that had been repressed in the Orisha and Hindu worship on the island, had replicated itself in the *mas* in the Trinidad Carnival.

Working with Peter Minshall in the late 1980's, I was able to observe him adapt and transform traditional *mas* characters through his own meticulous designs—the basic bat, the Midnight Robber, the burrokeet, the moko jumbie. I witnessed how he incorporated history (particularly the social and design history of the *mas*) into the present reality of performance without hampering it with nostalgia. Through this, I understood that traditions are most meaningful when they transform and evolve within the culture that produces them. Thus, it was important to re-examine the value of traditional, culture-bearing, *mas* characters, which embody the history of emancipation and the struggle for self-definition and independence. I went in pursuit and studied closely characters such as the Midnight Robber with his rapid-fire, grandiloquent speeches of revenge, and his imposing hat and gait. The Baby Doll with his/her instant social action theatre, which, openly on the street, insists on shaming renegade fathers into child support (Baby Doll was sometimes played by men); and the Badly Behaved Sailors satirizing the gay abandon of the Yankee sailor in drunken choreography along the street. I went in pursuit of all these and more.

What I began to understand was that in our everyday Caribbean performance culture, despite the different characters we try on for size all year round (play *mas*) to deal with daily exigencies and, thereby, discover our inner strengths, everybody has a character, or combination of characters (since the lines are never that clear), for which they have some specific affinity. And because the character can take a participant to a divine place which connects him or her to a new "cross-cultural" time-space concept of the universe, a refreshing, objective, egoless inner-self can be discovered in the process. Harris suggests that at least one of our many selves has an "affiliation with the divine" (www.l3.ulg.ac.be/harris/whintro.html).

The characters, therefore, become guides or guardians to empowerment and can carry participants to their fundamental truth, which already exists within them. Immersion in character became the cornerstone of JPTP. And, as I encountered different popular cultures around the world through the workshop, the character base broadened to include not just traditional *mas*, but also folk and religious characters, thereby embracing what each and every participant brings to the process. In this way, it is possible to pursue a new time-space concept of the universe. Caribbean people were brought from different places carrying with them this shipwreck of fragments, these echoes, these partially remembered customs, with which they created the Caribbean.

4. Emancipation: Cycle of Creativity–
the continuing circle of transcendence

– a revolutionary vision –
Transcending Reason and Logic
to 'awaken' or to *'jouvay'*
[ad infinitum in the *jamette* moment of NOWNESS]

1. Relaxation & Imagination
(musing on principles of creativity)

MEDITATION
2. Observation & Concentration
(preparing the artwork)

EMANCIPATION
5. Participation & Action (living as being)

MANIFESTATION
3. Possession & Characterization
(presenting the artwork)

LIBERATION
4. Reflection & Discussion
(reviewing the artwork critically)

TRANSFORMATION

1. Relaxation & Imagination
(musing on principles of creativity)
Leads to a state of MEDITATION . . .

2. Observation & Concentration
(preparing the artwork)
Leads to a state of MANIFESTATION . . .

3. Possession & Characterization
(presenting the artwork)
Leads to a state of TRANSFORMATION . . .

4. Reflection & Discussion
(reviewing the artwork critically)
Leads to a state of LIBERATION . . .

5. Participation & Action
(living as being)
Leads to a state of EMANCIPATION . . .

and then forward to No.1 again

Relaxation & Imagination
(musing on principles of creativity)
Leads to a state of MEDITATION . . . etc.

"A story refers life to an alternative . . .
Stories are one way of sharing the belief that justice is imminent"
(Berger 2006, 33).

JPTP—a *cross-cultural* workshop based on an *inter-cultural* life experience

This workshop takes its participants into seven spaces of activity:

[i] *FIRST SPACE*—Initiation, the assumption, a challenge

JPTP begins in a space of 'initiation' by acknowledging The Gatkha Calinda School's principles of prayers, chants, play, dance and fight in The Gayelle System of combat.

[ii] *SECOND SPACE*—Storytelling to find your guide or guardian

This second space assumes that the daily life of each participant reflects the essential drives and energies of any one, or combination, of the hundreds of religious, folk, or traditional *mas* characters in the emancipation traditions, seen as archetypes rather than historical figures. Next, workshop participants begin their search for the right character, or combination of characters, with which they may have some specific affinity (their daily "guardians" or "guides") through the telling of a story which begins: "I remember a time when". This is a story that may be based on an observed pattern of happenings, of an instant when an obstacle or barrier was overcome by some unexpected revelation or infusion of, what appeared to be, personal strength. It may seem as though the participant becomes somebody else in these instances, assisted by a 'guide' or 'guardian'.

[iii] THIRD SPACE–Finding your guide or guardian

In the third space, participants go through a range of theatre exercises and games, based on the street performances and other occurrences of the characters, to assist them (theatre artists, students, community persons, or employees) in their discovery of these characters as their 'guides or guardians' which manifest in their everyday life stories.

[iv] FOURTH SPACE–Exploring your guide or guardian

In the fourth space, participants explore discovered territory to better understand the specific performance elements that may constitute their 'guides or guardians' and their relationship to the manifestations in everyday life.

[v] FIFTH SPACE–Possessed by your guide or guardian

In this space, JPTP participants are asked to create short, improvised dramatic presentations based on their stories using elements of the occurrences of their chosen characters. In these presentations, they must play themselves, as the characters, in their own normal, everyday life situations. This can be related to the process of spirit possession, which is an important part of the traditional religions of many of the peoples who settled in the West Indies. The traditional characters, therefore, manifest in contemporary stories through the JPTP participants.

[vi] SIXTH SPACE–Green Corner: Your guide or guardian manifests

Take your stories to the street, GREEN CORNER, the sixth space, "the performance space" in the JPTP where "things" are revealed. In a performance called GREEN CORNER, the 'guide or guardian' manifests through the participant. We see this performance as trance, a ritual preparation for the crossing back to everyday life, a transition.

Here an awakening, a *'jouvay'*, is realized. This is what it means to see *jouvay* by GREEN CORNER. It is a way for the participant to explore cultural history as well as what their own lives may be about.

[vii] SEVENTH SPACE–A Ceremony (optional)

JPTP can evolve into a collective creation, a ceremony, a Communal Environmental and Street Theatre event, a *Jouvay* Opera using the Emancipation: Cycle of Creativity. The stories created to explore the characters are fused together collectively into one or more *'mas* band like' presentation(s), a 'habitable performance metaphor', preferably site specific, to consolidate, in a ceremony, the strategies of survival embedded in the many emancipation traditions of the pre-, post-, and post-post-emancipation eras.

"The Schooner 'Flight:"
"I had no nation now but the imagination"
(Walcott, *Star Apple Kingdom*, 1980)

Works Cited

Berger, John. 2006. "Dispatches: Undefeated Despair". *Race and Class*. Vol. 48, 1:23-41.

Best, Lloyd. 1999. "Making Mas with Possibility—Five Hundred Years Later." *Enterprise of the Indies*. Ed. George Lamming. Port of Spain: Trinidad and Tobago Institute of the West Indies.

Brathwaite, Kamau. 1974. *Caribbean Man in Time and Space*. Mona (Jamaica): Savacou.

Etherton, Michael. 1982. *The Development of African Drama*. London: Hutchinson University Library for Africa.

Harris, Wilson, and A. J. M. Bundy. 1999. *Selected Essays of Wilson Harris: The Unfinished Genesis of the Imagination*. London: Routledge.

Hill, Errol. 1972. *Trinidad Carnival: Mandate for a National Theatre*. Austin : University of Texas Press.

Mighty Sparrow (Francisco, Slinger). 1963. "Ten to One is Murder." *One-Hundred-and-Twenty Calypsos to Remember*. Port-of-Spain: National Recording Company.

Nichols, Bill. 1981. *Ideology and Image: Social Representation in the Cinema and Other Media*. Bloomington: Indiana University Press.

Walcott, Derek. 1992. 'The Antilles: Fragments of Epic memory', The Nobel Lecture. http://nobelprize.org/nobel_prizes/literature/laureates/1992/walcott-lecture.html

_____. 1986. *Collected Poems, 1948-1984*. New York: Farrar, Strauss & Giroux.

Warner, Keith Q. 1988. *Critical Perspectives on Léon-Gontran Damas*. Washington DC: Three Continents Press.

White, J. P. 1996. "An Interview with Derek Walcott." *Conversations with Derek Walcott*. Ed. William Baer. Jackson: University of Mississippi Press.

Masman/Artist

Peter Minshall[1]

Minshall: Once, I was asked to speak about my work. I had a few notes and I got a few slides together and I knew more or less what it was I wanted to say. I started off like this: I want to tell you who I am. I want to show you four images. The first image was an extraordinary carving of the crucifixion of the Christ, dark and wooden, against a deep red velvet background that accentuated the suffering, very beautiful. The slide came up and I said this is man and suffering. The second image was Shiva Nataraja in his circle of fire. I said this is the Lord of the Dance, the Creator and Destroyer of the Universe, dancing it into existence with one step even as he crushes it with the next. This is the cycle of life and death. This is man and celebration. The third image was a shining, slender golden Buddha. I said this is man and tranquility, man at peace with himself. And the fourth image, I said I will share with you an image now that is more about angels than any human being I have seen painted with wings at his shoulders. This is truly spiritual and other-worldly in a way that I have never ever before experienced. I showed them this image of five Bobo bush masks.[2] These are truly angels from Africa. Then I said all of these are me and they are so mixed up. All of these are who I am. I am a Caribbean. I am a magical

---

1   Peter Minshall in conversation with Maxine Williams and with Christopher Innes. Transcribed and edited by Anton Wagner.
2   From Burkina Faso and Mali: generally animal masks, particularly representing horned heads, representing spirits of the bush and worn during ceremonies associated with new crops, initiations and funerals, they are designed to reconcile the Bobo tribe with nature in purification rituals. While the animal face is the starting point, in form and pattern they are fantastically abstract.

creature of the universe. I so delight in who I am. I am like nobody else. Nobody else is like me. I am at the tip of the spear that leads into the future. If you want to see who I am, look at my work. I am Tan Tan and Saga Boy. I am *Tapestry*. I am *River*. My work is who I am.

I have the advantage of being an artist. As I look at the twentieth century, it strikes me that much of the creative work of the twentieth century has been done by three groups: the Jews, the Blacks, the Gays. They share in common persecution and suffering.

And then I went back to the early caveman. That mark he made, that animal he drew, those simple drawings: what did they say? They said to the dark, unfathomable universe: I am! So when I make the mas, I am saying, I AM! WE ARE!

I make mas for the Caribbean primarily, but for all the people of the earth, because I feel it is an extraordinary, universal form of expression that is not dependent on language. It really isn't the "I" that is operative here. There is no art form like the mas that is so profoundly a relationship between the artist, the participants and the audience. It teaches us: you are but a tool, you are but part of an extraordinary process. It teaches you on an island which already has an attitude, "Who you think you is?" I didn't choose the mas. It grabbed me by the foot and pulled me in—sometimes screaming—by a set of impossible, extraordinary accidents. But once the truth was revealed, I had but little choice.

It has been very difficult because I live in a society which believes that theatre, as in the proscenium arch, the curtain, the floorboard and the spoken language, is a much nobler thing to which to give your life as an artist.

Let's start from the beginning. You were in London training as a designer, so exposed to precisely that kind of attitude and artistic preconception.

Minshall: A little bit before that, the Beginning. Born in Guyana, through no fault of my own. Conceived in Trinidad. From then to the age of twelve like a shuttlecock between the two places. At the age of twelve until the age of twenty-one, Port of Spain, Trinidad, where there is an annual Carnival which is a combustive festival of the arts. It just grows out of the people. Songs! Dance! Apparel worn as art! I just grew up with it and took it totally for granted. In fact before I was trained in London I was unconsciously being trained in "that," whatever you want to call it.

From Guyana as a very smart, bright young man at school, I went to Trinidad, from the jurisdiction of a grandmother to a mother, and all my scholastic brilliance fell apart as I fell into the "bad" Trinidadian ways and got involved in all sorts of extracurricular activities. At the age of about fourteen, as the most natural thing in the world, like picking up a cricket bat and hitting a ball or making a kite and flying it on the Savannah, I, at four o'clock one Carnival Jouvay [*jour ouvert* or *j'ouvert*] morning, got up, and with a pillow over my stomach and a pillow strapped on my butt and my sister's debutante dress over it and stockings over the length of my arms and stockings over my feet and a cotton jersey mask with just two little holes to breathe and another wire mask superimposed on that and coconut fibre from the mattress as false hair and a big broad hat and a handbag and my mother's bedroom slippers, I went into town as a Dame Lorraine.

This is where it all started. As a Dame Lorraine in the throngs of the pre-dawn Carnival Monday morning, I was unburdened of gender, unburdened of age, unburdened of race. I was a totally free spirit. I can only now look back and realize that an extraordinary transformation had happened.[3]

Did you have words to go with the costume? Was there a script for the role, or did you improvise your own?

Minshall: At the corner of Park and Frederick Street, I saw standing on the pavement, well-dressed, come to view the Jouvay morning celebration, my mathematics master, his wife and girl children. He had made the mistake of giving me poor marks just two weeks prior to the Carnival. I really played, as far as a fourteen-year-old boy can imagine it, a cantankerous old whore in the streets. I attacked him verbally in front of his wife, asking what was he doing there with this lady when he was with me last night. He literally drifted back into the crowd as a letter might into an envelope. He just disappeared. And I was empowered.

---

3   Minshall's first mas design on record was an African witch doctor that he designed and wore at age thirteen. Made of "a cardboard box and Christmas bells turned inside out as eyes, and some silver and some green paint . . . and some grasses . . . from the hill behind the house, and bits of wire, and bones the dogs had left around the yard and dried in the sun and bleached," the mas won first prize for originality in his age group in the children's carnival competition. ("Peter Minshall: A Voice to Add to the Song of the Universe," an interview by Richard Schechner and Milla C. Riggio, *The Drama Review* 42, 3 [T159], Fall 1998)

Anyone could imagine the sheer pleasure of that reversal of power, that inversion of the social order, which is what Carnival is based in. So for you, the love of Carnival clearly came from acting out...

Minshall: I don't know if it was a love of Carnival. You see when you are on an island you are of a place that is inevitably small, and big places just seem bigger and better. All I knew of Broadway were twelve-inch LP's with pictures of the scenery and the actors on the back. My received knowledge was that real art and real theatre happened over there. It couldn't possibly come from a little place. And so I left at twenty-one on a journey to learn how to make real art and to make it in a place where it was appreciated. My Carnival in Trinidad was just a little island fling.

Going to London to the Central School of Art and Design, to the Jeannetta Cochrane Theatre,[4] was a revelation because, in learning what real art was, I realized that what was happening on the streets of Port of Spain was as real as any art anywhere. Not that I went running jumping back into it. That took some time.

I had left Trinidad thinking that the pinnacle of Carnival design was all about the Jaycees [Junior Chamber of Commerce] Carnival Queens that were so glamorous, lovely and manicured. But much of the finest stuff that comes from that island comes from the ground, from the bottom up, not from the top down.

Of course. But then Carnival did always come from the people at the bottom of the social pile, the slaves in historical times, and the outcasts.

Minshall. Yes, it did. Although you do—at every level of the expression—do require those shamans, those people whose devotion is to the art, whether it's the bottom, in the middle or the top. You do require the artist to give his dedication and devotion to the people.

It's interesting. You spend three years at the Central and the first thing is you sit down with all these other white boys. You arrive in Southampton. You take the boat train. For the first time in your life you are passing the cows and the sheep in the meadow. You have read about them They have been in your school picture books. You have to remember that in the Caribbean in my growing up, "A" in the Caribbean was for apple, and I had never seen one except in pictures. And "M" was never for mango. That's been corrected since. So I come to

---

4   The Cochrane Theatre opened in 1964 and was named after its founder Jeannetta Cochrane, a theatre practitioner specialising in costume and scenery design.

London. You have to understand that I've never seen so many white people in my life. I go to the Central and after a while I realize here I am with all the other white boys doing my drawing or designing my set. My drawing was always a little different from theirs. It's quite obvious when you live in a community you come away with bits and pieces of the community entering you and crawling around under your skin and you become who you become.

What did you find happening in the arts when you arrived in London?
Minshall: 1963 was the year of the Beatles, soon thereafter the Rolling Stones, Carnaby Street, the King's Road. There was a renaissance happening in London. I don't know if it's saying too much that it centered around the Beatles. They stormed the world. It seemed that England was the place where all the right stuff was happening. I was a little boy from the island and I came there. And there was my first opera, my first concert. But it was also the world theatre season and stuff was coming in at the height of the season—the best from Japan (Kabuki and Noh Theatre), China, Poland, America, Kathakali dancers from India at the Shaftsbury. I remember it was then and there that I saw *Umabatha*, the black *Macbeth* performed by Zulus at the Aldwych Theatre. When they thundered towards the castle from the back of the stage with no scenery... And I was there when Peter Brook was doing his most extraordinary work—God, it was such a gift to take through my life—his immortal production of *A Midsummer Night's Dream* in which he kicked out all the Victorian fairies, the flowers and everything and put it into what I would describe as a white-tiled bathroom. For the first time in a long time the words—the poet's words—went jumping off the white tiles into the audience and Titania was lowered from the ceiling reclining on a trapeze bed of red ostrich feathers and yes, actors kind of leaping onto the walls with their feet. It was magic. I remember clearly thinking, oh my god, for the first time I am seeing the words. Subsequent to that the mesmerizing *Marat/Sade*.... What theatre!

And how connected that is to the power of the Jouvay in the Carnival. And perhaps the most erotic expression of the male of the species, the Blue Devils of the Trinidad Jouvay, nonchalantly coming down the road, near-naked men with blue grease on their bodies, two horns—talk about theatre!— minimal costume, minimal music, minimal lighting, minimal text, and the audience is totally in the palm of the hand of the performer. These are the Blue Devils of the Jouvay of the Trinidad Carnival of my youth and my growing up and they are becoming less and lesser as people have become—so they think—more and more refined and sophisticated. "We don't want that sort of native stuff to seem to be the stuff that we are made of"—whereas people in the theatre are looking to try to find ways of expressing just that sort of stuff.

The middle class has been a problematic class in not understanding self, lack of personality and character. When you design for everyone...

Minshall: I wouldn't say problematic. Life has thrust and parry.... But perhaps you're right. Perhaps it is a problem, because I have lived in the space of these thirty-five odd years in a society believing that the pinnacle of design expertise was in fact the white Jaycees Carnival Queen. Everybody accepted that, and you know why? Because it was the nearest thing we did that looked like those things we saw in Hollywood films. So it had to be the best. I grew up and sponsors would come and say, Miss Jean, your son can draw! Oh God, come design a costume nah! And I would feel, oh Lord, I'm going to design a costume, and so on, you know how that happens.

And then I go away. You don't read it in a book. You then realize as you begin to learn about what people throughout history all over the world have worn and why they have worn it and why the Elizabethan moved through to the Restoration and to the Victorian and why people began to wear big skirts. You suddenly realize, my goodness—and I don't say this with nostalgia, they belonged to their time—but the Fancy Sailor and the Midnight Robber and the little Hummingbird girl dancing a dress that grew wings[5]—these were the thread where originality lay. Because these three things were—and I say it with such a lovely song in my heart—these three things were "Made in Trinidad." They did not happen in Europe or Africa or India—it was the mixture.

And it was also the mixture that produced pan. After the terror of the crossing and being brought to the island with your drum, you are exposed for the first time to an instrument which is also percussive played with the tips of the fingers and is called a piano. It makes not just the rhythm and beating of the drum but does all sorts of melodies.

---

5   *From the Land of the Hummingbird*, an individual children's mas designed by Minshall in 1974, played by his young adopted sister, that made a major impact on the Carnival: "[T]here can be no question that The Land of the Hummingbird, so ingeniously conceived and so stunningly executed by Peter Minshall, and so captivatingly presented by tiny Sherry Ann Guy, was truly the individual of the year for 1974 and for all years to date." ("The Land of the Hummingbird," by Roy Boyke, *Trinidad Carnival* magazine, Special BWIA Souvenir Edition, Key Caribbean Publications, 1974)

And this sinks into your unconscious for a hundred and fifty years. During that period of time other people come to the place with another drum, heated by fire to get its tone, the tassa, that is held around the neck with a piece of cloth and is beaten with two sticks in ritual street procession. And that too sinks into the unconscious. Then the universe, spinning and turning—and we do not know its plan—makes a point of putting into the island the very black fluid which mankind, after hundreds and hundreds of years and centuries travelling from place to place—fought wars, tilled lands—on horseback, suddenly developed a vehicle that needs this black fluid. Simple so, eh? Four wheels and some oil. And everything change. Everything. Because the universe determined that the fluid lay on the very tiny little island where she had brought with great pain all of these other things. What was this fluid stored in? A steel drum. And nobody knew what it was put there for until there was a war. At the end of the war the island—like everybody else—was celebrating, but it had no bamboo. So people pick up any piece of iron and old biscuit tin and went pong pong down de road. And one fellow went pong pong and he pong it too hard, and it dent, and it go ping pong. Dat is where de whole thing start. Two notes ring out on a piece of tin. The Universe saw fit that the lowest of the low, the Invaders, the Renegades, and the Desperados, who used to fight up with each other with guns and knives of steel should turn to drums of steel and make war with music.

You see how the universe does work? You see why this place is magical? And why it is now we are having all this trouble which everybody feels we are having? The ancients knew that if the gods blessed you with these blessings it was your duty to build a temple in praise to the gods. Up to now, we have not built a cathedral of a concert hall in which to put these drums of steel that are beaten with two sticks like a tassa and play music like a piano.

When you talk of going away and how your understanding of theatre changed the more history you understood and you saw our place in it— thinking how elsewhere theatre is year-round, and if you worked somewhere else you would have been involved in theatre on a continuous basis—instead this theatre, which is related to the Lenten season and to only these two days which are the pinnacle of it—how does this expand to fill a nation with theatre throughout its life, throughout the year for all of its time?

Minshall: There are two approaches to answer what you are asking. One is, we are a small place with a big heart and too much talent for our own good. The first thing we have to learn from young is to love our islandness and to understand there are things in this world we will never do and we mustn't feel bad about it but to understand equally that being small, we have great advantages and can do things—and have shown it with the pan and certain aspects of the mas—we can do things here that no one else in the world can do. You talk about Carnival and Lent. This goes back much further than that. This goes back to primeval time. We go back to the very beginning of the Bible: And God took a clump of mud and made man. That is universal. That is all religions. What we call Carnival took its passage through Rome and Christianity. The oldest living Carnival is the Holi festival of India, which here in Trinidad is called holy Phagwa. Here, because Hindus are surrounded and seemingly besieged by notions of Christian piety, they want to say that Phagwa is not that nasty thing like those drunken black people do. But it is the same Carnival.

My father described a Carnival on a Tuesday morning. Coming down the road, where there wasn't a band this way or a band that way, was a group of young boys. In one hand each one was holding a couple of coconuts, and in the other a piece of bamboo, hitting it on the ground, the phallic implications quite obvious, and they are singing, "Netty, Netty, give me the thing you have in your belly." Wow!

Many years later I am reading about the Holi festival of India, the personification of Lord Shiva, naked, with grey mud on his body, on a donkey, like Christ, going down the road, and all of these young boys are coming down the road with phallic symbols in their hands, hurling obscenities at the rich, yes, in the Holi festival of India. I tell you we are living in One Universe.

These are only words. Phagwa is a word. Carnival is a word. But it's the same root. It's a Spring festival. It's a religious ritual, to say: "God, thank you. Please, make us fertile. Make the things that we plant in the land grow."

People think that I am a masman? This is the only place that I know where, at the opening of the day which we call Jouvay, nothing I could ever do could be as strong or as powerful as the mud with which people paint themselves at Jouvay.

Here it is. The sun hasn't risen and the pan is pounding in your ear and you're pushing the steel and you're going down. And it's not just the music. It's the sweetness of that shsh, shsh, shsh, of a thousand feet on the road. You hear it in your feet. You haven't heard it for a year. It's as though you really understand that you are just the dust of which the universe is made. You have come out of your houses in the darkness. You have entered into this stream of humanity. Suddenly you find you are surrounded by throngs of people whose bodies are muddied as though they now come out of the earth.... I know enough about theatre to say that is brilliant theatre. It is vital. It has potency. It is improvisational in the extreme. It is where the audience is the participant. New York can't do it. Paris can't do it. London can't do it. I get very impassioned about that. The middle class wants to say, oh no, no, no, we're very ashamed of that. That's primitive. We want it to be pretty.

Yet you've said that primitive is what Carnival is, what mas is. Mas is mud.

Minshall: Not all of it. But it starts there. The wonderful arc of the mas is that it starts at the Jouvay. You mentioned Lent. The one good thing about Carnival passing through Christian Rome was this business of Lent. I'm a great traditionalist. Not from a religious point of view. But the idea of having this—it's called Fat Sunday, Dimanche Gras, Mardi Gras—and then after all this excess, after all this extravagance of expression, come the unfathomable, impossible to understand ideas of eternity, when you are born into this life-death space, and after all of that to go into a kind of quiet piety. I grew up with it.

I didn't realize any of this. I was very fortunate. I went to London in the year of Independence, 1963. Jackie Hinkson, Peter Minshall, Jeffrey Chock, leaning over the edge of the boat saying bye-bye to our families. Jackie was going to Paris and I was going to London. It was my father—this is the accident of life—I wanted to be a painter but my father said no, do the stage design. It will earn you a living.

And my first big break came in 1970. Again the Universe said: "Here, see, you have something to do, little island boy." I showed my work to Peter Darrell and he said, my goodness, you're the person we've been looking for. I designed both set and costumes for the inaugural production of the Scottish Ballet Theatre which premiered at Sadler's Wells Theatre.[6]

How did you translate who you were to that context?

Minshall: What was extraordinary was that Peter Darrell was looking through my portfolio and he came to a design I did for one of the

_____

6   The founder (with Elizabeth West) of the Western Theatre Ballet in Bristol in 1957. Renamed the Scottish Theatre Ballet, the Company moved to Glasgow in 1969, changing its name to the Scottish Ballet in 1974.

aforementioned Jaycees Carnival Queens, Ingrid Anderson, in a mas called Once Upon a Time. Interestingly, because of the consciousness that was falling upon me, Ingrid's costume was based on the lower class Fancy Indian of the streets. It was a big, big circle and instead of the teepee with the papoose and everything pulling behind her, I used the same geometric pattern but feminized it. It had trees with magic birds. It had all the confusion that one of them Fancy Indian mas would have except that it had a more delicate treatment. Darrell turned the page and said that he had never seen anything like it from any of the English designers. The Scottish Ballet Theatre premiere was a full-length production of Beauty and the Beast, more or less based on the Cocteau story, choreographed by Darrell, scenario by Colin Graham.

And carnivalesque costumes designed by you?

Minshall: Yes and no. Carnivalesque implies bawdy and gross. Mas is more the spirit and flesh combined, angels and demons dancing together in perfect harmony. Yes. Mas triumphed. Masks were used to great effect. I was a theatre designer. I was not some visiting exotic. There were truly surreal moments. One fantastical scene—it was night, a vast shimmering lake fills the space, a single billowing piece of silk played by three masked dancers (the lake as scenery personified), the moon enters in a darkly sensuous pas de deux with his living reflection, a pair of enormous silvery-grey moths hover mysteriously at the water's edge. Classic Minsh "dancing mas mobile" morphed with classical ballet. What a treat. The work of the masman/artist/designer must always be relevant to its time and place, always truthfully serve his director/choreographer/collaborators.

It was a lovely night for me. My mother had flown up. She was in the audience and people still did the whole black tie thing. I didn't know it but on a first night of a premiere, everybody gets their little turn on stage, Peter Darrell, Colin Graham, Thea Musgrave who wrote the original score, and the young designer who did the set and the costumes. I got a standing ovation. And my mum was in the audience.

But said mum, two years later passing through London: "Now Mr. Big Avant-Garde Designer, I want you to come home and design a costume for your little sister so that she can be Junior Carnival Queen! Further, I want it to be a hummingbird." I couldn't imagine anything more kitsch. But my mother knew things that I didn't know. The child was honey-brown, about twelve years old. She was the perfect hummingbird. I didn't know it at the time.

I put every kinetic theory I had by this time formed—after three years at the Central I was no longer into glamorous ladies for the Jaycees Carnival Queen. By this time I was fascinated by the articulation of the Bat, of how he would do these delicate little pirouettes. He never went with music. He was always around the Fancy Clown and dancing to somebody else's tune. I was into what the Bat did, the simple little bat of the Savannah, pirouetting with silk attached to the whole of his body and with a few canes dancing the mas. The thing about the Bat in terms of dance is that the creature led to the dance because the wing is attached right up the entire side of the body. If you look at my work on the Kings and the Queens—Tan Tan and Saga Boy are the canes and the silk of the Bat rearranged in spirals and attached to the human body so that whatever the dancer does, that too does. Joy to the World [HALLELUJAH, 1995]: the whole thing comes right down to her backbone so that if she just shudders, it goes right back up.

How could I take that and transform it into a hummingbird? Little did I know that the magic of the island, the Made-in-Trinidad brew of the bat plus the age and size of the sapodilla child, her glow, plus the very notion of the hummingbird from an island that for a century had been called The Land of the Hummingbird—whether because the Amerindians revered the hummingbird for being sacred or because the Victorians exported two thousand dead birds per week to put on their hats—finally, whatever, Trinidad was called The Land of the Hummingbird, and so we called our magical dancing little bird-child carnival creature "From the Land of the Hummingbird"—I just did not know how BIG this little thing was. I spent five months working out this single piece of geometry, which finally was a very simple dancing iridescent circle.

You have to put this in context. In those days, the Junior Carnival Queen costumes were worn and performed by the daughters of the rich. And the daughters of the rich were generally light-skinned people. Life goes on and on and on and the aristocracy—whether it is black, white, brown or tan—tends always to behave aristocratically. That is how it is. My challenge was not only how to translate the kinetic dynamics of the low-class street bat into a high-class hummingbird fit for the royal ballroom, but also how graciously to enter that ballroom, that light-skinned arena with its prevailing aesthetic, and conquer it with the vibrant energy and spirit of a little dark-skinned girl.

So I sit down in London and I'm now—besides the inherited unconscious Indo-Afro-Euro under-the-skin thing that's deeply embedded in me—I'm now trying to make this one contemporary piece of art, trying to work it out, doing hundreds of small thumb-nail sketches, trying to find it out, to discover, uncover, reveal its being. How? How does this ordinary nondescript little brown-black bat begin to transform into the beautiful jeweled hummingbird princess that wins the crown and saves the kingdom? Yes, How? How do I keep it to that utmost simplicity? I don't want it to be literal. She still wants to be a little girl. I want it to be abstract. I want it to be contemporary. I want it to be able to go tomorrow and sit in the Tate Gallery [London]. That's been one of my problems in the mas over the years. I'm not competing with these guys here, I'm competing with Japan, New York and Paris. So sometimes my work seems ridiculously out of place. I have to accept that. I can't patronize my audience. I was terrified because everybody else's thing was on wheels. It was like a great collection of trophies and floral decorations. Her costume was a little piece of geometry. She had an angular skirt and the skirt and the wings were one clean continuous circle.

I got very ill and she missed the first few competitions but managed by the grace of God—whoever or whatever—and all of the forces of the Universe—to get on the stage just in the nick of time when all the other competitors were parading for this coveted competition prize. The prevailing design ethic when I went back in 1974—not only in the kiddies Carnival then—my God, it's still the prevailing design ethic, I'm saddened to say—was a pair of wheels upon which you would pile your riches. And the bigger and the higher and the taller the pile of riches, the more likely you were going to win. Please, it's a little island. It's the Junior Carnival Queen competition. It's nothing to the rest of the world but it's everything on this afternoon in this place.

And this little child who had rehearsed for five weeks with me, who was grim-faced as any great method actor would be before entering . . . she entered . . . and she sidled to one side, just a shimmering little blue-green tent . . . and at the right moment she just—in the words of one observer—exploded like a sapphire . . .

Every time I envisage it, I feel water come to my eye, even right now, because I, who had by now a pretty good idea of what makes great art and what makes art great—I had seen Nureyev and Fontaine—I had marvelled at Callas—I had seen all of Brook—I who had myself taken a bow at Sadler's Wells—just saw something remarkable happening. The little child danced the mas, one, two, three turns, and in an instant ten thousand people were enlivened and were dancing with her. She went to that side of the stage and the people at that side of the stage were dancing. Honestly, the whole place—she jumped and they jumped. You looked around and there was such a connection. There

was such communication. It was so instant. I always remember Callas'
great comment: "Art is the highest form of human communication, and
music is the highest form of art." To use another quote, I think it was
Balanchine who said that you have succeeded when you were able to
hear the dance and see the music. In mas that is exactly the purpose.
You want to be able to see the music dancing. That's what happened
with the Hummingbird! Me who had learned art is communication, I'm
seeing this one little costume communicating better than anything I
had seen in all my time in London. The music, the dance, everything
was one. And the audience and the performer were one. At its best,
because the audience and the performer are so close, spirit and flesh
combined—at its best—when the mas works, it is as grand as grand
opera. I saw it happening that afternoon.

Besides the pan that the island invented, there is the innovation
that is the mas. In every other sphere of its existence the apparel as a
form of entertainment is secondary to the performance. An actor wears
a costume to help in his acting, as an opera singer, as a dancer. In the
Trinidad Carnival you play the mas. The apparel is performed. It is
primary to the performance. The mas is the work of art. That's what I
discovered. That's perhaps what sets my work apart from the herd. The
mas is not nearly so much how it looks as what it does. The traditions of
Africa are not paintings that hang on walls. The traditions of Africa are
in performance. The traditions of Africa are in the playing of the mask,
literally. To invoke the gods. The masks, for the rest of the year, are
hidden and sometimes buried and new ones have to be made.

I went back to London to do my London business and two years
later—because of the Hummingbird—one morning when I was preparing stuff for Notting Hill, which is where I first scratched the surface,
one of the big bandleaders [Stephen Lee Heung, who had previously
worked with artist Carlisle Chang] phoned me up and said: "Peter Minshall, you want to come home and do my band for next year?" He had
had a fall-out with his own designer, and because of their argument a
door opened for me that, whether it was the greatest mistake of my life
or the best thing that I could ever have done, I went back. And the band
I was doing at Notting Hill at the time in the early seventies, the name
of that band—what better name for a band in London at that time—
was *To Hell With You!* But from that I went straight to Trinidad with
the Carnival band version of a text that I had been taught at Queen's

Royal College: Milton's *Paradise Lost*.[7] It was the full Cecil B. DeMille production. It was taking all that I had learned from the Hummingbird and doing it large! *Paradise Lost*: the Burning Lake, the Fallen Angels, the Garden of Eden. Satan, the Sun in Eclipse was one of the characters.

The King was simply called The Serpent. It was audacious! It was a near-naked man. It was taking the elements of the Bat and—this was 1976, a lifetime ago. [*Minshall holds up his index finger.*] Here's the body of the man and looking at it as the single stem of a leaf. And using canes, just doing an arc in a radius of twenty feet around, and just canes from his ankles as veins and working it out and thinking, well, if the wind blows, you have to use a very broad-weave base, a sort of light fishing netting. And how do you colour it? Like Seurat did, a kind of pointillism on a grand scale so that when he stamps his feet electrical charges go through it. So his energy is legible in a great aura around him. And snaking through this abstract leaf that was the Garden of Eden was literally the Serpent, the head in one hand, the apple in another.

This was at a time when every other King costume was a great trundling trophy on wheels. This was at a time when Trinidad was experiencing its first oil boom and, as is happening right now, the purpose of the mas was to show how much money was spent. So these wheeled chariots would come on piled with riches. And in the midst of that came a fellow with his two bare feet on the ground. I had wanted to put him on platform shoes. I nearly broke his ankles. At the third try, I suddenly thought, he's going barefoot. He's Adam in the Garden of Eden. Stop trying to be so damn clever, Minshall! He went on in bare feet. And now I will give you the finest definition of a good mas that I have ever heard.

Is this your own definition?
Minshall: No, it was a fat Indian lady. After the Carnival I went down to see the costume on display in one of the department stores on Frederick Street by one of my competitors. And while there, this lady came: "Oh, Mister Minshall! I have to tell you, that King of yours. It was so beautiful. You see the moment where he bent right over and the top of the costume hit the ground in front of him, I held my breath. But

---

7   Queen's Royal College is one of the leading and oldest secondary schools in Trinidad—notable alumni include not only Peter Minshall, but also presidents and Prime Ministers of Trinidad & Tobago, George Maxwell Richards and Eric Williams, as well the Nobel Prize-winning author Sir Vidia Naipaul.

you see when he flicked it back as though it were the hair on his head, I have never seen anything so beautiful in my life, Mister Minshall."

When he flicked it back as though it were the hair on his head. When you are able by whatever means at your disposal, whatever inventions you fancy you can invent, when you are able to take a man's energy to place it in space out there, so the stamp of a foot and the swirl of a body or flicking back the mas as though it were the hair on his head—that is to me what the excitement is. And it comes from the Bat.

So by simplifying the costumes and making them less heavy and cumbersome, you can actually have people act out a story in a way you couldn't in the more traditional type of masking.

Minshall: Well, be careful how you use the word traditional. The traditional costumes of the Trinidad Carnival only started being traditional when Trinidad became independent. I suspect that the clue and key to that is when Trinidad became independent it wanted to look big and therefore mas started putting on wheels to build up massive and became crass. The Golden Age of that extraordinary island—the magic rising unconsciously out of the people—was over. That Golden Age was somewhere between the early fifties and the late sixties. When the oil boom came in the seventies, the steel band was at a creative zenith but its visual equivalent, the Fancy Sailor, began to seem quaint and old-fashioned.

The Fancy Sailor is so wondrously surreal and so superior to any kind of painting. I love René Magritte and am fascinated by Salvador Dali. But you see the Fancy Sailor: a man coming down the street with a kind of light butterfly gait, half balancing, half drunken, with a very studied step that's rhythmic but not overly pronounced, and the shape and form of him is of a sailor of the high seas, but the decorative embellishment of him is of fanciful tapestries of India and Persia and the Far East, and the head of him, where his eyes and nose and human mouth should be, becomes a surreal fantasy of a flock of butterflies or an eagle with a snake in its mouth or a strange head covered with cotton wool with the nose of a cobra and the ears of an elephant, or in fact, a B-52 bomber made out of tinsel and gauze. This harks back to all of those masks out of Africa that, I am sure, are not worn on the face but on the head, in celebration of the gods and in communication with one's fellows. Not to be precious about it. The subject matter can go from Walt Disney's comic cartoons—Donald Duck and Mickey Mouse—to all sorts of fanciful leaps of the imagination and philosophy. All of this was happening in the fifties and sixties.

It strikes me what you describe is individual artists doing individual things in the streets, or little groups doing group actions in the street. When you take on something like Milton's Paradise Lost, it's a grand story that needs a lot of people to act it out. Is there a difference in scale between the golden age of the fifties and your involvement in the seventies?

Minshall: I think I had the bold-faced audacity to walk a very high high-tension wire, which is to say that this art form of the street can communicate at the highest level. The apparel—what is worn—is primary, and the performance is largely of movement and gesture, but mas can also use the spoken word because speech is part of the Midnight Robber, and calypso has a song to sing and a tale to tell. If dance can wordlessly convey deep emotion and tell the story of Romeo and Juliet without a word being spoken, and if opera can accept the ridiculous notion that people are singing drama and is convincing and can make you weep, and a high note alone—again I am going back to Maria Callas because she made the music weep—so too it was my feeling that this little street festival at its best has the power to communicate. There is such a range of expressions. There are paintings. What does a painting do? I found myself saying to people in Trinidad, please, I love great painting but all painting is still-life. We are people who dance our art! Paint your paintings but do not abandon the dancing of the art as if it were some primitive throwback. If anything, it is the future.

The future needs the mas. When everybody is so passive in front of a computer screen or a television screen or a movie screen looking at somebody else doing the stuff, you need people to get together to take the road. The greatest thrill to any artist is to affect and profoundly move other people. There is this argument. Yes, Carnival is about having fun. But there is fun and fun and fun. Peter Samuel hits the stage as the Midnight Robber [*Danse Macabre*, 1980], which was my first experiment towards a puppet: a great skeleton where the performer's body is literally blacked out, like a dancer. The skeleton, anchored to his feet but actually sort of sitting piggy-back on his shoulders so that the crotch of the skeleton—it's some kind of symbolic statement—is a skull, and the skeleton is in fact a whole pile of skulls, comes on holding a cape which is a spider's web. He thunders onto the stage and the audience is immediately thundering with him. So you have the pretty little hummingbird that brings tears of joy to everybody's eyes in *From The Land of the Hummingbird,* but then at the other end you have the Midnight Robber come to get you—your money or your life! In between these dramatic extremes the playing of the mas offers unsurpassed fun.

The Midnight Robber, by Minshall (Trinidad Carnival 1980)

But you chose to communicate particular kinds of story, grand narratives, "The Garden of Good and Evil"...

Minshall: That was just one particular masband, *Paradise Lost*. That was epic. There were other bands in complete contrast to that. In my more recent work, there was a band simply called *RED* [1998], which told no story whatsoever, just communicated an essence, and an aesthetic. It was contemporary and abstract. The other problem is that on the little island there are some very antiquated Victorian ideas about what "art" is. One of my tasks is to be contemporary and relevant. In my mas called Mancrab [*River* 1983], I was unconsciously thinking, ok, the movies are doing Darth Vader. That's pretty stiff competition. Our Midnight Robber was fine with his big hat and everything where he was in the fifties. We need to update him. Mancrab hit the Savannah stage with a piece of cloth floating on top of him entirely reactive to his movement. But he didn't touch it. The cloth floated like a cloud. And at a point Mancrab just quivers to the tiny shivering finger cymbals that accompany the tassa drums. This dancing piece of silk starts to bleed in front of your eyes. I think that was a major moment in the mas. Because the other rule of the mas—in the age where everything is push-button—the only button in the mas is the belly button. It kind of earths you, it grounds you in reality.

But what you are doing with Mancrab is applying all of the magic of theatre to the mas. This is the kind of thing the Victorians would have loved in the scenic development, the magic of the illusion.

Minshall: I'm not sure we're speaking about the same magic. The magic of the mas is that it's very tactile. It's very out there, elemental, with the sun and the rain and the sweat. It does not answer to the polite advantages of indoors. It's not blessed with proscenium finesse and computerized lighting. In fact if I am doing anything to the mas I would like to think I am doing what Gordon Craig did when he turned a whole page and said, not so—so![8] It's very tactile. You know there is no electrical plug going in anywhere. It's human energy. There's mas that's there to terrify and frighten and disturb, which was Mancrab, and there's Joy to the World much later on, with Alyson Brown, just a floating ethereal angelic presence. And there's mas that's just kinetically splendid. WOW! It's the equivalent of Baryshnikov just taking off and he's just floating there for three seconds before he starts to descend and you go, wow!

And I'm sure everyone did go wow! Except the church. Why was the church so against some of your mas productions? Because the energy has a certain spiritual quality? What was the church objecting to?

Minshall: Especially one that was called *HALLELUJAH*. In that particular case I sat alone at home all day Carnival Tuesday of the year before, while my band went out on the road. I was pretty well exhausted from the effort of just getting it there. The troops were capable of taking it through its paces. And I sat, me one alone, pouring the rum in the orange juice and just quietly by myself looking at the whole Carnival on TV—not getting plastered but just keeping a steady lucid level— just seeing all of these people, all of these other bands just trundling across the stage in feathers and beads like so many sheep—bands being awarded prizes for going across as fast as possible and bands being awarded prizes for being "the most colourful band." You would not even award a prize for the 'most colourful' painting to a child. It is so infantile. An entire island people willingly at the mercy of crass commercial propaganda. Oh, so Kodak is colour—so therefore Carnival is colour. Here is the spirit just being herded across the stage like sheep. The feeling of excitement and celebration has been lost. Or sold.

When I was young we used to have what was called a jump-up. The music would go at a level and then hit PA-PAH! TA TA TA TA TAH!— no costume, no nothing. The people would jump up. In their physical action and activity there would be celebration. And the calypso had to

---

8   Gordon Craig was a ground-breaking scenic designer who "turned a whole page" in the prevailing style of stage design, with his dramatic departures from literalism to a sort of monumental minimalism.

have a chorus where the people could join in—whether "Ten to One Is Murder" or "Drunk and Disorderly, Me Friends and Me Family!"

I don't know. I really don't know what the answers are. I do know that in my own case, I thought, I've got to find some way to bring celebration back in the mas. How can I do that? I thought, I'll put the word on a banner. CELEBRATION. That word on the banner lasted for about a week. I was going to a corner shop to buy some groceries to make some lunch and it was like one of those moments when you just turn the corner and you see it. There is the banner and it's white and it has the word HALLELUJAH in gold on it. And I thought, that's it. This is a year before it happened. There is no better word in the world. The name of a work of mas is very important: *River, RED, Paradise Lost. HALLELUJAH* was right.

The preacher people got very mad. How dare this infidel who deals with this obscene revelry on the street call his band by this sacred word? I thought, that's a double standard. Ella Fitzgerald sings a song called "Hallelujah." How dare they turn *Jesus Christ, Superstar* into a Broadway hit? Why is this island so self-contemptuous? Why do you think that the Carnival is so lowly when all these other forms of entertainment from opera to jazz are allowed to deal up with all your sacred words? Why is it that you so boil with notions of self-disgust when it comes to your own thing?

How would you sum up your career as a mas designer?

Minshall: After all these years, it is still "only" mas. Tan Tan and Saga Boy [*Tantana,* 1990] was the last major big leap. It's funny. It took thirty years for a little island to come up with a puppet form that revolutionized universal notions of puppetry. One person. One puppet. It's so simple. It's so iconic. You extend the spine upward. You place a crossbar for shoulders up there. From it forms a torso. The legs go forward. The knees are out there. The feet are attached to the feet of the puppeteer. The arms go from the shoulders to its elbows, and the hands of the puppeteer with a fibreglass rod go from here to there. The spine of the puppeteer is the spine of the puppet. The hands of the puppeteer manipulate the hands of the puppet. Likewise the feet. Now, all this puppet is supposed to do is what a sunset does or a good gust of breeze does when it makes the leaves of a tree dance. It's not supposed to act or to speak or to say a part. It's supposed to express human energy in a way best described by Alyson Brown when she once played Tan Tan for four hours straight in the streets of Kingston, Jamaica. She came home at sundown, exhausted, and she said, "Mr. Minshall, I couldn't take it off. I was so tired. But a sea of smiles kept opening up all through the streets of Kingston before me. I just could not take it off. I had to play the mas till I drop."

On the streets! It's incredible. A puppet form so visceral, so essential, so simple—so Afro-Indo in its genesis. Because when you take it down and put her in a box to lie down and put it away, she is only at rest, until Alyson comes along again and the box is opened and she is resurrected. Again, it is to play the mas. Nothing like Tan Tan so immediately describes the power of mas, how it comes alive when Alyson breathes her energy into it once more.

Was it that kind of energy that you hoped to get when you designed the opening ceremonies of the Olympics?

Minshall: Let me say two things. Long before someone tapped me on the shoulder and said, come, we want you to try this kind of stuff here, with Tony Hall and Noble Douglas and every single dancer and artist that I knew on the island of Trinidad and Tobago we produced in a stadium on a Monday night of the Carnival something that had never before been done on the island of Trinidad. In the city of Port of Spain we produced a mas called *Santimanitay* [1989] which is a colloquial of *sans humanité* ("without humanity"). It was a terrible mas, a very frightening mas, and it truly was a kind of symbolic passion play. It was not by any means perfect but it had never been done before. I just want to say that long before Barcelona called, we had on our own done a mas in a stadium.

I don't have an agent for the work that I do in Trinidad and by divine providence we have a gig in Nîmes, for Tan Tan and Saga Boy to dance in a bullring before the bulls do their business [Feria de Musique de Rue, 1991]. And so the Barcelona committee drives to Nîmes and I showed them a few tapes and they say [*Minshall shakes hands*], "You're on." That's how it happened. I think the reason is in the integrity of the mas. I kind of think ordinary human beings are attracted to integrity. I learned from my father at a very early age the integrity that is required of the artist in dealing just with the canvas. That learning was broadened when I went to the Central. When you read the play and listen to the director, you start collaborating. The thing you need to apply most is a sense of integrity, that truth-beauty-love combination. When you start applying it to the mas, I think ordinary human beings everywhere, whatever their language, their colour, their belief, are attracted to integrity.

The thing about the Olympics is that the same rule applies. I think Barcelona turned a page. The theme of the story came from the Catalan imagination, the idea of giving to an Olympic ceremony—for the first time—a real sense of a beginning and a middle and an end, a development, a flow, a story. I think Barcelona turned a page that has carried on and brought a new "tradition" into the Olympics. In my case, my value to such an event is that I, unknowingly, had been doing work in the open air for some time and had been given this vast Savannah stage on which to put a single individual competing against others. So I was able to make a human being who is this big [broad gesture with his arms] without reducing his mobility. Now, imagine a great stadium floor. In Barcelona at the beginning of the story the arena is first flooded with the Mediterranean Sea. Before they gave me the task of trying to deal with that problem, the Sea consisted of nine thousand people. I came up with these nine-foot wide kinetic collars that echoed Gaudi's tiles[9] and nine hundred people made up the entire Sea.

My job, my value was, as with theatre, to work with the team, to define ways and means, working with people like the Barcelona committee. Then there's that other side, the Dame Lorraine knowledge, the business of seeing just one little detail, one small single piece of white confetti floating down in the big huge green of the Savannah. There is this memory I have of going back to Port of Spain and in a pre-Carnival fete someone had white streamers hanging from a Savannah tree and I remember seeing this young black man just dancing among the streamers with a few rums in him. Just these little moments of unsuspecting, un-stage-managed beauty that just happen so. There is always that moment on a stadium floor where one little boy with a hoop and a roller goes across the stage. It could be huge by just putting one, instead of a flood of nine thousand.

What inspires you now?

Minshall: Now you're going to send me into a stage of sadness. In my work as an artist I need to say, I am. I don't want Bats now. They belong to the 1950s. A Midnight Robber stalking around the Savannah—"Your money or your life!"—it's like a Bette Davis movie. It's lovely but it belongs to its time. Mancrab was, I dare say, the Midnight Robber of *his* time. Since our Midnight Robber, Spielberg and Lucas have come along

---

9   The Barcelona architect Antoni Gaudi characteristically clad his sculptural architecture in elaborate irregular tile, reworking a Spanish decorative tradition, most spectacularly in his Parc Güell.

with some wild visual imagery. We've met Darth Vader. Our Midnight Robber has to compete with all of that. So I come out with Mancrab. In the same way, I don't believe we can have Midnight Robbers and Bats today. The process of evolution is change. But I want the process to go forward. I don't want it to go back.

I sat out the Carnival in 2004. I understood the pain and loss of my people, the troops, who enabled the work to happen these many years. And the burden of that on top of my own personal pain and loss was not easy. I needed to make a public statement. In preparing the statement, I put together the following words with the help of my Callaloo colleague, Todd Gulick, the Company scribe:

> Our Carnival was once hugely broad in the expressions it encompassed: from let-go bacchanal to determined seriousness; from the tawdry to the magnificent; from frenzied to stately and dignified; from jump-in-the-road to clear-the-way, a mas coming; from nakedly revealed to fully disguised and transformed; from mindless to meaningful; from the self-absorbed to performance that reaches out to the pavement and the grandstand; from superficial glamour to profound drama; from rhinestones and beads and sequins to mud and bones and bush; from playing yourself to playing a mas. Now it is only bacchanal, tawdry, frenzy, jump-in-the-road, naked, mindless, self-absorbed, superficial glamour; rhinestones, beads, sequins, and playing yourself. This style, this aesthetic, so shrunken to a single dimension, now reflects little or nothing that is original to us. It is borrowed and derivative, completely foreign-used. And the entire social and cultural discourse accepts and legitimizes this, as if it were mas, as if it were Carnival, as if it were design, as if it were always so, as if this is all that we are and all that we wish to be.

I feel there is a fight on for the soul of this country, on every level, and I feel the other side is winning. Yes, I am ahead of my time, or far behind it, or way outside it, wandering somewhere, like mad old Lear. We did a trilogy: *HALLELUJAH, Song of the Earth* and finally *Tapestry* that had La Divina Pastora played by Alyson Brown and a great African god all in procession, Shiva played by Dave Williams, and Michelangelo's Pieta done in nasty Carnival gold just passing by you, using breadfruit leaves and all the baroque shapes and forms of the actual environment. Today the tapestry is in shreds.

Carnival is a mirror. The politics, the society, the criminal, the kidnapping, the Carnival—it's all one thing. What you don't realize is that the Carnival is no pretence. It's a living part of people's lives. And the tragedy is that the imagination—the collective pre-Independence imagination, that gave us the Bat, the Fancy Sailor and the Robber—is now giving us a wash of foreign-used Las Vegas. How did we get here? We still need to be like white people? Like Las Vegas?

The mas is so tactile. To play the mas you just have to get out there and do it. It is about human energy. It is as human as a kiss, or sex (as in making love). Even as I hold my head and I bawl that we are now foreign-used—because practically everything in the Carnival is straight out of the old Las Vegas book—IT'S NOT OURS!—there's nothing where you can say YES, WE DID THAT!—even with all of that—when you see that energy take hold of the road and start to do SO!—so that even the buildings look like they jumping up—you KNOW that something is happening here—that THIS IS THE PLACE!

Part of knowing yourself is loving yourself. Yes. This is the place. The first thing you have to start to do is to love your islandness. To understand all the things it can't do but also to understand the things it can do. We're not going to send a man to the moon. We're not going to invent whatever comes after digital technology. The one thing it can do is to give to us all a life of grace, the sort of gracefulness that a big city—for all its excitement—cannot. It started with a naked body in a forest clearing putting on a mask and some mud to connect to the god. It was Richard Schechner who visited us in the year of *Tapestry* and told us: "I want to remind you that great art comes just from such little places as yours. The Greeks were smaller in population than you and Athens much smaller than Port of Spain."

Yes. Love your island. Love yourself. I know this because somewhere in my early twenties I began to find out that my sexual self was not what I had been brought up to believe. I went through turmoil and confusion. My sexuality has been a source of much pain, and much ecstasy, and much love and learning, and perhaps has been one of the reasons why as a Caribbean I needed all the more to say, I am! One's own suffering through life gives one an inkling of one's brothers' and sisters' suffering through life. Whatever I have given you here, on this afternoon that has turned to night, I think you have given me a moment of believing still that I am a Caribbean, that I am a wonderful person and have important work to do, and other people have their work to do, and I am no more and no less than them. But I have to accept my responsibilities and show the world by fulfilling my and our destiny. I say we are all truly wonderful rare hybrids. LeRoy Clarke,[10] magnificent hybrid, is carrying on, brilliantly, the traditions of my ancestors. And I, equally hybrid, am carrying on the traditions of his. That is riches!

---

10   LeRoy Clarke is a Trinidadian artist, whose abstract-expressionist work includes a cycle of paintings on "de poet."

Contributors' Biographies

Modesto Mawulolo Amegago is currently in the Dance Department at York University and has taught at the University of Ghana, School of Performing Arts; and at Simon Fraser University, University of Arizona, and Arizona State University. He directs Nutifafa Afrikan Performance Ensemble, a Toronto based Performing group, and has performed extensively with artists from various parts of the world.

Loyce L. Arthur is a costume designer, an associate professor and Head of Design in the Theatre Arts Department at University of Iowa. She has designed costumes for carnival and numerous productions including *The Magic Flute* at the Chicago Cultural Center; and *The Brothers Sun and Moon* at the Kennedy Center for the Performing Arts, Washington D.C.

Suzanne Deborah Burke is a development specialist, trained in the areas of Psychology and Sociology, currently lecturing at the Arthur Lok Jack Graduate School of Business (UWI, St Augustine) in the Master of Marketing and the Event Management Certificate programmes.

Jeffrey Chock is a professional photographer of the performing arts in Trinidad. He has documented every single Carnival since 1979 and his photography has been exhibited in Port of Spain, Toronto, Hartford, Con., Hamburg and Martinique and were featured in the fall 1998 issue of *The Drama Review* and in *Carnival: Culture in Action—The Trinidad Experience* (2004). He is currently preparing a monograph on Narrie Approo, a legendary Carnival performance artist.

Donna Coombs-Montrose is President of CARIWEST/Western Carnival Development Association, Director of the Edmonton-based Caribbean Women's Network, and a founding member of the Caribbean Diaspora Initiative (CADI). She is also Consulting Archivist at the Alberta Labour History Institute a Member of Living History, with responsibility for recording the histories of Caribbean immigrants in Alberta.

Karen Cyrus is a PhD student at York University (Toronto). Her interests include the resources, rhythms, and repertoire for steel band classes and social functions of steel band groups in the Greater Toronto Area.

Jerry & Leida Englar: Jerry worked as a professional landscape architect, and taught at the University of Toronto. Since retiring, his work as a designer, painter, panoramist, builder, and jazz musician has been expanded to include working with Shadowland.

Leida's professional career includes cancer research and art education. She is a co-founder, Artistic Director, Designer/Builder, and General Manager for Shadowland Theatre Inc. She's been a Bandleader, Production and Costume Designer and Builder for the Caribana Festival, as well as working for the Trinidad Carnival.

Sabrina Ensfelder is a Phd student at the University of Francois-Rabelais in Tours (France). She is currently working on her thesis 'Marginal religions of the Americas' and focuses more specifically on the Caribbean and the Caribbean diaspora.

Lesley Ferris has chaired departments of theatre at Ohio State University, Louisiana State University, University of Memphis and Middlesex University. She has published widely on theatre and performance and her books include *Acting Women: Images of Women in Theatre* (1990) and *Crossing the Stage: Controversies on Cross-Dressing* (1993). She was the theatre consultant for The Saint Louis Art Museum catalogue/book for their exhibit entitled *Masks of Culture* (1999). She has directed over forty productions in United Kingdom, the U.S.A., and most recently South Africa.

Ray Funk is a criminal trial judge for the Alaska Court System as well as a fellow of the Academy at UTT. He has articles published in recent anthologies, *Music, Memory,Resistance: Calypso and the Caribbean Literary Imagination* (2008) and *Trinidad Carnival: The Cultural Politics of a Transnational Festival* (2007).

Tony Hall has worked internationally as an actor and a director. He has taught at University of Alberta, Canada, King Alfred's College, Winchester, UK and the University of the West Indies, St. Augustine, Trinidad. He is the founding director of Lordstreet Theatre Company [LTC]. His plays include: *A Band On Drugs* (1990), *Twilight Cafe* (2002), which won the 2002 Cacique Award for The Most Outstanding Original Script, *The Brand New Lucky Diamond Horseshoe Club* (2004)—a Calypso Musical, which won the 2005 Cacique Award for The Most Outstanding Original Music.

Jeff Henry has been involved in the Canadian theatre as an actor, dancer, director, choreographer, teacher and producer. A senior professor and past Chair of the Theatre Department at York University, designated Professor Emeritus and Senior Scholar, he is the founder and Artistic Director of the Black Theatre Workshop Montreal and Theatre Fountainhead Toronto.

Henry Lovejoy received his Ph.D. in History at the University of California, Los Angeles, in 2012. His Ph.D. thesis is entitled "Oyo Influence on the Transformation of Lucumi Identity in Colonial Cuba." He has published "The Shipping Records of the Havana Slave Trade Commission" in *African Economic History* (2010) and is a contributing member to The African Origins Project, www.african-origins.org/about. He currently holds a Post-Doctoral Fellowship from the Social Sciences and Humanities Research Council of Canada for 2012-2014 at the University of British Columbia.

Paul Lovejoy is Distinguished Research Professor in the Department of History, FRSC. He holds the Canada Research Chair in African Diaspora History and is Director of the Harriet Tubman Institute for Research on the Global Migrations of African Peoples. He has published 28 books, including *Transformations in Slavery: A History of Slavery in Africa* (3rd edition, 2010). He has been a member of the International Scientific Committee of the UNESCO "Slave Route" Project, Secteur du Culture, was Associate Vice-President (Research) at York University from 1986 to 1990 and was a member of the Social Sciences and Humanities Research Council of Canada from 1990 to 1997, serving as Vice President in 1996-97. He was awarded a Killam Senior Research Fellowship from the Canada Council in 1994-97 and was Visiting Professor at El Colegio de Mexico in 1999. In 2007, he was awarded an Honorary Doctorate by the University of Stirling and in 2011 received the Life Time Achievement Award from the Canadian Association of African Studies and the Faculty of Graduate Studies Teaching Award at York University in 2012.

Lionel McCalman is a Lecturer at the University of East London and a Steelpan Tutor. He is Governor at several London schools; and works on projects with disabled and socially deprived groups. Co-organiser of the first Steelpan Conference, London (2006), he is the main tutor and musical director of Steelpan Academy, UK - Workshop - "Pan-Around-The-Neck" (2008).

Peter Minshall revolutionized the Carnival in Trinidad—and consequently influenced Carnival throughout the world—with his designs for *From the Land of the Hummingbird* in 1974, the first of his "dancing mobiles," and in 1976 for *Paradise Lost* based on Milton's epic, which introduced complex story-telling into the mas parade. These were followed by a series of path-breaking mas bands in the 1980s and 1990s: *Papillon* where he costumed 2,500 masqueraders in ten-foot butterfly wings to create a great meditation on the ephemeral nature of life; an eco-protest mas, *River* which attacked materialistic greed and industrial pollution, and formed the first piece of a trilogy, staged over three consecutive years, that ended with *The Golden Calabash*: an epic clash of two full-sized bands, *Princes of Darkness* and *Lords of Light*, symbolizing the battle between good and evil. The pessimistic vision of *Santimanitay* (1989) is balanced by the joy and harmony of giant dancing puppets—the queen and king of the band, Tan Tan and Saga Boy—in *Tantana* (1990). A second trilogy (*HALLELUJAH, Song of the Earth*, and *Tapestry*) used creation myths and religious images in a baroque and openly theological song of praise, which aroused vocal denunciation from the Church. His social commentary and political messages continued in the late Nineties and the millennium through bands such as *The Lost Tribe* or *Ship of Fools*, while in 2006 *The Sacred Heart* presented an army of urban samurai cowboys and cowgirls marching against disease, and prejudice, explicitly focusing on HIV/AIDS awareness.

He has designed opening ceremonies for the Barcelona and Atlanta Olympic Games (1992, 1996), as well as the Salt Lake City Winter Olympics (2002), and has collaborated with the French composer-producer Jean-Michel Jarre on city-wide concert-spectacles for Paris in Concert at La Defense, Bastille Day 1991 before an audience of 2 million, and the 1995 Concert For Tolerance under the auspices of UNESCO for 1.5 million spectators at the Eiffel Tower.

Everard Phillips is a Psychotherapist and the Director of Training for Personal Power Unlimited, has worked as a mediator, and in the field of education and training. He has extensive experience in Alternative Dispute Resolution and has worked as an advocated in over 800 cases. He is a 1998 Winston Churchill Fellow.

Bruce Boyd Raeburn is a curator at Hogan Jazz Archive, Tulane University. Among his many publications is his newest book *New Orleans Style and the Writing of American Jazz History*. He has also served as an historical consultant for various media projects and has worked as a drummer for the past thirty-seven years.

Haroun Shah is the head of Molecular Identification Services at the UK government's Health Protection Agency new 'Centre for Infections', and he holds several chairs at different universities. He is the editor of 3 scientific journals and has published over 150 peer review scientific papers. For the last 10 years he has been a member of Nostalgia, and he was a co-organizer at the first Steelpan Conference in London (2006).

Phil Sher is an Associate Professor of Anthropology at the University of Oregon. He is the author of *Carnival and the Formation of a Caribbean Transnation* (2003), co-editor of *Trinidad Carnival: The Cultural Politics of a Transnational Festival* (2007) and editor of *Perspectives on the Caribbean: A Reader in Representation, Culture and History* (2008).

Teruyuki Tsuji is currently Associate Lecturer at Nova Southeastern University. His major publications include "Mothers–Hyphenated Imaginations: The Feasts of Soparee Ke Mai and La Divina Pastora in Trinidad" in *Man in India: an International Journal of Anthropology*.

Editors

Brigitte Bogar holds degrees in Music, Theatre and Dramaturgy from the University of Copenhagen. She is a production manager, who has organized a series of international conferences, including this one on Carnival, and is currently training as an opera singer. She has published several articles, and has presented at international conferences in Canada, the US, and Europe—the most recent at IFTR in Munich (2010).

Christopher Innes holds the Canada Research Chair in Performance and Culture, together with the title of Distinguished Research Professor at York University, Toronto. A Killam Fellow of the Canada Council, he is a Fellow of the Royal Society of Canada and of the Royal Society of Arts (UK). He is the author of 16 books—which have been translated into eight different languages—and over 100 articles on various aspects of modern drama, he is also General Editor of the Cambridge "Directors in Perspective" series, Co-Editor of the "Lives of the Theatre" series, a Contributing Editor to The Cambridge Guide to World Theatre, and has been Co-Editor of the quarterly journal Modern Drama. He has organized several international conferences, most recently "Carnival: 'A People's Art' and Taking Back the Streets".

Annabel Rutherford following a career in the performing arts as a dancer and actor in both the UK and USA, Annabel Rutherford has completed MAs in Dance History and English, as well as an inter-disciplinary MA in Russian Modernism. She has published papers on ballet, drama, poetry, literature, and art history and is dance editor for both *Journal of the Oscholars*, www.oscholars.com and the international Wilde online project.

Index

Abakuá 47, 127-131, 143, 144, 146-151

Abakuá Groups 47

Abrahams, Roger D. 174

Achong, A. 222

Ada Kese 31

Adae 31

African Art in Motion 288

Afro Pan 208

Afro-Asian Experience, The 184

Agee, James 278

Akashi, Kenji 245

Akinyeye, Yomi 41

Akryll, Lyle 97

Aloes, Sugar 265-267

Ambo, Sam 133, 139, 142, 143

Amerindian 5, 30

Ammon, Bobby 97

Anderson, Ingrid 324

Andrews Sisters 275

Andy Griffin Show 283

Apoo Festival 31

Approo, Narrie 99-102, 104, 105

Apter, Andrew 38, 39, 41, 46

Aristotle 26

Arts Council of England 229

Arythmics 190, 193

Ashanti 31

Ashe, Arthur 9

Awori 37

Babayemi, S. O. 40

Baby Doll 307, 309

Bacall, Lauren 279

Bacchanal 65, 336

Bacchus 65, 174

Bailey, George 97, 180, 181, 289

Bakatue 30

Baker, Houston 179

Bakhtin, Mikhail 73

Balanchine, George 327

Bamboula 82

Bando de Buen Gobierno y Policia 48

Bäng Bäng Marching Band 241, 242

Baradas, Miguel 223

Barbe, Marvin 233, 237

Barber, Anne 195

Barber, Karin 42

Bare Bones 196

Bariba of Borgu 45

Baryshnikov, Mikhail 332

Bascom, William 42
Bassilon, Harry 97
Bata 42, 45
Bateson, Gregory 264
Batiste, Terrel 170
Batra, Tamla 240
Bay 109, 223
Beatles, The 319
Beauty and the Beast 324
Beecroft, John 132
Belafonte, Harry 282
Belasco, Lionel 274
Belmont 95, 96
Benda-Beckmann, F. von 260
Benjamin, Robert 264
Bèrè Festival 39, 40, 43, 49
Berkeley, Wayne 97
Best, Lloyd 300
Betancourt, Sterling 221, 222, 228, 235, 236, 241, 246
Betsy 275
Bettleheim, Judith 288, 289
Bhabha, Hommi 61, 62
Black Indian 101, 102, 104, 105
Black Sage 279
Blair, Janet 274
Blue Devil 94
Blue Notes 223
Blues for New Orleans: Mardi Gras and America's Creole Soul 174
Blumenfeld, Larry 166
Bogart, Humphrey 272, 279
Bohannan, P. 258
Bollito Misto 234, 240
Bonfire Night 239
Bookman/Beelzebub 72
Bourian 33

Brathwaite, Kamau 299
Bride of Lucifer 72
Bridgwater 239, 240
Bridgwater's West Country Carnival 239
British Slave Trade and Public Memory 178
Brook, Peter 102, 319
Brown, Alison 190
Brown, David H. 37
Brute Force 281
Brynner, Yul 272, 282
Buber, Martin 207, 212
Buccaneer, The 272, 282
Buffalo Jump 195
Burke, Kenneth 252, 262, 264
Burrokeet 307, 309
Buschmann, Martin 236, 242
Bush, Robert Baruch 253, 254

Cabrera, Lydia 45, 128, 129
Caged Beast, The 73
Calinda 82, 302, 303, 305-307, 311
Callaloo 18, 336
Callas, Maria 4, 326, 327, 330
Calvary Hill 54, 56, 59
Calypsonians 108, 245, 251, 253, 254, 258-260, 262-265, 267, 268, 271-273, 284
Cameroon, David 115
Canboulay Riots 87
Canboulay Rituals 28
Candombe 27
Caribana 10, 109, 189, 190, 193-196, 198, 207, 208, 216, 271, 289, 290

Caribbean Festival arts 288
Caribbean Magic 244
*Caribbean Man in Time and
   Space* 299
Caribbean Night 242
Cariwest 197-200, 202, 204
Carmen 104
Carnival in Romans 89
Carnival Institute 114
Carnival Messiah 184
Carson, Jack 282
Casetta, Boots 273
Central School of Art and Design
   (London) 318
Chambers, George 261
Chang, Carlisle 289, 327
Chanock, Martin 257
Chapeaux, Pedro Deschamps 46,
   128
Cherrie, Pickers 223
Childs, Matt 147
Chock, Jeffrey 93, 323
Churchill, Sir Winston 273
City of London 229
Clapperton, Hugh 40, 50
Clark, Gerald 272, 338
Clarke, LeRoy 14, 338
Cobham, George 139, 142, 143
Cochrane, Jeanette (n.) 318
Cocteau, Jean 324
Cohen, Roger 3, 21, 157
Collier, Jane 257, 258
Comaroff, John 258, 260
Congada 27
Connor, Geraldine 290
Conquerors of Kishra 96
Constantine 65, 66
Contender (Mark John) 280

Cooder, Ry 284
Coombe, Rosemary 154
Coutou 94, 95
Coventry Steel Pan Academy 229
Cozart, Milla 292, 294
Craig, Gordon 332
Creole 25, 36, 44, 58, 60, 79,
   81-83, 85, 86, 88, 89, 105, 111,
   174, 300, 301, 303, 307
*Crime and Custom in Savage
   Society* 257
Cripps, Thomas 275, 278
Crowley, D. 76, 220
Cultural Olympiad 229
Culture in Action 292
Cumberbatch, Trevor 223
Cumuto 272
Curse of the Cat People 278
Curtiz, Michael 282

Dali, Salvadore 329
Dame Lorraine 28, 70, 191, 307,
   317, 335
Darrel, Peter 323, 324
Davidson, Philmore 235
Davis, Christine 233, 237, 335
Day, Charles 85, 87
Day, Doris 285
De Mille, Agnes 4
DeGeneres, Ellen 11
Delano, Pablo 16, 18, 20, 21
DeMille, Cecil B. 11, 328
Desperados 8, 321
Devil Dragon, The 71, 73, 77
Diabolitos 47
Disney 8
Dixieland Steel Band 223

Doody, Kathleen 189, 192, 195
Dosumu, Jubril Adesegun 42
Douglas, Gordon 278
Douglas, Noble 334
Dragon Band 71, 73
Dramatism 264
Duchamp, Marcel 4
Duke, Ntiero 134, 139-143, 150

Ebony Steel Orchestra 223
ECS Kiddrum 242
Edwards, Osmond Sr. 200
Egba 37
Egbado 37
Egungun 55, 67-69
Ékpè 127-144, 146-151
Ello y Oyo 48
English in the West Indies, The
    105
Entertainment Industry Devel-
    opment and Export Co. 114
Ephraim, Duke 128, 136, 139,
    142, 143, 148
Etherton, Michael 305
Eve Knew Her Apples 280
Eyo Honesty I 135
Fantastics (Kobe) 244, 245
Farrar, Max 290
Father Knows Best 283
Faulkner, William 283
Feld, Steven 173
Festival of Britain 221, 235
Fitzgerald, Ella 333
Fitzgerald, F. Scott 3
Folger, Joseph 253, 254
Fon 45
Fontaine, Lynn 326

Francis, Paul 240
Frankfort, Henry 27
Frazier, Philip 173
Freedom Song 184, 295
Frobenius, Leo 38
From the Land of the Humming-
    bird 320, 330
Froude, James Anthony 105
Fugiwara, Chris 278
Funland Serenaders 240

Ga 30
Gabriel, Carl 181-184
Galindo, A. 47, 50
Gambit Weekly 167
Gaye, Marvin 170
Geertz, Clifford 257, 292
Gelede 31
Gentleman Jim 73
Ghandi, Mahatma 184
Ghost Ship, The 278
Ghouba 82
Gill, Junior 240
Gilligan's Island 283
Gillman, Webster 82
Gilroy, Paul 179, 186
Gluckman, Max 258
Goffman, Ervine 264
Gomez, Raul 233, 237, 267
Graham, Colin 324
Graham, Martha 4
Grant, Rupert Westmore 275
Great Gatsby, The 3
Guy Fawkes 239
Gwari 45, 50
Gypsy 266, 279

Hale, Claudia L. 264
Hall, Stuart 179, 186
Hall, Tony 10, 13, 299, 334
Hallelujah 54, 325, 332, 333, 336
Hancox, Diana 239
Handel, George Friedrich 184
Handler, Jerome S. 44
Happy Go Lucky 274, 275
Harlem through Calypso Eyes 273
Harley, Brad 189, 195
Harris, Wilson 299, 300, 304, 309
Hart, Calder 15, 16
Hausa 45, 50, 55
Hawks, Howard 279, 283
Heartney, Eleanor 292
Henderson, Russell 217, 221, 235, 246
Henshaw, Jimmy 132, 139
Her Lucky Night 275
Herodotus 26
Herskovits, M. J. 36, 256
Heung, Stephen Lee 99, 327
Hill, Don 284
Hill, Errol 25, 183, 294, 302
Hill, Helen 172
Hogbetsotsoza 31
H2-Oh-Oh 194, 196
Holman, James 133, 134, 136, 140
Homowo 30
Hoover, Edgar G. 272
Hot 76, 165, 166, 170, 171, 191, 303
Houdini, Wilmoth 273
Howarth, Boris 190
Howarth, Maggie 190
Hughes, Langston 9

I Walked with the Zombies 275, 279
Ibgo 55
Ibibio 55, 58, 129-132, 134, 148, 150, 151
Idanre 41
Iden 41
Ife 41
Ijesu 37
Ile-Ife
Imps 71-73
In Trinidad: Photographs by Pablo Delano 16
Innes, Christopher 5, 88, 315
International Caribbean Carnivals Association (ICCA) 120
Isenhart, Myra Warren 254
Ishiguro, Akihiro 244
Island Follies 190, 191, 196
Itapa Festival 41

Jab Jab 191
Jab Molasses 58
Jamaica Canadian Association 209
Jamaican Gleaner 280
James, C. L. R. 87
Jamettes 84-90, 103, 104, 308
Jelepa 40, 43
Jesus Christ, Superstar 65, 333
Johnson, Jacob 170
Johnson, Samuel 39
Jolly Jumpers 241
Jones, Errol 13
Jonkanoo Band 199
Jonkonnu Parade 27
Joseph, Hazel 233, 237

Juego de los Congos 27
Jumbi 70

Karadzic, Radovan 21
Kathakali 319
Kawashima, Kiyoshi 245
Keate, Robert William 86
Keller, Charles 166
Kemet (Kemit) 26, 27, 29
Kemite 29
Key Imp 72, 73
Khan, M. H. 278
King, Martin Luther Jr. 184
Kings and Queens 10, 191, 200
Kobe 244, 245
Kong, Raymond Choo 10
Kongo 55
Kpoikpoi 30
Kwanza Harvest Festival 27

Laclau, Ernesto 156
Ladurie, Le Roy 89
Lady Africa 279
Ladypan 241
Lafitte, John 272, 282
Landaluze, Victor Patricio 47, 50
Landis, Stella Baty 166, 167, 171, 172, 174
Laroche, Sir James 142
Law, Robin 38-40
LeBlanc, Lumar 167
Lee, Jenny 190
Lee, Spike 171
Lefebvre, Hdenri 173, 174
Lesker, Jürgen 242

Lewton, Val 275, 278
Linda Be Good 281
Lingo 279
Liverpool, Hollis Urban Lester 28
Loesser, Frank 274
Lomax, Alan 273
London All Stars Steelband 223
Lorca, Garcia Frederico 21
Lord Invader (Rupert Westmore Grant) 275
Lord Kitchener 245
Lost Tribe, The 17, 20
Lovelace, Earl 12, 53-62
Lucas, George 335
Lucifer King of the Band 73
Lucumí 46 37, 43-50
Lucumí Calbido(s) 37, 45, 46, 48-50
Lugosi, Bela 278
Lux Video Theatre 283

Macbeth 319
MacFarlane, Brian 15
Magritte, René 329
Mahogany Arts Ltd. 183, 185
Maino, Yves 236, 240
Making mas with Possibility Five Hundred Years 300
Malinowski, Bronislaw 257, 258
Mandela, Nelson 184
Mandingo 55
Manfredi, Victor 147, 148
Mangrove Steel Orchestra 223
Manning, Patrick 13, 15, 16, 261
Marat/Sade, The 319
Mardi Gras 27, 108, 111, 116, 117, 122, 166, 169, 174

Marine Expo 244
Martin, Mary 274
Mashramani 110, 225
Mason, Bim 294
Mason, Peter 59, 294-296
Maultsby, P. 260, 261
Max Cherrie and the Cherrie
  Pickers 223
McCain, John 11
McCarthy, T. 228, 282
McHugh, Jimmy 274
McWilliams, Louis 306
Melody Makers 223
Merken, Betty 293
Messiah, The 184
Metronome 223
Meza, Ramón 47, 50
Midnight Robber 74, 77, 102,
  191, 194, 307, 309, 320, 330,
  331, 335, 336
Mighty Sparrow 302, 303
Mighty Terror 245
Miller, Ann 280
Miller, Ivor 128, 129, 135, 146,
  147, 149-151
Miller, Sarah 189, 195
Milton, John 328, 330
Minshall, Peter 3, 5, 9-13, 15, 16,
  21, 93, 98, 99, 181, 190-192, 287,
  289, 290, 292-294, 296, 309,
  315-321, 323, 324, 327-33
Mintz, Sidney W. 36
Misty Carnival Club 181
Mithras 66
Moko Jumbie 5, 191, 309
Mole 39
Money Talks 196
Mother Theresa 184

Mukpono 30
Murakami, Yuki 245
Musgrave, Theo 324
Musicking 210, 212
My Fair Lady 9

Nader, Laura 240, 257
Naipaul, V. S. 217, 328
National Alliance for Reconstruc-
  tion (N.A.R.) 59, 112, 261
National Carnival Bandleaders
  Association 109, 120
National Carnival Commission
  (NCC) 107-109, 113-120, 122
Neg gwo Siwo 58
Negue Jardins 81, 88
Nehusi, Kimani 26-30, 32, 220
New Birth 172, 173
New York Times 3, 21
Nicoletti-Tung, Monika 236, 241
Nkoranza 31
Nonaka Trading Co 245
Nostalgia Steel Band 217, 221,
  223, 224, 227, 229, 233
Notsie 31
Notting Hill Carnival 99, 180-
  183, 185, 217, 218, 220, 226,
  227, 233-236, 238-241, 243, 246
Ntoa 31
Nunley, John 288, 289, 294
Nupe 39, 45, 50
Nureyev, Rudolf 326

O'Brien, Pat 274
Oba 37, 38, 41, 42, 45
Obama, Barack 3, 9, 10, 295

Offbeat 167
Offor, George 132
Old Woman With a Rolling Pin 281
Olofin 41
Olympics Atlanta 13
Olympics Barcelona 13, 15, 128, 334, 335
Once Upon a Time 324
Orisha (Òrìsà) 28, 37-39, 41-43, 45, 46, 49, 50, 58, 181, 219, 309
Ortiz, Fernando 36, 45-48, 129, 146, 148
Orun 39
Osaka Expo 244
Osiris 27
Otin 42
Owa 41
Owo 37
Oya 58
Oyo 37-46, 48-50

Paddington Arts Youth Steel-band 237
Paddington Youth 223
Palmié, Stephan 121
Pamberi 244
Pan 15, 28, 32, 33, 96, 108, 111, 116, 147, 157, 158, 181, 190, 191, 199, 207-211, 214, 215, 217-229, 233-243, 245, 246, 271, 281, 301, 308, 320, 322, 327
Pan Alive 216
Pan Podium 246
Pan Village Steelpan School 245
Pan-African Festival 28

Pan-Am North Stars Steel Orchestra 223
Panday, Basdeo 60, 261, 267
Paninos 242
PanKultur 229, 241, 242
Pan-round-neck-steel band 233-237, 239-243, 245-247
Pans'n Roses 241
Pansonide 244
Pantheon of Evil, The 72
Pan-Trinbago 108
Papa Mas 13
Paradise Lost 11, 328, 330, 331, 333
Parks, Van Dyke 284
Parmasad, Ken 306
Parnes, Irwin 280
Parrinder, E. G. 38
Parsons, Robert 239
Patwa 69, 70
Pay Wo 69, 77
Pearse, Andrew 84, 85, 87
Peel, J. D. Y. 44
Pete, Bennie 190, 191
Pfafflin, Elisabeth 241
Philips, Terry 227
Phillip, Lyndon 194
Pierre, Curtis 223
Pierrot, Grenade (Pay-Wo Grenade) 69, 191, 307
Pinard, Donald 272
Pinard, Lancelot 270, 271, 281
Pinheiro, Christopher 190, 195, 288, 293
Pitres, Gretta 200, 202
Plato 26
Political Calypso: A Sociolinguistic Process in Transforming

Conflict 251-254, 260, 261, 267, 268, 273
Poro 127
Powell, Dick 274
Pradel, Lucie 57, 58
Price, Richard 36, 80
Prieto, Juan 48
Prince of Darkness, The 73, 75
Purge A Tory 196

Quinn, Anthony 272

Rabelais and his World 73
Rada 55
Ramdeen, Michael 185, 287, 290
Rampersad, Arnold 9
Ras Shorty I 264
Rat Race 191, 196
Raven, Olivia 233, 237
Rebirth Brass band 166, 173
RED 289, 331, 333
Reed, Lou 103
Reglamento de esclavos 48, 49
Reich, Howard 171, 172
Reisado 27
Renegades 244, 321
Rennie, B. 221-223
Rice, Timothy 207, 210
Riesgo, P. 46, 50
Riggio, Milla 25, 28, 292, 294, 317
River 15, 17, 18, 20, 26, 289, 293, 316, 331, 333
Roach, Charles 194
Roaring Lion (Ralph de Leon) 274

Roberts, Jacqueline 239
Roberts, Simon 258, 260
Robinson, Arthur 60, 261
Robinson, Michael 245
Rogers, James 142
Rohlehr, Gordon 55, 264, 278, 302
Romance on the High Seas 282
Roosevelt, Franklin 273

Sadler's Wells Theatre (London) 323
Saga Boy 11, 12, 316, 325, 333, 334
Sakakeeny, Matt 166, 167, 172, 173
Salandy, Clary 183-186, 287, 290, 291, 293-295, 297
Saldenah, Harold 96, 97
Sandflöö 234, 240, 241
Sango 39, 40, 42, 45, 46, 49, 50
Sanoir, Andrew 94
Santimanitay 13, 334
Savanna 8, 9, 13-17, 99, 119, 317, 325, 331, 335
Savary, Charlie 97
Schapera, Isaac 260
Schechner, Richard 8, 292, 317, 337
Schulz, Eckhard 236, 242
Scott, David 156
Scott, James 88, 89
Scottish Ballet Theatre 323, 324
Seeger, Pete 273
Seurat, Georges 328
Shadowland 189, 190, 192-195

Shame and Scandal for the Family 276

Shango 5, 38, 57, 58, 102, 105, 181, 182, 184, 219

Shavers, Dinneral 170-172

Shern Hall Methodist Steelband 237

Shern Hall Youth Gospel Choir 237

Shrovetide 79

Simpson, George Eaton 55, 56

Sir Lancelot (Lancelot Pinard) 271-284

Small, Christopher 210

Smart, Ian 26-30, 32, 94

Smith, Rudy 240

Smith, Whitney 189, 195

Snyder. F. G. 257

Soca Monarch 115

Social Aid and Pleasure Clubs 166, 168, 170

Socrates 26

Song of the Earth 336

Sonobe, Ryo 244

Soobii 30

Soros Foundation 166

Soul Rebels 165-169

Soul, Jimmy 274

Southern Symphony Steelband 243

Soyinka, Wole 67, 300

Spangl, Michael 254

Spielberg, Steven 335

Spitzer, Nick 174

Stark, Karen 241

Starr, June 257, 258, 274, 278, 282

Steelpan Academy 239

Sterling's Angels 236, 241

Street Theatre & Other Outdoor Performance 10, 108, 190, 191, 197, 198, 294, 313

Sukiyaki Orchestra 245

Sun of the Morning 72

Sweet Wheat 203, 204

Szwed, John F. 174

Tamboo Bamboo 219, 221, 233

Tan Tan 11, 12, 316, 333, 334

Tantana 11, 333

Tapestry 8, 17, 19, 20, 316, 336, 337

Tate Gallery (London) 326

Taylor, Deanne 190

Techiman 31

Terry, P. 219

Theory and Practice of Creole Grammar 303

There Ain't No Black in the Union Jack 179

Thomas, J. J. 303

Thompson, Robert Farris 32, 129, 174, 288, 289

To Have and Have Not 272, 279, 283

Todd, Henry 257

Tokai Trio 244

Tolliver, Jeremy 166-168

Tomita, Akira 243

Tompsett, Adela Ruth 177, 178, 181, 182, 186, 290-292, 294

Tony Charles Steel Band 217, 223, 224

Touch of Africa, A 184, 185

Tourism Development Co. 108, 113

Tourneur, Jacques 275-277

Toussaint, Fed 223, 301

Toyama 245

Trans-Atlantic Slave Trade Database, The 44, 148

Trees 'r Us 192, 194, 196

Trinidad All Steel Percussion Orchestra (TASPO) 221, 222, 235

Trinidad Carnival: Mandate for a National Theatre 183, 302

Trinidad Guardian 153, 280, 281

Trinidad Sentinel 86

Triumph 18, 27, 87

Trollope, Anthony 82

Tropicana 223

Tswana 260

Turner, Victor 258

Two Yanks in Trinidad 272, 274, 282

Umabatha 319

Unknown Terror, The 282

Valdez, Russell 223

Victor, Rubadiri 12

Video Cabaret 190

Vieira, Geraldo 200, 202, 203

Village Vanguard 272

Villaroel 222, 223

Waddell, Hope 132, 134, 136, 140, 151

Walcott, Derek 304, 305, 313

Walking Steel 241

Wallace, Elizabeth 178

Wallace, Henry 273

Warner, Keith Q. 303

Welfare State International 189, 190

Welles, Orson 279

Wenchi 31

West Country Carnival 239

White, J. P. 307

White, Michael 166-171

Williams, Dave 336

Williams, Eric 9, 10, 156, 261, 328

Williams, Joseph 170

Williams, Raymond "Dr. Rackle" 171

Wilshire Ebell Theatre 274

Winston, Samuel H. 167

Wolof 29

World Steelband Music festival 240

Wosorian Festival 26

Yemoja Festival 38

York University 58, 194, 207, 208, 233, 246

Yoruba 29, 31, 32, 35, 37-47, 49, 50, 55, 57, 58, 67, 288

Young Girls of Today 281

Zamora, Pérez 46, 47, 50

Zephaniah, Benjamin 177, 187

Zombies on Broadway 278